SHEPHERDS OF THE EMPIRE

SHEPHERDS OF THE EMPIRE

GERMANY'S CONSERVATIVE PROTESTANT LEADERSHIP—1888–1919

MARK R. CORRELL

Fortress Press
Minneapolis

SHEPHERDS OF THE EMPIRE

Germany's Conservative Protestant Leadership—1888–1919

Cover image: © iStock.com/Andyworks

Cover design: Laurie Ingram

Library of Congress Cataloging-in-Publication Data is available

Print ISBN: 978-1-4514-7295-0

eBook ISBN: 978-1-4514-7986-7

The paper used in this publication meets the minimum requirements of American National Standard for Information Sciences — Permanence of Paper for Printed Library Materials, ANSI Z329.48-1984.

Manufactured in the U.S.A.

This book was produced using PressBooks.com, and PDF rendering was done by PrinceXML.

To Ina

CONTENTS

Acknowledgements   ix

1. Introduction   1
   The Connection between the Theology of the Word of God and the Moral Leadership of the Church in Wilhelmine Germany

2. Christianity, Political Conservatism, and the Community of Believers   19
   Adolf Stoecker and the Organization of the Believing Community

3. How to Honor the Bible   45
   Martin Kähler's Theological Views of the Bible and Ethics

4. Receiving the Ancient Beliefs in the Modern Day   83
   Adolf Schlatter's Life and Work

5. Views from the Kingdom of God   141
   The Life and Preaching of Christoph Blumhardt

6. The Friends of Job   183
   German Sermons, 1888–1914

7. Confident in Jesus' Victory   221
   Germany's Protestant Clergy's Spiritual Guidance during the First World War

8. Conclusion   263
   The Relics of the First Modern Believing Theology

Bibliography   269
Index   281

Acknowledgements

Many have helped bring this project to fruition over the past decade, and all deserve my thanks. Spring Arbor University has given me enormous opportunities to craft my role as a historian, professor, and administrator. This community has proved everything I hoped for when I first arrived. I am thankful to my colleagues, administrators, and students for the confidence they have bestowed on me. I wish to offer particular thanks to Mark Edwards for his assistance in the publication process. Gary Burge and Mark Noll, my professors at Wheaton, have my enduring thanks for introducing me to the subject of biblical criticism and to the personal work of Adolf Schlatter and Christoph Blumhardt. The history faculty of the University of Florida provided me with the opportunity to begin this project. Frederick Gregory was the ideal dissertation adviser, leaving me a free hand to delve into the subject of my choice but offering poignant advice and criticism when they were most useful.

I am deeply indebted to the Deutsche Akademische Austauschdienst and the University of Tübingen for their generous support for a year of research in German archives. The provincial archives for the Protestant churches in Stuttgart, Speyer, and Kiel overwhelmed me with their support, assistance, and friendliness. Their abundant resources are sadly underused by academics. I would also like to thank the state and university archives in Göttingen and the state library in Berlin for the use of materials.

Thanks also to Fortress Press. When I first took a temporary job at Augsburg Fortress headquarters in 1997, I certainly could never have imagined having my own work published by the company. It is a happy homecoming, and I appreciate Will Bergkamp, Lisa Gruenisen, and Marissa Wold for their help producing the finished book.

My family also has earned my lifelong gratitude for their input on this project. My brother-in-law Matthew Miller was a helpful sounding board for my queries in historical research and interpretation. I am beholden to my in-laws, Wolfgang and Elfriede Schmidtpott, who allowed us to stay with them in Germany and always supported me, even when the purpose of my project remained rather abstract to them. I appreciate my parents, who encouraged me in my pursuit of history. Finally, to my children, I feel their support and love every day, and I am so thankful to my wife, Ina, for her support, love, and humor in this long process. It is to her that I dedicate this book.

1

Introduction

The Connection between the Theology of the Word of God and the Moral Leadership of the Church in Wilhelmine Germany

> *There are only two possibilities here: either the Gospel is in all respects identical with its earliest form, in which case it came with its time and has departed with it; or else it contains something which, under differing historical forms, is of permanent validity. The latter is the true view.*
>
> —Adolf Harnack, *What Is Christianity?*[1]

On July 23, 1900, leaders of the parish in the Brandenburg village of Neu-Trebbin wrote to the province's church-governing consistory. In the letter, they asked for the appointment of "an appropriate man to follow [their long-standing retired pastor], who is a proper messenger of the Gospel, who speaks from God's truth and love and who presides over us in godly peace."[2] The congregation had already found the pastor of its choice, vicar and interim pastor Max Lindenberg from Rossleben in Thüringen. However, their petition to the consistory was surprising. Why would a church need to ask specifically for a pastor who was a "proper messenger of the Gospel"? Every Protestant pastor

---

1. Adolf Harnack, *What Is Christianity?*, trans. Thomas Bailey Saunders (Philadelphia: Fortress Press, 1957), 14–15, originally published as *Das Wesen des Christentums* (1900).

2. Landeskirchliches Archiv Berlin-Brandenburg, J V 10 vi, 14/1289, #4310.

swore an oath to teach the gospel at his ordination. Yet their request for such a pastor was deliberate, and the consistory would understand the full meaning of it. In the opinion of the congregation of Neu-Trebbin, some clergy no longer preached the gospel of Christ. Only a certain sort of pastor would be acceptable in the parish. The theological landscape in Germany at the turn of the twentieth century was marked by over sixty years of ideological battle. The very essence of Protestant Christianity was under question, so much so that a rural congregation felt it necessary to specify to the highest church leaders in the land their desire for a pastor who spoke "God's truth and love."

Alongside these passions for right theological guidance lay other factors that complicated the situation. The parishioners of the rural Neu-Trebbin parish needed to submit their petition to Berlin, the capital and largest city of the sprawling empire. A difference in education separated the elders of the country church of Neu-Trebbin and the university-trained members of the consistory of the state church of Brandenburg. In their petition, the parishioners were asking the leadership of the church to bend the rules. Lindenberg was not yet fully ordained in the church. He still needed to complete the second theological examination required of all full pastors. Despite these differences and Lindenberg's inexperience, the congregation leaders of Neu-Trebbin implored their superiors to "not esteem the ecclesiastical rules more than the preservation and advancement of Christianity and the worship of the church (*Kirchlichkeit*) here."[3]

Members of the congregation of Neu-Trebbin were thankful for the interim pastor they had. They were also deeply concerned about what might happen if his time in Neu-Trebbin were not extended. If their request were not granted, they might receive a new pastor who had passed all the formalities of official ordination into the state church but did not feed their religious fervor. They feared having a new pastor who would undermine their most cherished beliefs. They worried that such a new spiritual leader would impose an outside piety on their congregation.

ADOLF STOECKER, MARTIN KÄHLER, ADOLF SCHLATTER, AND CHRISTOPH BLUMHARDT: OFFERING A NEW PATH FOR AN OLD BELIEF TO GUIDE GERMANY INTO THE TWENTIETH CENTURY

Adolf Stoecker (1835–1909), Martin Kähler (1835–1912), Adolf Schlatter (1852–1938), and Christoph Blumhardt (1842–1919) were four representatives of a new, self-conscious body of believing church leaders who understood

---

3. Ibid.

the pious Protestantism of congregations like Neu-Trebbin. While Stoecker sought to give churches like Neu-Trebbin the opportunity to voice their concern about new theology from the pulpit, the other three sought to span the anxious tensions that pulled apart the rural, simpler adherence to the traditional doctrines of historic Protestantism and the critical biblical research that excited a new urban, educated perspective on Jesus and his teachings. These latter three leaders created an explicitly modern theology that both affirmed the long-standing beliefs of Protestantism and adopted some of the methods and interpretations of the newest research. As they understood it, all that separated these two groups was their understanding of biblical authority. They squared the circle of the competing visions of the Bible for the modern faithful. Kähler's, Schlatter's, and Blumhardt's key to coordinating these two often antagonistic ideas was to reappraise the way the Bible was the continuing authority for the Protestant church. They believed that the Bible's character as the word of God—that is, its revelation of God in human history—was the means by which the Bible would continue to be the foundation for Protestant belief, but its historical nature permitted the critical research of its origins and meanings.

In their thinking and teaching, these three made it clear that Germany was facing an immense crisis. The results of the struggle between traditional beliefs and the critical questioning of biblical truths ranged far beyond the questions of biblical interpretation. Biblical teachings had been used by generations of Germans to create an image of Germany as it was and as it ought to be. Protestant doctrines were believed to be the moral underpinning of all positive aspects of German society. Theologians of all stripes were certain that the way that Germany interpreted the Holy Scriptures influenced every aspect of their lives. Kähler, Schlatter, and Blumhardt particularly believed that Germany's constructive advance into the future would come only as it asked modern critical questions of the Scriptures while maintaining a faith in the traditional doctrine of Protestantism that the Bible is the revealed word of God.

These three church leaders used the church networks founded by Stoecker to voice cooperatively a theological response to the religious, political, and social crises of their day. This study seeks to describe the creative theological impact of their thought in the greater practice of Protestantism in late-nineteenth- and early-twentieth-century Germany. It asks how these theologically conservative German Protestants reappraised the nature of the Scriptures in light of modern literary and historical critical theories and, in turn, how this new view of the Bible guided their moral leadership in Germany's Protestant churches.

Each of these leaders found the basis of the Christian life in the understanding of the Bible as the word of God. All three worked independently of each other, but their conclusions were remarkably similar. As a collective, they created a consistent presentation of modern theologically conservative Protestant dogma and ethics. They represent the leading figures of a robust community that affirmed their belief in the continued relevance of the Scriptures to guide life. Other prominent theological figures of the day supported and added to their work, but none could match their creativity in handling the pressing issues.

The result of their thinking was a modern theology that found the truths of Christianity emanating from its efficacy rather than its objective factuality. For Kähler, Schlatter, and Blumhardt, the Bible is the word of God because it is shown to be so through the changed life of the believer. In turn, this same changed life was the building block of the Protestant ethical society that all three envisioned.

From their positions of authority and renown, theologians and professors Kähler and Schlatter should have had a noticeable effect on the theology of the pastors who affirmed the same theological beliefs. Blumhardt's fame, and in certain cases infamy, as a preacher and politician should likewise have had its fair share of supporters and mimics among the Protestant clergy.

This is not the case, however. Among a clergy where the debates over the value and interpretation of the Bible as the word of God were not as imminent and pressing, there also seemed to be less of an attempt to find a constructive answer. An overview of the sermons of the age suggests that the parish clergy were unwilling and unable to translate Kähler's, Schlatter's, and Blumhardt's ideas into their proclamation of the gospel. In the place of their theology of the word of God and its application to ethical practice, the clergy adopted a theology of blessings and curses. Surprisingly, it was the least theological of these ideologues, Adolf Stoecker, who had the most lasting impact on the practical Christianity of pastors in Germany. The pastors preached, in effect, that God's blessings and curses were wholly dependent on Germany's communal righteousness. It is important to note that these ideas were not present in any of the theology, critical or conservative, coming from the universities. This theology was based on Germany's ascent to world prominence. A theology of blessings and curses was easier to present in sermons, and it justified the pastors' place of prominence in their respective communities, since they could then determine the proper course of action required for receiving God's blessings.

The Believing Christian in the Context of Nineteenth-Century Protestantism

Protestants in Germany were by no means monolithic. Some German observers of the time broke Protestants into three categories: confessionalists, biblicists, and liberals. In some ways, these paralleled the contemporary British breakdown of high church, evangelical, and broad church. This set of three groups, however, still did not adequately describe the divisions within German Protestantism.

Confessionalists defined themselves in accordance with the traditional doctrines of the Reformation as expressed in the Lutheran confession of Augsburg or the Calvinist Heidelberg Confession.[4] Biblicists put less emphasis on the institutional definitions of Christianity and a greater weight on the role of the Scriptures as the arbiter of religious truth. They were more likely to be suspicious of biblical criticism because of the centrality of the Bible for their beliefs. Liberals valued reason and conscience as the spiritual core of humanity. Liberals valued these faculties over all other forms of revelation and used them to freely question the Scriptures. They believed that Christianity's central focus was the moral code of Jesus in his teachings. They welcomed anyone who acknowledged the superiority of Jesus' ethical mandates, even if they differed with historical doctrines of the church.

None of these terms adequately describes the active voice of the believing theologians of this study. They were not confessionalists, slavishly adhering to Lutheran ideas (although Kähler does use Lutheran doctrine as his theological launching point). Indeed, few in the university lasted long with this viewpoint. Biblicists were often theologically close to the fundamentalists of twentieth-century America. While Kähler accepted the title for himself, Schlatter (whose theology was perhaps more traditional) strongly objected to the title. Among theologians, they called themselves *Vermittlungstheologen*—theologians of a middle way. This idea grew in the generation of the 1830s and 1840s as D. F. Strauss and F. C. Baur were developing speculative theories that were discarding the most treasured beliefs of the church. Many university scholars

4. Walter H. Conser Jr., *Church and Confession: Conservative Theologians in Germany, England, and America, 1815–1866* (Macon: Mercer University Press, 1984), 3–4, 26, 55, 315. Conser suggests that the liberalism of the early nineteenth century assumed the ability of individuals to make wise and correct religious choices. The confessionalists, for whom liberalism posed a terrible threat, reacted by returning to the corporate nature of creeds that bound confessional communities together through common doctrine. In the end, Conser portrayed a movement that was truly conservative in both a religious and political sense in that it drew its strength out of the romanticized memories of Reformation Germany's state and church.

were unwilling to accept the notional nature of Strauss's and Baur's theories but likewise could not support extreme conservative theologians such as Berlin's Ernst Hengstenberg.[5] The *Vermittlungstheologen* did not identify with either extreme. However, by the unification of Germany, only a small minority of theologians belonged to either extreme. So many theologians identified with *Vermittlungstheologen* by the foundation of the German empire that the term had lost its meaning. Very traditional scholars including Stoecker, Schlatter, and Kähler all fit within the tradition as well as the great liberal scholars Albrecht Ritschl and Adolf von Harnack. Needing a way to identify like-minded churchmen, they turned (like liberals) to a political name. They chose to call themselves "positive" theologians after the church political movement the Positive Union. This was the group that rose to the defense of the word of God in Wilhelmine Germany.[6]

But the labels *positive, biblicist*, and even *conservative* and *liberal* lead to interpretive confusion in the history of nineteenth-century ideologies, a confusion that is merely passed on if these categories are not clarified. For example, the positivist followers of August Comte separated themselves from everything important to the positive theologians; hence the name has had little staying power for theology. The widely used terms *conservative* and *liberal* could likewise easily be misconstrued with political connotations when theological affinity did not correspond to political affiliation. Liberal theologian Adolf Harnack was a staunch supporter of the kaiser and the Conservative Party. Christoph Blumhardt professed socialistic political beliefs while preaching "conservative" theological doctrines.

The best title for the conservative theologians who form the focus of this dissertation comes from Schlatter. He sometimes referred to himself and others as "believing Christians" (*Gläubigen*), meaning theologians and pastors who adopted a hermeneutic that assumed the Bible was supernaturally authoritative and the true word of God (while reserving the right to question it scientifically). Schlatter never used the phrase to classify a particular school of thought; rather, he meant it as a description of a type of biblical interpretation. The title then becomes applicable, admittedly anachronistically, to those before him and can be used broadly to include theologians of varying creeds and parties who upheld

---

5. Indeed, it may have been at this point that the German church avoided the bitter fundamentalist vs. modernist debates that were seen in the United States at the beginning of the twentieth century.

6. Cf. Paul Tillich, *Perspectives on 19th and 20th Century Protestant Theology*, ed. Carl E. Braaten (New York: Harper & Row, 1967), 4–5, 9–15. Tillich goes so far as to claim that the entire movement of modern theology has been to try to find the connection between the traditions of the church and the rational explanations demanded by modernity.

the authority of the Scriptures in the modern world as the divine revelation and therefore as superior to human reason.[7]

The use of *liberal* as a broad umbrella expression for all post-Enlightenment theologians who separated themselves from the traditional doctrines of the church was also something of a misnomer, although it was common parlance in the nineteenth century, as it is now. Theological liberalism was a specific movement coming out of the thought of Albrecht Ritschl and was developed by Wilhelm Hermann and Adolf von Harnack. However, the critical theologians were also not unified in their theology. Other schools of thought, especially the history of religions school, which stressed religions' evolutionary growth in the advancement of civilization, differed on important aspects of the centrality and uniqueness of Jesus. For this reason, the word *critical* is, generally speaking, a more appropriate term for these scholars, since they all perceived human reason as the ultimate arbiter of the Bible's enduring value for Christians.

The Word of God, Believing Faith, and the Question of Authority, 1888–1919

Some historians who study religion have assumed that secularization, or at least the exodus from the church, came about because Christianity became obsolete. They suppose that the Christian faith was incompatible with the social, economic, and intellectual pressures of the day. That is, the working class rejected Protestantism because it was not conducive to their social needs. They turned instead to social democracy. The liberal elements of the middle class tended to leave the church because of differences in ideology and questions of conscience.

These two factors were undoubtedly true to a large extent. It is especially understandable when one compares the Protestant clergy's antagonism to socialism with Catholicism's open acceptance of working-class civil-rights claims. However, if modernity and Christianity were mutually exclusive categories, then the exodus from the church should have been universal. The fact that Protestant churches still exist in Germany, a plurality of Germans still adhere to the church, and the churches have adopted modern life and

---

7. As will be discussed below in chapter 3, Martin Kähler proposed another term for this group, *Bibelverehrer* (literally, one who honors the Bible]. While the term would be eminently suitable for this study, it has no English equivalent that could be used without confusion. However, he used it in the same way that Schlatter referred to a *gläubige* reading of the Bible. For this reason, this study will refer to the *Bibelverehrer* as believing pastors and theologians.

modern philosophical standpoints suggests that the situation was significantly more complex.

The strong survival of these churches in Baden-Württemberg and Saxony indicates that the form of theological belief was crucial to the survival or atrophy of faith in Germany. Baden-Württemberg and Saxony shared a pietist, individualistic faith that survived despite the regions' differences in geography, location, and subsequent history (Baden-Württemberg was part of West Germany, Saxony a province in the German Democratic Republic, or East Germany). The similarity of faith and Christian adherence leads to the natural conclusion that pietism was more adequately suited for success in modernity. The fact that pietism carried over the traditional doctrines of Christianity (as opposed to explicit methods of modernism shown in critical theology) makes the causal connection between modernization and secularization in Germany untenable.

If declining church membership was not simply a result of modernization, one question that originates from the declining church participation is to what degree the clergy exacerbated the problem. The crisis was already mature by the death of Wilhelm I in 1888. However, the average citizen still came in regular contact with the church. Germans, even working-class members of the Social Democratic Party, were still identified in terms of confessional affiliation. The clergy had an opportunity to state its purpose and function in modern society, more so even than in the considerably more churched United States. Despite the opportunities available for the church, it failed to utilize its resources to win back disenchanted Germans. There never developed strong extra-church institutions as were used successfully in Britain, the United States, and even Catholic Germany (e.g., the Salvation Army, the YMCA, the Center Party). Instead, the German Protestant churches used their opportunities of influence to tie the fate of the church more closely to the power structures of imperial Germany. Simply put, the German church was not an authority because of its claims on the citizenry's adherence and connectedness; rather, it was an authority because it was part and parcel of the German nation. The leaders of the Protestant church in Germany (critical and believing alike) were not solely responsible for Germany's broad rejection of organized Protestantism, but they played a key role in deciding that the discourse of faith and morality was a discussion of German national faith and morality more than of an individual's faith and morality.

This study seeks to define and identify this particular stream of theology emanating from Kähler, Schlatter, Blumhardt, and their associated clergy of believing Christians at the twilight of Protestant Germany. It will first show that this body of church leaders was a unified, self-conscious entity that together struggled to defend the church's purpose in the modern world. This group sought to provide responses to the various pressures on the church—political pressures from Marxism, economic pressures from industry, demographic pressures from urbanization, and in the forefront of their minds, theological pressures from biblical critics, university scientists, and outspoken freethinkers. The nineteenth century was a period where members of the church were deliberately defining the boundaries of the church. The theological debates of the era forced the church to decide who was to remain in the church and who fell outside. To accomplish this, the finest believing theologians created a new language and theology that rested on the authority of the Bible as the word of God. Even though the understanding of the Scriptures in the early Reformation produced hard-fought decisions on many matters of theological importance, the German successors to the movement had surprisingly few resources at hand to continue discerning the trajectory of Protestantism in the nineteenth century.

The Reformation stood fast on the unquestioned, self-apparent authority of the Bible—exactly the point under question following the Enlightenment. The German Protestant church was forced to define itself exactly at the moment that its opponents put its main authority under siege. Outside intellectuals from Marx to Nietzsche challenged the church's privileged position in a modern kingdom. Internally, the theological debates inspired calls from both extremes to purge heretical or backward thought. Beyond this, the general populace threatened the church's standing by leaving the churches empty. To this, Kähler, Schlatter, and close colleagues created a new definition of spiritual authority. However, the theology of Kähler and Schlatter must be considered a failure. Few pastors turned to these ideas. Instead, when faced with these difficulties, the only unified recourse conservative church leaders could find in the decades leading up to the First World War was social traditionalism and an appeal to the strength of the monarchy.

The German state church, especially its parish clergy, proved extremely reluctant to change in all its potential facets. Most pastors ignored new theological interpretations that were tailored to fit the ideas and issues of the period. They showed themselves unsympathetic to the ordeals of working-class life in the newly industrial state. And they fiercely opposed any reform or political ideologies that threatened to compromise their standing as the official arbiters of religion in the state. Unsurprisingly, however, their opposition was indicative of their place in the hierarchy. Professors were open to reforming the pastorate, and clergy were willing to question the university chairs' authority over religious matters.

The religious establishment at the end of the nineteenth century already proved to be outdated and unwilling to face the social and cultural issues of the day. By the time of the cataclysm of the First World War, when war and revolution destroyed the whole imperial system, the Christian leadership had, in the eyes of the vast majority of Germans, already lost its credibility to interpret the spiritual ramifications of God's plan for the world. Sweeping interpretations of world events became the province of political ideologies in the Weimar period and following.

Beginning in the last year of the war, Karl Barth, who had fled Germany for his Swiss homeland just before 1914, set about establishing a new theology. The war shaped questions for Christianity that the theological groupings launched by D. F. Strauss's *Life of Jesus* could not address. In response, Barth rejected the whole of nineteenth-century theology, the good along with the inadequate from the elder generation.

The sharp break of twentieth-century theology from nineteenth-century theology, conservative and liberal alike, led some to blame theologians and pastors for shortsightedness. They asked for theology's answer to Nietzsche, who was able to see the darkness of the twentieth century coming. Stoecker, Blumhardt, Schlatter, and Kähler, like their liberal theological counterparts, were not able to foresee the problems of the twentieth century. Indeed, Stoecker bears particular blame for introducing anti-Semitism into German politics. However, all four were products of nineteenth-century thought who worked within the framework of their day. They were not responsible for the problems that would succeed them. They understood their responsibility to guide Christians of their day in their faith. This they did with their whole hearts. Their failing was that they were unable to muster the following necessary to provide the later generations with Christian thinkers to help them weather the brutalities of the twentieth century. The fault of the Christian leadership before the war, if there was one, was its incapability to rally around a single theological understanding of the modern world. Their responses to modern challenges resonate still to theologians finding meaning for the new world and historians looking to find the creative responses to modernity's challenges.

This study aims to follow these developments in the state church and the larger culture by tracing the changes in the use of the concept of the word of God as it was used at both the university level by prominent believing theologians and in the sermons of the period. It is crucial to understand that this book picks up in the middle of an ongoing discussion about the nature of spiritual authority that began in the eighteenth century with Lessing's biblical critiques and picked up steam with Strauss's *Life of Jesus.*[8] It covers the period from 1888 to 1919 because the last generation before the First World War experienced the greatest distance between theological progressivism and the appeal to social and theological conservatism.

In Germany, 1888 was the year of three kaisers. Wilhelm I began the year as kaiser. He was succeeded by his son, Friedrich III, whose death came just ninety-nine days after his succession. Finally, the young Kaiser Wilhelm II occupied the throne until his abdication in 1918. He promptly removed all of his father's advisers and set out on a path that he intended to be different from his father's. It was the year of a new generation of leadership coming to the fore.

The period covered here ends with 1919. It was the year of the Versailles treaty, and the succession of the Social Democratic Party of Germany in the Weimar Republic. It also saw the publication of Karl Barth's *Epistle to the Romans*, which signaled an end to Strauss's domination of the theological debates in the German academy. Beginning with Barth's work and the limited disestablishment of the church in the Weimar period, Protestantism charted a new course, this time as a minority faction of concerned faithful seeking to determine the best path for their select community in the face of difficult times.

8. In 1835, David Friedrich Strauss published the most important theological work of the nineteenth century, *Das Leben Jesu* (*The Life of Jesus*). It used modern historical-literary critical ideas and applied them to the biography of Jesus as he was portrayed in the biblical Gospels. Strauss was not the first person to interpret the Scriptures from Enlightenment principles of reason and objectivity. Gotthold Ephraim Lessing (1729–1781) possessed the courage to publish Hermann Samuel Reimarus's (1694–1768) *Wolfenbüttel Fragments* posthumously when the author proved unwilling to face the criticism during his lifetime. Strauss's book eclipsed Reimarus's, Friedrich Schleiermacher's, and others work in this area in that he incorporated the concept of myth. Jesus was not a divine entity come to earth from heaven. He was a powerful man with a powerful spiritual aura. Strauss's work spawned generations of imitation and refutation, both historical and literacy. His contribution to the field marked a transformation in the mind-set and driving questions of post-Enlightenment religion. Reimarus and others divided the Gospel accounts into the groupings of true and false. Strauss changed these categories into historical and mythical/spiritual. The Gospel writers for Strauss and subsequent scholars were no longer accused of intentionally writing false accounts; they simply saw the fulfillment of prophecy and the occurrence of miracles because they lived in a world where such thinking pervaded religious experience. Biblical scholars after Strauss, although standing in the shadow of the Enlightenment, no longer needed to explain away the miraculous accounts in reasonable ways. They only had to find and explain the enduring spiritual truth behind the mythical. Strauss established a mechanism to create a modern Christianity that no longer needed the Nicene doctrines of the Trinity and the Chalcedonian understanding of Jesus' divine and human natures. His thought made it possible to create a Christianity unfettered by miracles, complex doctrines, and unfathomable mysteries. He promised a new, modern Christianity pared down to eternal moral truths that could be properly applied to modern life.

Protestant clergy held a tenuous position in the last days of the German Empire. They still had the official position as the arbiters of religious truths to the laity at the end of the nineteenth century, but their actual situation looked much bleaker. They were pushed to the margins by academics and shunned by the working class. Even middle-class Protestants often remained merely nominal listeners. The clergy's strength came from their ties to imperial authority, but even here, their fortunes waned. Bismarck's *Kulturkampf*, meant to weaken the strength of Germany's Catholic minority, took a heavier toll on the less unified Protestants. In its attempts to decrease the power of Catholic clergy, it also stripped Protestant clergy of their legal rights (e.g., the right to have schools and the right to perform legally binding marriages). The Catholics responded to the persecution with greater unity and strong political opposition. The Protestant leadership advanced the ideas of the *Kulturkampf* until they proved to be as much an embarrassment for them as they were for the chancellor.

THEOLOGY AND CULTURAL HISTORY

Considering the continued marginalization of Germany's Protestant institutions through the twentieth century, it is expected that those theological ideas from before the First World War should receive less attention than the ideas that eventually eclipsed them, like Barth's Crisis Theology. However this overlooks the creativity of the era as these theologians and pastors concerned themselves with the questions that surround this difficult period in Protestant history including questions of authority, order, class, conservatism, liberalism, social hierarchy, and faith. Correspondingly, the failures and successes of the Protestant state church cannot be measured simply in terms of its practicality for modern Germans, but also should weigh all of these realities of the late-nineteenth and early-twentieth centuries. The Protestant state church's elaborate infrastructure still allowed it to disseminate its ideas as effectively as any political party throughout Germany. Historians, by omitting conservative theological voices from the broader discussions of the era, fail to gain a whole picture of the major issues that defined the church in the period.

Fortunately, some historians have begun to see the usefulness of the efforts of theologians to understand their world in spiritual terms and to struggle to make the faith present and real to others. Interest in the field of history began with work on early modern Catholicism fueled by creative writers such as Natalie Zemon Davis and Lynn Hunt. Raymond Jonas has shown how conservative theological ideas continued to exercise huge influence even in the secular nineteenth century. In German Protestant historiography Thomas Nipperdey, Hugh McLeod, and Helmut Walser Smith have begun to resuscitate religious history as an aspect of general secular history.[9]

Despite the growing literature on European religion, theology's role in the shaping of Germany's religious experience has been largely neglected. Theology has typically been written as an independent source for inquiry, in which case theological developments are outlined at great lengths, but their influence on or intentions toward laity are not addressed. In other examples of literature on German religion or German intellectual thought, specific doctrines and theological ideas tend to be seen as tangential to the supposedly real issues at hand, whether philosophical tradition, anti-Semitism, or political persuasion. Few works have addressed the theological root of Germany's clerical crisis of faith. The central doctrines of Protestantism, the motivation for action and belief in all other aspects of life, have remained unclear and ignored. This is a book that hopes to begin to overcome this failing by taking seriously the content as well as the context of theological thought.[10]

9. Natalie Zemon Davis, *Society and Culture in Early Modern France: Eight Essays* (Stanford, CA: Stanford University Press, 1975); Lynn Hunt, *Politics, Culture, and Class in the French Revolution* (Berkeley: University of California Press, 2004); Raymond Jonas, *France and the Sacred Heart: An Epic Tale for Modern Times* (Berkeley: University of California Press, 2000); Thomas Nipperdey, *Religion im Umbruch: 1870–1918* (Munich: Beck, 1988); Hugh McLeod, *Religion and the People of Western Europe, 1789–1989* (Oxford: Oxford University Press, 1997); Helmut Walser Smith, ed., *Protestants, Catholics, and Jews in Germany, 1800–1914* (New York: Berg, 2001).

10. Scholars of the history of religious life and thought in Germany in the nineteenth century have approached the subject from two angles. The first scholars to take a significant interest in the area were members of the theological community. They turned the tools and methods of historical theology to the interpretation of the nineteenth century even before the First World War, but particularly following Karl Barth's assessment of the era in his work. These works have focused solely on the theological development of the era with an almost exclusive interest on the contributions from academic theologians in Germany. The disproportionate concentration of critical theologians in the university faculties in the nineteenth century meant that the historical theologies naturally centered on the advancement of liberalism and critical thinking. Historians of Germany and church historians approached the era later, but their work has brought with it numerous alternative means of studying the period's developments. These works brought social aspects of Protestantism to the fore. They turned the focus away from the ivory tower and put it on the parishioners. In doing this, they were forced to recognize a distinction between religion as a popular activity and the church as a selective, particular institution. This is a balance they have not yet resolved. The move away from the exclusive study of the institutional church has issued a corrective to the long-standing belief that Germans abandoned Christianity absolutely. Instead, these historians have shown that popular piety continued even when it was not directly attached to the church. On the flip side, however, this work's exclusion of theology has its limits in being able to judge matters of dogmatic importance, namely, determining at what point piety is no longer Protestant or Christian altogether. Little of the recent work in either field, however, has acknowledged the

Much of the newest, most exciting research on religion in late Imperial Germany is challenging the idea that secularism replaced religion in modern Germany. The new historical work is discovering that religious expression outside the normal forms of Christianity blossomed in this period. Volunteer organizations and the inner-city mission grew in this period to supply religious outlets for urban Christians. Other Christians found the conservative *Gemeinschaftsbewegung*, a free-church-like movement within the state church, as a way to express their faith in otherwise critical parishes. Finally, as Lucian Hölscher and other contributors to Helmut Smith's anthology of works on modern German religion have related, Protestant piety was moving away from the church and into the home. A Christian family life became the central characteristic of the good Protestant. Germans were still religious at the beginning of the twentieth century; they simply found other means of expressing their faith than under the auspices of traditional German state-church worship.[11] A question must be further pursued, however: Why did the state church prove incapable of providing avenues for faith in modern Germany? This study indicates a few possible reasons.

This book offers a look at the theologians' and the clergy's role in forging the compromises that hurt the continuing influence of the church in the long run. It also appraises whether some alternatives were proposed that could have staved off the mass exodus from the state church. The picture that begins to appear shows that some had proposed a real alternative solution that built on a subjective, almost mystical understanding of the relationship of the believer to God through the auspices and direction offered by the word of God. The centrality of the word of God in this new theology offered a modern foundation for ethics that recognized authority but removed it from the realm of objective discourse that tied it absolutely to pre-Enlightenment institutions of royal authority and the absolute doctrines of the Reformers.

---

community of traditionalist Christian thinkers and clergy in the last decades before the First World War. When referred to, scholars acknowledge that the majority of Christians remained at least nominally attached to congregations who affirmed the traditional doctrines of the church. Yet these churches' and individuals' influence on German Protestantism and their cooperation with each other has been largely ignored.

11. Smith, *Protestants, Catholics, and Jews in Germany*, 5, 33–48. Willfried Spohn suggested something similar by noting that socialist groups in Germany adopted religious ritual in their political action, thereby changing the nature of the sacred but incorporating German's faith into their practices. Willfried Spohn, "Religion and Working-Class Formation in Imperial Germany, 1871–1914" in *Society, Culture, and the State in Germany, 1870–1930*, ed. Geoff Eley (Ann Arbor: University of Michigan Press, 1996), 179–81.

This work sketches this modern theological system by following the architect of the believing community, Adolf Stoecker; the two creators of the systematic theology, Adolf Schlatter and Martin Kähler; and an exceptional preacher, Christoph Blumhardt, who shows the possibilities within the new system. It then inspects the broader thought of the clergy through their sermons. The hope of this study is to present a picture of the dissemination of theological ideas from their inception in the universities and the church hierarchy through the pastors and finally to the parishioners.

This project is explicitly and unabashedly a "top-down" history. The church as an institution with rules, boundaries of membership, and a hierarchy strove to retain relevance in the German nation. Church leaders perceived their own obligation to set the moral direction for the nation. The parishioners had ultimate veto power, in that they could choose to accept the teachings of the church or to reject them by either joining with other sectarian groups or by leaving organized Christianity altogether. They ended up doing both. However, this does not negate the fact that a small number of church leaders exercised a disproportionate amount of influence in shaping the expressions of piety, determining the proper interpretation of the Scriptures, and formulating the understanding of right ethics. As mentioned in this chapter, we are fortunate to have a growing number of works that look at the lay responses to religious faith in Wilhelmine Germany. This book hopes to add to their findings by studying the largest faith institution in Germany.

The study is divided into two sections. Chapters 2 through 5 look at the political origins of the believing community, particularly through the work of Adolf Stoecker, and moves onto the developing theological consensus of its leading thinkers: Martin Kähler, Adolf Schlatter, and Christoph Blumhardt, who abandon Stoecker's nationalistic model of Christianity. This section introduces the four principal church leaders in sketches that trace the reaction of believing theology to the various social and religious influences of the age. The believing theology of Kähler, Schlatter, and Blumhardt shows a path available for believing church leaders at the beginning of the First World War.

None of these three meant his work to remain esoteric. Each had an explicit hope that his system of theology, his understanding of God's Spirit and the Christian's ethical response would practically change the nature of the Christian faith in Germany for the better. Each encouraged the propagation of his ideas to a broader audience. Each believed that God's message, as it was recorded in the gospels of Jesus Christ, needed to be a part of German public life and heritage.

Somehow, however, the connection broke down, and the hopes of the leaders of the community were not realized. The second section of the book, in chapters 6 through 8, is an inquiry into why Kähler's, Schlatter's, and Blumhardt's theoretical and practical theologies were never widely put into practice by a largely sympathetic clergy. Through an examination of sermons from the time, it is possible to ascertain some idea of what actually did percolate through to the broader German churchgoing public. These sermons show that only a minimal portion of the clergy wrestled in their sermons with modern theology in either its critical or believing manifestations. Three separate reasons seem to play a role in this condition. First, pastors were unable to view the church as an autonomous authoritative institution that existed alongside the state. The predominant view of the church by the opening of the First World War was that the church was subordinate to the authority of the state. Second, the pastors did not adequately understand the foundations for their theology. Third, the clergy were far more concerned with issues of social standing than they were of advancing the standing of the faith in Germany.

The combination of these three qualities greatly hindered the rise of a strong, independent clergy that could weather the brutalities of the First World War. The resulting church was unable to deal with the radical political changes brought about by the revolution of 1918. By 1919, the new generation of theologians opted to disassociate themselves from nineteenth-century theology and the problems that came with it, both theological and practical.

The question remains: Can pastors, with their vested political interests and their often obtuse rhetoric, function as a mirror for their time? Or more properly, do the sermons they delivered give the twenty-first century a glimpse into the life in the nineteenth? The sermons certainly cannot be used to claim specific insight into the thoughts and beliefs of churchgoers in Germany. They do, however, provide useful perspectives on German social hierarchical structures. The sermons paint an eloquent picture of the middle-class civil service dependent upon the patronage of the king and the aristocracy. The pastors understood that they were an important voice of the establishment to their communities. Their sermons, therefore, were carefully crafted presentations. While this meant that some pastors remained guarded in expressing any opinions that threatened to rile up the populace, it gives a better picture of the church as a collective.

One more difficulty must be expressed. The theologians and pastors—even those who were historians by trade—understood their beliefs to be timeless and transcendent. Accordingly, most sermons were seldom written to respond to immediate issues. They said little about current events or news subjects and remained abstract in their ethical teaching. Despite their shortcomings, the pastors were intriguing specimens of the nineteenth and twentieth century because many of the most influential leaders and pastors truly sought to shape their worldviews to reflect their theological beliefs. These clergy, critical and believing, believed that Christianity continued to offer productive means of understanding the modern world and guiding modern Germans in their decisions. These pastors provided a sincere, if one-sided, view of their world as they sought to do God's will in it.

2

Christianity, Political Conservatism, and the Community of Believers

Adolf Stoecker and the Organization of the Believing Community

For someone raised within the church in mid-nineteenth-century Germany, the end of the century certainly appeared menacing. While challenges to the authority of Protestant Christianity were not unheard of before midcentury, they were growing every year at an accelerating pace. Challenges appeared everywhere. The traditional authority ascribed to the church was eroding from various directions. The Protestant majority in the state was shaken by the addition of many Catholics as a result of the annexation of the southern kingdoms. The rapid industrialization of the cities had left large population centers underserviced by the institutional church. New philosophies and ideologies arising in the intellectual centers appealed as alternatives to orthodox Christianity to many of the burgeoning middle class and educated elite. Christian clergy facing diminishing numbers within their churches on a Sunday were aware that Christianity's responsibility to provide the moral foundation of the empire was weaker than it had ever been.[1]

THE RELIGIOUS CONTEXT OF BELIEVING GERMAN PROTESTANTISM

From the viewpoint of the university, this institutional weakness was not as apparent. At the end of the nineteenth century, German biblical scholars were the uncontested worldwide masters of their craft. Their critical scholarship over

1. Cf. Hugh McLeod, *Religion and the People of Western Europe, 1789–1989* (Oxford: Oxford University Press, 1997); Thomas Nipperdey, *Religion im Umbruch: Deutschland 1870–1918* (Munich: Beck, 1988).

19

the previous century brought significant "lower critical" (textual) improvements to both translations and original-language texts of the Scriptures. Their advanced knowledge of Greek and Hebrew and the improved manuscripts that began to be produced in the nineteenth century uncovered meaning and thoughts in the original texts that enabled even lay Christians to better understand the origins of their faith.[2]

The so-called higher critical (contextual) pursuits led these scholars to study the history of the ancient Middle East, to give cultural context to the biblical passages, and ultimately directed them to pose queries concerning the authorial intent and date of authorship of many of the texts. While the academics who asked these questions certainly built on the assumption that the Bible continued to be an important authority in German Christian history and culture, their work was also unsettling for many whose beliefs were nurtured in a far less skeptical era. The critical scholars themselves believed that their work was finally uncovering the essence of spirituality and religion that had been obscured by millennia of dogmatic misunderstandings. However, many other Christians (both in the academy and in the churches) felt that the critical scholarship went too far, destroying the most important tenets of historical Christian orthodoxy.

Critical scholarship engaged in a massive project to reevaluate the received texts and beliefs of Christian history. Put simply, the purpose of this project was to discover the true origins of Christianity. These scholars held that the new historical methods and scientific criticism prepared the way for an unimpeded knowledge of the early church and the life of Jesus. If intellectuals found the origins of Christianity, so the thought went, then they would also correspondingly discover the essence and importance of the faith.

This venture implied two main assumptions. First, it supposed that the traditional Christian beliefs neither were still relevant in the modern world nor were divinely revealed truths. These scholars believed that the teachings of Christ and early Christians were not intentionally falsified. Rather, they posited that later Christians writing the book of the New Testament changed the original ideas of Jesus to deal with contemporary problems. Since these

2. Peter Bergmann acutely notes that despite its reputation for genius, Germany's prewar generation, which he titles the generation of 1866, lacked figures of enduring brilliance. This is certainly the case with German theology. Some arguments could be made that Albrecht Ritschl fit into this category, but in retrospect, his influence seems not to be as great as many contemporaries supposed. The developments in the field during the latter half of the nineteenth century were in the details, not in the systems. Cf. Peter Bergmann, *Nietzsche, "the last Antipolitical German"* (Bloomington: Indiana University Press, 1987), 58.

problems had ceased to exist by the nineteenth century, the critics believed that the true history of Jesus and the disciples could be uncovered.

The second assumption was that scholarship (especially since David Friedrich Strauss's 1835 work, *The Life of Jesus* (*Das Leben Jesu*) suggested that Jesus and his disciples lived in a radically different context. Strauss and his followers argued that the early Christian writings related more closely to the mythic worlds of the ancient Greeks and Romans than to enlightened nineteenth-century Christians. This meant that the thought world of the early church and of Jesus needed to be translated into a modern idiom. Scholars performed this by stripping the mythical elements from the four Gospels (or more properly stated, from the three Synoptic Gospels) that recounted Jesus' ministry, in order to find his timeless ethical teaching.

Biblical critics pursued this massive project by attempting to determine the authentic life and sayings of Jesus of Nazareth, the founder of Christianity. They posited that this could be discovered by finding the oldest texts within the Gospels and by inspecting Old Testament texts and first-century Roman culture to understand Jesus' context. Once the critics accomplished this, they could accurately and effectively explain the apostolic faith and culture to nineteenth-century readers. The second half of the project required them to write a history of the earliest church. Such a history was meant to explain how and why the unnecessary doctrinal additions were formulated.

Despite the worldwide prominence of German Christian scholarship, there was no blossoming of the church at the parish level. The German Protestant church in particular was facing unprecedented attacks. The cult of science and objectivity in the universities led some scholars to question whether theology, one of the three original higher faculties of the German university, belonged at all.[3] Socialist and freethinking ideologies joined with the large Catholic minority to oppose the close alliance of the state with the Protestant state church.

Perhaps the greatest threat of all to the success of the state church, however, was the growing religious apathy in the populace. At the close of the nineteenth century, the majority of Germans were no longer regularly attending or participating in church life. Most did not leave on the basis of particular ideological disputes; rather, the church simply no longer met their needs in the

---

3. There is an added level of irony involved, as indeed, the modern German university system was built with theology as one of its core disciplines and creators of German university culture. Cf. Thomas Albert Howard, *Protestant Theology and the Making of the Modern German University* (New York: Oxford University Press, 2009).

modern world. Many of the workers were loath to spend their precious few leisure hours attending church services.

While the kaiser's regime still proved strong and resilient in the face of industrialization and urbanization—even with the growing threat of socialism—the church's place in society grew more uncertain. The Christians of Germany, the land of Luther, faced a crisis of modernity that threatened Germany's whole structure from the universities and the political establishment all the way to the parish congregation.

Theologians in the traditional theological community believed that the difficulties of modernity did not lessen the importance of the Bible for German society. If anything, they believed that the Bible's basic ethical teachings and its teachings about the value of community were more important than ever before. As a result of this conviction, they developed an active program to reinforce the Bible's authority for German society.

The initial steps to underscore biblical inspiration were clumsy, defensive techniques that aimed simply to attack critical methods. There was no attempt to build something constructive from which confessional or biblicist theologians could reform Christianity for the modern world as Luther had for his generation. Conservative theologians relied, for example, on the doctrine of verbal inspiration, which held that the Bible came word for word from God. They forced Strauss out of all theological faculties. They prophesied moral anarchy. But they were unable to find effective modern responses to modern issues raised by Strauss's successors.

It is important to note that these conservative Christians were not fundamentalists in the modern sense of the word. They did not reduce Christianity to a minimum set of absolute doctrines. They affirmed the traditional creeds of the church and of Protestantism, but the understanding of these creeds differed significantly within the broader context of theological conservatism in Germany.

As the century wore on, the efforts of conservative believers solidified into a unified, concerted effort. They focused on the question of authority to attack the most harmful elements of critical theology and the belligerent characteristics of modernity. They inquired about the point at which critical assumptions totally undermined the Scripture's authority. They posited that unlimited critical attacks on the Bible would eventually undermine everything the Bible stood for. At some point, they believed, the Bible would be so divided and its message so contested that the critical work would cease to be Protestant.

As in any conflict, the rhetoric and dialogue of the conflict changed over time. Critical theorists forced believing clergy to adopt Enlightenment language, even though that language acknowledged reason and scientism as the only certain source of truth. Using the language and discourse of archaeology, historical method, and textual criticism, historical biblical research by believing scholars in fact surpassed traditional systematic theology in the nineteenth century in both quality and prestige.

While Kähler, Schlatter, and Blumhardt were willing to question the critics' a priori assumptions about the Bible, they were explicit about developing an equally modern believing theology in response to post-Enlightenment Germany's needs. From their perspective, the problem was that the new world of objective theology and historical studies in the nineteenth century appeared to make Reformation doctrines and apologetics obsolete. Strauss and his successors never doubted justification by faith alone; they questioned the object of that faith.

Clergy who affirmed the traditional Reformation confessions were the majority in every aspect of the church leadership except for university chairs of theology. While the laity was generally only lightly informed about the new forms of critical scholarship, there were some church leaders who believed it was an imminent threat to Christianity in Germany. They were willing to take any steps to keep the contagion of critical theology cooped up in its ivory tower. Of these, perhaps the most prominent after 1871 until his death in 1909 was Adolf Stoecker. Stoecker, alongside his fellow court preacher Rudolf Kögel, was the leading organizer of a community of believing church leaders and theologians. He called the members of this group "positive" theologians to contrast them with their critical opponents. Stoecker forged this group to provide a powerful force in synodal politics to counteract the critical theology still growing in prominence at the universities. He was the leading figure and a master of networking and closed-door politicking. While the group calling itself "positive" theologians soon outgrew and at times abandoned the church-political goals set by Stoecker, they retained the name to define the particular theology of the believing community as opposed to more traditional or more fundamentalist versions of doctrine.

Stoecker's career saw successes and influence in a remarkable breadth of public life. His career rose meteorically before succumbing to a similarly drastic downfall. In the meantime, he became a nationally known preacher and was promoted to being one of four court preachers; he established a church political party; ascended to the head of the Berlin City (Inner) Mission; and became a demagogic voice in Berlin politics, even to the point of becoming Germany's first politician to use anti-Semitism to win over working-class citizens to a fundamentally conservative party. Despite the seeming disparity of his various endeavors, all of his religious and political actions were motivated by a common uniting conservative ideology of a united people following the benevolent leadership of the monarch and church.

THE LIFE OF ADOLF STOECKER

Adolf Stoecker was born December 11, 1835, in the rural community of Halberstadt in Prussia. Despite being born into a working-class family, it seems that he was brought into the company of the privileged elite while still in school. He grew close to the family of a high-level civil servant (the city's *Geheimen Justizrat*) Krüger, where he was also introduced to a particularly conservative brand of political thinking as well as pietistic Christianity. This led him so far that he felt no sympathy whatsoever with the liberal 1848 revolution taking place at the time of his confirmation. It was in the house of the *Justizrat* that he had what he would later term his conversion. It was also in this house that he met his future wife, Anna, the niece of the *Justizrat*. Anna Krüger's family was also connected to the broader theological world, as she was the sister-in-law of Martin Kähler, whose extended family possessed chairs in theology and pastorates throughout German-speaking Europe.[4] Kähler was to become a lifelong correspondent of Stoecker. Although the two did not see eye to eye politically, they were closely aligned in their hopes and expectations for the defeat of critical theology.

Stoecker continued with his upper-class fascination and lifestyle while at the Universities of Halle and Berlin. As a student of theology, he joined one of the *Korporationen*, an upper-class fraternity. These groups were known for their support of social hierarchy and the military. However, Stoecker did not seem to be a part of the most notable aspects of these institutions, the dueling clubs. Again he put himself into social circles that praised hierarchy and a respect for the Prussian institutions of state.[5]

His later theological leanings also were already showing in his college career. While at Berlin, Stoecker was able to take theology classes from some of the most liberal theologians in Germany while also attending the classes of Germany's most famous conservative, Ernst Hengstenberg. Hengstenberg, like Stoecker in his later life, was also one of the court preachers (for Friedrich

4. Hans Engelmann, *Kirche am Abgrund: Adolf Stoecker und seine antijüdische Bewegung*. Band 5. *Studien zu jüdischem Volk und christlicher Gemeinde* (Berlin: Selbstverlag Institut Kirche und Judentum, 1984), 14–16.

5. Ibid., 16–17; cf. Kevin McAleer, *Dueling: The Cult of Honor in Fin-de-Siècle Germany* (Princeton, NJ: Princeton University Press, 1994), 125.

Wilhelm IV as well as for Wilhelm I). However, Stoecker never viewed the Old Testament texts so ultra-literally as Hengstenberg. Hengstenberg's brand of ultraconservatism—the closest parallel to American fundamentalism—did not find many adherents in Germany after the Berlin professor's death. Surprisingly, perhaps, Stoecker seemed to gravitate toward neither of the extremes, and instead felt himself theologically at home in the classes of Karl Immanuel Nitzsch, a member of the moderate critical school, known as *Vermittlungs* theologians. These scholars tried to reconcile orthodox faith with the best scientific knowledge. Nearly all of Stoecker's later church political allies and theological allies belonged to this school of thought.[6]

After completing his education and apprenticeship, in 1866 Stoecker was assigned to the pastorate at the industrial, Catholic town of Hamersleben. He was the first Protestant pastor to be assigned to the village in 150 years. After active volunteering with the Berlin Inner Mission, Stoecker was thrilled to be in a community where he could engage evangelistically with the community. He saw himself in a competition with the two Catholic priests in the village for the souls of the inhabitants of Hamersleben. Indeed, a competition with Catholicism seemed to be central to his mind during his short tenure there. This idea had already taken form during his vicarage as he took a vacation to Italy and played with the idea of remaining in Italy as a missionary.[7]

His years in Hamersleben also brought out further characteristics of Stoecker's thought. First, this was his initial exposure to the harsh conditions for industrial workers in Germany. He noted particularly how vulnerable the workers who were unable to unionize were to the machinations of business leaders. A social awareness arose in Stoecker that the church needed to speak on behalf of the working poor. He would champion the cause of the poor for the rest of his life, but he also lamented that this exploitation of the workers led them to be susceptible to a greater threat than poverty and the dark side of industrialization; it made them susceptible to the ideas of the socialist party in Germany. The socialist parties at this point were thoroughly secular and staging a long campaign in opposition to the government.[8]

While Stoecker could sympathize with the workers, he could never sympathize with socialists' subversive politics. The year of his placement at Hamersleben, Prussia went to war with Austria. This excited a vociferous patriotism in Stoecker, who began to see anything less than the full support of

6. Engelmann, 18; Grit Koch, *Adolf Stoecker, 1835-1909: Ein Leben zwichen Politik und Kirche* (Erlangen: Palm & Enke, 1993), 16–17.

7. Koch, *Stoecker*, 19; Engelmann, *Kirche am Abgrund*, 19.

8. Koch, 21.

the kaiser and Bismarck as base treachery. He began to preach from the pulpit a pro–Prussian message and was rewarded with a quick, dramatically successful victory by the Prussians. He saw God's hand at work through the victory of Protestant Prussia over Catholic Austria. Furthermore, he saw God bringing his people together to support the nation. Clearly, God's hand brought forth a strong Germany united together to carry the gospel through the world and to the lapsed Protestants of the nation.[9]

So as Prussia continued to march toward war with the "godless French," in 1870 Stoecker firmly supported his king and chancellor. As the war broke out, he began to write weekly pro-German articles in the *Neue evangelische Kirchenzeitung* (NEKZ ([New Protestant Church Newspaper]). In these articles, he outlined a clearly providential view of God's actions in Germany. The war offered Germany an opportunity for change and cleansing. He wrote, "There have been those robbed by false prophets of their treasure, these have been influenced by the French dogma of godlessness and have become bestial. We need not wonder why France has become a scourge in the Hand of God to wake us from our sins. We must arm ourselves in the strength of God."[10] Stoecker perceived no tension in describing France as both a Catholic country and a secular one that was also both a tool of God to punish Germany's leanings toward apostasy (most clearly shown in the liberalism of the 1848 revolution) and at the same time the target for punishment at the hands of the newly united (in Christ) German military. In this, Adolf Stoecker created a template for all nationalist military sermons that were to come through the rest of the Franco-Prussian War, but even more for the forthcoming sermons of the First World War. Stoecker's war sermons were possibly as well known by Germany's pastorate at the end of the nineteenth century as any other modern voice in theology. This can be seen in countless repetitions of the same themes in 1914 as Stoecker preached in 1870.

Stoecker's enthusiasm for missions and the German triumph led him to take a post as pastor in Metz in the French province of Lorraine. Where Alsace was heavily Germanic and German speaking, the province of Lorraine was French. He did not remain long in Lorraine; however, his writings had become known in the highest offices, and in 1874, he was invited to fill the post for the fourth court preacher responsible for preparing one sermon in four at the national cathedral in Berlin.

In Berlin, Stoecker was able to continue considering the possibility for combining Christianity with political action. He reconnected with the Berlin

9. Ibid., 21–22.

10. Quoted in ibid., 26.

Inner Mission, in which he had participated during his university career. Even more than his work as the court preacher, his work with the Inner Mission made him an empire-wide famous preacher, known as "Father Stoecker." The Inner Mission distributed copies of his sermons throughout the empire. Again, in his work with the Inner Mission, Stoecker came face-to-face with abject poverty amidst the rising industrialization of Germany. His sympathy to the workers rose, as did his fear of the increasing influence of the socialists amidst the poor. Seeing these workers abandoning the church and the traditional morality it protected led Stoecker to his eventual decision to found the Christian Social Party in Germany a few years later.

STOECKER'S CONSERVATISM AND POLITICAL CHRISTIANITY

Despite his outreach and missions activity in Berlin, Adolf Stoecker is best remembered for his political actions. He deserves infamy as the bringer of anti-Semitism into mainstream political discussion. His anti-Semitism, however, was not the central theme of his political discourse, as one could make the case for Hitler later. Instead, Jews were one of Stoecker's multiple targets. His politics grew out of a single conservative vision of Germany as a state of faithful subjects to king and cross. For Stoecker, as long as this union held true, Germany was destined to receive God's blessing. His Germany, however, was being attacked from enemies within the state. He certainly believed that his patriotism could be seamlessly blended with his Christianity. So when he arrived in Berlin and Bismarck's *Kulturkampf* was in full swing, he supported it fully and was greatly disappointed when Bismarck backed down to both Catholics and socialists later in the decade.[11]

11. The principal reflection on Stoecker within the wider historiography has been focused on his anti-Semitic politics. Considering the developments of German politics in the twentieth century, this scholarly focus on Stoecker's political bigotry is unsurprising. He was deserving of historical condemnation, as his role in adding anti-Semitism to German politics was an important transition taking anti-Jewish sentiment from a fringe position held by a disregarded minority into one that was used by politicians to gain access to the poorer populations in urban Germany. However, even in his anti-Semitism, historians have differing opinions. Some see his anti-Semitism as being central to his person and his worldview. Others, however, suggest that Stoecker saw anti-Semitism as a means of gaining a wider electorate. These scholars point to Stoecker's lack of original ideas in his anti-Semitic statements. This historiography of Stoecker is one-sided and misses the political skill of Stoecker to maneuver himself into the national consciousness in the first place. For Stoecker's spiritual supporters, he was not particularly renowned for his anti-Semitism during his lifetime. Certainly, his anti-Semitic demagoguery attracted its share of rebukes, especially from what he termed the "Jewish press." However, within the theological community, there are nearly no comments about Stoecker's political enterprises. Contemporary theologians regarded Stoecker's anti-Semitism as something of an embarrassment,

Stoecker's later political and religious career was defined by a deep sense of disappointment in the failed aspirations of the ideal Germany he envisioned being created by the dramatic victories of the 1860s and 1870. In 1870, he reflected there was an "awakening" of the "national spirit" (*Volksseele*) that could only be explained in supernatural terms.[12] He believed that God was calling Germany to a central role in a divine plan for the world.[13] This generation was called to world evangelism and to the ending of secularism and liberalism within Germany. God had used Germany to punish the godlessness of France and to make Germans aware of the spiritual gap between the two nations. Nevertheless, the following decades had not fulfilled their promise. Instead, new leaders who were not conservative Christians came to the forefront. University professors advocated both political and theological liberalism. Even the mighty Otto von Bismarck failed, in Stoecker's opinion, to continue his drive to German Christian ascendency. This was perhaps best seen in the Iron Chancellor's seeming defeat to the pope. The heights of German political power had failed to translate God's victory into a Christian Germany.[14]

When the elite of Germany proved unable to elevate Germany, Stoecker resolved that the salvation of Germany needed to come from below. The strength of Germany was its people, Stoecker believed. Yet the simple people had been neglected by both the church and the national government. Stoecker's attention to the poor had started during his college career in Berlin, when he was assisting with the inner mission. It grew into a passion during his years in Hamersleben among the working-class parishioners.[15] After working with them, however, he came to the belief that they were being bombarded with lies and myths that were taking them away from true obedience to the church and to the state. These constituted the threats of the modern world. As he developed his political vision, he turned his political activism to thwarting these perceived threats and protecting his unified conservative vision of the state.

---

especially after his fall from the good graces of Wilhelm II. (This is likewise disturbing, as none of his colleagues within the theological world thought his anti-Semitism was even worth addressing.) At Stoecker's death, in the first memories of him, his eulogists treated it as a nonissue. Hans Engelmann, *Kirche am Abgrund: Adolf Stoecker und seine antijüdische Bewegung*, Studien zu jüdischem Volk und christlicher Gemeinde 5 (Berlin: Selbstverlag Institut für Kirche und Judentum, 1984), 11–12.

12. Adolf Stoecker, quoted in ibid., 21.

13. Adolf Stoecker, *Wach' auf Evangelisches Volk! Aufsätze über Kirche und Kirchenpolitik* (Berlin: Berliner Stadtmission, 1893), 312–13.

14. Ibid., 290.

15. Koch, *Stoecker*, 59.

ADOLF STOECKER'S CHURCH POLITICS

While the threat to Christian Germany seemed universal to Stoecker, he believed the solution would come in separate religious and political reforms. Stoecker turned first to the religious issues. After ascending to the position of court preacher, Stoecker used his position to aid in the organization of an ideological party within the state-church government. Stoecker arrived in Berlin at a fortuitous time; in 1874, Germany codified its first national church constitution built upon reformed synod structures. The varying confessional origins and theologies coalesced into political parties to take advantage of the influence and popular elections for the new German general synod (Evangelisches Oberkirchenrat, or EOK). As critical biblical scholars were monopolizing chairs at the elite German universities, Stoecker was afraid they would likewise rise to the heights of the church synods. So he put his energy into the organization of the Positive Union.[16]

Stoecker perceived an immediate threat in the rise of critical theology at the universities. He did not yet despair for the people, as the threatening theology had remained at the level of academic discourse, and most pastors remained uncritically attached to Reformation-era theology and preaching. Nevertheless, Stoecker's conservatism led him to believe that the German church was on the precipice of falling into theological error. So the immediate step that needed to be taken was to separate, as far as possible, the critical spirit of the universities from the laity. His attack came in three directions: first, to bar any critically minded church leaders from the highest levels of the synods; second, to require a certain number of conservative chairs at each of the universities, even those like the University of Berlin whose reputations were driven by their advancements in new theology; and finally, to remove the power of church decisions from potentially freethinking provincial leaders and instead to create a united *Volkskirche*, which would be governed by the high

---

16. Three general parties developed in the church synods: The confessionalists (Neu-luthertum) objected to the forced integration of reformed liturgy and church structure into Lutheran churches. The liberals (Deutschen Protestantenverein) contended that requiring creeds limited Christian freedom, and they celebrated the new critical theology. The final party was the middle party (the *Volkskirchliche-Evangelisch Vereinigung*), who believed there could be a united German Protestantism behind a devotion to the Bible even as individual German Christians maintained varying interpretations of the Bible. The Protestant Union, the conservative wing of the Middle Party, broke off in 1876 under the leadership of another court preacher, Rudolf Kögel (it was often also called the Court Preachers' Party), and it dominated synodal politics until the First World War. Claus P. Wagener, "Die evangelische kirche der Altpreußischen Union," in *Kirchenkampf in Berlin, 1932–1942: 42 Stadtgeschichten*, ed. Olaf Kühl-Freudenstein, Peter Noss, and Claus P. Wagener (Berlin: Institut Kirche und Jundentum, 1999), 24–25.

synod and emperor alone. In these intentions, Stoecker had a powerful ally, the emperor, who perceived that a conservative, nationalistic church could help counterbalance Otto von Bismarck's coalition with liberals during the 1870s.

To achieve these three goals, Stoecker recognized the need for a party of like-minded church leaders to wrest control in church elections and to guide their decisions. For this reason, he joined and advocated the Positive Union to counter the critical spirit of the universities. This group, founded in conjunction with his fellow court preacher, Rudolf Kögel, set its aims to preserve the preaching and teaching of conservative theology.[17] Kögel founded the group on strict theological terms and eventually separated from Stoecker on the question of the state church versus the *Volkskirche*. Nevertheless, together they formed a theological party whose name would soon be used outside of the strict boundaries of church politics. Indeed, within a generation, all anticritical theologians would be using the term *positive* to describe their believing theology.

In two of these campaigns, Stoecker was remarkably successful. The Positive Union was able to dominate church politics through the First World War. Critical theology was prevalent only in university communities, and proponents of liberal theology were not able to get enough votes in church elections to be able to challenge for a more prominent voice in the church. Likewise, the Positive Union and other like-minded conservative Christians were successful in lobbying to win chairs strictly reserved for conservative theology at numerous universities. The greatest of these successes came in 1888 as the kaiser and the cultural minister bent to the wishes of the Positive Union and agreed to the need for a conservative voice in Berlin, especially to counteract the perceived growing heterodoxy coming from Berlin's preeminent theologian and church historian, Adolf Harnack. The cultural minister first offered the position to the elder statesman of the believing theologians, Martin Kähler, who was Adolf Stoecker's cousin by marriage. However, comfortable in his seniority at Halle, Kähler turned down the hotly disputed chair. The cultural minister then turned to the junior member of the Greifswald faculty, Adolf Schlatter.

Although long forgotten by historians, perhaps the most influential role Stoecker played during his lifetime was that of constantly networking with other conservatives and holding together the Positive Union. He created a group of conservative theologians who all saw the inherently destabilizing ramifications of critical attacks against the Scriptures. Although he was hardly a

---

17. Johannes Wallmann, *Kirchengeschichte Deutschlands seit der Reformation*, 6th ed. (Tübingen: Mohr Siebeck, 2006), 210.

deep theological thinker and others—Schlatter, Kähler, and Cremer, to name a few—would lead the group intellectually, Stoecker's political sensibilities forged a unified community. He met Martin Kähler through his family. He guided Christoph Blumhardt through Berlin when the celebrated Swabian healer arrived as part of the funerary ceremony of Kaiser Friedrich III. Stoecker and Schlatter were regular acquaintances in Berlin, although politically they did not see eye to eye. The Swiss theologian Schlatter never accepted Stoecker's ultranationalist German political ideology, for example.

Stoecker did fail to achieve his third goal to end the traditional idea of a state church (which divided the German empire into historical regions and divisions). Interestingly, here he differed from his cousin Martin Kähler, who was an opponent of the idea of a *Volkskirche*. Stoecker's motivation for the creation of a *Volkskirche* grew from the experiences of his own generation. Certainly, other conservative theologians of earlier eras had expressed frustration with (particularly Prussian) attempts to reform the church by royal fiat. Stoecker however, mostly championed a *Volkskirche* to roll back the new restrictions on the church enacted by Bismarck during the *Kulturkampf*. In the *Kulturkampf*, Bismarck, who believed that the Roman Catholic church was a foreign threat undermining the absolute authority of the emperor, removed religious legal privileges from both Protestant and Catholic churches; these included the legal recognition of church marriages and parochial education.[18]

Stoecker hoped that as the control of church decisions was transferred, clergy and elders under the guidance of the Positive Union could also begin to police the doctrinal beliefs of the church's members, thereby ensuring that dangerous apostasy and heterodoxy would be prevented in the proposed *Volkskirche*.[19]

Stoecker believed that the *Volkskirche*, independent of Germany's rulers, would also be a perfect complement to the godly leadership of the emperor. It would be protected from the possibility of a weak or heterodox prince and would be able to stand as an independent observer and moral police of the state. He argued that the church can act in these ways only if it is free of state control.[20] In this, Stoecker was advancing Martin Luther's idea of the church and government as the two swords of authority in the state, separated in their function and purpose, but united in the protection of the faith and souls of their subjects.[21]

18. Stoecker, *Wach' auf*, 165, 167, 572.
19. Ibid., 170.
20. Ibid., 185–86.

Stoecker understood that his appeal to party politics to silence the rising tide of critical theology was objectionable to many. This was particularly true of the Lutheran churches from areas of the country only recently annexed by Prussia after the wars of the 1860s and 1870s. The Prussian state church was a united Calvinist and Lutheran liturgy created by King Friedrich Wilhelm IV. If Stoecker's *Volkskirche* came to fruition, then many of these Lutherans were afraid that they too would be forced to adopt the Calvinist liturgies of Prussia. So they objected to Stoecker's political maneuvers. He, however, warned the Lutherans that the threat of critical theology was far greater than the threat of a united church, for both churches had already been infested by critical teachers who had united under their own party, the Protestant Union (*Protestantverein*). So despite his success at uniting believing theologians of all stripes, he continued to fear critical-minded clergy's and theologians' access to church leadership because of the failure to create a *Volkskirche*.[22]

Stoecker saw a far-reaching threat if his Positive Union of believing theologians were unsuccessful at damming the rising tide of critical theology. Undermining the Bible was essentially undermining the German spirit that was at the core of Stoecker's nationalistic vision. Germany was the nation of the Reformation.[23] If the land could no longer call itself the land of the Reformation with a church of the Bible, then Germany would lose its core identity. Indeed, Stoecker saw this as the express intent of the antinationalistic elements of public life to which he turned his attention after he had used the Positive Union to effectively block the aspirations of the critical theological party, the Protestant Union.

While the religious ideology was enough to fend off the attempt by liberal church leaders to relax doctrinal control from the church leadership, it was not enough to stop the increasing power of freethinkers, liberals, and Jews gaining political leadership. Here, too, Stoecker believed that a separate party, utilizing the tools of the government, needed to step forward to promote the ideals of conservative Christians who paternalistically cared for their laity. This would be the focus of the state political part of his public life.

---

21. Ibid., 562–63.

22. Ibid., 146–47.

23. As a proud member of the Prussian united church with both Calvinist and Lutheran elements in the leadership and liturgy, Stoecker is explicitly making no distinction between the two reformers. He seems willing to overlook Calvin's Francophone Geneva in favor of its belonging within the Holy Roman Empire.

ADOLF STOECKER'S POLITICAL LIFE: THE FORMATION OF THE CHRISTIAN SOCIAL PARTY

At the height of his church influence and as a growing presence in the court, even having the ear of Crown Prince Wilhelm (who would become Wilhelm II) and his wife, Adolf Stoecker began to agitate politically. In 1877, Stoecker helped create a political organization under the auspices of the Berlin Inner Mission to lobby on behalf of the poor. His experiences in launching this movement inspired Stoecker to start his own political party to speak on behalf of the poor. Unabashedly, Stoecker called his party the Christliche Sozial Arbeiterpartei (CSAP), or Christian Social Workers' Party. He set out to speak on behalf of the workers of Germany with his own brand of paternalistic politics.

The motivation for this political party and the means of organization mirrored the foundation of the Positive Union exactly. Both were formed to counteract a perceived threat against the uneducated and simple populace of Germany. In the case of the Positive Union, it was the threat posed by university professors and their critical appraisal of Scriptures. In the case of the CSAP, the threat was the growing influence of the socialist party in these same populations. Ironically, this meant that his party would often be willing to work alongside the liberals (whom most biblical critics supported politically), who governed with Bismarck against their common enemy, the socialists. [24]

Both the Positive Union and the Christian Social Worker's Party were also strictly paternal in nature. Neither side wanted to allow the common citizens a chance to voice their opinions, as the poor tended toward radicalism in both venues. Instead, Stoecker's CSAP spoke on behalf of the poor. Stoecker did not challenge the highly unequal voting rules present in the empire. Likewise, his idea of social politics was not based on an idea of equality of merit or the redistribution of wealth. Instead, it was a model of paternalism wherein wise leaders in government, such as the emperor, would act on behalf of the workers to lessen the evils of unchecked capitalism. [25]

The idea of a Christian social safety net came from Stoecker's belief that such selfless protection of the poor was possible only if the leadership of the state was Christian. This attempt to care for the workers was not a revolutionary movement, but rather a movement of love and charity. The wealthy and capable had a Christian responsibility to care for the poor that the market alone was never able to really grasp. Likewise, only the church had been exercising

---

24. Koch, *Stoecker*, 65–66
25. Ibid., 21–22.

this kind of love all along. It was the church that provided for the care of the poor, elderly, and sick. Politically engaged Christians would be able to transition this aspect to governance.[26] For this, he needed to move away from the strictly religious elements of his position as court preacher and begin to work in the realm of politics.

As Stoecker had strongly rejected the intertwining of the state and the church in church affairs, how could he possibly stand for the church playing such an active role in government? In reality, he would have desired no such intertwining if the state had been fulfilling its original duty as prescribed by Luther. As they had failed to do so, particularly through the cartel capitalism of the second industrial revolution, the poor had found no recourse but to flee to Marxism. Therefore, Stoecker believed that in the face of these two unethical political-economic ideologies, the church needed to right the ship through continuing evangelization, charitable action, and now political activism.

Initially, Stoecker's strength in preaching served him well in politics. He had a penchant for political engagement and public speaking. The launch of the CSAP at first appeared extremely successful. He quickly became a celebrated political speaker who attracted large crowds. He was able to find enough supporters to form the foundation of his political party and to have real chances, locally in Berlin, of winning seats in parliament.[27]

As his politicking grew closer to demagoguery, the high council of the state church sent him official censure. In 1878, they warned him that he risked splitting the church over his political actions, and recommended that he give up his political agitation.[28] Stoecker ignored the warning of the church with great expectations for the elections of the same year. However, his growing celebrity did little for his political success. The elections were a disaster for his political dreams. Running as an alternative option for the working masses of Berlin against the Social Democratic Party (SPD), the CSAP was able to garner only 1,421 votes, or one vote for every forty votes cast for the Socialist Party.[29] After this unmitigated disaster, Stoecker brought his skills and his party and rolled them into the Conservative Party of Otto Bismarck. This helped advance his cause. He was even elected to a seat in parliament from the district of Siegen, which had elected him despite being on the other side of the empire from Berlin and having little connection with the court preacher.[30]

26. Ibid., 33.
27. Ibid., 75–76.
28. Ibid., 76.
29. Ibid., 76.
30. Ibid., 98–99.

While he was able to organize church politics through his informal collection of relationships, on the large scale of national politics, he was much less successful. He proved inept at the massive structural needs to run the political party. So while his speeches were well attended and appreciated, and while he became an ever more successful preacher and political speaker (both his sermons and his political speeches were reproduced and distributed nationally, especially through the Inner Mission), his party languished, winning only a few seats in each subsequent election.[31] At this time the party abandoned the term *Workers* in the party's name, becoming the Christian Social Party (CSP).

STOECKER'S POPULISM AND ANTI-SEMITISM

After his initial attempt to win over workers failed, Stoecker try to gain support by turning to a populist message. Stoecker honed this message and held it with little change over following years. It is well represented by speeches Stoecker gave in 1888, which carried the same themes from his earliest campaigning. In these speeches, Stoecker described how the Christian Germany he had seen in its ascendency was under attack. In Stoecker's cultural picture, the German people were at heart good, hardworking, prosperous, and obedient. However, they were often trusting of outsiders and therefore at risk for corruption. Outside the monarchy, forces of evil and destruction were circling to prey on the German populace. Freethinkers, liberals, Catholics, socialists, and uncontrolled capitalists all sought to either leech off of the populace or to corrupt them and lead to the destruction of the German state in favor of international Catholicism or socialism. At the heart of all of these forces (excepting Catholicism) were Jews. Using the press under their control and the capital in their industries, plus their influence in socialism, Jews sought to undermine the Protestant foundations of the German Empire.[32] All of these groups were tied together by their common victim, the poor, and by their common trait of not being truly German. With such political peril, Stoecker knew that a new political voice needed to rise up to return the common Germans back to the vision cast in 1870. This was particularly true of the working poor of the cities; they were most clearly caught up by each of these enemies of the state. Indeed, as Stoecker saw it, socialists had turned their atheistic and international gaze toward entrapping the working poor. The Jews, particularly bourgeois factory owners, put the poor into places of destitution through poor working conditions and low pay.[33] Catholics were working

---

31. Ibid., 67–68, 72.
32. Stöcker, *Wach' auf,* 286–87, 294, 295, 297.

toward building their own central party that owed allegiance to the foreign pope, and liberals were insensitive to the plight of the poor. If these groups continued in their advancement, Germany would lose God's blessings forever. So his political aspirations began with a call to repentance and a rejection of these enemies of Christian Germany.[34]

In 1888, Stoecker's political aspirations were growing rapidly as he saw the rapid changes around him. Of particular concern for him were the transitions between the three kaisers Wilhelm I, Friedrich III, and Wilhelm II. None of the offspring of Wilhelm I could possibly live up to their elder when it came to being the ideal ruler. Nevertheless, Stoecker was confident in the smooth transition of power, because Germany was led by a Christian family and was God's chosen people to spread the gospel. Interestingly, Stoecker proved willing to support Wilhelm II despite the young kaiser's rejection of Stoecker's political maneuvering a few years earlier. His image of an idealized German Protestant state remained in his speeches. He saw the movements of his lifetime thusly:

> Whoever thinks back on the struggles and pains of the German nation (*Volkes*) in the last millennium from Charlemagne to the last Habsburg, and then realizes what God has brought about in our generation. God gave us in a few years what did not come to pass in a thousand. Anyone needs to recognize that this is visibly the product of the hand of the Almighty. What the Catholic era of Germany could not win was made possible through the Reformation. What the Holy Roman Emperors could not complete with their inner struggles against the Popes and the princes, was brought to perfection through the peaceful unity (*Bunde*) between peoples and princes under the leadership of a Protestant king.[35]

No kaiser of such a blessed country could bring with him its downfall.

At this point, Stoecker realized that his vision of a future for Germany was not capable of capturing the imagination of common Germans. So he turned more and more to radical extremes of rhetoric. He first turned to conservative university students, who like him, were part of the social world of the fraternal

33. Indeed, Stoecker's greatest condemnation here was not that the Jews made profit from German labor, but that they were unwilling to participate in the same work themselves. Jews, he claimed, were unwilling to a day's hard labor for themselves or any of their fellow Jews.

34. Stöcker, *Wach' auf*, 182, 290; Adolf Stöcker, *Das moderne Judenthum in Deutschland, besonders in Berlin: Zwei Reden in der christlich-socialen Arbeiterpartei* (Berlin: Wiegandt und Grieben, 1880), 3.

35. Stöcker, *Wach' auf*, 287.

societies that aped military lifestyle and honor. They, like him, were entranced with the idea of a greater Germany at the center of Europe. During this period, Stoecker's political agitation mimicked the extreme nationalism of the historian Heinrich von Treitschke.[36] He called for the University of Berlin to block Jews from teaching classics and biblical languages to future religion students. The students who were already in support of Treitschke's ideology likewise supported Stoecker.[37] So ironically, the court preacher who set out to start a workers party to help the working poor of Berlin found his voice and a modicum of political success only with the children of affluent and powerful families.

Stoecker celebrated Kaiser Wilhelm's adoption of the Christian-Social proposals of social welfare reform from 1881 to 1889 with the advent of retirement, injury, and unemployment security as developed from fellow CSAP founding member Adolf Wagner. Certainly it was in this moment that Stoecker reached the apex of his political significance with the attempt by conservative parties to undercut the Marxist SPD by accepting various social welfare programs.[38]

Due to the prominence of Treitschke, Stoecker's embrace of extreme nationalist rhetoric and his forays into anti-Semitism were largely overlooked. Stoecker's political agitation was frowned upon by the kaiser himself. In 1885, the crown prince, Wilhelm (later Kaiser Wilhelm II), was an outspoken supporter of the court preacher. He appealed to his grandfather, the kaiser, that Stoecker was a bulwark against antimonarchical forces in the capital.[39] Kaiser Wilhelm I, however, warned his grandson to avoid being too closely aligned with Stoecker. The elder monarch wrote that too closely aligning with one political party risked an open partisanship that left the monarchy vulnerable to political attack. The younger Wilhelm seemed to take his grandfather's advice to heart and slowly removed himself from his association with Stoecker. Later, it would be Wilhelm II who forced Stoecker's resignation from his position as court preacher.[40]

Despite winning a seat for the Conservative Party, Stoecker still saw himself as a voice for the working class.[41] As a sitting parliamentarian he happily announced:

36. Koch, *Stoecker*, 99.
37. Ibid.
38. Ibid., 104–105.
39. Ibid., 127.
40. Ibid., 131.
41. Ibid., 110.

What I want is clear to anyone who would like to see. Over the past four years, I have stood in the spotlight of Berlin to fight the hegemony of capital, secret speculation, the exploitation of labor, and general corruption in industry. I have recognized the hoarding of wealth in a few, largely Jewish hands as a danger that plays into the hands of socialist revolutionaries. So I have sent the warning call out not only against the problem of mammon, but also I have warned against the social democrats who make impractical and impossible promises of a socialist people's republic (*Volksstaat*). In order to undercut the social revolution, I have called for a social reform based on a Christian foundation.[42]

Clearly Stoecker continued to believe that any disregard of the possibility of a socialist revolution came only at the state's own danger.

From his own writings, it is clearly evident that Stoecker never held out hopes that his party would ever be anything more than a minor party that would express its voice through alliances with other, greater parties. That being said, he still saw his party through an absolutist ideology rather than simply playing to a single-issue political ideal. He saw his party offering focus to the other conservative parties both in reminding them of the importance of catering to the poor as well as in recentering conservative politics around Christian values. He even saw this as the ultimate solution to the Jewish problem. A revitalized and revived Christian Germany would certainly fulfill the conversion of the Jews (a particularly Protestant belief going back to Luther).[43] Likewise, a Germany confidently moving forward in its manifest destiny would certainly recapture the greatness that led to the triumphs of 1870. So it is clear that Stoecker was not driven solely by anti-Semitism or even a quasi-theocratic ideology; rather, it was an all-encompassing conservative utopianism that saw a union of a godly kaiser, a true church, and an obedient population.[44]

STOECKER'S FALL FROM GRACE

Stoecker's political star fell rapidly in 1896. While the young kaiser had long followed his father's advice and abandoned alliance with Stoecker, he had, since the rising tenor of Stoecker's anti-Semitism, sought a way to extricate his connection with Stoecker altogether. Stoecker had also strained his relationship

42. Adolf Stoecker, *Wach' auf*, 106.
43. Adolf Stoecker, *Wach auf*, 303–304.
44. Adolf Stoecker, *Das moderne Judenthum*, 3, 5.

with the royal family when he openly criticized the royal family's Jewish acquaintances and allies. The opportunity arose to dismiss the court preacher when Stoecker was connected to Freiherr Wilhelm Joachim von Hammerstein, the chief editor of the *Kreuzzeitung*, an archconservative newspaper, who was convicted of check fraud. Stoecker was ousted from his post as court preacher and from his position in the church synod. While this did not end his political activism and participation (indeed, he sat on the national parliament from 1898 until 1908, just one year before his death), in terms of real political influence, Stoecker was greatly weakened from this point.

While still sitting in the parliament, Stoecker turned the focus of his activity back principally to the spiritual poverty he saw in Berlin's working class. He redoubled his efforts with the Berlin Inner Mission. He remained a national celebrity, and his sermons were printed and distributed throughout the empire. He certainly never renounced his anti-Semitic viewpoints, but references to them were notably diminished at the end of his career.

It seems to have been largely Stoecker's believing-theologian and Positive Union friends who stayed with him even as he lost his official status within the German church. Adolf Schlatter, who came to the University of Berlin because of the pressure that the Positive Union put upon the cultural ministry, defended Adolf Stoecker's positions and importance to the church. This led Schlatter's critical colleagues at the University of Berlin to redouble their own pressure on Schlatter. Nevertheless, while not condoning much of Stoecker's ultra-Prussian nationalism or his anti-Semitism, Schlatter continued to point to Stoecker's tirelessness in appealing to the well-being of Germany's poor as a true model for devout Christians throughout Germany. Schlatter would write years later of his admiration: "Among the Berliners he stood there . . . with one of a kind gravitas with a view on the whole of the populace and with a stouthearted love that did not only think, but also acted."[45]

Years later, as Stoecker lay dying, his cousin Martin Kähler wrote to Stoecker's wife, "The closer his servants stand to him, the more they will suffer in the crucible. Of Adolf it is true, that in his service he absorbed 'beatings with fists on his body,' but he only preached Christ and made himself reprehensible. In this he seems to me to be in a similar situation as [the apostle] Paul, when he took sufferings on himself on Christ's behalf." Kähler believed that Stoecker had been attacked because of his Christian ministry.[46]

45. Werner Neuer, *Adolf Schlatter: Ein Leben für Theologie und Kirche* (Stuttgart: Calwer Verlag, 1996), 313–14.

46. Martin Kähler et al., *Theologe und Christ*, ed. Anna Kähler (Berlin: Im Furche-Verlag, 1926), 351.

STOECKER'S PREACHING OF THE WORD OF GOD

Like his fellow believing theologians, Stoecker built his theology from a defense of the scriptural authority. He had less theological education than Kähler and Schlatter, and his ideals surrounding the Scriptures as the word of God were less nuanced and less explicit. He held a high view of the Scriptures as the word of God. This fed into both his religious and his nationalistic worldview. Harnessing the scriptural authority was the means through which both the church and the state would be transformed to once again become the leaders of the world, as he had seen in the religious excitement surrounding the Franco-Prussian war early in his pastorate. Such an outpouring of support was possible, Stoecker believed, only because the Bible was a living document to the faith of the believers.[47]

The Bible became vital in the life of the believer only through an appropriate reading of the Scriptures. In a speech given while campaigning for election to the state-church synod, Stoecker proclaimed that the time had not yet passed where the nation needed a historically grounded belief in confessions and the Scriptures. For Stoecker, the Scriptures were to be read as they had been read by Protestants since Luther. They were the foundational doctrines of Christianity, authoritative and unquestionable. This does not mean that Stoecker appealed to an uncritical innerrantist argument. The Scriptures were to be brought into the present and used by Christians to interpret and engage in current political, social, and theological issues. The documents, he insisted, were living documents that needed to be seen as such. To see them solely through the abstract methods of historical criticism was to strip them of their God-given character.[48]

This was the perfect place for the church. Stoecker understood that the fight for the soul of the universities had been largely lost; with the exception of the university seats held by supporters of the Positive Union, including Martin Kähler, Adolf Schlatter, and Hermann Cremer, the majority were held by advocates of critical theology. Nevertheless, for Stoecker, even with their education in these universities, the pastors were capable of carrying through the true teachings of the church. It was through the preaching of the pastors that the Bible was made present and living to the congregations. So, even though he politically advocated for university seats for believing theologians, he knew that the true impact on the nation would come from the pulpits of the churches, not the lecterns in the university halls. Ultimately, it was for this

---

47. Stoecker, *Wach' auf*, 576.

48. Ibid., 578–79.

reason that he founded the Positive Union to advocate for believing theology in the church leadership, because he wanted to ensure that at least the pastorate remained uncontaminated from overly critical theology that undermined the cultural shaping power active in the historically valid Scriptures that he believed in so readily.[49]

Stoecker forged the template for his life's sermons already in his time as an observer and later as a military chaplain during and after the Franco-Prussian War. He formulated a preaching theology of blessings and curses. In its essentials, it ran something like this: God is on the lookout for righteousness, and his anger against sinfulness is ever present. Thus, the larger outcomes of this world can be explained by the need for God to enact revenge on the disobedient or to protect the obedient. While wars (and other political and social movements) seemed to be over human efforts and human desires, in truth they were God's way of enacting justice. For their sinfulness, secularism, and wanton ways, God punished the French during the Franco-Prussian War. Since Germany was the more righteous nation, God blessed Germany. Nevertheless, Germans could not rest assured in God's pleasure, considering the current trends of mammonism, greed, sexual lasciviousness, and atheism that were present in Germany and needed to be countered before God punished Germany as God had punished France.

In a very real way, Stoecker modeled his preaching on the preaching of the Old Testament prophets.[50] The blessings and curses of this world were played out by God at a national level for the collective sins (or righteousness) of the people. This meant that Stoecker was calling for a great vigilance among the people to avoid not only the sin of their own doing, but also the sin of their neighbor. This may have also been the root of Stoecker's fundamental popularity. Indeed, his model published during the war and regularly read

49. Ibid.

50. This may seem ironic, considering the anti-Semitism of Stoecker. However, Stoecker was always a religious anti-Semite. The Jews were so abysmal as far as Stoecker was concerned not because they were Jews, but because they had less excuse than anybody else to misunderstand the ways of God. Their rejection of Christ as God and savior was what made them so repulsive to Stoecker. Stoecker himself developed during his studies a high respect for the Old Testament; this may have even been some of the connection that drew him to the Positive Union. The church party was started as a continuation of the work of a former court preacher and Old Testament scholar, Ernst Hengstenberg, who had been the greatest champion of conservative theology at the University of Berlin in the first half of the nineteenth century. This may also be the foundation for Stoecker's political theology as well, as the Old Testament is far more conducive to a theology of blessings and curses than are the relatively apolitical teachings of the New Testament. For just one such example of Stoecker's use of Old Testament texts, cf. Adolf Stoecker, *Das Leben Jesu in täglichen Andachten* (Berlin: Vaterlandische Verlags und Kunstanstalt, 1908), 2.

afterward would provide the essential model for most German preachers of the era. Its calculus of good and evil was easy to understand and helped a largely disenfranchised population understand its own participation in national affairs, and drew the people together in a common purpose. Finally, it added the strength (as noted in Stoecker's complaints about the abstraction of criticism) of making the Bible present and real to readers and hearers in the nineteenth and early twentieth centuries.[51]

Other than the nationalist overtones, Stoecker's politics were muted in his sermons; he never explicitly voiced his anti-Semitism. His defense of orthodoxy against the threats of modern criticism, however, remained at the forefront.[52] In this, Stoecker separated himself from the vast majority of German pastors. Every opportunity he had, he spoke in favor of the miraculous readings of the Scriptures, defending traditional orthodoxy. During a Christmas sermon, he advocated for the virgin birth of Christ, underscoring its importance to the doctrine of the incarnation.[53] Likewise at Easter sermons, he forcefully affirmed the bodily resurrection of Jesus.[54] He often couched these affirmations in terms of a general lament over the growing godlessness of Germans. These suggested a weak and dying critical spirit, in contrast to his synodal speeches, where critics were a cancer growing and threatening the body of the church. But clearly this was also intentional to encourage the members of his congregation that they were on the right side of belief as they fought against the sins of their nation.

Despite the grandiose meaning of sin in the world of Stoecker's spiritual calculus, the moral appeals he made to his listeners were largely personal. Certainly he lamented a broken justice system, but more often he mourned the breakdown of family, the perceived desacralization of Sundays, and hatred of one neighbor against another. In his prayers for his congregation, he also prayed at a personal level, asking God for strength to lead a personally pious life with a personal salvation and sanctification.[55]

Conclusion: Adolf Stoecker as the Architect of the Believing Community

Fundamentally, Adolf Stoecker is both the hero and the villain of the believing community. He built the community and created the networks between the

51. Adolf Stoecker's sermon printed in Engelmann, *Kirche im Abgrund*, 26.

52. Koch, *Stoecker*, 138; cf. Koch, *Stoecker*, 139.

53. Stoecker, *Das Leben Jesu*, 4–5, 15.

54. Ibid., 176, 179, 182.

55. Ibid., 8.

believing university theologians and the orthodox clergy. Without Stoecker's efforts, it is possible that the self-identity of the believing community would never have developed or that universities would have been more effective at blocking orthodox thinkers from their universities. However, Stoecker also laid the foundation for the clergy's crisis of the First World War. His theology of blessings and curses led to the clergy's rejection of the subtlety of believing epistemology during the First World War.

Certainly, from the level of theological innovation and subtlety, Adolf Stoecker hardly deserves to be included among the other principal subjects of a study concerning the leading believing thinkers of a generation. His theology did not have the depth of Martin Kähler or Adolf Schlatter, nor did it have the surprising nuance and flexibility of Christoph Blumhardt. Nevertheless, he played a crucial role in the debate over the nature of God's word and its moral place in Germany for the believing theologians. First, he played the crucial developmental role to link believing theologians together. Because of Stoecker's party, these similar-thinking church leaders already possessed a corporate unit when questions moved beyond the church-political realm of the initial positive union. The relationships there were significant enough that Kähler, Schlatter, and others continued to call themselves "positive" theologians, a direct reference to the church group advanced and continued by Stoecker. Stoecker also seems to have played a direct role in the creation of a chair of theology at the University of Berlin that was to go to a conservative scholar. This chair ultimately was given to Adolf Schlatter, but only after he had been recommended by Martin Kähler, who turned down the chair himself. While in Berlin, Schlatter and Stoecker were well acquainted, and at least at one event, Schlatter was the guest speaker for one of Stoecker's student gatherings. Stoecker also hosted Blumhardt when he came to the funeral for Wilhelm II. Considering the very different politics, it was most likely coincidental, but shortly thereafter, both Stoecker and Blumhardt embarked on political careers.

Stoecker also provided another crucial link for this study. He seemed to have been incredibly influential in the creation of a template for a general nationalist sermon. As the chapters that interpret the sermons of the time period cover, the main ideas of the pastorate seemed to have paralleled Stoecker's. In the main, they were conservative in their theology, differing little in their scriptural interpretation from Luther or Lutheran scholasticism. However, a common trait throughout the pastorate was the nationalist overtones of the sermons. The pastorate most likely followed (although it may have only paralleled) Stoecker's nationalist calculus wherein God blessed Germany in direct proportion to the obedience of the nation. This was a new theology—one that would have been mostly foreign to Martin Luther and, indeed, most pastors before the creation of a nationalist theology at the turn of the nineteenth century. Certainly, this theology was never so clearly enunciated as in the wake of the Franco-Prussian War. And it is clear that Stoecker was one of the lead voices at that particular moment.

What is perhaps most important to note in the link with Stoecker's later infamy is that while Stoecker seemed to be unable to gain any political allies out of his religious allies, none of them likewise spoke out against Stoecker. In fact, the believing community as a whole remained silent on the rising force of German anti-Semitism until well into the Nazi rule. So while Stoecker's anti-Semitism seemed to be unusual for this population, it was not seen as so outside the sphere of Christian thought that it raised condemnation. Considering the outrage that did come from kaisers and other political opponents, the silence on the part of the theologians is deafening. There may have been several reasons for this; the most compelling, however, is that Protestant theologians were unwilling to consider openly distancing themselves from one of their own who had reached such a position of leadership within the German government.[56]

56. This point is also made effectively by Hans Engelmann. Engelmann sees Stoecker's anti-Semitism as being more central to his worldview than I do, but his criticism of the religious community's silence to Stoecker's anti-Semitism is excellently presented. Engelmann, *Kirche am Abgrund*, 5.

3

How to Honor the Bible
Martin Kähler's Theological Views of the Bible and Ethics

*We Pietists and Confessionalists in the
churches, at the pulpits, and in the teacher's
lecterns are those who honor the Bible (sind
Bibelverehrer). The deepest foundation for
this honor is that we do not merely hear
other pious men and women who wrote
about God in the Bible, we hear God speak
to us. That is why the Bible is our best
friend, and our interaction with it, in
deepest trust and without interruption, is
crucial for our lives.*
—MARTIN KÄHLER, *AUFSÄTZE ZUR
BIBELFRAGE* (*TREATISES ON BIBLE
QUESTIONS*)[1]

In his identification of the *Bibelverehrer*, those who honor the Bible, Adolf
Stoecker's brother-in-law and Halle systematic theologian Martin Kähler tried
to find a unifying concept for orthodox Christianity. Nineteenth-century
German Christians experienced a confusing proliferation of conflicting voices.
Kähler believed that the appropriate interpretation of the Bible was being
attacked from two sides. On the one side, critical scholars wrote of the Bible

---

1. MARTIN KÄHLER, "UNSER STREIT UM DIE BIBEL: VORLÄUFIGES ZUR VERSTÄNDIGUNG UND BERUHIGUNG FÜR
'BIBELVEREHRER' VON EINEM DER IHRIGEN," IN MARTIN KÄHLER, *AUFSÄTZE ZUR BIBELFRAGE*, ED. ERNST KÄHLER
(MUNICH: CHR. KAISER VERLAG, 1967), 20.

as one of many ancient texts that could be understood only through modern historical critical methods. Their in-depth scholarship of Scripture's origins questioned every tenet of orthodox Christian belief. On the other side, certain adherents to traditional doctrines ended up destroying a true interpretation of the Bible in their attempts to salvage it. They reacted so extremely to the critics' attacks on the Bible that they began retreating from academic inquiry. In its stead, they affirmed stringent beliefs in verbal inspiration. This doctrine held that God dictated every word of the Scriptures to its authors. These tenets excluded any possibility of questioning the intent of the biblical authors and thereby undermined academic but pious scholarship.

In this theological climate, where each new book and sermon claimed to bring new insight into the very nature of Scripture, the schism in authority threatened to tear Germany's Protestant churches apart. Martin Kähler had little interest in innovation when writing about the place of the Scriptures in Christian life. Rather, he sought to find a middle ground for modern *Bibelverehrer* to understand and find God's continuing word through the Bible.

Martin Kähler's situation aided his attempt to mediate. His position in the university allowed him to interact with Christian thinkers on both sides of the divide. During his tenure, the trend in theology was that students of the Scriptures devoted themselves to minor debates over particularly difficult texts. The natural consequence was that their knowledge of the broader importance of their ideas was limited. However, Kähler's work as a systematic theologian gave him a perspective that allowed him to look at the large questions concerning the Bible and its authority. Furthermore, his scholarship gave him literary contact with theologians from the previous century, who guided him in his own careful definition of the Bible. In the end, he defined a middle path for his fellow *Bibelverehrer* to travel into the twentieth century.

The great achievement of his theology of God's word was that it respected the position of the Scriptures for traditional belief without relying on an anti-intellectual reaction that restricted the free access to the Bible. Kähler's defense of the Scriptures had important ramifications in redefining the makeup of the church, describing and motivating the ethical Christian life, responding to the changing world, and knowing how to follow Jesus Christ.

In spite of Kähler's pioneering work, his efforts have been largely forgotten or misinterpreted. His attempt to bridge the rapidly separating elements of the church came too late. His efforts, though impressive, occurred at a time when the differences could no longer be brokered. The minor status later scholars assigned him does not, however, diminish the important perspectives on nineteenth-century German Christianity that arose from his writings. For an orthodox scholar, he displayed a surprising flexibility to contextualize his beliefs in a rapidly changing intellectual climate.

MARTIN KÄHLER'S LIFE: THE FORMATION OF A BELIEVING THEOLOGIAN

A brief summary of Kähler's life sheds some light on his intellectual career. Kähler was born January 6, 1835, in Neuhausen near Königsberg in East Prussia. He possessed an impressive pedigree for an academic theologian. Both his father and his maternal grandfather were Protestant pastors and published theologians. He later remarked dryly in his autobiography that his birth year coincided with the publication of David Friedrich Strauss's epochal *Life of Jesus*. Kähler's father read the book shortly after its publication. He struggled with it but in the end abandoned Strauss's skepticism for the orthodoxy of his heritage. Following this direction, Kähler's father taught his son the traditional piety of northern German Christianity.[2]

Kähler remained in Neuhausen for only his first six years, but in his mind, the village remained the ideal childhood home. Neuhausen lay only an hour outside Königsberg, home of the famous philosopher Immanuel Kant. The church, built during the reign of the Teutonic Knights, towered over the town. It stood as a beacon to the spiritual heritage of the village. Kähler's childhood was, by his own memories, idyllic. He was born well after the Kählers' eldest child, a daughter, who died in infancy in 1826. Martin's brother, Otto, was the second child in the Kähler family. He was five years older than Martin. His life followed a very different path from Martin's. He gained great prestige in the military and made his fame in the reorganization of the Turkish army under Field Marshal Colmar von der Goltz (1842–1916). By the time of his death in 1885, Otto had earned the rank of general in Prussia and pasha in Turkey. The Kähler family also included Martin's mother's sister, who lived with the family for many years, even after the death of his mother.[3]

Kähler's road to academia began with a sputter. His first experiences with schooling were negative. Only in 1848, amidst the excitement of revolutionary fervor, did he begin to dive into reading. Around this time, his family hired a private tutor, who helped harness his excitement to turn his explorations into productive academic development. Kähler also went through confirmation during the furor of 1848. However, the excitement over politics distracted him enough that this early religious training failed to exercise much influence on him.[4]

---

2. Martin Kähler et al., *Theologe und Christ*, ed. Anna Kähler (Berlin: Im Furche-Verlag, 1926), 1–2.

3. Kähler, *Theologe und Christ*, 2–3.

The possibility of a career in theology began to open in his mind only after Kähler had already begun his university training in law. A near-death experience during a significant bout with typhus led him to question his original intentions for law and instead convinced him to change his field of study from jurisprudence to theology. In April 1853, at the heart of this decision, he wrote, "I came to my decision without any great crisis or revolution in my life. I felt no pressure for my decision. I came to a point where I felt my development led me naturally to this decision. Now I feel for the first time solid ground under me."[5] At least at the beginning of his studies, he was little concerned about giving up a potentially more lucrative or famous career in politics.

Kähler set out to find a theological home and a mentor to guide his development in theology. He began at Heidelberg in the duchy of Baden, where he fell into the influential sphere of Richard Rothe (1799–1867), a so-called mediating theologian—a theologian who attempted to combine critical thinking with received doctrines. Rothe opened up the world of literary criticism to Kähler. Rothe and the Heidelberg faculty introduced Kähler to the radical thought of the Tübingen school and Eduard Reuss's (1804–1891) history of the New Testament, *Die Geschichte der heilige Schrift* (1842). Kähler later described this first involvement as his "cold shower" awakening him to critical scholarship.[6]

Nevertheless, Kähler continually encountered conservative voices that presented a counterpoint to radical critical ideas. While at Heidelberg, Kähler was influenced by the writings of Johann Christian Konrad von Hofmann (1810–1877), head of the Erlangen school of theology, known for rejecting Lessing's claim that the Bible is a textbook for humanity. Hofmann and his followers insisted that the Bible is a portion of God's salvation history (*Heilsgeschichte*). Therefore, its contents are supernatural and holy. His experience with both the Tübingen and Erlangen schools of thought at Heidelberg introduced him to the struggle between developing critical schools and conservative theology. In a marked demonstration of the animosity between liberal and conservative theologians, Kähler's professor of systematics,

4. Ibid., 26, 54–57. Despite being excited by the revolutions he lived through, he later developed sympathy for the king. In his autobiography, written over thirty years after 1848, his principal memory of the revolutions was the story of his schoolteacher. The ill-fated teacher/revolutionary believed he had intercepted a package from the tsar offering the kaiser his support. When he opened it before the revolutionary crowd, he discovered to his embarrassment that it contained only a ball gown.

5. Ibid., 79.

6. Ibid., 76, 79, 88, 89.

Daniel Schenkel (1813–1885), held a candle up to his lips and said, "Even as I say the name of Hengstenberg the candle blows out and all is dark."[7] Through all this, Kähler began to see in Rothe a way to work with modern criticism that was not wholly destructive to the faith of his upbringing. He perceived in his favorite professor a great love for the life of Jesus and the history of the Gospels. However, the climate at Heidelberg was not satisfactory for Kähler, so he transferred to the Prussian university at Halle, where he met the most formidable force in his own development, Friedrich August Tholuck (1799–1877).[8]

In his clearest exposition of his views on the Bible, "Unser Streit um die Bibel: Vorläufiges zur Verständigung und Beruhigung für 'Bibelverehrer' von einem der ihrigen" (Our Struggle for the Bible: An Explanation to "Those who Honor the Bible" from One of Their Own to Understand and Be at Peace with the Current Debates), Kähler dedicated his book to his fellow *Bibelverehrer* (Those who honor the Bible). The story of his academic life at Halle was the discovery of academically involved pastors and theologians who sought to defend the traditional respect for the Bible among German Christians. In "Unser Streit," he took the time to name twelve *Bibelverehrer* who were the most influential in shaping his own academic and spiritual life.[9] These twelve turned Kähler's own outlook away from even the moderately critical view of Richard Rothe and the Heidelberg faculty and returned him to the traditional outlook of his upbringing.

In his first period at Halle, Kähler familiarized himself particularly with the thought of three of his *Bibelverehrer*, Tholuck, Julius Müller, and Ernst Hengstenberg. His first experiences with Friedrich Tholuck failed to indicate the future intimacy that these two thinkers later developed. Kähler was immediately impressed with the older, blind scholar, but the esteem was not mutual. Kähler introduced himself to Tholuck by leading him on walks around Halle. Here Kähler's positive impression of Rothe put the fledgling relationship

---

7. Kähler, *Theologe und Christ*, 92. Ernst Hengstenberg (1809–1862) was the editor of the *Evangelische Kirchenzeitung*, the main voice of conservative theology in Germany during the middle of the nineteenth century.

8. Ibid., 90, 92, 93, 105.

9. Gottfried Mencken (Dorpat, Bremen: 1768–1831), Ernst Hengstenberg (Berlin: 1802–1869), August Neander (Berlin: 1789–1850), Friedrich August Tholuck (Halle: 1799–1877), Julius Müller (Halle: 1801–1878), Johan Bengel (Württemberg: 1687–1752), Heinrich Rieger (Stuttgart, 1726–1791), Tobias Beck (Tübingen: 1804–1878), Johann von Hofmann (Erlangen: 1810–1877), Franz Delitsch (Leipzig: 1813–1890), Otto von Gerlach (Berlin: 1801–1849), Theodor Fliedner (Kaiserswerth: 1804–1864), and Johann Wichern (Hamburg: 1808–1881). From Kähler, "Unser Streit," 19–20.

with Tholuck at risk. Tholuck's conservative positions were incompatible with Rothe's adoption of critical methodology. Tholuck only offered to supervise Kähler's amanuensis, a scholarly work that would authorize him to become a professor, after thoroughly checking Kähler's theology for any negative effects of Rothe's influence. But once Tholuck committed himself to supervising Kähler, he took every measure to enrich Kähler's experience. Eventually, Tholuck encouraged Kähler to write a dissertation defending the Christian origins of the concept of the conscience.

In the progress of his education at Halle, Kähler also discovered Julius Müller's work on sin, practical theology, and symbolism, Kähler wrote that Müller's thought gave him "courage to stand up to all philosophies and theosophies."[10] When Kähler escorted Tholuck to a church conference in Berlin, the elder scholar introduced Kähler to Ernst Hengstenberg, professor of Old Testament and the editor of the theologically archconservative *Evangelisches Kirchenzeitung* (Protestant Church Journal). Even though Hengstenberg expressed skepticism over Kähler's promise at their first meeting (Hengstenberg thought Kähler's father and grandfather were not devoted enough to the conservative cause), Kähler continued to hold him in high esteem.[11]

In preparation for his dissertation, Kähler took a trip to Tübingen in Württemberg. The Swabian region was the center for pietistic religion in the German-speaking world. Here Kähler met and read words from another three members of his *Bibelverehrer* pantheon, Johann Bengel, Franz Delitzsch, and Johann Tobias Beck. At Tübingen, Kähler formed a deep relationship with a fellow theology student, Hermann Cremer (1834-1903).[12] Cremer introduced him to Bengel's pietistic thought and to the system of reading prophetic theology developed by Delitzsch. Also at Tübingen, Kähler met and sat under Tobias Beck, the conservative professor of Old Testament. While in Württemberg, Kähler took a short trip to the spa at Bad Boll. There he met the renowned spiritual healer Johann Christoph Blumhardt. He must have also come across Blumhardt's young son Christoph at this meeting.

Kähler made full use, then, of the community of conservative churchmen who assembled themselves in Tübingen and its surroundings. The outbreak of war between Italy and the Austrian Empire in 1859 forced him to shorten his trip and return to his Prussian homeland and Halle. Nevertheless, the trip was

10. Kähler, *Theologe und Christ*, 127.

11. Ibid., 120–25, 127.

12. Cremer later gained notoriety in his own right when he published a biblical-theological dictionary of New Testament Greek.

an important formative experience for Kähler. The tutelage he received from Beck and convening with the pietist theologians led him into a greater respect and love for the New Testament and the trustworthiness of its contents. From this point on, Kähler called himself a biblicist. By this, he meant someone whose theology was derived from the Bible's revealed authority, superior to human reason or confessional tradition. This moment was a turning point in Kähler's life and discipline as well. Previously, he had enjoyed literature and poetry and played with the idea of being an author and poet as well as a theologian and member of the clergy. He came to see, however, that the purification of religion needed to be an all-encompassing passion for it to be done properly. Upon his return from his trip to Württemberg, Martin Kähler fully devoted himself to theology and destroyed his poetry notebooks. He dedicated himself wholly to the advancement of a sound biblical theology.[13]

Kähler's reaction to the unification of Germany through a series of wars from 1864 to 1871 was initially positive, but it cooled considerably over the following years. He acknowledged the remarkable era in which he lived. When writing to his friend Dr. Carl Bertheau, head of the Verein für evangelische Mission (Union for Protestant Mission) in 1866, shortly after the astounding victory of Prussia over Austria, Kähler exclaimed "God has used Germany to pass wonderful judgments; we have lived through great events."[14] Kähler hoped that Germany's victory would allow missionaries to present the gospel unimpeded to the Slavic peoples in Austria. Twenty-two years later, after the death of Kaiser Wilhelm I, Kähler's enthusiasm seemed to have cooled. His only comment in a letter to Bertheau was skepticism about the future and the capabilities of the kaiser's young successor, whose generation had succeeded and ousted the generation of 1870.

Kähler never indicated a great disappointment, as others of his generation did, that Friedrich III did not survive long enough to initiate a liberal rule. His lifelong interest in politics, however, suggested that he was certainly among the number of his generation who reacted with disappointment when their generation was passed over after Wilhelm II's ousting of Bismarck. If anything, the young emperor's drastic break with the ruling class of 1870 only further influenced Kähler's move away from politics. Kähler instead turned to a social conservatism wherein he hoped the church would take a greater role from the state in guiding the empire's moral decisions.

In another example, he borrowed from the spirit of Germany's unification as an opportunity to buttress conservative theology's militancy in 1896. He

13. Kähler, *Theologe und Christ*, 168–69, 171, 173–74, 176.
14. Ibid., 332.

wrote that conservatives needed to fight the battles before there could be peace because, "even German unification did not come without its wars."[15] Certainly Kähler's remarks about Otto von Bismarck's memoirs showed that his initial enthusiasm about the positive religious significance of Germany's unification had fully abated. He was shocked and disappointed with the old chancellor's arrogance and self-importance. The chancellor never attributed his success to God, but rather to his own heroic strength. Kähler penned with dry irony that it was little wonder that Bismarck was replaced when he showed himself to be such a disagreeable person. In the end, Kähler wrote, "The 'magician' [as Bismarck was called] manipulates superhuman powers with secret, unnatural materials. Bismarck's comments, just like his celebratory speeches as chancellor, reserved no place for belief in God. This was not the case for other great orators of public service—no, political successes are his gods, he must serve them, and that is why he initiated neither joy in life nor friendliness to those around him."[16]

Kähler's advancement into the prestigious ranks of academia was a slow and difficult process. His first major book, *Das Gewissen* (The Conscience), was finally published in 1877, when Kähler was already forty-two years old. The long delay caused his prestige in academia to slip. The lowered expectations from his peers brought Kähler to question his own place in the university.

In 1875, Kähler attempted to break into church politics instead. He joined the congress of the Prussian state church. Shortly after the unification of Germany, the congress debated the form and scope of the future German state church. While the German Empire was unified, German Protestants were divided into a series of small provincial bodies (the Prussian union church had not expanded with the Prussian state after 1866), each with its own independent hierarchy. Many at the meetings, such as Kähler's brother-in-law and court preacher Adolf Stoecker, sought a state church that would encompass all German-speaking lands. Others suggested expanding the Prussian state church merely to the borders of the new German Empire.

Kähler, however, believed that any change in the system would be counterproductive. He was a believer in the separation of church and state. He feared that an enlarged state church would become a *Volkskirche* defined more by its German characteristics than by its Christian ones. However, Kähler was even less successful in church politics than he had been in academics. Outside of his friend from his Tübingen trip, Hermann Cremer, he found no audience for his message. Instead, he returned to academics to finish his amenuensis.

15. Kähler, "Unser Streit," 28.
16. Kähler, *Theologe und Christ*, 332, 340, 323–24, 326.

His church political ideas were, however, later justified. The move to expand the Prussian state church within the German Empire brought no permanent growth to the church.[17]

Finally, as he was finishing up his dissertation, he read the writings of Bremen pastor Gottfried Menken. Kähler adopted Menken's idea that real (*echten*) Christians were *Bibelverehrer*. The ideas of this early-nineteenth-century preacher underscored Kähler's resolutions from his experiences among the conservative Swabian scholars of Tübingen. At this point, Kähler concluded that all conservative, traditionalist theologians could be identified through their high respect for the full authority of the whole Scriptures. This simple definition identified a select and easily discernible group for Martin Kähler and others like him. Kähler called them the *Bibelverehrer*.[18]

Kähler had his work cut out for him. Through the work of scholars like Hengstenberg and Tholuck, northern conservative scholars possessed a tradition of combating liberal theology through academic institutions and methodology. However, the earlier thinkers provided no systematic unifying principles to build a contemporary theology. Kähler saw some advantages to the theology of southern German pietism and used them to lay the foundation for a new variety of orthodox systematic thought. These were found in his first broadly successful book, *Wissenschaft der christliche Lehre* (Systematics of Christian Teaching), a systematic theology text for students and seminarians.

The *Wissenschaft der christliche Lehre* failed to shed conservative theology's slavish ties to its Reformation past, however. In the work, Kähler used Luther's foundational Protestant principles as the themes to systematize his whole theology. While this was popular, it kept Kähler from truly finding his modern theology for another twenty years.

Once Kähler shifted his focus from the Reformation to the question of the Bible's authority for Protestantism, his theology blossomed. In the 1890s, German Protestants were fighting over the truth of the Scriptures on a very public level. In 1892, the Christoph Schrempf controversy over the Apostles' Creed finally forced the regional state churches to define a point theologically where certain Biblical interpretations ceased to be Protestant. Kähler began to weigh his own response to Schrempf. The result was a new appraisal of the Bible's authority that no longer relied on Reformation theology formed in a time where such questions were never asked. His writings in the 1890s, especially *The So-Called Historical Jesus and the Historic, Biblical Christ* and

17. Ibid., 252–53.
18. Ibid., 178–79.

"Unser Streit um die Bibel," both written after he turned sixty, marked his career's apex in poignancy and cultural significance. During this time, he reached back to ideas he had developed for decades, but his theology became something new: a modern, post-Enlightenment defense of the Bible's authority for twentieth-century Protestantism.

He hoped that this new theology could combat the skeptics outside the church, such as David Friedrich Strauss and Ernst Renan, whose works still created difficulty for conservative theology. Even more importantly to Kähler, however, it questioned the doctrines of critical-minded theologians and preachers who were still inside the church, such as members of his former faculty at Heidelberg. He believed these internal threats presented the greater challenge to belief in Germany, because they were still inside the church but had a misplaced trust in their own intellect. These liberal rationalists' "foundation centers more on 'ideas' rather than on the living God, the living savior."[19] In Kähler's thinking, these threats were insidious and more tempting to the typical German believer than the radical rejection of the entire gospel of Jesus Christ.[20]

After his successful completion of his habilitation in 1877, Kähler was promoted to a full professorship at the Halle faculty.[21] He stayed there for most of his career, except from 1863 to 1867, when he took a visiting position at Bonn, where the great liberal theologian Albrecht Ritschl was on the theological faculty. Apart from guest professorship semesters at Berlin and Göttingen, he remained in Halle for the rest of his career. His writing, though considerable, tended to be short theological treatises, which were collected into two volumes in 1907 under the title *Dogmatische Zeitfragen* (Contemporary Dogmatic Questions), with a third posthumous volume published in 1912. In the end, he spent three successful decades at Halle as a popular professor. He and his wife had seven children, a number of whom went on to have successful theological academic careers of their own. During his last few months, he moved to the health resort town of Freudenstadt in the Black Forest and died there of pneumonia on September 9, 1912. His last words were the Lord's Prayer and a loud "Amen, Amen."[22]

---

19. Ibid., 200.

20. Ibid., 181–82, 199–202.

21. German professors were expected to complete a second academic work after their dissertation to be elevated to the status of professor and have their income guaranteed by the state. Instructors who had not yet completed the *Habilitation* were paid solely from student fees for particular courses.

22. Ibid., 203, 262, 266, 280–82.

Kähler's biography illuminates a few crucial aspects of believing Christianity in the second half of the nineteenth century. His life parallels the arc of a significant portion of the German populace away from the liberal-nationalistic ideals of the 1848 revolution. Like these other Germans, he grew up in a charged environment and was excited by the possibilities of change and greater personal freedoms. The humanistic possibilities that derived from a fascination with Goethe and the later German Romantic writers grew in him. The residue of these beliefs led him to pursue a life in politics and law as he first entered the university. The realization of corruption and the possibility of death by typhus was an extreme means of finding his way back to his familial heritage as a member of the clergy, but the general trajectory he took was hardly uncommon. By the end of his life, his anti-revolutionary, anti-Enlightenment mentality put him in good company.

An equally important aspect of his biography arose from his experience during his studies, especially his tour of Tübingen and Württemberg—namely, the existence of a self-conscious conservative theological community. Although this community was divided into separate groups of pietists, confessionalists, and biblicists, they found they had more in common with each other than separation. The unity they achieved through their common enemies of theological liberals and skeptics forged ties between confessional lines (Lutheran and Reformed) and regional differences, where fierce competition existed earlier. For this reason, by 1896, Kähler could identify a number of *Bibelverehrer* historically and would find a similar group in his academic contemporaries, notably, Hermann Cremer and Adolf Schlatter. Kähler, too, would occasionally refer to this same group by the name of Adolf Stoecker's church party, the Positive Union. Kähler's travels through Germany and his professional associations meant that when he was writing to the believing theologians, or *Bibelverehrer*, he was writing to a group of people whose major figures he personally knew.

Contra Critics: Kähler's Opposition to Literary and Historical Criticism

Two works outlined Kähler's view of the Scriptures, "Unser Streit um die Bibel" and *The So-Called Historical Jesus, and the Historic, Biblical Christ*. In these, Kähler suggested that both extreme critics and reactionary believers threatened believing theology. According to Kähler, the principal challenge to German believers' acceptance of Scripture's authority and authenticity came from critics who wanted to question traditional views of the Bible.

These scholars' conclusions often varied radically from traditional Protestant doctrines. Kähler located the origin of the critical threat in Gotthold Ephraim Lessing's challenge to Enlightenment scholars that the Bible ought to be read using the same critical tools that scholars used on every other classical text. Kähler argued that modern scholarship took Lessing's advice so thoroughly that the nature of the Scriptures changed. For over a millennium, the view of Christians was that the Bible was a revelatory book of surpassing value to all Christians. Answering Lessing's call, the critics began to look at the Scriptures as a collection of historical documents that readers could access only though complicated scientific methods.[23]

Kähler's critique of such contemporary biblical scholarship was fourfold. First, he fought against the atomization of the Bible. When scholars read the various Scriptures as individual texts, they took them and researched them in isolation, without regard to how their passages interacted with earlier and later biblical texts. Kähler saw this as a direct outgrowth of the research that Lessing proposed. Critical academics and skeptics took Lessing's challenge to extremes when "source criticism" further divided the individual books of the Bible in an attempt to locate their oldest and truest materials. The scholarly distillation and reconstruction of "God's word" out of the Bible appalled Kähler. The practice suggested that certain elements of the Scriptures were unimportant additions that could be discarded without any loss to Christian piety. As a systematic theologian, he found this practice unacceptable. His whole career (indeed, his whole field of systematic theology) was based on finding unifying principles found throughout the Bible. Individual texts could be studied in isolation to determine their themes and content. However, the Bible only *worked* as it was meant to through reading it in its entirety.[24]

Kähler's second difficulty with the direction of modern criticism was the impression scholars gave that the Bible could be understood only through the use of the modern critical apparatus. Lessing and his successors portrayed the Bible as foreign and in need of scholarly interpretation as esoteric and ancient texts. Kähler thought this assumption took the Bible away from the individual lay Christian. He feared that scriptural interpretation would become the solitary realm of the higher critic. This was a grievous error, because he still believed that Protestant Christian faith depended upon the individual believer growing in faith through careful reading and study of the Bible. This would not work if

---

23. Martin Kähler, *The So-Called Historical Jesus and the Historic, Biblical Christ*, trans. Carl E. Braaten (Philadelphia: Fortress Press, 1964), 117–18, 123–24.

24. Kähler, "Unser Streit," 57–58.

the Bible became the sole possession of trained academics. Kähler condemned this tendency as being a result of intellectual hubris.[25]

The third issue Kähler drew with post-Enlightenment scholarship was that critics claimed to be able to find information that was impossible to substantiate. Kähler believed these claims unfounded because there simply were insufficient sources adequate for the type of modern historical research that the scholars claimed they were accomplishing. The whole life-of-Jesus movement was a flawed endeavor, because the critics hoped to reconstruct Jesus' biography without the materials historians relied upon for balanced research. For instance, the Gospel of John was discredited as a source for the life-of-Jesus studies because the author held dogmatic viewpoints. However, in Kähler's lifetime, scholars had established that all of the authors of the gospels wrote to persuade readers to accept Jesus' messianic claims. If John was excluded, then all gospels would need to be excluded as sources for the life of Jesus for the same reasons. If critics applied their methodology consistently, no sources would remain. The critics had sawed off the branch they were sitting on. All of the gospels were meant to guide readers to a saving faith in Jesus Christ. They were never intended to give a dispassionate narrative of Jesus' ministry, Kähler stated bluntly; the gospels were meant to inspire belief. Any biographical details that were found in the materials only served this endeavor. They could never function as objective biographical sources to describe the life of Jesus.[26]

Kähler recognized that the uncertainty regarding the actual chronology of the life of Jesus formed his final contention with critical scholarship. The varying chronologies from the gospels created a vacuum of real knowledge—with no certain resolutions. He condemned critics' works as fraudulent when they made theories to explain this. The researchers' only choice was to fill the vacuum with their own preconceived notions. In this case, the critics' biographies of Jesus and their histories of the church were nothing more than veiled presentations of the scholars' own presuppositions and worldviews. The resulting scholarship ironically took readers further from real knowledge. In the end, Kähler lamented that "the historical Jesus of modern authors conceals from us the living Christ."[27] In this confrontation with the life-of-Jesus movement, Kähler anticipated some of the eventual damning conclusions that Albert Schweitzer would publish eight years later. In essence, all of Kähler's critiques against modern scholarship centered around the one major difficulty that he had of nineteenth-century scholars who dealt with first-

25. Kähler, *The So-Called Historical Jesus*, 123–24; Kähler, "Unser Streit," 37.

26. Kähler, *The So-Called Historical Jesus*, 44, 58, 90.

27. Ibid., 43.

century accounts: they believed that their own modern assumptions were more factual than the eyewitness accounts of the first century.[28]

FINDING A MIDDLE GROUND: CRITICISM'S VALUE IN KÄHLER'S THEOLOGY

Kähler still believed that the critical, scholarly exercises of modern methods brought much good to Christians. He freely asserted that orthodox believers ought to heed scholarly literature, despite his sharp criticism of many of the most grandiose endeavors of the scholarly community. He pointed out to his traditionalist readers that the object of critical science in biblical scholarship was the study of the ancient languages and the history of the ancient Middle East.[29] These two studies in themselves only aided the general understanding of the Bible's language and its cultural context—two aspects that most Protestants longed for in their personal study. Kähler assumed that so long as the critical scholars remained in the field of knowable and verifiable history, these studies provided a tremendous asset for Christians. Such scholarship would serve to enhance the respect and honor of the Scriptures instead of diminishing them.[30]

Therefore, his opposition was not to critical historical study of the Scriptures per se, but rather to the critical preconceptions that the Bible's miraculous content be discounted purely as relics of a pre-critical society. He agreed wholly with critical scholars that the history surrounding the authorship of biblical texts was as crucial as the subjects of the texts themselves.

In this point, Kähler was willing to go beyond the comfort level of many of his traditionalist contemporaries. He used the histories of Genesis as an example. Kähler assumed that these stories certainly were not penned during the patriarchal epoch, but rather at a later time. So these texts told stories at two levels, and both were useful. On the first level, the story told of the original historical events during the age of the patriarchs in Genesis. The second layer told of the time and place of the authorship. In the context of Genesis, these second-level stories portrayed the world of Moses and the prophets. The description of the context and justification for the histories' authorship were as crucial as the histories that were the subject of the narratives. Even here, Kähler paid homage to the ideas of the critics. He mentioned in his footnotes that most experts built on the thought of Old Testament scholars such as Julius Wellhausen that much of the Pentateuch dated well into the monarchy and prophetic period. Yet Kähler never suggested that even this significant

---

28. Ibid., 56, 43; Kähler, "Unser Streit," 56–57.

29. In this, Kähler likely had Schlatter's groundbreaking work on first-century CE Judaism in mind.

30. Kähler, "Unser Streit," 61–62.

challenge to traditional Biblical interpretation undermined the ancient stories' value to modern Christians.[31]

Later, Kähler sharply contrasted this constructive scholarship with the insidious threat to biblical orthodoxy: the critical schools of thought that arose from the writing of David Friedrich Strauss. In his *Life of Jesus*, Strauss undermined the authenticity of the gospels by characterizing their writing as mythic. This differed from the Old Testament scholars, whom Kähler praised. The good critics poured over their texts to find their origins and the importance of the stories to the stories' authors and editors. Strauss used myth to obscure any factual foundation. On this point, Kähler wrote, "We are not fighting against the practice of literary criticism itself, but we have significant concerns about the typical destructiveness in the form of their critical history, historical research and specifically their retelling of history."[32] In essence, he accused Strauss and others of taking their unsubstantiable theories as fact and thereby impugning the honor of the Bible. Kähler took an important position on criticism that differed from that of most conservative thinkers. The threat for Kähler was not the act of critically analyzing the history of the text; it was overestimating the value of their historical findings.

Kähler had no problems writing historical criticism along the lines he proposed. His dissertation on the conscience was an example to which he could point. It was a historical critical inspection of the foundation of the modern idea of the subject. His findings indicated that the modern conscience was a product of ancient Christianity. It developed with the church and continued through the Middle Ages because of the church. By using modern historical methods, Kähler used historical critical work to strengthen the honor of the Bible and to underscore its claims as the source for modern conscience.[33]

At the core of his message, Kähler called on scholars to have a believing hermeneutic, an interpretation of the Bible that accepted, at the very least, its authority to make claims about itself. The books of the Bible repeatedly asserted that they told of God's works and originated from God's will. If that were true, according to Kähler's logic, then they must be authoritative in their entirety. Kähler promised to acknowledge critics' victory if they could definitively and absolutely negate the Bible's claims about its divine origins in part or in its

---

31. Ibid., 63.

32. Ibid., 65.

33. Martin Kähler, *Neutestamentliche Schriften in genauer Wiedergabe ihres Gedankenganges dargestellt und durch sie selbst ausgelegt* (Darmstadt: Wissenschaftliche Buchgesellschaft, 1968), 52; Martin Kähler, *Das Gewissen: Ethische Untersuchung; Die Entwicklung seiner Namen und seines Begriffes* (Darmstadt: Wissenschaftliche Buchgesellschaft, 1967), 6–7, 11–12.

entirety. However, so long as such logical defeats of the Bible proved elusive, Kähler believed that there was no recourse but to accept the Bible's claims about itself. In the realm of theology, belief must supersede skepticism as the foundation for knowledge.

Certainly, Kähler's claims here paralleled the anti-liberal trajectory of his life by the late 1890s. If liberalism was the protection of the rights of the individual conscience against the received authority of ruling institutions, Kähler had no place for it. Beginning even with his dissertation on the conscience in the 1860s, he showed that the conscience could not be separated from its Christian moorings. Therefore, he concluded that moral character could not exist outside of the church. Authority was not individual, but corporate, growing from the received doctrines of the state and church. They were to remain fixed until their rule could be undoubtedly shown to be without reasonable grounding. Since authority was thus received and not logically arrived at, the onus to challenge authority fell upon its detractors.

In such political sentiment, Kähler would have found many supporters within the church. Theologians and pastors sought to exercise their moral leadership in a Germany that was increasingly callous to their calls. The authority of the Protestant church in Germany had been endowed by historical mandate and Biblical sanction. Theological liberalism had bent too far to modernistic, Enlightenment principles when liberals identified the individual conscience as the voice of God in every individual. In his dissertation, Kähler claimed that the community of true believers possessed the correct knowledge of right and wrong only with guidance of the Scriptures and the Holy Spirit. The threat of individualism and the liberty of conscience were insidious and unfounded. If such radical ideas should gain widespread appeal, especially among the lesser-educated masses (although Kähler would not have made the distinction), then Germany risked moral chaos. Right action among the populace was possible only as long as the authority of the clergy and the state was respected.[34]

34. Fritz Stern understood this moral alarm as part of a larger trend, which he referred to as a "conservative revolution." In his view, the churches, Catholic and Protestant, were the largest groups calling for an end to liberalism and a return to a moral past. But he did not think they were the vanguard. The prophets of *Kulturreligion*, Paul de Lagarde, Julius Langbehn, and Moeller van den Bruck, fused their thought with the cultural pessimism of Nietzsche and Dostoyevsky in creating a new conservatism that held a place of uncommon prominence in Germany. The differences between the churches' conservatism and the *Kulturreligion* was the churches' ties to traditional orthodoxy, but they both shared a hope for the future built on a romanticized past taken from Germany's rural, Christian past. Fritz Stern, *The Politics of Cultural Despair: A Study in the Rise of the Germanic Ideology* (Garden City, NY: Anchor, 1965), 6–7, 11.

Contra Verbal Inspiration: Kähler's Call for Moderation from Traditionalist Extremism

In response to the criticism of the nineteenth century, many traditional church leaders resorted to the Reformation-era doctrine of verbal inspiration. The proponents of this doctrine stated that because the Bible is God's word and "God breathed" (2 Tim. 3:16), then every word of the Holy Writ necessarily emanated directly and exactly from the mind of God. If this doctrine were shown to be true (or at least universally accepted), traditional biblicists would gain the upper hand against critics who gainsaid parts of the Bible. As wholly God's word, adherents of verbal inspiration argued, the Bible would be above and beyond the probing questions of the critics, since the authors of the texts were mouthpieces of the eternal God. After all, God would not give contradictory or inaccurate information.

The advantage of verbal inspiration for biblicists was that it engaged in the same post-Enlightenment epistemology as the critical scholars. In theory, verbal inspiration could be proven or falsified with the same techniques of modern science that critical scholarship valued so highly. Proponents of verbal inspiration held that all the supposed contradictions and inaccuracies of the Bible brought up by the critics had, in the end, a logical explanation. At some point biblical scholarship would discover this truth either through archaeological evidence or through a proper understanding of the text itself and put the argument to rest.

Kähler believed that retreating into a dogma of verbal inspiration was a significant step away from a constructive interaction with the best scholarship. Verbal inspiration had shown itself historically to be an ineffective method of dealing with problems of biblical interpretation. He pointed to the church battles of seventeenth-century England, where the doctrine of verbal inspiration was invoked. It neither resolved the doctrinal difficulties between Christian factions nor strengthened the position of the Bible for future doctrinal struggles. Rather, the dogma embittered Christians against the all-supreme "Bible-pope." On the continent, the dogma similarly did not resolve the issues that divided the Lutheran and Reformed traditions, much less the schism between the radical reformers and the Catholics. What is more, all of these traditions held to the authority of the Scriptures as divinely inspired. Kähler asked how modern biblicists hoped that verbal inspiration, with its past impotency, could possibly resolve conflict with Enlightenment critics who did not even see the Scriptures as originating in any way from God. Comparing verbal inspiration to weaponry, he wrote, "One lets a rusty weapon go when he has fresh arms from a blacksmith."[35] In his opinion, verbal inspiration had already shown itself incapable of advancing the church.

The second problem with the doctrine of verbal inspiration for Kähler was that it undermined the authority of the apostles and early church. In Kähler's view, the apostles, as leaders chosen by Jesus, received from him the authority necessary to write letters of admonition to other churches and for the Christian church as a whole. They were authoritative because of their position within the church and their proximity to Christ. The doctrine of verbal inspiration, though, in attempting to strengthen the authority of the Bible, ended up destroying the authority and responsibility of its authors. Verbal inspiration depended upon the belief that the Bible was written in such a way that every word was absolutely as God intended it. In effect, under verbal inspiration, God was the sole author instead of the prophets and apostles. Instead of buttressing the authority of the early church, Kähler argued, verbal inspiration sapped the apostolic church of its remaining creativity and power. Verbal inspiration turned the authors in effect into human "quills" writing the dictated words of God, rather than allowing them to be creative messengers sharing the work of God that they witnessed. This was not the believing, obedient hermeneutic that Kähler argued was necessary, but rather a rote, slavish submission.[36]

Thirdly, Kähler believed that dogmatic verbal inspiration forced scholars and readers to focus on secondary and less important passages of the Bible instead of looking at the most important texts. As mentioned earlier in this section, the belief that God inspired every word of the Bible led dogmatists of verbal inspiration to conclude that, as God is perfect, so too must the Bible be perfect. Again Kähler argued that this dogma put *Bibelverehrer* in a difficult position. Holding verbal inspiration, traditionalist believers needed to defend the accuracy of every word and fact. Even minor grammar errors could not be excused without impugning the character of God. For Kähler, this belief was a terrible waste of time. He asked why orthodox Christians should be forced to support their position by chasing down the proof of every minor biblical jot and tittle. Those minor elements were unessential for salvation. A frustrated Kähler pronounced that nit-picking over minor details had little or nothing to do with the essence of the faith. Minor biblical details were nothing more than a distraction from true faith.[37]

Verbal inspiration's methods were backward, according to Kähler. This approach looked for the truth in the major things by proving the minor. He, in

---

35. Kähler, "Unser Streit," 44–46.

36. Ibid., 44.

37. Ibid., 44.

contrast, expected to see that attacks on minor issues would prove unimportant when the major points were lined up. He held that extreme forms of verbal inspiration were ultimately destructive to faith. He asked, for example, what would result if critics discovered one single, definitive error in the text. The only recourse for verbal inspiration would be to scrap all faith in the Bible. Since no self-respecting adherent of verbal inspiration could accept such a possibility, this forced promoters of the dogma into a position of being unable to look at the critics' problem with an open, objective mind. Seen positively, verbal inspiration was a strengthening of the Bible's authority by tying its perfection to the faultlessness of God. Negatively speaking, however, the doctrine of verbal inspiration meant that if the Bible were partially in error, it would be fully in error. This was a level of certainty about Biblical accuracy that Kähler thought unnecessary and damaging. In the end, Kähler thought the doctrine of verbal inspiration idolized Biblical factuality and created an unrealistic image of the text.[38]

BLAZING THE MIDDLE WAY: THE BIBLE AS GOD'S WORD IN MARTIN KÄHLER'S THEOLOGY

Kähler found his middle ground between destructive criticism and dogmatic verbal inspiration through a theology of the word of God built upon its efficacy for believers. This subjective proof did not allow for a certainty of verifiability that his opponents on both sides sought. However, it helped him to avoid the pitfalls of overly stringent dogmatism while allowing criticism its proper, controlled place among traditionally orthodox Christians. To do so, Kähler used systematic theology to begin defining the makeup, intent, and authority of the Bible, and to ascertain its divine aspects. By logically following the doctrines of traditional Protestant belief, he expected to find the best way to show the Bible's continuing authority for the Christian community. This aspect was crucially important, as the Bible remained the sole source of dogma for Protestant churches and needed to remain an authority to combat heresies from the critical sphere and elsewhere.

Kähler acknowledged the critics' principal claim against the adherents of verbal inspiration—namely, that the Bible is not an infallible text. But he did not believe it is merely a pious artifact from premodern unenlightened authors, either. For him, the Bible still had significant importance and authority. Drawing a comparison with the author of 1 Peter's description of the perfect church made of fallible human stones, Kähler asked whether the Bible could

38. Ibid., 47, 49, 70; Kähler, *The So-Called Historical Jesus*, 114.

not also be made up of fallible human texts that came together into a perfect Bible through which God speaks to God's people. In this respect, the value of the whole of the Bible is greater than the sum of its individual parts.[39]

Despite his willingness to acknowledge certain inaccuracies in the Bible, Kähler set out to authenticate its veracity as a historical text from radical literary critics who questioned any authenticity of its historical accounts whatsoever.[40] For Kähler, the artless description of the gospels leads to the reader's intuitive belief in Jesus' authenticity. The gospel narratives bring their readers face-to-face with the historical Jesus. They do not possess the characteristic quality of poetry. Jesus was an actual person with personality, not a mere abstraction of the finest qualities of humanity, as one would expect in an epic.

Kähler turned the argument back on the critics and asserted that the very desire to write the definitive "life of Jesus" came from this instinctive knowledge. The direction of Jesus' life is so difficult to comprehend and pin down precisely because he was a real person with a real person's complexity. While the gospels do not provide the source material to write a thorough biography of the life of Jesus, Kähler emphasized that they give true glimpses of Jesus' character. Kähler described the gospels as Jesus' disciples' memories of the life of their lord. As Kähler suggested, these recollections were Jesus as they remembered him—that is, Jesus as he typically was. This typical behavior shines through so powerfully that in each of the stories within the gospels, the whole personality of Jesus is clear and accessible. Kähler wrote, "In every drop of bedewed meadow the light from the sun is reflected; likewise in each little story the full person of our Lord encounters."[41] Even though the gospels are sorely lacking as historical sources appropriate for a proper biography, they are adequate to bring all future generations face-to-face with the living Jesus Christ.[42]

But if the stories of Jesus are historically authentic, what is to be done about the miraculous stories? Here Kähler's answer strayed even further from the critical scholarship of his day. He acknowledged that the nature of the miraculous events was not such that they can be recognized as historical (i.e.,

---

39. Kähler, *The So-Called Historical Jesus*, 52.

40. Bruno Bauer is perhaps the best known of these critics. In his scholarship, he questioned whether even the Markan tradition was based in fact. In the end, he answered in the negative and believed that the author of Mark created a completely legendary Jesus from the Messianic expectation of the Jews. William Wrede would renew Bauer's claims a few years after Kähler's publication of "Unser Streit um die Bibel" and *The So-Called Historical Jesus*.

41. Kähler, *The So-Called Historical Jesus*, 81.

42. Ibid., 79.

historically viable in the scientific sense of his day), because they did not change the natural succession of causalities. However, here he drew a line between historical verifiability and theological necessity. The miraculous events of the Bible affirmed in the historic confessions of the church—the virgin birth, the resurrection, the ascension, and Jesus' return—cannot be researched with historical certainty, but they are necessary for a correct understanding of the Bible. In such situations, theology supersedes historical objectivity, and in that case, believing Christians are beholden to the authority of the Scriptures and their inspiration as preserved in the text. In this respect, Kähler's work on systematic theology drew unquestionably from the entire Bible, even those parts which were subject to attacks by the critical pen. So, with the exception of the supernatural accounts wherein a Christian must rely on faith, Kähler did not believe that the appropriately conceived perspectives of the critical and the traditional doctrines of orthodoxy were mutually exclusive.[43]

Regarding the authority of the biblical writers, Kähler noticed that, with a few exceptions (that proved the rule), the authors of the New Testament never explicitly wrote that they were receiving the text from the Holy Spirit. He believed that the doctrines concerning scriptural inspiration came at a later date from an understanding that the apostles wrote the messages necessary for the church's success from authoritative positions (i.e., apostles, prophets, or teachers) within the church. Hence, in retrospect, the church viewed the Scriptures to have arisen from God for the church. However, inspiration was not their original source of authority. The authority of apostolic ancestors came from their experience as they sat at the feet of Jesus and had firsthand reception of his teachings. Jesus trusted them with the responsibility to pass these teachings down to successive generations. So for Kähler, the apostolic writings' principal value was not derived from their perfection, but from their testimonial witness to Jesus' life and ministry. This did not dampen his belief that the Bible stands as the supreme authority for Christian faith. The Bible continues as the source for all belief and knowledge of God. Its authority is undiminished even if the Bible was not written through the auspices of verbal inspiration. Christians can be certain that even though the Bible is potentially factually flawed in portions, it is true in its essentials.[44]

Regarding the Holy Spirit's work and influence on the Bible, Kähler was less clear. On the one hand, he did not want to give credence to the adherents of verbal inspiration, who gave the Holy Spirit credit for every word of the Bible. On the other hand, he desired to respect and continue the beliefs of Protestants

---

43. Kähler, "Unser Streit," 22.

44. Ibid., 63–64; Kähler, *The So-Called Historical Jesus*, 138–39.

concerning the Holy Spirit's formative role in the writing and collecting of the biblical texts. These beliefs were upheld by Christian leaders from the Reformation through the revival movements of the nineteenth century. In doing this, Kähler never gave a clear delineation of where the inspiration of the Holy Spirit ended and the independent (and fallible) action of the biblical authors began.

Kähler judged that the Holy Spirit's hand was in every step of the work, from its authorship to its collection and preservation through generations. He justified his lack of a strong position by looking to Jesus' response to the mockery of the Pharisees in Matt. 12:31-32. In this passage, Jesus explained that insults and affronts against him would be forgiven; so, too, would misconceptions of the Holy Scriptures. So while Kähler disagreed with extremists in the verbal-inspiration camp about the means of inspiration, he agreed with them fully concerning the authority and source of that inspiration. That the Scriptures contain the living word of God and point to the saving work of Jesus Christ is beyond question.[45]

THE SUBJECTIVE WORD OF GOD AND BELIEF

In Kähler's middle way, the Bible functions as the word of God because it is the way to the truth of God and God's Son, Jesus Christ. Kähler wrote, "The Christian, though, does not seek the truth in every direction only for his or her own benefit. For the Christian its goal is *the* Truth that teaches the way to life. That is, to where one can gain knowledge about the true God and his son, Jesus Christ (John 14:16, 17:3). The pursuit of this life is salvation. To discover salvation and the knowledge of this salvation, we study the Bible."[46] Kähler argued that Jesus Christ was, after all, the center and origin of Christianity as well as the principal focus of the Bible. The prophets anticipated his arrival, and the apostles preached his death and resurrection. Kähler began with the fact that the gospels were the only written account available for Christians to begin to know Jesus' character. From this, Kähler followed the long tradition of orthodox theology. He argued that because Jesus was the image of God, the very Word of God (John 1), the gospel's portrayal of Jesus is also the means by which Christians can begin to know God's nature as well. Unlike the critical histories of the life of Jesus, Kähler affirmed that the gospel's proclamations are distinctly spiritual. Its purpose is to inspire faith in Jesus as the son of God, rather than to provide a historically verifiable biography. Through the supernatural

---

45. Kähler, "Unser Streit," 42–43, 79–80; Kähler, *The So-Called Historical Jesus*, 140.

46. Kähler, "Unser Streit," 37.

authority of the Bible and the biblical authors demonstration of God through Jesus, Kähler wrote, the Bible puts the reader into the very presence of God.[47]

Kähler asserted that the Bible functions as God's Word when it reveals God's testimony to the world. It does this by providing an enduring witness to the earliest examples of faith. This aspect was so important to Kähler because the Bible reveals qualities of God that are inaccessible to reason alone. The revelatory character of the Bible makes known the divine message of what is necessary for salvation. One cannot know about God, Kähler argued, unless God reveals himself.[48]

Nevertheless, this still did not answer the principal question Kähler set out to address—namely, how it can be knowable that the Bible is God's word. The common measures of the time to ascertain the Bible's divinity were tangible and measurable. Critical theologians waited until it was historically verifiable for it to be potentially true, and traditional dogmatists who adhered to verbal inspiration determined its divine origins due to its proscribed infallibility. Kähler pointed instead to its efficacy in the life of the church and the individual believer. He wrote, "We feel the effective power of the Scriptures in the words set appropriately in the text. We feel it in the way we have questioned its testimony in a thousand ways, and learned its effects in history. It has stood the test of time and for this reason we affirm that the Bible speaks from the acts and Word of God. Seek and ye shall find in this book."[49] Even though the Bible gives true testimony of Jesus, this is not enough. The Bible is God's word because it affected and changed the history of the world in ways that transcended the lives of individuals. For Kähler, this was proof of its origins and sustenance in the spirit of God, even if the Bible's exact influence on the history of the world was as difficult to ascertain as the historicity of its subject.

Kähler here set the stage for Schlatter to develop the form of theology that could best be described as critical mysticism. Christianity's power and authority in the modern world came from the sense of togetherness the believer received from his or her interaction with the Bible. Once oneness and certainty with God were established, then measures of modern epistemology were powerless to shake that foundation. In an age of increased popular objectivity and positivism, this tendentious doctrine must have come across as a sign of weakness to others around them. This would have been doubly true for the

---

47. Kähler, *The So-Called Historical Jesus*, 61, 86, 104–105, 127; Martin Kähler, "Jesus und das alte Testament," in *Dogmatische Zeitfragen: Alte und neue Ausführungen zur Wissenschaft der christlichen Lehre,* 2nd ed. (Leipzig: Deichert, 1907–1913), 3:111.

48. Kähler, "Unser Streit," 55, 39–40, 70.

49. Ibid., 40.

lesser-educated masses, to whom the modern critiques of so-called scientific objectivity made by Schopenhauer and Nietzsche had not yet filtered down. Even though Kähler and Schlatter were taking on the post-Kantian revolution, they could not wholly shed the transcendent picture of religion as an immeasurable phenomenon that exists alongside the knowable realities of the physical world.

A Response to Christ's Sacrifice: God's Word and Christian Ethics

As the inspired revealer of the salvation enabled by Jesus' sacrifice, the Bible is God's message to the church. For Kähler, then, it follows that the Bible is the means by which God communicated God's wishes and plan to believers. In so thinking, Kähler drew from the Protestant tradition of Martin Luther, who held that the Bible is the means of directing and organizing the church. He believed that the church gives birth to ethical action through the believers' common experiences of Jesus. The Bible's standing as the word of God and the means to any knowledge or encounter with Christ meant that the church needs to fall back on the complete Scriptures as its exclusive authority. Kähler portrayed this in sharp contrast to the critical spirit of the academics of his era, who sought to use rationalism (or religious consciousness) to detect the word of God within the Bible. For Kähler, this indicated a significant misappropriation of priorities. Latter-day believers do not have the authority to judge or discard Scripture's moral prescripts. As a guide to right action, the Bible needs to be kept whole as the authority of the church, no matter the current state of critical research at the time.[50]

Kähler's definition of the word of God as the foundation for ethics was dynamic. For Kähler, the Bible receives its full potency as the word of God only when a Christian reads, believes, and acts upon the message in the Bible within the Christian community. The ethical life of the Christian validates the Bible's existence and therefore makes it even more supernatural, even more the word of God. A changed life is the ultimate testimony to the efficacy of Scripture, and thereby is proof of its supernatural character. Certainly, if the reader failed to act on the leadership of the Scriptures, however, the Bible would remain wholly God's word to judge the reader's immorality. The purpose of Scripture is to

---

50. Martin Kähler, *Schriften zu Christologie und Mission: Gesamtausgabe der Schriften zur Mission mit einer Bibliographie,* herausgegeben von Heinzgünter Frohnes, *Theologische Bücherei: Neudrucke und Berichte aus dem 20. Jahrhundert,* vol. 42 (München: Chr. Kaiser Verlag, 1971), 82; Kähler, *The So-Called Historical Jesus,* 133, 134–35.

bring about God's will. So the Bible is fully God's word only as it brings about God's will.

Kähler's mechanism for ethics was simple by comparison. Through the revelation of God and the sacrifice on the cross, God's word carries the message by which sinners can be redeemed. Christian ethics are the natural response of Christians to the salvation they received through Christ. For Kähler, ethics are the transformation of the Christian's life in response to and in proportion to the salvation that has been given.

For Kähler, true Christian morality is the act of making good on Jesus' salvation by living as much an exemplary life as a justified believer as one had lived a sinful life before conversion. As a Protestant, he did not define this as justification by works, but rather acts of gratitude. Although the debt can never be truly repaid to God, the Christian perceives the changed life as verification of the word of Christ in him or her.[51]

ETHICS IN PRACTICE

In these respects, Kähler's model of ethics as a response to Christ's salvation in hope of eternal rewards differed only minimally from traditional Protestant ethical teaching. Kähler was certain that his model also functioned in his contemporary world. His published ethical teachings were not as thoroughly developed as his systematic theology. For this reason, his specific ethical directives were less complete than his theological justification of them. Work and mission were two examples he used to provide insight into the specific mechanism of his understanding of the Christian life.

Kähler compared the work of his turn-of-the-century world with the discourses on work in the Bible. God assigned work to Adam even before the entry of sin into the world, and the Bible describes God's creation of the world as work. For this reason, work is a necessary and godly pursuit for everyone. Likewise, this showed that the Sabbath law that people should work six days and rest on the seventh still held true, because the work of human hands is similar to the creation by God's hands. Despite the changes in work patterns between the ancient world of the Bible and the modern era, Kähler wrote, "Even today, the word unemployment brings fear and trembling."[52]

Kähler recognized, however, that in his experience, work often came with suffering. He attributed this to the effects of sin. Again he delved into Scriptures

---

51. Martin Kähler, *Wissenschaft der christlichen Lehre: Von dem evangelischen Grundartikel aus* (Neukirchen: Verlag des Erziehungsverein, 1966), 470, 476.

52. Martin Kähler, "Einleitung zur Ethik: Zwei Eröffnungsreden zu Vorlesungen über die Ethik," in *Dogmatische Zeitfragen* (1913), 3:110.

to defend his point. He pointed to Isa. 43:24, where the prophet spoke the response of God, "You have burdened me with your sins and wearied [made work (*Arbeit gemacht*) in Luther's translation] me with your offenses." He used this to indicate that God, too, suffers with work due to the sins of humanity. However, Kähler wholeheartedly encouraged his readers by noting that work combined with prayer would achieve godly ends again. Here he pointed to the success of the church from its institution by Jesus through the Reformation and up to his own day. Kähler wrote that the root of all spiritual success is work, charged from the will of God, combined with prayer, wherein God gives the believer sustenance.[53]

According to Kähler, one of the natural ways for Christians to respond to God's forgiveness is through mission: the proclamation of God's word to those who do not yet know it. Mission is the most elementary action of the Christian believer who receives the word of God. It is sharing one's gratitude for salvation with others. Mission was sacramental for Kähler. He compared mission with partaking in Communion. If Communion is the act of remembering Jesus' death through the symbolic eating and drinking of his flesh and blood, then mission is the act of remembering Jesus' resurrection by its proclamation to the world. The act of preaching the gospel, or *kerygma*, was for Kähler how the Bible takes its final step to become the realized, effective word of God. Kähler believed that as it is preached, its truth changes lives.[54]

It followed that Kähler grew excited about the possibilities for world mission through the expansion of colonialism. The Christian West finally possessed the opportunity to share the gospel freely in the world. This included evangelizing both those whose faith had lapsed and those who had never before heard the Christian gospel. As he told it, this expansion was not only a commandment of Scriptures, but also the completion of them. The Scriptures began with the creation of the world by God, followed by the fall of humanity into sin. However, through mission, the world would be restored to God in the culmination and completion of history.

Because Jesus' atonement was meant for all humans universally, it needed to be proclaimed throughout the world. Kähler observed, "*The will of God* that was revealed in Christ, *is Evangelism.*"[55] He therefore wholeheartedly supported the burgeoning Protestant missions movement. In this respect, like most theologians in the nineteenth century, liberal and conservative, Kähler was

---

53. Ibid., 109–10, 114–15.

54. Kähler, "Die Bedeutung der Mission," 71; Kähler, *The So-Called Historical Jesus*, 131.

55. Kähler, *Schriften zu Christologie und Mission*, 100.

optimistic about the advancement of the Christian church via the advancement of European imperialism.[56]

Even though ethics were the natural outcome of salvation, Kähler admitted that their effects were difficult to quantify. In contrast, the extreme outcomes of sin and evil could be measured through criminal studies. This asymmetry was due to the fact that a pure Christian community of believers who truly imitated Christ had never existed. He acknowledged that there was no Christian community in the past that had wholly lived up to its calling of a life lived in holy gratitude. His explanation for this phenomenon was that no Christian community was ever wholly separated from the world.

Kähler's explanation of this was twofold. First, every Christian setting included some who lived in the Christian community but were not truly believers and did not yet know the gratitude that comes from salvation. Second, even healthy Christian community would continually bring in new members and new converts whose Christian lives were not yet mature or fully dedicated to the imitation of Christ. Life within the Christian community was a cycle of maturation and numerical growth. The continual attempts of Christians to model themselves on the will of God through the imitation of Christ would inspire the belief and entry of new Christians into the church through evangelism, and they, in turn, needed time to mature.[57]

Kähler's ethics fell comfortably into the common vision of German nineteenth-century culture and religion. It exuded optimism about the character of humanity and the perfectibility of human knowledge. Despite his warnings about contemporary misinterpretations of the Scriptures and his acknowledgment that a perfect society had never existed (and would never exist), his image of the Christian community was of one always approaching perfection. He optimistically described the mature Christian believer as one who approaches sinlessness.

Karl Barth's postwar critique of nineteenth-century theology would skewer this optimism as one of the lead causes for the church's inability to understand or condemn the great bloodshed of the war years. Barth's response to such optimism was his own reevaluation of Calvin's doctrines on the depravity of humanity in the light of God. Yet without hindsight's wisdom, Kähler could hardly be blamed for his views. In comparison with many of his contemporaries, his optimism was moderate. It was hard to see the advancements in culture, art, sciences, technology, and the long-standing peace, and not imagine that the world was advancing to a moral society.

56. Kähler, "Die Bedeutung der Mission," 72–74.

57. Kähler, *Wissenschaft*, 473–74, 485.

Furthermore, Kähler, and Schlatter after him, would claim the possibilities of the prospect for true moral advancement with the help of God, but they both carried significant critiques of the unbelief that surrounded them. Perfectibility in their theology was not a passive act. They did not hold that society and culture were swept up in a wave of progress beyond human efforts. Morality was a goal to be pursued, and it was possible only with the strength of God. This must be understood as an unresolved tension within the German Christian community of the time. On the one hand, in certain areas of reflection (mission most notably), the church leaders were ultimately optimistic about their society. They saw the forced westernization of the colonized world (and the corresponding growth in church rolls) as an unmitigated good. On the other hand, when looking at urban culture, poverty, crime, and conspicuous consumption by the wealthy, the general tone of believing pastors was pessimistic, and ideas of the decay of culture were commonplace. Here Kähler, like the more vociferous Stoecker, marched in lockstep with others. Clearly his middle way could not resolve this tension.

Defending the Young and Protecting the Church: Kähler as Teacher

Kähler carried his passion for the Scriptures and his fervency about its interpretation into the classroom in his role as professor of theology at the University of Halle. Perhaps because it took him so long to get published, he took his responsibility of mentoring young upcoming church leaders even more seriously than his published scholarship. He wrote a few short pamphlets aimed at helping students adjust to their university experience.[58] He also fulfilled his mentoring role from the lectern, teaching courses throughout his career at Halle. His extant lectures testify that his teaching was passionate and frank. He went beyond the mere framework of factual knowledge necessary for the course subjects, sharing his greatest fears and hopes connected to the work of theology. Through these writings and lectures, Kähler imparted to his young listeners some of his most candid thoughts on the state of Christianity.

In the final lecture in a course on the history of nineteenth-century theology, Kähler summed up the semester with this thought: "That is what remains and is great from the historical projects [of the nineteenth century] that we undertook: the historical Christianity, the historical Christ. Even though

---

58. Martin Kähler, *Wie Studiert man Theologie im ersten Semester? Briefe an einen Anfänger*, 2nd ed. (Leipzig: Deichert, 1892); Martin Kähler, *Der Lebendige Gott: Fragen und Antworten von Herz zu Herz* (Leipzig: Adeichert'sche Verlagsbuchhandlung Nachf. (Böhme), 1894).

the academic pursuits were purely historical, they were not merely historical, because in Christ came something timeless into our ever-changing life. And indeed the whole historical research of the nineteenth century was about the Christ! What was the result? The result came from the need—and it is so, gentlemen, so little one likes to hear it—for authority!"[59] He knew that his students were being bombarded with various claims of authority. The most potent of these authorities for the day's young theologians were the claims of science and knowledge on one side, and the revelation of the Scriptures on the other. He used his lectures and his writings to persuade his students principally to seek submission to the latter.

In his short pamphlet *Wie Studiert man Theologie im ersten Semester? Briefe an einen Anfänger* (How Should One Study Theology in the First Semester? Letters to a Beginner), Kähler urged students to set in motion their relationship with the Bible before inaugurating a relationship with their professors. He suggested that beginning students ought to commence reading segments of the Bible in Greek and Hebrew before the start of the first semester. Without this early preparation for the first semester, they would never be able to develop a true relationship with and love for the Scriptures, even if they were to use the Scriptures for their whole career. From his own experience, Kähler wrote that when students waited for the semester to begin and waited for their professors to direct their reading, their professors became the spiritual authority instead of the Scriptures. Initially, reading the Bible in its original languages was difficult, but it would pay immense dividends in the future.

Here, too, the Bible was an authority that transcends human reason. Kähler promised that if the students began to read the Scriptures, they would be nurturing a relationship they would carry through their entire theological career. Even if a student was certain he already knew the Bible, his present knowledge was not enough. Kähler learned in his own career that he needed constant review and rereading of the Bible. In return, the Bible promised to give continually new insights to its reader. He also reminded students that this personal devotion would continue to serve them in their own faith even when they were studying the Bible in its purely historical aspects.[60]

Kähler wrote that this spiritual piety would also advance the academic careers of his readers. Academic research required an open mind and an open eye to new detail in the Scriptures. Students could not interact with Scriptures at the highest level simply by accepting the authority of the church, school,

59. Lower Saxony State and University Library, Göttingen, Cod. MS. Martin Kähler, Box 12, Ansätze und Entwürfe, #9, Letzte Vorlesung: Geschichte der Dogmatik des 19. Jh., 1.

60. Kähler, *Wie Studiert man Theologie?*, 18–19, 20, 22, 26.

or parents. The Bible needed constant study to be truly understood. The advancements and ideas that theological students received when they studied in a university could be productive only when the students first knew the Bible for themselves. He encouraged his readers that the necessary experience of Christianity came solely from the intimacy with the biblical source of information about Christ and the church.[61]

In his lectures, Kähler presented similar themes. The authority he spoke of in his lectures on nineteenth-century theology came from Scriptures alone. In the course, he divided nineteenth-century theologians into camps of "positive" (confessionalist or biblicist) thinkers and critical scholars. After drawing out the bitter divisions within German Protestantism, he acknowledged that nineteenth-century theology seemed more capable of dividing Christians than of formulating the ultimate purpose of modern Protestantism.

Yet he saw indications of direction and purpose in the theology of the nineteenth century, despite its contested points. The direction for future Christianity came solely from the positive theologians. For Kähler, the positive scholars were the only ones who made true steps to define constructively the authority for the church and the historical veracity of the Scriptures. The critical scholars were of little value to Kähler because they were unwilling to submit to any authority outside of their own thinking. He had these thinkers in mind when he wrote a short pamphlet directed to students and younger believers, *Der Lebendige Gott: Fragen und Antworten von Herz zu Herz* (The Living God: Questions and Answers from Heart to Heart). In this pamphlet, Kähler wrote, alluding to Psalm 14, "There have always been 'fools' who say in their heart, 'There is no God.' 'Fools' are the people who make their own thoughts more important and respect them more than truth and reality. They were satisfied with themselves."[62] He encouraged his students to continue in the positive, orthodox tradition and to continue the Protestant traditions of scriptural authority that began in the Reformation.[63]

Kähler never imagined nor desired that his students would accept a blind submission to the Scriptures. He was always ready to guide his students with honest interjections from his own piety. However, this practice never limited him from covering the academic aspects of theology. He felt free to share his most profound findings from his academic research with his students. In his

---

61. Ibid., 22–23, 25, 26–27; Lower Saxony State and University Library, Göttingen, Cod. MS. Martin Kähler, Box 12, Ansätze und Entwürfe," #10, Vorlesung, "Geschichte der Dogmatik des 19. Jh., 5.

62. Kähler, *Lebendige Gott*, 6.

63. Lower Saxony State and University Library, Göttingen, Cod. MS. Martin Kähler, Box 12, Ansätze und Entwürfe, #10, Vorlesung, Geschichte der Dogmatik des 19. Jh., 1–3.

lectures, he included the same theological insights and conclusions that made up his academic writings.

Just as in his short work "Unser Streit um die Bibel," Kähler wanted to push his students away from both the false dogma of verbal inspiration, as well as from the other extreme of the overly critical views of his liberal colleagues. He praised the nineteenth century for its work in overthrowing the stubborn reliance on verbal inspiration that only weakened Christianity.[64] As a potential solution to the authority question, Kähler shared with his students his middle-ground dogma that he defined in his most profound theological writings. Namely, Kähler explained to his students his own belief that the Bible is the account of the super-historical become history. In so doing, he lent his support to the study of historical Christianity and the mandate of the university, because even its criticism was crucial for the study of the revelation of God's action.[65]

The tendency of theologians of all stripes to actively undermine what Kähler perceived as the function of the church gave him his greatest worries. His passion for his students to practice good theology often came out in a choleric harangue against the opponents of his faith. Even though Kähler wrote polemically in his theology against the errors of both his overly critical opponents and his overly conservative ones, his written works maintained an academic and collegial mien. In his lectures, however, he spared no bile for his opponents. His fiercest attacks were aimed against modern atheism that he saw originating in the Enlightenment and the godless French Revolution of 1789, and even in the Roman Catholic Church. Kähler described the French Revolution and the following Napoleonic Empire as the tyranny of anthropocentrism. The following restoration of the Catholic Church and the Jesuit Order throughout Europe was just as evil as anything unleashed by the preceding revolution. His opinion of later Catholicism was no better. He accused the Catholic Church of the greatest misuse of theology when the First Vatican Council in 1870–1871 took the historically developed devotion for the pope and canonized it into the timeless dogma of the pope's infallibility. Perhaps in no other venue did Kähler so openly display his adamantly conservative political and social preferences as in his mentoring role with his students.[66]

64. Ibid., 6.
65. Ibid., W.S. 1909/10, 5.
66. Ibid., 1, 4.

BUILDING THE BELIEVING COMMUNITY'S INFLUENCE: KÄHLER AND THE HIRING OF BELIEVING FACULTY

Kähler's concern for the spiritual mentorship of his students also drove his academic politics. Throughout his career, he continued to express his thanks toward his former mentor, Friedrich August Tholuck, for his position at Halle. Kähler worked hard to encourage the hiring of other theologians who could follow him and his believing theology. This included the hiring of conservative scholars Wilhelm Lütgert and Julius Schniewind. Kähler also actively campaigned to invite Adolf Schlatter three separate times to join the faculty. He personally wrote Schlatter with the invitation to succeed him at Halle in 1910. Schlatter eventually refused the honor, but Kähler wanted to be sure that the students at Halle continued to get active encouragement for orthodox theological positions.[67]

Despite his belief that he and his students were opposed by powerful enemies, Kähler transmitted great hope to his students for the direction of modern, believing Protestantism. During a lecture in 1910, he prophesied that the twentieth century would be a century of conflict between Protestantism, Catholicism, and Islam. He noted that with the rise of the critical school, Protestantism appeared broken and divided, yet this did not dampen his hope for an eventual victory. Instead, he hoped that the theological debates of the nineteenth century especially prepared Protestants to carry the banner of right doctrine and the power of their faith into this upcoming spiritual Armageddon. The Protestants understood the historical aspects of their faith from the theological debates of the past century and at the end of the century were able to rest their faith with greater certainty on its historical veracity than any of their opponents. Kähler told his listeners that the new knowledge accrued through the century's work enabled modern Christians to take their message boldly into the realms of spiritual conflict and mission. And in the end, he promised his students, "many enemies—much honor!"[68]

Kähler concerned himself with his students because he wanted them to be prepared for their ministry as preachers of the word of God. He based this goal on his understanding of theology. While theology fit into the modern academic environment, its goals differed from the modern sciences. Since he argued that efficacy and inner conviction were the principal concern for theology, its responsibilities grew out of the necessity to provide answers for people in

---

67. Protestant State-Church Archive, Württemberg, Adolf-Schlatter-Archiv, "Briefe von Kähler an Schlatter," D 40 #426, letter dated March 1, 1910.

68. Lower Saxony State and University Library, Göttingen, Cod. MS. Martin Kähler, Box 12, "Ansätze und Entwürfe," #9, Letzte Vorlesung "Geschichte der Dogmatik des 19. Jh.," 3, 5, 7.

their specific life situations. This practical responsibility took priority over the objective observation required for theology to be a modern academic subject. Kähler summed up for his students his division of theology from the other sciences and history, saying, "Theology derives its motivation from intuition and inspiration, not from reflection."[69]

In Kähler's lectures, theology also divided itself from the other sciences by adopting strict limits to its conclusions. He delimited theology to its confessional obligation because of Christianity's origin as a religion revealed to humans from God. Since theology is the expression of belief, theology necessarily excludes total skepticism. He explained to his students that their future profession in theology would be the act of expressing and explaining belief. Pastoral theology was the explanation of God's revelation for both those within and outside the church. Therefore, the theology he wanted to pass on to his students was principally pedagogic in nature, and not scientific. In this respect, the fundamental apologetic function of theology remained unchanged since the first theologians in the second century. Kähler was satisfied with his own role as teacher and mentor so long as his students were prepared to share the gospel and present their knowledge of the Scriptures with their parishioners.[70]

In the meantime, Kähler encouraged his students to attend sermons and to understand the function of the church as a member and lay participant of a congregation before they would begin to guide a congregation of their own. To his anonymous correspondent in *Wie Studiert man Theologie?*, he wrote:

> In would be all wrong to think that a theologian only needs to know the Biblical literature in order to advise others or to use it in their church functions. It is the same thing with visiting worship services, too. Young men who are not called into the pulpit early enough to try their own hand at preaching often go every Sunday as zealous students and critics into the church in order to belittle and criticize the clergy they observe. In all probability they will also eventually be preachers, but they will never be witnesses [of God], witnesses who inspire life. Those who do not submit themselves with a hungry spirit to the pulpit and receive their bread of life from it have a difficult time later to know what it takes to nourish the souls of others.[71]

69. Lower Saxony State and University Library, Göttingen, Cod. MS. Martin Kähler, Box 12, "Ansätze und Entwürfe," 16d, "Theologie," March 13, 1900, 1–2.

70. Ibid., 1–3.

Kähler strongly believed that the theologian's supreme goal was in the service of the church and in the support of belief.

Kähler's teaching sheds light on his hopes to initiate a return to a faithful scriptural Protestantism. He put his principal professional efforts into mentoring and teaching his students. To a degree, his lectures present the clearest intentions of his writings and academic pursuits. Kähler hoped his message and his theological interpretation would principally flow to the general populace through the pastors he trained, not through the books he penned. His clearest dogmatic assertions came from his teaching as well. In his books, as the historiography has proved, some misunderstandings could arise when they were read individually, but his lectures leave no question that he remained a strict theological conservative.

CONCLUSION: MARTIN KÄHLER'S VOICE FOR A RETURN TO A FAITHFUL COMMUNITY UNDER GOD'S WORD

In the generations following Martin Kähler's life, a remarkable number of epochal theologians have chosen elements of Kähler's writings to grant authority to their own work. Most notably among them was a student of his at Halle, Paul Tillich. However, in doing this, Tillich and others have obscured the historic Martin Kähler in favor of their own legendary Kähler. Unfortunately, in the process, they have also whitewashed Kähler's legitimately innovative thought. [72]

---

71. Kähler, *Wie Studiert man Theologie?*, 39.

72. In terms of the historiography, generally speaking, Martin Kähler is a forgotten theologian. Although he enjoyed an active career that ran from 1877 to 1907, the vast majority of historians and historical theologians interested in this period have overlooked his numerous volumes of systematic theology, philosophy, devotional literature, and biblical studies. When he was mentioned in English-language texts, in nearly every case scholars only showed a familiarity with his best-known work, *The So-Called Historical Jesus and the Historic, Biblical Christ* (1896). Certainly, English-speaking scholars are at a disadvantage, since this is the only work that has been translated and published in the United States. Because the whole spectrum of Kähler's thought remains underresearched, modern scholars have taken the ideas from *The So-Called Historic Jesus* out of the context of Kähler's entire canon of writings. Recent scholars portray Kähler as a precursor of either Albert Schweitzer, Paul Tillich, or Rudolf Bultmann. The scholars who draw comparisons to Schweitzer's critique of the life-of-Jesus movement compare the common assessment of the historical critical research as nothing more than hollow ideas and opinions. Those who paint Kähler as a precursor to Bultmann are fascinated by his separation of the two forms of history, *Geschichte* and *Historie*, which Bultmann later used so powerfully. While the comparisons to these epochal theologians are flattering to Kähler's memory, they are anachronistic. Kähler and Schweitzer may have agreed on a number of criticisms of the life-of-Jesus movement, but their conclusions were astonishingly different. Kähler dismissed the entire attempt to find the historical Jesus

Many thanks ought to be given to the historical theologians who have read and studied the thought of Martin Kähler over the past fifty years. They hoped to restore his prestige in a generation of theologians and churchgoers who forgot about the Halle scholar. Nevertheless, it is time to correct their presentism. They clouded his message by tying him to Rudolf Bultmann, Paul Tillich, and twentieth-century existentialism. Kähler cannot continue to be

Christ in the hopes of returning instead to the orthodox understanding of Jesus from traditional Christianity. Schweitzer found a Jesus Christ who erred greatly in his expectation of the end of the world. The Strasbourg theologian then proceeded to reduce Jesus to an ethical benchmark for all succeeding Christians. Furthermore, Schweitzer never quoted nor alluded to Kähler, and it is unlikely that he was familiar with the works of the elder scholar.Unlike Schweitzer, Rudolf Bultmann read and appreciated Kähler's *So-Called Historical Jesus*. Bultmann acknowledged Kähler's formative role in his own work on form criticism. He adopted, for example, Kähler's distinction between *historische* and *geschichtliche* truths of the Gospels. But despite Bultmann's use of Kähler's ideas, the ultimate conclusions of the two theologians could not be more dissimilar. Kähler attempted to discredit the quest for the historical Jesus based on *Historie*. He only accepted the faith in the *geschichtliche* Christ as a true and accurate portrayal for the church. The details of Jesus's life were for him those of the scriptural accounts. Bultmann, on the other hand, used existentialist thought to justify investigations into both the *geschichtlich* and *historisch* facets of the life of Jesus as equally true and valid for modern Christians.Paul Tillich, a student of Kähler's at Halle, also saw his mentor's thinking in existentialist lines. Tillich's history of the nineteenth century reserved a special demarcation for Kähler as a prophet outside his own time and likewise ignored by his peers. In his recount, Kähler's seminal ideas waited for the thought of the twentieth century to be plumbed to their depths. Tillich, like Bultmann, saw Kähler's separation of *Geschichte* from *Historie* as the key to unlocking the true synthesis of modern Christian theology. They both saw the theological, biblical Jesus' values as independent of their historical veracity. Because of Kähler's clearly polemical teaching, it is strange that Paul Tillich, who studied under Kähler at Halle, had what must have been an intentional misreading of Kähler. In seeing Kähler as a prophet of neoliberalism, Tillich completely rewrote the historiography of Kähler. Albert Schweitzer, *The Quest of the Historical Jesus: A Critical study of Its Progress from Reimarus to Wrede* (New York: Macmillan, 1964), 98; Paul Tillich, *Perspectives on 19th and 20th Century Protestant Theology*, ed. Carl E. Braaten (New York: Harper & Row, 1967), 214–15.For examples of reading Kähler through the lens of Bultmann and Tillich, cf. Friedrich Karl Schumann, "Gedächtniswort des Dekans der theologischen Fakultät," in *Zu Martin Kahlers 100. Geburtstag*, Hallische Universitätsreden 64 (Halle [Saale]: Max Niemeyer Verlag, 1935), 1, 7; Carl Braaten, "Introduction," Kähler, *The So-Called Historical Jesus*; Alasdaire Heron, *A Century of Protestant Theology* (Philadelphia: Westminster, 1980), 55–56; John Reuman, introduction to Albert Schweitzer, *The Lord's Supper in Relationship to the Life of Jesus and the History of the Early Church*, trans. A. J. Matill Jr. (Macon, GA: Mercer University Press, 1982), 21. In one recent work, Susannah Heschel wrote that Kähler's work protected Jesus as a reasonable founder of Christianity because of the existential separation of *Historie* and *Geschichte*. She claimed that his subjective definition of Jesus *protected* liberal Christian sentiment even as the life-of-Jesus movement was nearing failure. By reading Bultmann's tradition and theology into Kähler's thought and word, she credited Kähler with saving the very endeavor he meant wholeheartedly to defeat. Susannah Heschel, *Abraham Geiger and the Jewish Jesus* (Chicago: University of Chicago Press, 1998), 231–32.

placed within this worldview. He neither practiced nor believed in Bultmann's theology. To think so is anachronistic. Unlike Bultmann, Kähler was a firm believer in the historical validity and actuality of Jesus' ministry, speech, and miracles.

Kähler's justification of separating the concepts of *Historie* and *Geschichte* was that the two prominent views of his day—dogmatic verbal inspiration and historical criticism of the life-of-Jesus movement, which both claimed objective knowledge—were untenable. His thought was much plainer and more traditional than historical theologians of the twentieth and twenty-first centuries ascribed to him. He never claimed to want to demythologize the *Geschichte* of Jesus, and his critique of the life-of-Jesus movement came and went with relatively little comment.

But does taking Martin Kähler out of the role of prophet for twentieth-century theology necessitate his return to obscurity? Certainly not. The life of Martin Kähler has important repercussions for historians and historical theologians who have an interest in the German theology of the late-nineteenth and early-twentieth centuries. First, Kähler's experiences at Halle as a student of Tholuck and his community of *Bibelverehrer* testified to a self-conscious, assertive conservative community. Notably, when referencing this body to his students, he did not refer to them as *Bibelverehrer*, but rather as positive, using the political terminology from Adolf Stoecker's church party. This collective group saw their first responsibility to be the return to the traditional orthodox creeds of the church. Kähler found his own niche in this community by writing a systematic theology based on conservative creeds. He laid the foundation for the early twentieth century's believing theology. He also dedicated himself to teaching theology students to be the next generation of believing theologians and pastors.

Second, Kähler identified the theology of the word of God as the unifying belief and the demarcation for believing theologians and pastors. With this belief clearly stated, he gave a more profound challenge to those who questioned the traditional dogmas of the church. They were not destroying dead remnants of a bygone era, but the continuing foundation of authority that sprang from the living word of God. In the end, Kähler engaged the intellectual community, with its own shortcomings, in a call to return to a state of belief in the message of Christ without falling into dogmatic absolutism. He did this with a subjective definition of the word of God that found the Bible's validity for Christians of all eras on its efficacy to change lives.

Finally, Kähler translated the theology of the word of God into a Christian ethic, driven by Christians' gratitude in response to their salvation. He expected the outcome of readers and listeners being affected by the writing and preaching of believing Protestants to be faithful work, evangelism, and the imitation of Jesus Christ. With these ideas, Martin Kähler developed a conservative, believing theology that engaged the Scriptures with the beliefs of the Reformation in an idiom suitable for the turn of the twentieth century and paved the way for a more thorough expression of believing theology by his junior colleague Adolf Schlatter.

4

Receiving the Ancient Beliefs in the Modern Day

Adolf Schlatter's Life and Work

In 1885, the relatively obscure Bern theologian Adolf Schlatter burst onto the wider theological landscape with an encyclopedic study of the New Testament's use of the word *belief*. From this point on, Schlatter became the most esteemed and prolific believing theologian of his generation. The great neo-orthodox voices that followed—Emil Brunner, Paul Althaus and Karl Barth, to name a few—acknowledged the intellectual debt they owed to Schlatter's work. Schlatter's historical insights have found a greater lasting audience than any other scholar of his age, even the significantly more widely read contemporary, Adolf von Harnack. Schlatter fulfilled the ideas of Kähler and wrote a believing systematic theology using the most sophisticated academic tools available. His theology was recognized in his lifetime for its daring independence from the field and its adherence to the faith of Protestant orthodoxy. However, despite the accolades he won during his career, despite the praise offered him by the leading lights of the following generation, and despite his continued renown as an authority about first-century Palestinian history, generations of theologians after Schlatter's death in 1938 all but ignored his greatest works: his histories of New Testament thought and his systematic thought on dogma and ethics.

Adolf Schlatter was the first of the believing theologians to create a wholly modern systematic theology, even as it retained the core traditional doctrines of the church. His background made him a perfect candidate to redefine Protestant theology. He was born in Calvinist Switzerland, moved to Lutheran Union Prussia, and finally ended his life in Lutheran Pietist Baden-Württemberg. This broad Protestant perspective gave him the tools he needed to free believing theology from its inflexible Reformation moorings. In his theology, Schlatter followed Kähler's lead and credited the word of God with its divine character because of its role in creating a relationship between the creator God and God's human creations. Schlatter wrote that the Bible acts as the conduit of expressing God's qualities to humanity. According to this definition of the Bible, the Bible brings the believer into a personal relationship with God. Finally, Schlatter developed a systematic ethics with a specificity and thoroughness that no other believing theologian had attempted. He defined ethics as the loving response to God's relationship. Schlatter understood ethical behavior in the light of his theology of the word of God because the believer discovers ethical mandates from the Scriptures as they reveal God's will to the reader. Schlatter eventually turned his whole experience as a systematic thinker to explaining and supporting the German war effort in the First World War. His thought encouraged many troops on the front and families who stayed behind. Yet despite Schlatter's monumental work, he quickly faded out of the theological limelight following the First World War. The dialectic theologians of the 1920s laid Schlatter's monumental systematic works aside in their general rejection of nineteenth-century theology. Despite individual calls to reappraise Schlatter's place in the German theological pantheon, he has remained a generally forgotten and ignored voice in German theology.

"My Experience with the Bible": A Biographical Overview of Adolf Schlatter's Life

Reflecting on his own life, Schlatter divided his major formative experiences into four categories, or better said, four relationships. Importantly, the first relationship he described was his relationship with the state, which was the relationship over which he had the least control. Through his life, his relationship with the state changed from it being a benign presence in his childhood, to it being an employer when he served in both the pastorate and the university, and finally to the state being the exactor of great sacrifice during the First World War. Schlatter described the other three relationships with joy and thankfulness for the role they played in his life. His relationships with the Scriptures, with the church, and with nature were love relationships that he freely joined.[1] Together, these four relationships colored the theological

---

1. Schlatter's special emphasis on nature brings our discussion to an interesting tangent to Frederick Gregory's inspection of the specifically German interaction of theology and science in *Nature Lost?* Schlatter fell comfortably into the orthodox understanding of nature that Gregory describes through the

questions he asked and defined the convictions he held for his whole life. He remained fully convinced of the important role his own biography had on his beliefs, freely admitting that his life story kept him from adopting a perfectionist's view of objectivity as if he could somehow separate his own tenets of belief from his academic, scholarly, familiar, and ecclesiastical life.[2]

Adolf Schlatter, the seventh of nine children, was born in 1852 in St. Gallen, Switzerland to the pharmacist, grocer, and lay preacher Hektor Stephen Schlatter (1805–1880) and his wife, Wilhelmine Schlatter (née Steinmann, 1819–1894). Theology and the Christian religion were the most definable characteristics in his parents' household. His paternal grandmother, Anna Schlatter (1773–1826), was an active participant in the early-nineteenth-century revivalist movement (*Erweckungsbewegung*). She had an active correspondence with the leading lights of the movement, both Protestant and Catholic. Her spirituality so shaped her family that by 1935 seventy-two of her more than nine hundred descendants were actively involved in full-time church ministry or were career theologians. Certainly, Anna Schlatter's piety deeply affected her son, Stephen Schlatter, the youngest of her eleven children. Stephen Schlatter originally rejected the ministry, opting instead to study the sciences. He opened a pharmacy in St. Gallen; however, in 1834 he closed the pharmacy and took over the administration of his parents' grocery store. Upon assuming the care of the grocery, he moved into his parents' large house in the heart of St. Gallen, where Adolf Schlatter was later born.[3]

In 1838, Stephen Schlatter experienced a conversion after listening to an itinerant preacher. Stephen Schlatter chose to be baptized as an adult and consequently was required to leave the state church of Switzerland, which did not recognize adult rebaptism. His excommunication from the Swiss Reformed Church did not dampen his newfound religious fervor; rather, it led him to found a free church in St. Gallen, where he also was an active preacher.

---

theology of Schlatter's colleague at Greifswald, Otto Zöckler. Schaltter never explicitly wrote about Darwinian science, and he acknowledged the brutal aspects of nature, but he never rescinded his belief that even this brutality is an essential element of God's creation and a revelation of God's character. In this sense, Schlatter's rejection of Ritschlian liberalism would also imply a rejection of Herrmann's distancing his theology from his religion. Cf. Fredrick Gregory, *Nature Lost? Natural Science and the German Theological Traditions of the Nineteenth Century* (Cambridge, MA: Harvard University Press, 1992), ch. 4.

2. Adolf Schlatter, *Erlebtes*, 4th ed. (Berlin: Im Furche-Verlag, [1926?]), 7, 19, 21, 28, 35, 40, 42–45, 47, 55.

3. Werner Neuer, Adolf *Schlatter: A Biography of Germany's Premier Biblical Theologian*, trans. Robert W. Yarborough (Grand Rapids: Baker, 1995), 17, 23–24, 26.

The younger Schlatter never attended his father's church and instead chose to join the clergy of the same church that refused to recognize his father's spiritual decision. Nevertheless, Adolf Schlatter was profoundly influenced by his father's spirituality, counting it as a greater influence on his life than his mother's. Later in life, Schlatter recalled fondly that his father's congregation called itself simply "a church of Christ in St. Gallen." The most important detail for Schlatter was that the congregation never claimed to be "*the* church of Christ in St. Gallen." Adolf Schlatter remained immensely grateful that in his father's life, Christianity was not defined by the denomination, but by the individual belief in Jesus Christ. Adolf Schlatter later recalled one clear example of his father's understanding of Christianity. An English traveler once approached Stephen Schlatter in his grocery store. Convinced of the imminent return of Jesus Christ, the man was traveling the globe to get the signatures of God's chosen 144,000, mentioned in the biblical book of Revelation. The elder Schlatter refused to sign the list he was offered, for he believed that his salvation only had to do with the grace of God and did not come from his signature.

The meeting of Swiss Calvinism and English dispensationalism also left a deep mark on Schlatter's later hermeneutical principles. For Schlatter, belief is not imposed from above through an inerrant, unquestionable Scriptures, but rather it manifests itself in the believer's willing submission to the Scriptures in all their complexity.[4]

Stephen Schlatter's wife never followed him out of the Swiss Reformed Church. She and the children were baptized into the state church and remained active members of the local parish church. Adolf Schlatter never believed that the confessional divide within his family hindered his own spiritual development or that of his siblings. Certainly, in the first years after Stephen Schlatter's conversion, several social difficulties arose. At the time, the elder Schlatter was branded a "sectarian." Adolf Schlatter recalled that the house was always locked at night because of the fear of violence from their neighbors. Schlatter's father maintained the strict separation from the Swiss Reformed Church that his excommunication had forced on him. Even at the burial of his daughter, he carried the coffin with his sons only to the doors of the church and refused to cross the lintel. He also missed Adolf's confirmation and ordination. But the tensions between the faiths were kept out of the family relations. By the time Adolf Schlatter was old enough to understand his parents' difference of faith, they each had learned to respect the other's decisions and respected the other's spirituality and Christianity.

---

4. Ibid., 32; Schlatter, *Erlebtes*, 52–53; Adolf Schlatter, *Rückblick auf meine Lebensarbeit*, 2nd ed. (Stuttgart: Calwer Verlag, 1977), 18, 23.

In retrospect, Schlatter maintained that the situation was advantageous for him. He claimed that from his earliest memories, he had two impressions of church life in his own home that were strictly separated from each other in practice and rite, but united in true love and partnership. He saw the twofold Christianity of his parents as an aid to understanding Christianity beyond the confines of a single confession or denomination. He credited his parents' different church membership as the perfect lesson for him to learn to differentiate between theology and faith. He knew that neither his father nor his mother believed that his or her method of baptism was essential for salvation. He stated that his parents attributed their salvation to their respective faith in Jesus. For Schlatter's entire life, the example of his parents' dedication to their respective churches bound church and Jesus together, but their marital love for each other elevated Jesus as the more important of the two. This happy situation made it clear to Schlatter for his entire life that the church was a safe environment for him, and it encouraged him in his own decision to study for the church.[5]

Schlatter's cross-denominational perspective marked a major change in his theological work later in life. During the first half of the nineteenth century in Prussia, especially facing the kaiser's increased meddling with the church liturgy, German conservatives mostly founded their defense against heterodoxy based on the particular church confessions of their heritage. Lutherans pointed to the Augsburg Confession, and the Reformed Churches to the Heidelberg Confession. While these documents provided the ideal starting point for their traditional views, it atomized conservative-leaning clergy and alienated potential allies. Schlatter's new draft of a believing theology went even further than Kähler's by suggesting that the traditional Protestant creeds were no longer the starting point for Protestant piety. In so doing, Schlatter was able to unite the various confessional groups against their common enemies, defuse the clergy's latent hostility against the government (considering all their protests against the government had accomplished little in furthering Protestant goals), and provide a foundation upon which future conservative scholars such as Barth and Brunner could build their own systems of thought.

Beyond church participation, Stephen and Wilhelmine Schlatter made the Scriptures an integral part of their family relationship. Schlatter remembered various occasions when the Bible had played a key role in family life. One such experience stood out candidly to Schlatter later in his life. While he was still a boy, one of his older sisters died, and his parents did not try to hide the death

---

5. Schlatter, *Rückblick*, 18–22; Neuer, *Schlatter: A Biography*, 32; Schlatter, *Erlebtes*, 24, 27.

from the family. Instead, they invited the other children to see their sister's corpse. Afterward, the parents read the end of the book of Revelation to them. At the time of suffering, the Schlatter parents used the Bible to remind their children of the hope of the resurrection.[6]

Schlatter's parents attempted to create a safe, Christian environment for their children. This went beyond introducing them to the Scriptures and participating actively in the church. Stephen and Wilhelmine Schlatter possessed a worldview in which they, as Christians, were responsible to take a stand against the sinful character of the world. Furthermore, they believed that their children needed to be protected from the evils of the world. Therefore, Adolf Schlatter's parents set strict rules for the family's behavior and social engagements. The Schlatters established their social relations so that their children would always be in an environment where their most important adult interaction would be with "believers" (*Bekehrten*), namely, those who held the same social and religious values as themselves. Even as an adult, Schlatter could write that he never saw the inside of the St. Gallen theater. He was protected from anti-Christian or erotic literature. He also never saw the inside of pubs except when visits were required to get food during school outings.

In retrospect, Schlatter never perceived these strict rules as some form of imprisonment or as overly restrictive. He believed that his parents' rules differed from other extreme forms of fundamentalism because the parents' admonishments were coupled with evangelistic fervor. The family was set against the sinfulness of the world but never left the world. His father set the example of this "in the world, but not of it" lifestyle. Schlatter wrote that his father continually sought interaction with non-"believers" in order to share with them the Christian gospel. This practice impressed on the son that while the world was corrupt, it remained redeemable through the Christian faith. Schlatter always understood the message of this strict upbringing. His father believed that his children needed a safe environment to grow in, but they never needed to be afraid of going into the world so long as they were accompanied by their Christian faith.

For the Schlatter family, the voluntary separation from the worldly environment also kept them apart from the liberal church movement of Switzerland. At the time of Adolf Schlatter's youth, a significant liberalization that went under the name of the "reform" movement was sweeping the Swiss state church. Both parents believed that these new ideas were every bit as much a threat to the well-being of their children as any form of profligate living. As

---

6. Schlatter, *Erlebtes*, 51–53.

a result, the whole Schlatter family refused to enter any liberal church. Schlatter later wrote that, for his parents, the "reform" movement summed up everything that was corrupt and wrong in the world.[7]

Schlatter's parents also introduced him and his siblings to a love of nature. His father was a trained pharmacist and passed his love of the natural sciences on to all of his children. Schlatter remembered fondly the long hikes the family took, introducing the children to northern Switzerland from the shores of Lake Constance to the highlands around Zurich. Schlatter credited the early acceptance of nature, even its unpleasant aspects, with forming much of his ethical outlook. He realized early on that nature has its brutal elements, but that as part of God's creation, it also is being restored through Christ's act of redemption. His eldest brother was mentally and physically handicapped. However, Schlatter could not recall that his parents ever allowed this son's disabilities to decrease his value in the family's eyes. This understanding of nature as being redeemed helped him accept the loss of his parents, his wife, and his son, because he always saw nature as laying the foundation for his belief in Jesus.

Schlatter's scientific upbringing also took its form in his theology. Like many theologians of the late nineteenth century, he saw his academic research as scientific in the best possible sense. He saw his work as providing a firm, knowable foundation for personal faith. He believed that knowledge of the Scriptures and thereby knowledge of the living God could progress and grow. Schlatter never pretended that his knowledge would ever be complete; he was by no means a scientific positivist. Despite the close, mentoring relationship he had with Karl Barth (1886–1968) after the First World War, he would eventually disassociate himself from Barth's existentialist rejection of "scientific" modernist theology.[8]

Schlatter's entry into the upper school (*Gymansium*) opened up a world of intellectual interest and skill. Schlatter showed particular gifts in linguistics. He eventually received private lessons from his teacher, Franz Misteli (1841–1903), who would later become professor of comparative linguistics at the university in Basel. During his schooling, Schlatter tackled the classical authors Julius Caesar, Ovid, Virgil, Hesiod, and Homer in their entirety in their original languages, as well as engaging in the German philosophies of Kant and Hegel. The advantage of reading these works at such a young age was that Schlatter was already beginning to differentiate the rational religion of the Greeks from the religion

---

7. Schlatter, *Rückblick*, 15–17, 26.

8. Schlatter, *Erlebtes*, 97–99, 103–104; cf. Gregory, *Nature Lost?*, 6.

of Jesus. This topic would often come up in his interaction with the liberalizing, modernizing theology.

At school, Schlatter also first came into contact with the reigning Hegelian biblical-critical ideas of the Tübingen School of David Friedrich Strauss (1808–1874) and Ferdinand Christian Baur (1792–1860). His religion teacher had abandoned his training as a clergyman (Schlatter described his action as fleeing) in order to teach in a school where he would have more freedom to question the tenets of traditional Christianity. Because of Schlatter's unusual linguistic abilities and his concern about the critical ideas of a university theology department, Schlatter briefly considered studying philology. After some introspection, Schlatter decided that he could not justify avoiding theological training out of the fear of critical thinking. In following years, having lacked any one moment where he accepted the Christian faith as his own, he would point to his decision to study theology as his conversion. It took the form of conversion because he believed himself to be stepping out in faith that his religious conviction and God's grace could not be shaken by human reason. After graduating from school, he took up his university studies in Basel in the spring of 1871.[9]

Indeed, Schlatter's theological studies were as critical as he had feared. The University of Basel's theology and philosophy departments, each in its own way, confronted him with animosity toward the traditional viewpoints of his parents' Christianity. Schlatter's Basel theological professors and their liberal theology made little lasting impression on him; instead, his philosophy professors—Karl Steffensen (1818–1888), Jakob Burkhardt (1818–1897), and Friedrich Nietzsche (1844–1900)—challenged and advanced his academic interests.[10]

9. Schlatter, *Rückblick*, 28–29, 31–32, 36–38; Neuer, *Schlatter: A Biography*, 36–39.

10. For his theology degree, Schlatter was required to take four semesters of philosophy. Karl Steffensen was Schlatter's favorite. Schlatter appreciated Steffensen's Socratic method of teaching. In giving his praise, Schlatter used the religiously applied word *devotional* to describe Steffensen's art from the lectern. Indeed, Schlatter wrote that his philosophy professor approached the great philosophers as a theologian approaches religious works. Eventually, Schlatter rejected Steffensen's adoration of philosophy, but he attempted to emulate his professor's pedagogical style. Schlatter never felt empowered in his own thinking from listening to the typical lecture style. However, he blossomed in Steffensen's open discussions that required every student to make his or her own judgments about it. This teaching style, more than any other element, was the lasting heritage from his years in Basle. He fondly remembered Burkhardt, too, for his presence as a teacher. Schlatter credited Burkhardt with the ability to create stirring, living portraits of the past that brought his students a new appreciation of it. Just as Schlatter rejected Steffensen's adoration of philosophy, Schlatter eventually rejected Burkhardt's pessimistic outlook toward the world. However, he continued trying to take Burkhardt's living portrayal

For three semesters in 1873–1874, Schlatter attended the University of Tübingen in the German kingdom of Württemberg.[11] The instruction Schlatter received in Tübingen, particularly from the biblicist theologian Johann Tobias Beck (1804–1878), gave him the focus he needed for his future theological interests. Beck provided the young Schlatter with a model for unifying personal faith with the highest level of scholarship. In retrospect, Schlatter, who idealized both true Christianity and true knowledge, gave Beck the greatest compliment he could give to an academic when he wrote that Beck was a true thinker and not merely a scholastic. Beck's sincerity in his theology differed greatly from the many other theology teachers Schlatter met who relied on trendy methods and an awkward combination of theology with modern German philosophy.

In one aspect above all others, Schlatter desired to emulate Beck in his own academic studies. Beck's confident trust in the continuing value of the biblical Scriptures impressed Schlatter. In Beck, Schlatter saw a serious academic who never denied his Christian belief. Schlatter wanted to have Beck's uninhibited *Christian* scholarship that arose out of his belief.

However, Schlatter had some serious complaints about Beck that kept the senior scholar from ever converting his young Swiss admirer into a total disciple. Beck's pedagogy differed greatly from Steffensen's open "devotional." Beck considered the lecture hall his domain, and his ideas were to rule in the room—much in the way Kähler taught twenty years later. He lectured with the expectation that the students were to know and learn his ideas. This differed greatly from Schlatter's own independent academic spirit and ambition.

of the past into account in his own writing and teaching about ancient Palestine. In contrast to Schlatter's appreciation for his other two philosophy professors, Schlatter had no kind words for his experience with Nietzsche. He later wrote, "The chief impression that I internalized from his lectures arose from his offensive haughtiness. He treated his listeners like despicable peons. He convinced me of the principle that to throw out love is to despoil the business of teaching—only genuine love can really educate."Schlatter's exposure to critical ideas and the critical philosophy, like that of Baruch Spinoza, through Burkhardt and Steffensen's seminars, brought Schlatter to a minor crisis in his faith during his first semesters. He eventually weathered the struggles and made the conscious attempt to bring his faith more consistently into interaction with his intellectual studies thereafter. Neuer, *Schlatter: A Biography*, 43–44, 46–47; Schlatter, *Rückblick*, 40–43.

11. Although Germany was united in 1871 under the German Empire, the southern kingdoms of Württemberg and Bavaria remained autonomous kingdoms. Each kingdom also had an autonomous cultural ministry responsible for its respective universities. Later in Schlatter's life, his decision to move from Berlin to Tübingen was bitterly contested by the Prussian cultural ministry precisely for this reason. He was leaving the Prussian civil service in order to become a civil employee of Württemberg. The confederation of kingdoms, and correspondingly the reign of the Württemberg kings, ended after the revolution of 1918.

Theologically speaking, Schlatter had strong aversions to Beck's ahistorical theology. Beck rejected modern historicism entirely. Instead, he attempted to build a theology of timeless statutes from the Scriptures that could not be touched by historical criticism. Schlatter's own scholarship could not be more different. He believed that historical criticism could be a boon to believing theology, as long as it was practiced by humble, believing scholars. Finally, he never adopted Beck's criticism of the Reformation doctrine of justification. For Beck, belief and theology were one and the same, but Schlatter divided the two concepts in his thinking. For him, possessing right doctrine could not guarantee a saving faith, just as a saving faith did not indicate perfect doctrine.

Schlatter's separation of the presence of belief from knowledge of theology allowed him more freedom for self-criticism in his theological assertions. At the same time, it led him to invest in a theology that he himself admitted had no essential purpose. As a whole, Schlatter complimented the Tübingen theological faculty of his student days. He gave praise even to the critical scholars, Maximilian Landerer (1810–1878) and Carl Heinrich Weiszäcker (1822–1899). But it was Beck's theology that spoke to Schlatter's receptive ear.[12]

His entire university education imparted to him a fascination with the study of historical criticism, and he remained convinced that the study of the history of the New Testament and ancient Palestine was a crucial task for Christian leadership. None of the systematic professors of dogma could impress him in the way that his historicist professors of philosophy, Steffensen and Burkhardt, along with Weiszäcker in theology, had. Schlatter only began to involve himself in serious systematic theology when he was required to teach it at Berlin. Schlatter's initial interest in historical criticism led him to study the ways in which Jesus adopted the practices and thought of first-century Palestinian Judaism. Of course, Schlatter approached the study of Jesus with all the Christian beliefs of his divinity and his importance as the atoning sacrifice. Schlatter insisted that the best way to understand these eternal concepts of Jesus came by understanding Jesus within his own historical context. Schlatter phrased this in doctrinal form, writing, "God uses history. In that in history the perfection of his grace is revealed as he brings out the complete life. Only through this act in history could we have a God that is truly one of ours."[13]

Schlatter did credit his university education with showing him the importance of historical fact for Christian historical scholarship. It taught him that theological interpretation could be properly undertaken only after the historical facts were collected and understood. This, he claimed, was the

---

12. Schlatter, *Rückblick*, 44–46, 49; Neuer, *Schlatter: A Biography*, 52–54.

13. Schlatter, *Rückblick*, 52.

principal way in which his theological writing differed from the theological methodology of Schleiermacher and Ritschl before him. Schlatter accused the two great modern theologians of drawing their systems of theology from abstract rationalism before looking at the course of history. In 1875, Schlatter took his university exams, receiving the highest possible score (*sehr gut*) in every examination subject. The Basel faculty invited Schlatter to remain for graduate studies, but he instead accepted a call to the pastorate within the Swiss state church.[14]

As Schlatter was taking his university examinations, Switzerland was experiencing a severe shortage of clergy. Due to this shortage, Schlatter received a position before he had even finished his exams. At twenty-three years old, he received a position as interim pastor in Kilchberg on Lake Zurich for three months. The congregation had recently fired its pastor, and Schlatter was called in to serve until the members could find a suitable replacement.

Following the short work in Kilchberg, he was called to work in the congregation at Neumünster on the eastern shore of Lake Zurich. The large congregation was split between its liberal minister with the liberal parishioners and a large traditionalist contingent who were unsatisfied with the pastor's liberalism. The congregation came to the unusual compromise of calling a conservative assistant pastor and invited Schlatter to fill the position. This was Schlatter's first calling to be a theologically conservative voice in an otherwise liberal environment, a pattern present in later university positions as well. The church had other significant issues, as Schlatter later wrote: "There was a theology professor who entered the pulpit drunk; an education director who would occasionally be found passed out on the street; a congregational leader who had amassed considerable power for himself, who publicly stated that he made use of the local houses of prostitution, yet was confirmed in his church office by a raucous majority."[15]

Despite the adverse conditions, Schlatter made the most of his year and a half in Neumünster. His preaching enjoyed success, the church saw growth, and the compromise situation of having two pastors continued even after he left. Schlatter felt he could leave with a good conscience, knowing that other believing pastors would be there to take his place. In the end, although the liberal minister, G. Hiestand, had originally opposed the calling, the two were able to carry a fruitful and animated discussion of their respective beliefs.

Schlatter's fundamental convictions remained unchanged by his experience in Neumünster. He wrote retrospectively that at Neumünster, he discovered

---

14. Ibid., 51–52; Neuer, *Schlatter: A Biography*, 56.

15. Quoted and translated from Schlatter, *Erlebtes*, in Neuer, *Schlatter: A Biography*, 60.

that despite liberalism's dynamic and complex systems of thought as they were presented in book form, they could never be turned into truly motivating sermons. He later accused his colleague Hiestand of standing at the pulpit fully helpless. He was unable to do anything with his powerful bass voice but offer meaningless phrases. Nevertheless, Schlatter's experience in Neumünster helped prepare him for his lifelong commitment to working with and interacting with his liberal colleagues in a sense of academic camaraderie.

Finally, in 1877, Schlatter accepted a call to the rural congregation at Kesswil-Uttwil on Lake Constance.[16] His three years in Kesswil were idyllic. He enjoyed his ministry to the three congregations there. He was able to put his theological convictions to practice in the ministry to his "farmers." He met and married his wife, Susanna (née Schoop, 1856–1907), and they were to have a happy, if short, marriage. Schlatter would eventually outlive his wife by more than thirty years. Together they had five children—two boys, Paul and Theodor, and three girls, Hedwig, Dora, and Ruth.

In Kesswil, Schlatter believed he found the strength of the church in the modern era. For Schlatter, the rural church life was the foundation of the whole state. He wrote in his reflections after the tumult of the First World War, "Let the industry and its rewards by all means leave, just build up the rural communities!"[17] His later experience living in the anonymity of Berlin only advanced this conviction.

Schlatter's rural sentiments, like Kähler's reaction to the 1848 liberal revolution, put him squarely into the larger conservative sentiment in German thought. Cities were widely perceived to be the festering wound of modern civilization, the center of vice, crime, and revolutionary sentiment. Schlatter paralleled the growing secular conservatism that looked to the ancient towns and romantic countryside to find their hope for the future of Germany.[18]

By his own accounts, Schlatter would have loved to remain in the active clergy. However, when the associations of Bern pietists requested that he join the academic faculty at Bern as a conservative voice in an otherwise liberal faculty, he believed that he dared not refuse the opportunity.[19]

Much to the chagrin of Bern's Pietist Christians, the city's university theological faculty had been a bulwark of liberal theology for the two decades

16. Schlatter took up residence in the Kesswil parsonage, the birth house of psychologist C. G. Jung, who had been born two years earlier, Neuer, *Schlatter: A Biography*, 65.

17. Schlatter, *Erlebtes*, 36.

18. Fritz Stern, *The Politics of Cultural Despair: A Study in the Rise of Germanic Ideology* (New York: Anchor, 1965), 20.

19. Schlatter, *Rückblick*, 55, 58, 68, 72; Neuer, *Schlatter: A Biography*, 57–61, 65–66.

preceding Schlatter's calling. These conservative Christians actively campaigned to bring like-minded theologians onto the faculty to loosen the grip that liberal theologians had on the curriculum. The Pietists' first successful calling was that of Samuel Oettli to be professor of Old Testament in 1878. From his position within the faculty, Oettli encouraged Schlatter to write a doctoral dissertation and to begin teaching alongside him at Bern. Schlatter initially showed little interest in leaving his position at Kesswil, where he enjoyed all aspects of his work. However, Oettli's persistence soon convinced him that the sacrifice would be worthwhile if it meant that the students at Bern would get a constructive Christian voice in their education.

In the German-speaking universities at the time, young professors (*Privatdozenten*) who were not yet advanced to full-professor status were required to raise their salaries through fees from their students. Only full professors received funds from the state. Since Schlatter needed to raise his funds in a hostile environment, he needed to have outside earnings to guarantee him a living income. The Bern Pietists were aware of these difficulties and prepared for him two teaching positions at a private conservative Christian high school (*Gymnasium*) and a Christian teachers' college.

At his interview with the leaders of the schools, the principal of the private high school, Theodor von Lerber, grilled the young pastor on his theological viewpoints. Lerber was entrenched in Bern's theological divide between traditional creeds and the growing influence of liberalism in politics, education, and the pulpit. As a strong adherent to the ultraconservative doctrine of Scriptural inerrancy, Lerber had set expectations about the hire's beliefs. He began with serious doubts about Schlatter's value, because of Schlatter's greater openness to critical thoughts. However, despite this initial skepticism, Lerber offered the position to Schlatter and prepared the way for him to come to Bern. The schools offered him teaching positions in religion and Hebrew and a salary to supplement the funds he would receive for teaching at the university. Now that his financial situation was resolved, Schlatter needed to earn a position on the theological faculty. He moved to Bern without the certainties that the faculty would offer him the opportunity to write his dissertation there or that they would ever offer him permission to teach.[20]

The Bern theology department was unimpressed with the Pietists' means of bringing new conservative faculty members into their midst. They were fully against Schlatter's participation from the first. Upon his arrival in Bern, Schlatter visited church historian Friedrich Nippold (1838–1918), the most important

20. Schlatter, *Rückblick*, 71–72, 74, 77; Neuer, *Schlatter: A Biography*, 66–69.

member of the faculty. Although Nippold could not restrict Schlatter's dissertation attempt, he made it clear that he did not approve of Schlatter's attempt to join the faculty. Nippold told Schlatter upon their first meeting, "The only thing you need to do is pack your suitcase immediately and go back where you came from."[21]

Despite this initial discouragement, Schlatter began to write a dissertation on John the Baptist with significant time constraints to finish his work so that he could begin teaching at the university. Beyond the dissertation work, Schlatter taught every day at the Pietist schools, and his father fell terminally ill. Nevertheless, Schlatter finished his two-hundred-page dissertation in a matter of weeks and submitted it to the faculty on July 1, 1880.

The work that he began in his dissertation gave him the principal historical question that would guide his career: How was early Christianity a product of first-century Judaism? Schlatter believed that modern Christian theology did not know the religious environment of first-century Judaism well enough to discern the importance of Jesus' Jewish heritage. Even in this point, Schlatter was providing a critique of the newest branches of higher historical criticism. The main movement of the growing History of Religions (*Religionsgeschichte*) school at the time was working on tying Jesus to Greek movements of the first century and separated him from all Jewish thought. Schlatter quickly jumped into the historical work and became an expert on first-century Jewish writings and the Talmud. Upon completion of his dissertation, he left immediately to visit his father before his death.[22]

Schlatter had the unusual experience of holding a moderate ideology in a polarized atmosphere. His colleagues from Lerber's school, where he taught, eyed him skeptically as someone too open to modern ideas and critical thinking. At the same time, the Bern faculty viewed him as tied too closely to naive traditionalist viewpoints. However, Schlatter noted a deep difference between these two critical groups. He noticed that even though Lerber kept him on a short leash and was worried that his teacher might lead his students in the wrong direction, the two had an open discussion of their opposing viewpoints with the firm knowledge of their common Christian faith. The Bern faculty, in contrast, considered him only in terms of how his presence could help or hinder their department. They believed that allowing a conservative voice might diminish their collective appeal in academia.

For Schlatter, this fruitful relationship with Lerber and the stalemate between him and his university colleagues remained unchanged from his arrival

---

21. Quoted and translated from Schlatter, *Rückblick*, in Neuer, *Schlatter: A Biography*, 71.
22. Schlatter, *Rückblick*, 87; Neuer, *Schlatter: A Biography*, 72.

until he left for Greifswald eight years later. Schlatter later wrote that, despite these differences with his colleagues, his situation remained positive and fruitful. This productivity stemmed from the situation that Schlatter and his ideological opponents on both sides maintained a common central focus on the Bible. Each group had its own interpretation of the Bible. The academics sought to inspect the Bible scientifically, and Lerber and his associates used the Bible as the means for their belief. However, the fundamental place of the Bible as the Christian's authority was the same for all.

Likewise, Schlatter's position between two opposing groups helped him solidify his own position. He tried to find a middle ground by denying that the two viewpoints of belief and criticism were mutually exclusive. He came to the point where he wrote that he was a critic because he believed. Criticism was the only way for him to understand the subject of his belief. This also formed a second corollary for Schlatter—namely, that those who put belief and criticism as mutually exclusive misunderstood both. Lerber and the ultraconservative traditionalists saw only the antireligious polemic that came from the radical voices in the critical camps: D. F. Strauss, Ludwig Feuerbach (1804–1872), Bruno Bauer (1809–1882), and William Wrede (1859–1906). While Schlatter somewhat shared this wary view of critical voices, he was convinced that it still did not require the total uncritical acceptance of everything in the Bible. This mediating position would help him survive in a hostile academic world where he could expect few allies.[23]

Finally, the exam committee settled on its requirements so that Schlatter could take his final exams. They resolved that Schlatter would write exams in eight subjects, and he was required at least a magna cum laude for his overall effort. The Bern faculty never required other professorial candidates to meet such rigorous requirements. The conditions were obviously drafted for the purpose of keeping Schlatter from receiving a post at the university. Six months after submitting his dissertation, Schlatter took his exams. He passed magna cum laude, and the examining professor, Friedrich Nippold—the same professor of church history and dogma who had given him such a cool welcome—admitted that Schlatter's answers were excellent and gave him marks of summa cum laude.

Despite Nippold's grudging admiration of Schlatter's competence, he continued to remind Schlatter that he did not approve of his viewpoints or his allies. Nippold submitted an editorial to the *Berner Post* entitled "Wer beruft den eigentlich die Professoren an der Berner evang.-theologischen Fakultät"

---

23. Schlatter, *Rückblick*, 79–81, 83. Certainly, despite there being no indications that he was familiar with Kähler's works, his theological moderation paralleled the Halle scholar.

(And just who calls the professors to the Bern Theological Faculty anyhow?) to express his displeasure at Schlatter's conservative allies and their means of forcing him onto the faculty. Despite their initial hesitance, Schlatter's success forced the Bern faculty to recognize his remarkable intellectual giftedness. Their respect for Schlatter grew enough that in 1883 the faculty requested that Schlatter's chair be supported from university funds. In 1888, they recommended his promotion to full professor. Despite this, Schlatter never had a close relationship with the other theology faculty members in Bern, and although they accepted Schlatter and his work, they never welcomed him as a colleague.[24]

Through their political maneuvering, the pietists also burned bridges with the institutional administration. Shortly before his exams, Schlatter met with the culture ministry's education director, Albert Bitzius (1835–1882), who oversaw all university hires. Schlatter asked Bitzius to expedite the examination process because Samuel Oettli had fallen ill and needed Schlatter to teach his courses. Before his entry into government service, Bitzius was himself a pastor, and as an adamant theological liberal, he was a leading member of the "reform" theological movement. Bitzius replied that he had no problem with Schlatter teaching courses but would never advance him to professorial status. As Schlatter recounted his words years later, Bitzius said, "If I make you a professor, the pietists in this land would call it an answer to their prayers. And I refuse to give them this pleasure." Originally, Schlatter believed Bitzius to have made the comment in jest, but when he told his conservative friends, they knew that Bitzius had meant it seriously. Ironically, Bitzius's eventual death in 1882 allowed Schlatter to advance unaided to the full professorship given to him in 1888. Despite Bitzius's open antagonism toward the young scholar, Schlatter later noted that he was the only person in Bern's liberal Christian circle who had openly and honestly rejected Schlatter because of his beliefs. This was in stark contrast to the theological faculty, which tried to discourage him by attempting to belittle his academic capabilities.[25]

In 1882, Schlatter stumbled across the project that would bring him international renown. The Hague Society for the Defense of Christianity offered a book award based on the subject "belief and believing in the New Testament." Schlatter assumed that the character of belief in the New Testament was essential to Christianity. He reasoned that belief must be discernible for Christianity to have any real meaning. Schlatter held that if

---

24. Schlatter, *Rückblick*, 84; Neuer, *Schlatter: A Biography*, 73, 75–77; Werner Neuer, *Adolf Schlatter: Ein Leben für Theologie und Kirche* (Stuttgart: Calwer Verlag, 1996), 146.

25. Schlatter, *Rückblick*, 89; Schlatter, *Erlebtes*, 11–12; Neuer, *Schlatter: A Biography*, 74–75.

he and the rest of the academic community left the question unanswered, Christians would despair. So he set out on a word study of the use of the Greek word, *pistis* in the New Testament and the corresponding Aramaic word from the contemporary Jewish religious literature. His work was accepted by the Hague Society and approved by its liberal members as well as its conservative ones. The resulting six-hundred-page work, *Der Glaube im Neuen Testament* (Belief in the New Testament), first published in 1885, became his generation's definitive work on the definition of New Testament belief. Schlatter's work was not merely a conservative definition of belief from the New Testament. He showed true ability in critical and comparative scholarship by interpreting many first-century Jewish works that had never before been seen in the context of New Testament studies.[26]

Der Glaube im Neuen Testament introduced Schlatter into the broader German-speaking theological circles. Over the following three years, he received invitations for positions at the universities in Halle, Kiel, Greifswald, Heidelberg, Marburg, and Bonn. Shortly after his promotion in 1888 to full professor at Bern, Schlatter was approached by Hermann Cremer (1834–1899), professor of theology at Greifswald and one of the premier believing scholars of the era. Cremer invited Schlatter to be his colleague at Greifswald on the Baltic Sea. Finalizing the process, Schlatter received the formal invitation from Prussian Culture Minister Althoff. The Greifswald position offered Schlatter better lecture facilities and more students, as well as the chance to be in a faculty that actively cooperated with him. Schlatter accepted the new position and left his beloved Switzerland. He would never again return except to visit.[27]

The Greifswald position returned even more than it had promised. Schlatter found an intimate and helpful colleague, mentor, and friend in Cremer that he missed in Bern. Cremer and Schlatter were united both in their desire to write good Christian scholarship and in the characteristic of their faith that put the love of Christ above petty doctrinal differences. So despite dissimilarities in their denominational upbringing (Cremer was the son of a North-German Lutheran pietist), they found they shared a mutual faith. In Cremer, Schlatter found a common academic spirit he had never found in his formative academic years, not even with J. T. Beck. Cremer was someone with whose entire work and spirit Schlatter could cooperate. He was amazed by Cremer's singularity of focus to combat the predominant Ritschlian theology in German universities. Up to the point of his entry in Greifswald, Schlatter remained aloof from the

---

26. Schlatter, *Rückblick*, 100–101; Neuer, *Schlatter: A Biography*, 78–79.

27. Schlatter, *Rückblick*, 114, 126; Neuer, *Schlatter: A Biography*, 79–80, 82–83.

written polemical attacks of the conservative-liberal battles. Cremer's extreme disgust with Ritschlian thought drew Schlatter's own irascibility into the fray of theological and university politics. In the five years Schlatter spent at Greifswald, Cremer and Schlatter together turned the university into the center for conservative theological studies in Germany. Beyond Cremer, the other faculty members at Greifswald, who for the most part shared Cremer's and Schlatter's conservative conviction, provided useful allies and sounding boards for Schlatter's burgeoning scholarship.[28]

However productive his time with Cremer was, Schlatter was again thrown into the heat of the German traditionalist-modernist controversy. In 1893, Prussian Culture Minister Althoff visited Schlatter again, this time to call him to Berlin. An 1892 publication against the Apostles' Creed by Berlin's premier liberal theologian, Adolf Harnack, incensed conservative Christians around the empire. These traditionalist church members petitioned the kaiser to create a new chair of theology for a conservative scholar to counterbalance Harnack. The kaiser accepted their proposal in 1892 against the expressed wishes of the Berlin faculty. Prussian Culture Minister Altoff, who had formally offered Schlatter his position in Greifswald, visited Germany's three premier senior conservative theologians: Martin Kähler (who was the Berlin faculty's choice for the position), Hermann Cremer, and Reinhold Seeberg (1859–1935). When all three rejected the offer, Altoff turned to his final choice, Adolf Schlatter. Schlatter likewise balked at the prospect of heading to Berlin and leaving the collegial environment he enjoyed at Greifswald. After refusing Althoff a number of times, the minister stood up and in a huff replied, "If that is your final response, then I must head to Königsberg." Schlatter believed that Althoff meant to suggest he would ask the professor of New Testament at Königsberg, R. F. Grau, to take the new chair. Schlatter was not particularly impressed with Grau, but it was no concern of his whom the Prussian ministry accepted. Althoff then turned and told Schlatter that there was a misunderstanding. Althoff said that if Schlatter refused the position, then he would be forced to return to his home in Königsberg. As a Prussian civil servant, his honor was tied to fulfilling the command of the kaiser. If Schlatter rejected his proposal, then Althoff could not return to Berlin, because his Prussian honor would be compromised. Althoff was a proud and powerful man. Schlatter had seen the minister greeted and honored by academics on a number of occasions, but here Schlatter had absolute control over the fate of the Prussian minister of culture. Once again, Schlatter had his choice in a major life decision

28. Schlatter, *Rückblick*, 138–40; Neuer, *Schlatter: A Biography*, 88–89; Thomas Nipperdey, *Religion im Umbruch: Deutschland, 1870–1918* (Munich: Beck, 1988), 79.

thrust upon him. Reluctantly, Schlatter accepted the invitation to Berlin, as he replied to Althoff, "If that is the case, then I will go with you."[29]

Once again, just as in Bern, the faculty opposed the decision to advance a religio-politically charged chair to Adolf Schlatter. However, Berlin differed in one important facet from Bern. The theological faculty in Berlin (with the important exception of Bernhard Weiss) made attempts to reach out to Schlatter and to engage him in the debates and intellectual endeavors of the faculty, once it became clear that he was to join them. This came principally from the most unlikely source, Adolf Harnack. Harnack wrote Schlatter shortly before Schlatter's arrival. Harnack honestly admitted that he was against the new chair for a conservative scholar, but he penned that he was happy Schlatter was coming to Berlin. In fact, Schlatter's encouraging relationship with his faculty colleagues was perhaps the greatest surprise of his tenure in Berlin. It was a pleasant contrast to Bern, where he had joined a faculty that begrudged his entry into academics and never warmed up to him. Most likely, the difference between the two schools lay in the comparable quality of the two faculties. Bern was a small faculty that lost all its best scholars as soon as they established themselves. In Berlin, the other scholars had already established themselves as the finest faculty in Germany. They did not need to worry about the influence of a conservative voice within their ranks.

The other elements of Schlatter's stay in Berlin were not as ideal. He never felt comfortable in big cities, and he never warmed up to Berlin. The situation was uncomfortable enough for Schlatter that, when conservative Protestants in Württemberg urged the king of Württemberg to found a chair for conservative scholarship at the kingdom's flagship university in the considerably more rural Tübingen, Schlatter had no hesitation accepting the position.[30]

In Berlin, Schlatter came into contact with the political circles in the German Empire. His calling to the university completed his transformation from a foreigner into a high state official. During this time, he also met Adolf Stoecker (1835–1909), the official court preacher (*Hofprediger*) as well as the founder and leading member of the Christian Social Party. Stoecker and Schlatter met and worked together on a number of social and church-political projects. However, the two differed in their view of the higher members of the political circles and their respective roles in leading a nation. Stoecker was a friend and supporter of the first kaiser and his chancellor Otto von Bismarck. He was concerned that Bismarck's successor, Caprivi, was not able to continue Bismarck's skillful guidance of the country. Certainly, Caprivi showed

29. Schlatter, *Rückblick*, 159, 163; Schlatter, *Erlebtes*, 13; Neuer, *Schlatter: A Biography*, 92–93.
30. Schlatter, *Rückblick*, 188–89; Neuer, *Schlatter: A Biography*, 95–96, 105–106.

that he did not have the exceeding genius for diplomacy that his predecessor possessed. Nevertheless, Schlatter believed that Caprivi's inferior capabilities were no reason for concern. Schlatter held a lecture seminar with Stoecker for young Christians in Berlin. In his speech, Schlatter told his listeners that German leadership did not need to have a series of geniuses along the lines of the renowned Bismarck to continue in its greatness. Schlatter declared that Germany only needed true citizens to continue on its path as a leader of the world. Stoecker gravely disagreed with Schlatter's assertions, but political differences notwithstanding, Stoecker helped guide the young Swiss scholar through the mazes of German higher politics. Also despite these differences, Schlatter later called his acquaintance with Stoecker, "the greatest that was given me in Berlin."[31]

While Schlatter had been chosen as a conservative response to critical theological faculties in his positions at Bern and Berlin, he had been passive in both of these decisions. He believed it was essential to have believing voices training pastors, but he never actively agitated for these until 1895. Perhaps we see here Stoecker's greatest influence on his friend during his time in Berlin. In 1895, Stoecker called together believing church leaders (who belonged both to the Positive Union and to the Neu-Luthertum confessionalists) to propose on behalf of the EOK (general church synod) a general policy that some conservative theologians be at every university. As somebody who had seen firsthand the difficulties faced by devout theologians foisted onto an unwilling faculty, one might expect Schlatter to maintain his silence about the practice. However, he was convinced to come to the meeting and also brought his friend from Greifswald, Hermann Cremer, who had first introduced Schlatter to Stoecker.[32]

At the convention, many of the speakers were extremely conservative in their theology and railed against academic theology as a practice and the universities undermining of verbal inerrancy. Schlatter and Cremer, who agreed with Kähler's assessment that verbal inerrancy was just as dangerous as extreme critical perspectives, were rankled by the speakers. The hotheaded Cremer threatened to leave the convention altogether. It seems it was Stoecker in his public speeches who was able to turn the convention as a whole toward a united fight against the common threat of critical theology departments. This turned the discussion away from such divisive issues as inerrancy. The convention chose to accept a more tolerant, charitable interpretation of Christian scholarship that adhered to Kähler and Schlatter's beliefs that the

31. Schlatter, *Rückblick*, 187; Schlatter, *Erlebtes*, 15–16.
32. Neuer, *Schlatter: ein Leben*, 313.

Bible is unquestionably authoritative even if it bears the marks of human imperfection. Stoecker spoke to the assembly, saying, "Revelation is not simply truth, but it is a life lived [*Leben*]."[33]

At the convention, resolutions were passed that supported the right of the church hierarchy to influence hiring decisions at the universities. Schlatter drafted the language that was adopted for the resolution. It read, "The convention implores the state to measure not only the intellectual and research [*wissenschaftlichen*] capabilities of the professors it hires but also the professors' Christian confession as it relates to the Word of God. The convention also recognizes the right of the [state] church to influence and guide the calling of professors of theology."[34]

After seven years of peaceful coexistence between Schlatter and the Berlin faculty, this active politicking on behalf of Stoecker's Positive Union created intense strife between Schlatter and the rest of the Berlin faculty. None less than Adolf Harnack, Berlin's most prominent faculty member, led the attack, surprising Schlatter. Nevertheless, Schlatter defended his point as he wrote, "The community of faith lies above any other," and later, "My [membership] in the church was higher, in my view than my position in the university."[35] The public fight that erupted as the faculty fought to defend their right to choose their own numbers certainly played a role in Schlatter's eventual departure from Berlin two years later and likewise influenced Schlatter's decision to eschew church politics from that point on.[36]

In 1897, after four uncomfortable years in Berlin, Schlatter returned to the site of his three semesters studying with J. T. Beck. In Tübingen, Schlatter found his niche and was able to consolidate his experiences from his first three professorial chairs. Tübingen saw his greatest output of literature, including his four famous systematic works of hermeneutics and theology, *Das Wort Jesu* (The Word of Jesus: 1909), *Die Lehre der Apostel* (The Teachings of the Apostles: 1910), *Das christliche Dogma* (Christian Dogma: 1911), and *Die christliche Ethik* (Christian Ethics: 1914). The first two works were a history of early Christianity that provided a conservative response to liberal outlines of early church history and dogma. Although not as visible as the life-of-Jesus movement, these critical reappraisals of the early church (most notably by F. C. Baur and Albrecht Ritschl) were the fundamental building blocks of critical theology. The second two works were Schlatter's attempt to create a wholly modern system of

33. Adolf Stoecker, quoted in ibid., 315.

34. Adolf Schlatter, quoted in ibid., 315.

35. Adolf Schlatter, quoted in ibid., 314.

36. Ibid., 317, 320.

believing theology that was no longer dependent on Reformation confessions. Tübingen also offered him the opportunity to spend time again in the church pulpit. While at Tübingen, Schlatter preached once a month in the theology department's chapel (*Stiftkirche*). Schlatter continued to teach in Tübingen until 1930. He continued to write until shortly before his death in 1938.[37]

Tübingen also saw the most difficult years for his family. His wife, Susanna, died in 1907 at the age of fifty-one. Schlatter never remarried, but his two eldest daughters, Hedwig and Dora, remained with him until his death. His eldest son, Theodor, took up church work as well in Tübingen as pastor of the theological faculty church and later as professor at the Bethel Theological Seminary near Bielefeld. His youngest daughter, Ruth, and her husband, Pastor Friedrich Hinderer, stayed nearby as well. His son Paul died from grenade-inflicted wounds in the opening months of the First World War. Schlatter himself died at the age of eighty-five. Heart and breathing troubles had become apparent shortly before his death. He died quietly on May 19, 1938.[38]

Setting a Foundation for Modern Belief: An Overview of Schlatter's Academic Work

Adolf Schlatter's theology pulled together various semi-systemized strains that were developed by fellow members of believing scholarship. Various biblicist and confessionalist theologians tried to respond to modern challenges that arose from Enlightenment rationalism and to the threats posed by new sciences and the political and economic growth of the German Empire. As with Kähler, the idea of the word of God laid the groundwork for his theology. He not only incorporated the same subjective understanding of faith and openness to critical thought from a believing hermeneutic, but also added to it a total picture of the results of believing Christianity for the individual, the church, Germany, and the world. Schlatter's systematic theology and system of ethics were the culmination of nineteenth-century theologically conservative thought.

As Schlatter's biography bore witness, his entire career was defined by the contemporary conflict between believing theologians and their critical opponents. From his second pastorate to his last professorship, Schlatter was continually brought in as a champion of orthodox, confessionalist teaching. His creative, unique appreciation of the traditions of the church made him a popular ally, even though at many points he separated himself from extreme conservative standpoints.

37. Ibid., 145, 147, 152, 158; Schlatter, *Erlebtes*, 46.
38. Neuer, *Schlatter: A Biography*, 113–15, 153.

Despite his public profile as a conservative voice in an increasingly iconoclastic profession, with a few notable exceptions, he eschewed polemical writings against his critical opponents. This was a sharp break from the defensive mentality that defined the works of many of his conservative predecessors—and that will also bear surprising contrasts in his view of Christian ethics. Nevertheless, his writings testified to the burden he carried as the leader of the pious theological camp in the new century. He took it upon himself to construct a new, tangible theology of Scriptures for modern believing Protestantism.

Schlatter's prolific writings covered the whole spectrum of modern academic theology, including historical theology, systematics, and exegesis. The vast majority of the over four hundred publications in his bibliography were historical theologies where his principal area of interest was the study of first-century Palestinian Judaism. These works continue to be the texts most often researched by professional historians and theologians. Schlatter's primary historical theologies,[39] his exegetical works, which were very popular during his lifetime,[40] and his two major systematic theological works[41] identified Schlatter's own justification for his professional work and his Christian faith. These works laid the interpretive foundation by which the rest of his works may be measured.

Schlatter's genius was his ability to process and synthesize conservative doctrines in a modern idiom. He was a canonizer, not a theoretician. His works were solid, straightforward, and well organized, even if they were seldom controversial or methodologically innovative.[42] His works collected and systematized the various contributions of the other principal conservative

39. Adolf Schlatter, *Zur Topographie und Geschichte Palästinas* (Stuttgart: Calwer Vereinsbuchhandlung, 1893); and Adolf Schlatter, *Kleinere Schriften zu Flavius Josephus* (Darmstdt: Wissenschaftliche Buchgesellschaft, 1910).

40. Adolf Schlatter, *Der Glaube im Neuen Testament* (Leiden: Brill, 1885); Adolf Schlatter, *Einleitung in die Bibel* (Stuttgart: Calwer Vereinsbuchhandlung, 1889); the two volumes of Adolf Schlatter, *Die Theologie des neuen Testaments: Die Lehre der Apostel* (Stuttgart: Calwer Vereinsbuchhandlung, 1910); and the series of popular commentaries of the New Testament, Adolf Schlatter, *Erläuterung zum Neuen Testament*, 11 vols. (Stuttgart: Calwer Vereinsbuchhandlung, 1887–1910).

41. Adolf Schlatter, *Das christliche Dogma* (Stuttgart: Calwer Vereinsbuchhandlung, 1911); and Adolf Schlatter, *Die christliche Ethik* (Stuttgart: Calwer Vereinsbuchhandlung, 1914).

42. Elements of his works drew criticism from the conservatives; however, those were never so decisive that they threatened to alienate Schlatter from the confessionalist circles in Germany. Schlatter's works were compared to those of his contemporary Adolf Harnack, who polarized Christianity in Germany, but Schlatter clearly never crossed any lines that would have separated him from his conservative base.

scholars of post-Enlightenment Germany: Kähler, Beck, Cremer, and Hengstenberg, to name a few. He built on long-standing traditions of Protestantism without bending to them as an infallible tradition. He made important inroads for certain forms of critical thinking into the conservative hermeneutics of his tradition, but he made no attempt to overhaul the whole of modern Christian piety.

SCHLATTER'S SYSTEM OF BELIEVING THEOLOGY

Schlatter was the first Protestant believing scholar to set out to define conservative Protestantism wholly in modern terms. Previous confessionalist and orthodox thinkers repeatedly fell back on the Reformation doctrines of Luther and Calvin to provide the backbone of their systematics. Schlatter recognized that the meanings of these Reformation doctrines had changed over the intervening four centuries. He desired to build a new theology that was faithful to the traditional creeds of the church while remaining comfortable with the best modern academic study and modern forms of knowledge. To do this, he felt the need to be able to criticize the Reformers' early modern doctrines while still recognizing their importance for Protestantism.[43]

He also arrived at the perfect time for such work as well. The conservative theologians were at a point of relative peace, common unity, and enduring status quo. They had achieved an uneasy truce with the government with cessation of the *Kulturkampf*.[44] Capitalism and industrialization created slums, unemployment, and urban vice, but their threat to the faithful had declined. The urban masses had already been outside the church for a generation, practically speaking, and industrialization showed few ill effects on the remaining middle-class parishioners.

All indications suggest that Schlatter was on his way to completing a unified believing theology when the First World War arrived. The calamity of the war and its effects on the mentality of Europeans obscured Schlatter's considerable efforts. They do not, however, negate Schlatter's intentions or his success. What follows is an attempt to define his theoretical foundations for a believing theology.

The way that Schlatter found to bind together the different strains of Protestant believers in a modern theology was through a form of mystical

---

43. Schlatter, *Rückblick*, 202.

44. As mentioned in the introduction, the *Kulturkampf* was a series of actions and policies set by the German government under Otto von Bismarck in an attempt to weaken the ties of German Catholics to Rome. The unintended consequences of the *Kulturkampf* ended up weakening the Protestant churches by equally limiting their legal privileges.

pietism, built surprisingly on a modern historicism. Indeed, this was a monumental task. Since the Enlightenment thinker Lessing, the historical nature of biblical revelation was seen as Christianity's greatest weakness. Schlatter offered many constructive suggestions concerning the place of theology in the modern world. However, he was careful never to substitute theology where faith belonged. For Schlatter, faith and knowledge were two separate entities. Theology is valuable because it articulates truth about God, but this knowledge is not an essential key to faith or to salvation from sins and damnation. Faith is a matter of personal piety, equally endowed to the brilliant and the simple. Theology is an act of Christian piety, not the hope of a believer's righteousness.

Schlatter did offer a new idea to Pietism that was missing from its seminal thinkers. He defined Christianity as a religion of the will. Faith is the believer's choice to submit himself or herself to the authority of God. Faith requires the acknowledgment of the Bible as the revelation of God's work with and through humanity. However, it does not require the absolute comprehension of the Scriptures. By proposing this, Schlatter introduced something new to the Protestant theological battles of the preceding four centuries. It was in this way that Schlatter affirmed Kähler's concept of a believing hermeneutic. Certain aspects of the Bible are simply beyond rational comprehension and need to be believed because of the Bible's authoritative claims.

Since the Reformation, orthodox Protestants defined faith largely as the possession of the right creed and doctrine. In practice, this elevated theologians to the pinnacle of importance in Protestant worship, because they were the interpreters of the Holy Writ for the whole church. Pietists challenged that statement. They defined faith as the proximity of God to the soul. This risked allowing thinkers like Schleiermacher to make individual God–consciousness superior to biblical teaching. Schlatter proposed that the *act* of orthodox Christianity proves the presence of God in the believer's soul. The faith shown in the act of the will claims supremacy over the Christian acknowledgment of spiritual truths. So, for Schlatter, the greatest Christian is not the theologian with encyclopedic understanding, but the missionary (in its broadest definition) who bends his or her will fully to that of God.[45]

---

45. This is naturally an interesting parallel to Schopenhauer's and Nietzsche's philosophies of the will, but turned on their heads. In Schlatter's understanding, the will of sinful men and women is naturally corrupt and deficient, but with God it can be restored and perfected. Barth would later reject Schlatter's premise that humans can change their will, even with the power of God. Neuer, *Schlatter: A Biography*, 179, 182.

Nevertheless, for Schlatter, theological knowledge and faith work hand in hand. Theology's pursuit of the knowledge of God makes the submission to God and to the Scriptures easier. The New Testament can successfully make its claim for faith only in proportion to its ability to convince Christians of the value and truth of its contents and its continued importance for the Christian life. True Christianity is participation with God in word and will together. For Schlatter, good theology is that which interprets the New Testament in such a way that faith is inspired. This faith in turn creates a transformation in the ethics and actions of believers—not the least of which includes the further pursuit of knowledge that comes from theological study. In the end, faith, as an act of the will, is the only possible way to transfer sacred knowledge into a life lived as God intends it to be lived.[46]

Schlatter was able to put knowledge below choice because he believed that reason is at best a receptive tool. For him, God is the ultimate supplier of knowledge about the Scriptures. For this to happen, the Cartesian starting point of the self must be willingly suspended occasionally. When interacting with the Scriptures, the believer transitions from being a subject reading the Bible into an object whom God can transform. Schlatter stated that it is blasphemous to believe that a true thought about God can be deduced from human reason alone. If God is infinite and transcendent, then any knowledge of God by a finite person must be a gift from above.

Since faith grows in combination with the New Testament's veracity, Schlatter declared that criticism is justified and allowed by the Scriptures. Naturally, this requires the right balance and diffidence to God's authority. Schlatter juxtaposed his own view about "believing" scholarship with the popular tenets of modern criticism. His description of faith as an act of the will brings the believer into a practical theological dialogue with the New Testament. Dogma and ethics result from this dialogue. The act of faith is submission of the will (ethics) to the will of God (dogma) as determined through the believer's interaction with the Bible. Too much modern criticism, in contrast, struggled for dominance over the Scriptures. Schlatter accused critics of using their methods to rule the Scriptures with violence. Modern criticism abandoned dialogue for hegemony.[47]

In Schlatter's writings, dogma is bound by its responsibility to the Bible. His foundation for dogma was those beliefs that Christians of all stripes held

46. Ibid., 179–81, 207, 209; Adolf Schlatter, "Meine Erfahrung mit der Bibel: Ein Rückblick" (originally published in 1924), in Adolf Schlatter, *Die Bibel Verstehen: Aufsätze zur biblischen Hermeneutik*, hrsg. Werner Neuer (Giessen: Brunnen Verlag, 2002); Schlatter, *Das christliche Dogma*, 11.

47. Schlatter, "New Testament Theology," 180, 181, 207–208, 209–210.

in community—above all, the precedence and importance of Jesus Christ as preserved in the Scriptures. Dogmatic work through all generations was principally the preservation and renewal of the historical message of Jesus Christ and the apostles for each generation. Recognizing the temporal nature of Jesus' revelation of God forced Schlatter to break from the predominant views of biblical inspiration. Traditionally, the Bible's meaning was thought to be perfect and unchanging. Schlatter, however, used a historicist perspective to assert that the words of the Scriptures are never simply handed down from one generation to another. Every new generation needs to phrase the same question, "What does the Scripture mean *for us*?"[48] This means that both historical and dogmatic works of theology are of utmost importance, because the community of faith continues to change through time. Since connections to the past and connections to each other need to be maintained, both forms of theological study remain important.[49]

Schlatter did not stop with the simple justification of the practice of theology and the recognition of its contribution to the general realm of knowledge. He laid the foundation for a critical, modern theology based on a believing hermeneutic. His key to a modern system of dogma was highly unusual. Modern theology was to be built on the recognition of the temporal forms of God's revelation. No conservative scholar had made such a bold claim. In the past, the historical narratives of the Bible were more likely to be seen as an embarrassment to theology, not its saving grace. Even critical scholars did their best to discard and discredit the temporal elements of the Scriptures' claims to possess eternal truth.

Despite the difficulties involved in bridging the gap between the early church and the modern one, Schlatter had great hope in achieving just that. He passionately argued that the understanding of the ancient belief was crucial for the survival of the church in the modern world. He still respected the Bible as the word of God, even when its writings were produced by human authors in their context. The understanding of God's revelation through Jesus and the

48. Ibid., 183.

49. This belief led Schlatter to something of a tautology: Since dogmatic writings were in his definition a *Christian* product, it was impossible to create (in Schlatter's opinion) an anti-Christian systematic theology—Ludwig Feuerbach's *Wesen des Christentum* (1841) was a good example of such an attempt—and the only possibility was a false or untrue dogma. Thus, the only recourse for anti-Christian critiques of Christian thought was through philosophy (e.g., Nietzsche) or through historical criticism (e.g., D. F. Strauss). But as the following makes clear, Schlatter also rejected anti-Christian critiques in historical theology for the astute reason that atheism is a dogmatic viewpoint, hence defensible only in the realm of systematic theology—which was already excluded due to extreme critics' separation from the church.

early church would strengthen Christians' thankfulness and broaden their faith. This was all the more important for him because he contended that modern faith was weakened by the broken connection to the early church caused by the modern theological pursuits. Those scholars who saw the essence of Christianity separated from the history of the church did a great disservice to true belief. Schlatter also laid out a plan of action for renewing the connection and the dialogue between modern Christians and the practice and belief of the early church. He wrote, "What we need for this is **renewed, intensified Scripture reading.**"[50] The purpose of the Bible is not to deliver a series of eternal precepts that are unbreakable and unchanging; rather, the purpose of the Bible is to bring the reader into the history of God's salvation.[51]

Schlatter believed that the results of his proposed theology would offer a clear doctrinal interpretation of the Scriptures and explicit ethical imperatives for the good, Christian life. Once the historical study of the biblical texts and the formation of Christian dogma were working in harmony, the theologian would be finally able to listen to the Scriptures. In the end, this is the ultimate act of theology: to discern what elements of the Bible were meant for the present and how they can be applied to the Christian life. Schlatter proposed that such an affirmative theology necessarily recognizes the authority of the Scriptures even as it reads the Bible critically.[52]

While Schlatter was ready to acknowledge the helpfulness of critical thinking for German Protestants, he did set specific limits on the sort of material it was to reach and the sort of truth claims it could make. For Schlatter, criticism is a tool helpful in gaining background information to the Scriptures that would make dogmatics more closely mirror the biblical authors' intent. He rejected any attempts to move historical criticism out of this narrow definition.

DISCOVERING THE WORD OF GOD IN SCHLATTER'S THOUGHT

Adolf Schlatter rallied all his resources from his wide-ranging talents to organize a theology of the Scriptures. He flipped traditional thinking about inspiration on its head. For Schlatter, the Bible is sacred because of the content of its pages rather than the means of its authorship. Like Kähler before him, Schlatter

---

50. Adolf Schlatter, *Der Dienst des Christen in der älteren Dogmatik*, "Beiträge zur Förderung christlicher Theologie," ed. A. Schlatter and H. Cremer, 1. Volume, First Year, (Gütersloh, C. Bertelsmann, 1897), 81. Emphasis in original.

51. Ibid.; Adolf Schlatter, "Die heilige Geschichte und der Glaube" (originally published in 1896), in Schlatter, *Bibel Verstehen*, 60.

52. Schlatter, *Das christliche Dogma*, 374.

affirmed that the Bible's authority springs from its ability to change lives, its power to bring the creation into relationship with God, and its role in unifying the church for a common mission. His deep trust in the Bible's authority was the starting point for the rest of his doctrinal teaching. His view of the Bible was explicitly modern but still protected the most important elements of traditional reverence for the word of God. In effect, he created a theology of the Scriptures that fused the greatest strengths of disparate and at times oppositional groups from traditional doctrines of inspiration to modern criticism, to the thought of modern believers, Martin Kähler and Søren Kierkegaard.

Schlatter asserted that the divine characteristics of the Bible arise from its divine subject. The Scriptures entail the revelation of God, as God gave it to and through creation. Their divine origins endowed the Scriptures with the highest authority for the Christian life. Yet Schlatter had no illusion that the Bible fell out of the sky complete and unerring.

Schlatter's portrait of the word of God was more complex than the predominant theologically conservative views of his day. He separated himself from the common belief that the Bible possesses an unambiguous, unvarying view of God. In viewing the Bible as a historical document, Schlatter recognized its plurality in its authors' portrayals of God and history. Even the very core of God's relationship with creation varies in the parts of the Bible. As an example, he drew attention to the fundamentally different images of salvation in the Old Testament and New Testament. The Old Testament built on the faithful fulfillment of the law by God's chosen people. The New Testament understood salvation as the result of faith in God's grace and redemption. These two systems of salvation work together in their entirety, but he would not insist that the revelation of God was wholly static and equal from the oldest writings of the Old Testament Law to the revelation of God in Jesus.

Schlatter recognized the Bible's limited breadth of knowledge. Despite the expansive subject matter addressed by the Bible, significant areas of knowledge are untouched and unacknowledged in the Scriptures. So he wrote that the Bible does not have the material necessary to be read to find a rationalistic all-encompassing system. However, he did not perceive this as a weakness. The less-than-total system of knowledge encompassed in the Bible does nothing to undermine its authority. He was convinced that the Bible is the word of God because it is the revelation of God's work in humanity and in history. What makes the Bible the word of God is its content, not its form or its factual inerrancy.[53]

53. Schlatter, *Einleitung*, 480–81; Schlatter, "New Testament Theology," 197–98; Schlatter, *Das christliche Dogma*, 369.

Schlatter's definition of the word of God offered an opportunity to question Lessing's "ugly ditch." Schlatter lectured that the Bible refers to the word of God as eternal. However, he believed that this claim did not hinder his move to join with the rest of modern academia (most notably including the critical-liberal schools of thought) in accepting that the Bible's writing was bound by historical causality.

Schlatter took Lessing's attack seriously and made every effort to rebuff its harsh rejection of traditional Christian beliefs. Schlatter responded to Lessing by defining the Scriptures as the word of God because they contain within them the very nature and knowledge of God. In this, Schlatter admitted that the texts of the Bible are temporal but the subject of the Bible is God, who is unchanging and eternal. Schlatter told his students, "A history can be eternal? Is there a solution? This word is poetry and prose from God, its content is the godly essence and thought, and *so it is* eternal. The Scriptures is the *revealed* Word, the Word as it was transformed in human possession, and here it gained its history, the history of human receptivity, its acceptance and acquisition, not of its production."[54] The Bible's historical account is the human history of the reception of God's eternal revelation. [55]

54. State Church Archive, Stuttgart, Adolf Schlatter Archive, "Die älteste Christenheit und die Bibel," D 40 #193.

55. Schlatter was convinced that the temporal narratives of the Bible prove God's personal nature. He used this unlikely claim in two ways. First, it allowed him to move past the Enlightenment's dismissal of a personal God. Second, he theorized that it supports an essential doctrine of Christianity—that God and God's creation are not fundamentally at odds with one another, but that God uses his eternal existence to redeem creation. Schlatter broke from other systematic theologies that worked outside the realm of historical theology and biblical studies. Rather, Schlatter's theology built from these very fields. New Testament studies of ancient Palestine and the critical inspection of the texts defined the form for theology. Historical theology was Schlatter's means to understand the temporal form of God's revelation. In claiming this, Schlatter took on Lessing's famous "ugly ditch." Lessing had challenged the Christian doctrine that an ternal God acts temporally in a finite world. No certain response was ever formulated against Lessing by theologians, critical or believing. Schlatter knew that many contemporary theologians undertook historical theology of the New Testament precisely because they believed the discipline of theology fundamentally areligious. They agreed with Lessing, and when they compared Jesus's actions with the temporal surrounding of first-century Palestine, they expected to find that the history of Jesus effectively denied the eternal qualities of God. Even scholars allied with Schlatter's beliefs effectively agreed with Lessing's pronouncement. Schlatter's former professor J. T. Beck, for example, refused to acknowledge the historical nature of God's revelation to humanity. Schlatter disagreed with this understanding of revelation and the fundamental concept of God that underlay it. He went so far as to wholly reverse Lessing's premise, claiming that every act of God in the created universe is temporally bound. This is not because God is temporally bound, but because God knows the inner workings of God's own creation. For Schlatter, the causal connections of the statements of Jesus and the apostles to the cultural setting of the time did not diminish their divine message. He showed that the repudiation of

Even though this historicist interpretation of the New Testament seemed to put the validity of Scripture on a more transient footing, Schlatter believed it was the best answer against both liberals and ultraconservative Biblical inerrantists. In this way, Schlatter contested theological liberalism, a movement made up, broadly speaking, of Albrecht Ritschl and his disciples. The Ritschlian liberals sought to extract the eternal religious truths within the temporal New Testament. Schlatter accused his theological opponents of ahistoricism. They avoided the challenges that historicism laid at theology by explicitly searching for eternal religion. He claimed that they replaced the concrete, historical reality of Christianity with abstract, timeless ideology.[56]

Ritschl first became a significant voice for modern theology as a conservative backlash against the conjectural historical work in the Hegelian theology of F. C. Baur's Tübingen school. Ritschl and his followers (most notably Adolf Harnack) saw the best way of determining the character of the early church to be tracing its doctrinal development. Therefore, historical theology drove their theological work. They believed that once the temporal elements of church doctrine were stripped from belief, then modern Christians could embrace the "essence of Christianity."[57]

Schlatter refused to create a timeless Christianity. The pursuit of eternal truths was seductive. However, from his first pastorate on, he noted that liberal theology lost its connections with truth or with any form of practicability as it attempted to apply these eternal tenets to modern reality. Timeless statements of religious morality were always tempting for any New Testament theologian. Schlatter could comprehend the attractiveness of these eternal statements because they seemed to make the sometimes-confusing New Testament eminently understandable and applicable. Yet it was exactly this activity, undertaken by so many in the Ritschlian theological circle, that Schlatter found so irresponsible. They were using historical methods to extract the essential "kernel" from the temporal "shell." Schlatter wrote that they were misusing their historical tools. The historian, in Schlatter's empiricist model, has the sole responsibility of making the meaning of the New Testament evident to modern readers. It is the dogmatist, the systematic theologian, who needs to bear the

any human connections that Jesus may have had in his revelation of God only opened the way for an even more subversive logic of Christian belief. If God could not work through sinful, flawed, and cultural means to deliver God's revelation through Jesus, then God could also not use the transitory culture and history to work in the lives of any Christian, ancient or modern. Schlatter's God was one whose acts purified and sanctified the setting in which they entered; God's history became sacred history. Schlatter, "New Testament Theology," 198.

56. Ibid., 183–84.

57. Schlatter, "Meine Erfahrung," 114–15.

responsibility of making the New Testament's message applicable to modern Christians. Schlatter took this view because he believed there is no elusive kernel under the shell. By removing the temporal from Christianity, the liberal theologians destroyed the value Christianity had. Schlatter boldly responded that faith is bound to the time and place of the believer.[58]

So Schlatter agreed with Kähler and flatly rejected the traditional view of the Scriptures being God's word because of the means of the transmission of their message. In its place, he developed an understanding that God's eternal word is in the message that humans sought to express. The Bible by this perspective contains the unerring, eternal word of God, but it was written by fallible humans set in a particular historical context. These two aspects, the historical and the eternal, are bound so tightly that they can never be separated. They are the perfect example of human and divine cooperation. This subtle change in understanding allowed Schlatter to open up his dialogue to include even the proponents of the most radical biblical criticism. He did not shy away from reading and struggling with biblical criticism. Likewise, he did not discourage his students from wrestling with biblical criticism's issues. In the end, he rejected these radical critiques, but on grounds of differences in theological results, not from an unwillingness to consider their points of argument.[59]

Schlatter saw inspiration as one aspect of a beautiful dance between creator and creation that results in the purification and perfection of the world. In Schlatter's description, both dancers work in cooperation to create something beautiful. By using humans to reveal himself to the world, God imbued the Bible with infinitely more value than a Scripture brought about through the means described by verbal inspiration. In the act of revelation, God gave the gift of the Spirit of truth to the Bible's authors, and God's truth was wholly perfect. If God gave the gift of the Holy Spirit to the prophets and apostles, then Schlatter was confident that God would also give the Spirit to the rest of the world.[60]

However, by emphasizing God's sanctification of humanity's efforts, Schlatter removed the Scriptures from their evangelistic role. The Scriptures were no longer believable because they were objectively fact. Rather, the Bible is true because it is the product of the same sort of God of which its

---

58. This obviously also excluded the radical pristinarian pursuits of many orthodox Protestant theologians to recapture the exact faith of the apostles of the early church. Schlatter, "New Testament Theology," 182–84.

59. State Church Archive, Stuttgart, Adolf Schlatter Archive, "Die älteste Christenheit und die Bibel," D 40 #193.

60. Schlatter, Einleitung, 480.

message proclaimed. Schlatter understood the Bible's authority and authorship to be completely defined and explained within its pages. He admitted to the tautology of his modern biblical Christianity. The Bible's authority is only evident as it is accepted. The Bible possesses no power to coerce. It only becomes authoritative as individuals submit to its message. This gives the Bible a mystical authority but removes its defensibility and provability in the modern discussion of scientific fact. He acknowledged that the Bible was no longer the first proof of Christianity's validity to the skeptic, and instead suggested that the validation of its truth and authority would come only as the result of God's gift of faith.[61]

Perhaps in this way, Schlatter tried to explain why the truth of the Bible is self-evident to some and rejected by others. He was certainly aware of the decreasing influence of the Bible on public thought and debate. The Bible played an ever-decreasing role in education. Political stances were no longer built on theological definitions of royal authority. Movements like socialism rejected the Bible outright as a belligerent tool of the ruling classes. Discussions of civic virtue no longer acknowledged God's providence and divine law. Evolution rid science of natural theology. By Schlatter's height of influence, more people than just the radical critics like Feuerbach had rejected the Bible as their personal guides for morality. By limiting the acknowledgment of the Bible's truth to the elect, Schlatter found a way to underscore the Bible's authority in an age when many chose to move the Bible to the margins of public discourse.

Since the Bible is God's gift to creation, Schlatter posited that God must have given the church the tools it needs to understand the Bible. He was fully aware that significant difficulties arose from the historical nature of the written revelation of God. Questions of meaning in the Bible came from the above-mentioned scholars who found difficulties synthesizing the text's historical and eternal claims. Naturally, these difficulties were acute for the church's lay members, who were not trained to understand and interpret the historical context of what they were reading.

In this sense, Schlatter separated himself from the Reformation doctrine that the Bible is understandable and accessible by all Christians alike. However, Schlatter did not despair. While he separated himself from the Reformers who claimed that all Christians have equal access to the Scriptures, he proposed that the church as a body possesses all the tools necessary to fully comprehend the Bible's meaning. Since individuals are so prone to error in interpreting

61. Schlatter, *Das christliche Dogma*, 366–68.

the Scriptures, Schlatter concluded that the Word of God achieves its greatest efficacy only as it is read by the church, both in its local and universal sense. (He understood his own work in the interpretation of the Scriptures as a cooperative labor in and for the church). The Bible is truly effective at awakening belief in the individual Christian only as it is read in community.

Schlatter's thoroughgoing historicity needed to be suspended in the realm of personal belief. In an about-face from his view on research, he adopted a presentism in his description of Christian piety. Revelation needed to be read as historical. A pious response to revelation, however, may echo Kierkegaard's question, "What does the Bible mean for me?" While Schlatter was insistent on seeing the Bible's revelation as set in history, he could only define its applicability as compressed into the believer's own life and reading. Piety and mandates for moral action proved incompatible with anything but an immediate response by the believer and a reading of the Bible that sees everything in it focused on the personal faith of the individual. For the believer, in stark contrast to the researcher, the Bible is always immanent.

In effect, the relationships between the reader and the Bible and, correspondingly, between the reader and God is remarkably democratic. The Bible demands absolute authority, but the expression of that authority in the individual's life is personal and internal. Each believer has equal access to the authority and the same right to interpretation with the same Spirit within the context of the church. What at first appeared to be a variation on a *Führer*-cult—that is, an absolute, unquestioned authority in all matters moral—actually was a complex issue of virtue and internal accountability to a divine moral standard. While there existed considerable parallels between religious conservatives and social conservatives, they remained opposed in some key beliefs.

By tying the interpretation of the word to the church, Schlatter strengthened the church's continued prominence in German society. He validated the reading of the Bible as an essential element of Christian piety by which a believer would know and receive moral guidance. Putting these together, Schlatter asserted that the church leadership, however it was constructed, had the authority to construct the interpretation of the Bible with its moral imperatives as a community. Schlatter recognized that most people outside the church would not recognize pastoral authority, but that made it no less bound to God's commands.

The Calling and the Life: Schlatter's Ethics

Schlatter's explanation of ethics grew out of his understanding of the word of God. In his mind, right Christian action in all its facets is intimately intertwined with the Scriptures. Ethics are the product of right doctrine and right faith as it changes the human will. The will can change only when the faithful believer actively unites his or her will to God's holy will. God's will can be known only through the relationship between the individual believer and the creator God. And this relationship can develop only as the believer learns, reads, and knows the word of God. No one has a mooring to right action without the presence of the word of God revealed in the Bible.[62]

For all of Schlatter's creativity and flexibility in laying the framework for a believing theology, his ethical pronouncements gave a relatively straightforward justification for the sort of society and morality that was already current in Germany at the turn of the century. Like Stoecker before him, Schlatter portrayed the ideal state as a modern authoritarian monarchy with limited parliamentary institutions that governed in close interaction with the church. Only when imagining Christianity as a minority religion in a pluralistic culture did Schlatter begin to contemplate creative Christian responses to government and society.

Schlatter explained that once the believer through faith acknowledged that the Bible is God's word, then he or she thereby also accepted the Bible's portrait of God's will. Ethics are the natural outcome of the Christian, biblical life. Yet he distanced himself from the belief that the Bible is a book of law or of propositional statements. The Bible has commandments for the believer, but these commandments become clear only when predicated on the relationship and intimacy of the believer with Jesus Christ. Theology (as well as pastoral ministry) cannot sustain itself merely by learning the interpretation of the Bible. True knowledge of God is found only by learning the word of God as it is practically lived out in the Christian life. Salvation comes from faith alone, but

62. Schlatter was the only believing theologian of his day to write an independent systematic ethics, since most others included ethics as merely one arm of their dogmatic teaching. Twenty years later, Karl Barth mercilessly attacked Schlatter for the division between doctrine and ethics that he implied. Barth claimed that such a divide between doctrine and practice was a gross error of theology. But Schlatter never saw his action as fundamentally separating two elements of Christian belief. He simply held that these two elements of Christianity, its faith and its action, require a different verbiage and formulation. He pointed to the New Testament authors and argued that they, too, created a bipartite division in their writings, separating the practice of Christianity from faith in Christ. In Paul's writings, the apostle uniformly began his letters with theological treatises and concluded with practical application. Schlatter insisted that morality and faith are inseparable even if their systematic description, as an academic exercise, separates them.

that faith makes itself manifest and shows itself true in the good works of the Christian who does God's will as expressed in God's word.[63]

Since ethics are actions, the will played the central role in Schlatter's theological ethics. He particularly emphasized the will of God as it is expressed in the historical narratives of the Bible, writing that the will, both human and divine, is the dynamo of history. It is the catalyst to action. In his portrayal, Christianity is not passive, nor is God distant. God has an active plan for the world that involves guiding its history toward its final state wherein God's sovereignty and grace will be immanent in everything. It was for this reason that God chose to reveal himself in the Bible through its historical narratives. In these cases, the word of God took the form of history because history showed the result of God's will tangibly. A god who was merely an abstract force and timeless being would be a god unable to enact any movement in history. Such a god could have no will. The dynamic God that Schlatter saw in the Bible unmistakably created and moved history.[64]

Since God's will was always transparent in the historical narratives of the Scriptures, believers can be confident that God will show God's will in the present. Schlatter sketched out how. As believers are made aware of their intimacy with God, they inevitably face the question, "What is the proper response to God's gift of relationship through Jesus Christ?" Like Kähler before him, Schlatter saw ethics as the loving response that the Christian makes. As the new believer grows in intimacy with the word of God, the Bible directs the reader to God's will. One of God's gifts to Christians was a clear presentation of his will for their lives in the Bible. The result of Christian faith is that the Bible's ethical leadership, generated from the will of God, leads to harmony with others, harmony with oneself, and peace.[65]

In his systematic ethics, Schlatter attempted to explain the explicitly Christian grounds for ethics. Because Christians believe that God is omnipotent and sovereign, they know that God has no need to receive services from them. Schlatter stated that Christianity believes that God is the giver of all gifts and talents. This makes the idea of doing something for God ludicrous. The proper response is to use those gifts in praise of God. God gave these gifts for the benefit of the community. Believers act ethically when each individual offers his or her gifts and services for the good of the whole community. Certainly, individual's lives as they know themselves to be parts of larger communities are

63. Schlatter, *Die christliche Ethik*, 258–59.

64. Schaltter, "Die heilige Geschichte und der Glaube," 53–54.

65. Schlatter, *Das christliche Dogma*, 374–75; Schlatter, *Einleitung*, 7–8; Schlatter, *Bibel Verstehen*, 100–101.

the central motivation for ethics. An individual can practice Christian ethics only when that person understands himself or herself to be an integral part of a larger community. Once this bond has been created, ethical behavior will be the natural outcome.[66]

POLITICAL ETHICS

The Christian community has a special claim to its members' obedience, according to Schlatter. Other ethical systems and communities make claims for an individual's behavior. Schlatter realized that the rhetoric of acting for the good of the community is also the proscription of behavior within the state. The difference between Christian ethics and state-based morality is that Christian ethics has an absolute foundation and justification. The belief in God as the giver of all good gifts and as the perfect creator of all human community grounds behavior in place as a by-product of God's goodness. A state that misses these divine principles risks tyranny. He wrote,

> Every community that calls us to work is mandated through the godly Government, not through our own creative acts. For this reason, our service that we complete for God in obedience is only pure once we follow the will of God that he has made known to us . . . . When we slip from the teaching of the [Christian] calling to the satisfaction of obligation, then we put our egotism in the place of love and subsequently break down the community. This is the origin of every despot who seeks to subjugate all others.[67]

For Schlatter, ethics, even within the context of the state, are truly pure only as they arise out of the holy will of God.[68]

Schlatter moved his attention to expounding how Christians ought to understand and order ethical action. Ethics are borne in the interplay of two complementary ideas: rights and love (or mercy). Schlatter also made an institutional divide between these two concepts. The state bears the responsibility to create and govern the community of rights. The church is the community of God's love. All people can submit to the community of rights, but love is a gift of God. Schlatter again underscored the unique ethical relationship of Christians by claiming their exclusive membership in the loving community of the church.[69]

---

66. Schlatter, *Die christliche Ethik*, 19–20.

67. Ibid., 21.

68. Ibid., 20–21.

Schlatter noted that both justice, which the state embodies, and love, which is the purview of the church, are ethical qualities that arise out of the character of God. Since God is righteous, the state's responsibility to protect the rights of its citizenry is holy. Likewise, since God loves, the church's responsibility to love grows out of the church's relationship with God. However, Schlatter's descriptions of the two institutions differed greatly. The state is a coercive body that requires the means to power and violence to protect the rights of its citizenry. The church, in contrast, acts ethically because it gives generously and never seeks to protect its own rights against encroachment.[70]

Indeed, for the church to carry out its function as the community of God's love, Schlatter saw that it requires a mystical believing connection within the church, not simply passive attendance at the worship services. The church is imbued with God's particular love and strength for the fulfillment of its ethical duty. To administer these responsibilities, the church takes its form as a community of life and sacrament. It alone has the power to coax out good, generous, and selfless decisions from its members. Ethics in the church are possible only through the special power and strength that God lends the church through God's grace. Then the service from individual believers is both a means of showing God's grace to others (through distributing God's gifts) and a means of experiencing God's grace oneself (by receiving the power to give).[71]

For Schlatter, the state protects the private sphere and life of the individual, but only the church can enrich that life to be worth living. Both the community of rights and the community of love are necessary for right ethical action. A society without the community of the church relies solely on the satisfaction of an individual's obligations, as established by the rights garnered by the state. While such a society can function, it will be stunted and limited in its ability to grow, mature, and develop. The satisfaction of obligations and the protection of rights only defend the society's status quo, but it lacks a motor to drive it forward.

As Schlatter described it, a member of such a society would only seek to satisfy his or her own individual obligations. Once those were satisfied, he or she would cease actively participating in the community. As a result, the larger, most productive aspects of life—those aspects where individual gifts can be poured into others' lives and cooperate with others' talents—would never be used to the mutual benefit of all. For proof of this, Schlatter pointed to the manifold cultures outside Christendom that could not match the West's

69. Ibid., 52.

70. Ibid., 56, 58.

71. Schlatter, *Die christliche Ethik*, 53; Schlatter, "Dienst des Christen," 5.

progress. He attested that other religions and other ideologies of state, while able to protect the rights of their members, were unable to build constructively because they lacked the selflessness of the church community of love.[72]

Not surprisingly, Schlatter used this idea to combat secular utopian ideas that suggested history has within itself a motor for progress and betterment. Nearly unanimously, these latter-day successors of Hegelian philosophy, most notably Communism, desired to shed the church, claiming it retards society's true development. They claimed that virtue arises from the state, not from religious belief. Perhaps Schlatter should be credited with remarkable foresight into the post-Christian Communist state. Schlatter warned that any such state could demand little love from its citizenry, or extra effort for the society's communal success, since power and coercion are unable to inspire love, generosity, and selflessness.

Schlatter also contended that a society built only upon the Christian conception of love is doomed to failure. A community that abandons the rights and obligations that it possesses because of the state risks anarchy and arbitrariness. The rights of society protected by the state are the basic fundamentals of life. They need to be provided to all members equally and faithfully. A community where generosity and love are the only guiding principles may fail to meet these essential needs or to administer them fairly. Schlatter suggested that only once the basic needs of a citizenry are satisfied is the foundation laid for an effective outpouring of loving action. So for Schlatter, both forms of ethics (those of rights and those of love) and both institutions (the state and the church) are fundamental for the satisfaction of true, Christian ethics.[73]

Schlatter's theoretical ethical apparatus gave him the framework he needed to develop a system of practical ethics. He wrote that this core relationship between God the creator and individual humans, the creatures, form the foundation for interpersonal ethical relationships. Schlatter gave particular ethical direction in three categories. He outlined a code of conduct governing the Christian's responsibility to his or her own people, to the world, and to the state.

Schlatter's most basic community for all humans, Christian and non-Christian alike, was the ethnic community, or *Volk*. He contended that all other communities (even those with universal adherence, like the church) function and are administered within the *Volk*. As an example, Christians necessarily

---

72. Schlatter, *Die christliche Ethik*, 59; Schlatter, *Bibel Verstehen*, 32–33.
73. Schlatter, *Die christliche Ethik*, 64–65.

work within a national church (*Volkskirche*). Bonds of culture, language, and local habits (*Sitten*) create a natural affinity to fellow members of the church within one's own people that runs deeper than a connection to the Christian church universal. The unique qualities of the *Volk* even determine the form of the worship service. Therefore, a German church service is necessarily different from a French service. By claiming this, he created a hierarchy of the church community's claims to service of love from an individual. The church members' duties of service begin at the individual's own group and widen out in circles of lessening connection.[74]

CHRISTIANS AND WAR

Without ever stating it as his explicit purpose, the Swiss-born, nationalized German developed a nationalist foundation for his theological ethics that was custom-built to sidestep the ethical questions that would arise when "Christian" nation took on "Christian" nation shortly after *Ethik*'s publication. As shown in chapter 7, the particular relationship that Schlatter drew between the Christian and his or her people would play a significant role later in his justification for the First World War.

This was also a point of contention between Kähler's ethics and Schlatter's. Kähler remained suspicious of the concept of a *Volkskirche* because it gave the ethnic divisions authority over religious universalities. If he was familiar with Kähler's opinions, Schlatter apparently was unmoved by such logic. He saw nationalities as the common, obvious division of people. This division was immutable and static. Since it was within the nature of humanity to be divided into ethnic groups, then it was not contrary to the will of God to use those divisions within church life.

Schlatter recognized that any time a national church was founded within a Christian state, it would work in cooperation with the state. While he had no issues with a church-state alliance, he did warn the church to avoid becoming a coercive power alongside the state. He stated it as a natural law that a decline in faith inevitably followed a church coercing its citizenry. Such churches always replaced true faith with a forced and unnatural attachment to the practice of church liturgy and sacraments. He did claim the right and obligation of the people's church to evangelize those members of a society who did not adhere to the essential doctrines of the faith. Yet for him, this was a greatly different idea than forcing belief through coercive means.[75]

74. Ibid., 160.
75. Ibid., 160, 164–66.

Schlatter outlined a basic code of Christian conduct in international relations as well as domestic ones. Even as the church had obligations to evangelize within its own culture, the believing community ought to engage in Christian missions to evangelize the non-Christian world. Looking at the merchant and military advancement of European imperialism, Schlatter contended that the spread of Christianity was of the utmost importance because it helped balance the godless and amoral elements of Western advances. He foresaw a massive conflict in cultures and worldviews in imperialism. Western science and political structure would lay waste to the religious landscape of the non-Western world, whose cultures were built upon religious myth. Schlatter encouraged the advancement of Christianity into the world to productively fill the religious vacuum that was left in European culture's wake.[76]

Schlatter claimed that Christians in the church possess a particular responsibility to submit to an efficient and righteous state. However, he put Christian citizens in a hierarchy of authority. He stated that, for Christians, the community of the church and the actions that arise from the loving will of God trump and limit the demands of the state. The church then, as the culture Christianized, would balance the state's power because the church knows its principal duty is to enact the will of God before the church fulfills the whims of the state. Schlatter took this complementary understanding of state and church to such a degree that he claimed that a state that guided its law on Christian religious principles would be a stronger and more successful state. He wrote, "Christianity protects the state from being shaken because it brings clarity and security in the relationship between the people and God. For this reason every prince and official only fulfills his duty to protect the state when he confesses freely (not only with words) and gives God the glory. Contrarily, those who trumpet atheism destroy their state."[77] Schlatter expressed confidence that the Christian state would be the superior state because the church in that state would exercise the love that the people need so that they learn to appreciate the protection the state provides for their rights. Schlatter was confident that believers make great citizens.[78]

Since the state is essential to life, he argued, the church needs to accept the state's authority over the natural elements of life. He accepted the right and the obligation of the church to defend its independence from the state. Christ spoke his commandment to be separate from the world in ethical and spiritual terms, not absolutely. The church should not pursue the same greedy goals of honor

76. Ibid., 204–205.
77. Ibid., 113.
78. Ibid., 111–13.

and wealth as the state or its unredeemed citizens might. Therefore, the church's separation from the world ought not create a sense of antipathy (*Feindschaft*) against one's own people, or the rejection of one's own state.

This relationship between the natural and spiritual was certain because both originate in the creation of God. Therefore, Schlatter could accept the ethical validity of revolutionary uprising only in dire circumstances. Drawing from just-war language, he justified such extreme political action only when the revolution and any ensuing civil war were fought to create a new society with a longer, more enduring peace. In normal situations, Christians were obliged to support any moderate government that protected the people from the extremes of anarchy and despotism.[79]

On the face of it, Schlatter's understanding of church-state relations shows many striking similarities to the picture of the ideal state proposed by Adolf Stoecker. However, the underlying view of the church's position in the modern world is fundamentally different. Stoecker's entire worldview was built from an extreme conservative worldview that saw various aspects of God's blessing—the nation, the government, and the church—as being assailed by modern godless institutions. The church was just one of many institutions under attack. In Schlatter's description of ethics, even as the picture of the ideal state looks much like that described by Stoecker or, better said, as the existing situation in Germany, the image of church-state relations was not born of the extreme pessimism of the court preacher. Schlatter's understanding of the church is fundamentally optimistic and positive. The church is a blessing to the state, rather than a fundamentally endangered pillar of the state. It has an opportunity to strengthen the state whenever and wherever it is effective. Schlatter betrays no sense of foreboding about the future of the church in Germany as Stoecker did.

GENDER ROLES

Schlatter also addressed the growing women's movement in his *Ethik*. In his theology, women are in the same spiritual relationship with God. So women receive the same grace and rights as men in a Christian state. Schlatter saw this manifested in a woman's supreme calling in her role as mother, but Schlatter addressed this calling positively. Maternal importance increased significantly in a spiritually oriented Christian society, because mothers take on the primary role of teaching their children the ways of faith. Addressing women's role in the Christian culture, Schlatter wrote,

---

79. Ibid., 112, 115–16, 125.

Following through on the statement that there are not two Christian ethics, one for men and another for women, also sets a morality into motion. This morality sets aside the limits that constricted the life of women and their participation in Christian community. This law gives women similar rights in society and in worship as men. As to the division of work, the norm to observe is that women ought to perform the service for which they are most suited, and they should not slacken on that work (*Leistung*) which is their greatest, their motherly role.[80]

Women were to fulfill their calls as mothers because that was where they were most suited and where they could best fulfill the ethics of love required for their place in the Christian community.[81]

Schlatter worried that the attempt of some women to enter into grocery and food production work was both unsuited for their physical stature and a degradation of their calling as mothers. He called it a "national travesty (*Schuld*)" and a "public misfortune" when women were brought into the workforce. He claimed that such work would reduce women's natural propensity for religious piety. The hectic pace of the daily work world would rob women of their quiet and the time they needed to consider their faith and they used to enrich society through the proper upbringing of their children. He saw women as the bedrock of a spiritual society because of their inborn superiority over men in serenity and their irreplaceable role as the formative voice on following generation.[82]

Schlatter never indicated his opinion of domestic servants and other unmarried women who were obligated to earn a living. His picture of the ideal Christian situation was clearly that of a middle-class family of leisure where the women had time for serenity, reflection, and Christian fortitude. This seems to lend credence to Hugh McLeod's contention that in the modern period, Christianity became increasingly identified with a middle-class lifestyle. It demanded ever-increasing moral standards and piety that were unfeasible for most working-class families.[83]

---

80. Ibid., 126.

81. Ibid., 125–26.

82. Ibid., 126–27.

83. McLeod does suggest that despite the middle-class culture of the church, the wealthy middle class in Germany was generally quite secular. It was the lower middle class and some rural communities that maintained strong connections to the church and kept up regular church attendance in Germany. Hugh McLeod, *Religion and the People of Western Europe, 1789–1989* (Oxford: Oxford University Press, 1997), 98–102.

Schlatter's insistence that women remain out of the workforce did not mean he precluded them from public work and participation in the government. Schlatter roundly dismissed the critique of what he labeled the growing "political right" that the nation (*Volk*) would become womanly if the citizenry included women in the function of the state. He welcomed an increased role for women so long as they remained centered at the same time in their relationship to the church.[84]

A CHRISTIAN ETHIC AS POLITICAL PLATFORM

In general, Schlatter accepted the Christian participation in party politics. In a situation where the general populace was not Christian, Schlatter accepted the necessity of a Christian party to guide a state along Christian principles. Yet he warned his readers that a Christian party would be ethical and right only when the Christians of the country (and the party) consistently put their faith into action. A Christian party that spoke Christianly but did not behave in a Christian manner would defeat its own goals. Furthermore, it would be disastrous for the witness of the national church. His other prerequisite for a Christian party was that it would use its voice for the good of the whole nation and not just the advancement of the church's members.[85]

He also reminded any people interested in starting a Christian party that the party could never expect that the government would lead people to obey God. Obedience to God, as he pointed out earlier in his text, came only when an individual turned his or her whole will to fulfilling God's will. This was an individual decision and a calling from God; it could not be enforced through state action.[86]

Schlatter justified a Christian political party by arguing that every political system, no matter its own claims to the contrary, presented a dogma of its own. Socialists followed their materialist dogma, liberals that of the Enlightenment, and the center party adhered to Catholic dogma. No objection could be made if Protestants developed a politicized form of their dogma to join in the national discussion as one legitimate worldview among many (although in his opinion clearly the best). He recommended humility in this endeavor. Only a twisted fantasy could claim to develop a political system from the teaching of Jesus.[87]

---

84. Schlatter, *Die christliche Ethik*, 126–27.

85. Ibid., 140.

86. Ibid.

87. At first glance, it may appear that Schlatter here opposed Blumhardt's political claims that the Socialist Democratic Party (SPD) was the party of Christ. Yet Blumhardt clearly acknowledged that the SPD was flawed in its political claims. Blumhardt merely contended that it was the nearest approximation

Any Christian political platform would draw from the present cultural milieu and in many policies would not differ from the decisions and policies of other political parties. In situations where Jesus's teachings did not provide clear guidelines for action, he welcomed political compromise with other existing parties.

Schlatter's ideal of a political party fit well into German's multiparty system. He argued that in political systems where only two parties existed, one wholly conservative, the other wholly progressive, Christian politicians would not find a home in either party. Christianity was neither wholly concerned with preserving culture nor wholly supportive of certain progress. Schlatter's Christian party would at times need to be conservative and at other times progressive in its calling to be fully Christian.[88]

Interestingly, Schlatter drew up this plan for a Protestant party seemingly independently of Adolf Stoecker's Christian Social Party. Schlatter fostered a good acquaintance with Stoecker during his tenure in Berlin, but the two men never saw eye to eye politically. Schlatter supported Bismarck's Conservative Party. Stoecker, he wrote, defined his party "Christian Social" too narrowly. He critiqued Stoecker's restricted focus on Christian perspectives of economics and work policy, ignoring the other obligations of the state. Schlatter listed these unaddressed obligations as the creation of rights, the protection of the people, and the advancement of health, art, knowledge, religion, and international trade.

Schlatter finally followed his own advice on this point in the late 1920s and 1930s when he was an outspoken member of the Protestant Evangelischer Volksdienst Partei (Protestant People's Service Party). He wrote in conclusion to his discussion of Christian politics in *Ethik*, "A healthy national life (*Volksleben*) can only come about when every citizen contributes his share to the advancement of the whole. The Christian character of the state advances the nation as it can only when the whole of Christianity gives its strength and its knowledge from all its members to the benefit of society. We are the Christian Party, only insofar as we work with our Christian gifts for the good of our people."[89] His hope was that a Christian voice in politics could be beneficial to

---

to a Christian party that existed, a surprisingly similar justification to Schlatter's support of a Christian party given before the warning that a wholly Christian platform was an impossibility. The two (although opposing in party affiliation) argued here essentially the same idea: the Christian is called to act on his or her faith in the public, political realm using any and all means available to enact God's will.

88. Schlatter, *Die christliche Ethik*, 142–43.

89. Ibid., 146.

the nation as a whole. He remained confident that a nation that was Christian would see the greatest political health possible.[90]

CRIME IN THE CHRISTIAN STATE

Schlatter also turned his ethical system to addressing the penal system. Crime undermines a society's unity. For this reason, he fully supported government's policing and punishing criminal activity. Such justice is a Christian act. The state in its responsibility of protecting the rights of its citizenry requires the power to remove those rights from society's enemies. In his postwar revision of his *Ethik*, Schlatter wrote that the sixth commandment of God. "Thou shalt not kill," does not apply to state punishment. To support his claim, he pointed to sayings of Jesus and writings of Paul. The sixth commandment was intended to sanctify life, not to eliminate all killing. The criminal who had already killed had already desecrated life and therefore no longer stood within the protection of the spirit of the commandment. The state needs to retain its right to take life as a form of punishment. However, he restricted capital punishment in a Christian state to crimes of murder. He worried that if the state exercised the death penalty too often, it would obfuscate the forgiveness available to all, even the worst criminals. Heinous crimes should not preclude the open preaching of the forgiveness of sins to the criminals that they may receive salvation in the next life, even if they are punished in this one. For other crimes, Schlatter suggested other forms of punishment—fines and imprisonment.[91]

He drew a parallel between spiritual sin and crime, the social sin. The most difficult activity of the Christian is the purification of his or her soul. From this, he commented that the punishment and purification of society is the darkest and most difficult obligation of the state. However, he held out great hope that the idea of purification in the spiritual sense could shed light on penal codes for society's ills. He suggested an alternative form of punishment for lawbreakers to what was commonly practiced.

Schlatter continued his comparison of the two sins. Even as the central message of Christianity is the forgiveness of sin and the sacrificial atonement of Christ, society's aim in punishment ought to be the restitution of the criminal to the state of innocence and restoration to a functioning place in society. It is at this place of restitution of the criminal that the church can play a role. The church has the special duty to show criminals the worthlessness and invalidity

---

90. Ibid., 141–42.

91. Ibid., 131–32; Adolf Schlatter, *Die christliche Ethik*, 3rd ed. (Stuttgart: Calwer Vereinsbuchhandlung, 1929), 159–60.

of crime. However, this true testimony of crime's evil is impossible when the criminals are removed from society through imprisonment.[92]

Schlatter argued that the isolation of criminals puts them into an even greater danger. Imprisonment leaves the criminal to the powers of his or her own broken fantasy. Furthermore, any community a criminal might find in prison is with other lawbreakers. In short, prison only hardens criminals. He was convinced that it was precisely at the moment when people in their crime had the greatest need for a supportive community that the state took them out of productive society. To resolve this problem, Schlatter suggested deportation as a criminal punishment. He recommended the formation of supportive communities of Christians where convicts would be welcomed into their midst and given employment in agriculture or forestry or some other physical work in nature. He was confident that useful employment, a change of locale, and a supportive, Christian community would help eliminate the criminal intents of a significant portion of lawbreakers.[93]

Since his ethics were effectively the second volume of his dogmatics, Schlatter limited his writing to commonly held ethical assertions of the church. Since the majority of German churchgoers were politically conservative, it is unsurprising that Schlatter's ethics too leaned conservative and questioned political leftists. Schlatter used theology to strengthen the ties between the state and church, the traditional view of families and gender roles, middle-class lifestyles and morality, and the authority of the state. At the same time, he condemned the evil of revolution, atheism, and socialism.

Despite these limits and obvious personal leanings toward religious conservatism, Schlatter showed surprising flexibility and independence in his political ethics. His plan for penal reform matched progressive ideologies from around the world. It created an opportunity to minimize the menace of the city and return criminals back to nature for healing. His limits on capital punishment offered a strict challenge to the martial law of old Prussia. Although by no means radical, his pre–World War I openness toward women in politics must have surprised many of his readers. Perhaps the most intriguing discussion was his discourse on Christian politics. By endorsing a Christian party, Schlatter acknowledged the end of Christian Germany. Protestant Christianity was but one worldview in an ever more pluralistic empire. He also admitted that a Christian party, when it was formed, would contain a plurality of views on areas not firmly covered by Scriptures. He never advocated a theocracy, because too much of God's will was unknown, and human civilization had too great

---

92. Schlatter, *Die christliche Ethik* (1914), 127–29, 131.

93. Ibid., 127–29, 131.

a tendency toward corruption. He proposed his ethics as but one set of suggestions among many possible Christian variations.

SCHLATTER'S ETHICS AS PART OF HIS SYSTEMATIC THEOLOGY

Adolf Schlatter was the most capable of the believing theologians of his era. He fleshed out the framework laid out by Martin Kähler. Schlatter's systematic expression of ethics provided a framework from which to understand someone like Christoph Blumhardt. In Schlatter's four systematic works, all published between 1909 and 1914—*Das Wort Jesu* (The Word of Jesus), *Die Lehre der Apostel* (The Teachings of the Apostles), *Das christliche Dogma* (Christian Dogma), and *Die christliche Ethik* (Christian Ethics)—Schlatter finished up the program initiated and promoted by positive theologians since they first set out to counter Schleiermacher's theology. Schlatter created a system of theology that used the most modern ideas and dialogued with the most radical critical program but still defended the traditional doctrines of the church. Finally, he established the definitive believing system for the long nineteenth century.

Schlatter's theology showed the perceived link in theologically conservative Protestants' thinking between an embattled understanding of the word of God and an eroding ethical standard in Germany. Schlatter used his modern theology to construct a new ethical foundation to combat the negative influences on German society. This was Schlatter's ultimate achievement; he was able to systematize the conservative thinking from a century of wrestling over the nature of Scripture's authority over the Protestant church to construct a means to address the pressing moral issues of his day.

However, this work of Schlatter's is exactly what has been deemed outdated and has been ignored by the greater theological community since Karl Barth. Schlatter's specific works on archaeology, Judaica, textual criticism, commentaries, and historical theology all continued to have their supporters, but the most admired works of his lifetime have been eclipsed. Schlatter completed the paradigm just as the First World War brought a new age of theology to pass.

Looking at the specifics of Schlatter's theology, some inherent difficulties existed that spelled its doom before it was written. The theology to which he was responding was inherently complex. The subtleties of historical research that defined the nineteenth century marked the new era. Schlatter's theology implied an expectation that progress was inevitable and many of society's ills were slowly being eradicated. The church played an integral role in this progress. Therefore, change in his system needed to be evolutionary, and improvements gradual. When society's appearances of improvements turned out to be a mirage in the First World War, Schlatter's system of ethics lost their moorings. Perhaps these reasons, as much as weaknesses in the theology, explain to a partial degree why Schlatter's draft of a believing theology was passed over in favor of Barth's system following the war.

SCHLATTER'S POSITION IN THE THEOLOGICAL ACADEMIC SCENE

By his own accounts, Schlatter's awareness of and interaction with the larger theological debates in the German-speaking realm progressed slowly. Besides the inherent isolation of the small, obscure Bern faculty, the problem was compounded by the faculty's unwillingness to introduce Schlatter to the larger academic world. He lived blissfully unaware of his colleagues' expectations that all scholars ought to be familiar with the entire literature of their subjects. Instead, Schlatter embarked on his first projects with an unusual independence of thought that was formed more by his ignorance of the general debates than by maverick intentions. The result was Schlatter's creative approach to well-known themes. This general seclusion from the German theological world ended quickly with the publication of his treatise on New Testament faith, *Der Glaube im Neuen Testament* (Belief in the New Testament). With the publication of the massive word study, Schlatter established himself as a rising star. His newfound fame brought him into the circles of many of the leading theologians of the German-speaking realm.[94]

SCHLATTER AND KÄHLER

One of the first job offers Schlatter received after the publication of *Glaube* came from the theological faculty in Halle. Although he refused the job, this offer brought him into contact with Martin Kähler. When Schlatter finally accepted the position offered him at Greifswald, he was able to build on his contact with Kähler. Schlatter's close friend and colleague at Greifswald, Herrmann Cremer, was a good friend of Kähler's from their student years. As a result, Kähler and Schlatter remained in friendly, if sporadic, communication with each other until Kähler's death in 1912.[95]

Schlatter sent his theological publications to Kähler when they appeared, and the two enjoyed an enduring academic interchange. For his part, Kähler indicated that he always enjoyed receiving Schlatter's works and was impressed by the breadth and capability of Schlatter's thought. On multiple occasions, Kähler replied with admiration to Schlatter's work. He noted that the younger

---

94. Schlatter, *Rückblick*, 115.

95. Kähler, *Theologe und Christ*, 168; Neuer, *Schlatter: Ein Leben*, 217.

scholar's breadth and insight easily resolved problems that had long perplexed Kähler himself. On another occasion, he encouraged Schlatter to write his polemical article "The Atheistic Method in Theology." The article was written in response to Paul Jäger's diatribe against Wilhelm Lütgert, Kähler's colleague and Schlatter's former protégé. Schlatter wrote the article defending the application of dogmatic assertions in academic theology. He bitingly asserted that Jäger's assumption that theology could be advanced through the adoption of atheistic scientism was a contradiction in terms and a philosophical impossibility. Kähler knew that Lütgert was shaken by the attack, and Schlatter's fame and philosophical ability could do important work in restoring Lütgert's prestige.[96]

Despite the close feelings and compatible goals in their theology, Kähler's responses to Schlatter's works were not universally positive. The elder scholar also did not shy away from admitting that Schlatter was occasionally more open to critical methods than he was. He brought up significant reservations with Schlatter's work *Die Lehre der Apostel* (The Teachings of the Apostles), and his systematic theology, *Das christliche Dogma* (Christian Dogma). In the end, however, Kähler seemed to acknowledge that Schlatter was a significant ally for his biblicist cause and that the theological differences they had were not enough for him to abandon his admiration for his junior colleague.[97]

Once Kähler had concluded his teaching responsibilities at Halle, he used his correspondence with Schlatter to continue assisting with the advancement of conservative students and academics. He began to advise students to seek out Schlatter and to study under him. On a few occasions, Kähler wrote Schlatter to recommend particular students from Halle for their doctoral dissertations. Kähler also used his letters to ask Schlatter to aid him in finding appropriate conservative candidates for open professorships at Halle.[98]

The two professors also cooperated in academic and spiritual ventures. In 1896, Schlatter and Kähler (as well as Cremer) were invited by Erich Schaeder, the professor of systematic theology at Göttingen, to an assembly of conservative theologians. At the meeting, Wilhelm Lütgert urged Schlatter to begin a conservative theological journal as a positive response to the successful liberal journal *Die christliche Welt* (The Christian World). Schlatter eventually

96. Neuer, *Schlatter: Ein Leben*, 495; State Church Archive, Stuttgart, Adolf Schlatter Archive, Briefe an Schlatter von Martin Kähler, D 40 #426, letters dated April 23, 1904, March 25, 1909, January 3, 1910, March 15, 1910, and December 24, 1910.

97. Ibid., letter dated January 3, 1910; Neuer, *Schlatter: Ein Leben*, 495.

98. Briefe an Schlatter von Martin Kähler, D 40 #426, letters dated March 8, 1910, August 5, 1910, and December 24, 1910.

took up this challenge with Cremer and Lütgert, and together they edited the theology series *Beiträge zur Förderung christlicher Theologie*. Kähler submitted his submission, *Das Kreuz* (The Cross), for publication in 1911.[99]

Schlatter and Kähler collaborated in planning a weeklong seminar for church leaders in at the Bethel Retreat Center near Bielefeld, organized by the leader of the center Friedrich von Bodelschwingh. These seminars, which were originally conceived by Schlatter, Bodelschwingh, and Cremer, met every two years at the conference center and eventually laid the groundwork for a theological seminary in which Schlatter would play an advisory role. Kähler and Schlatter were scheduled to be the two principal speakers at the retreat in 1904, but a bout with pneumonia forced Kähler to cancel his speaking appointments. However, Kähler met with Schlatter at other Bethel summer seminars.[100]

Several times, Kähler actively lobbied to bring Schlatter to Halle as his successor. As late as 1910, Kähler held out hope that Schlatter would be open to coming to Halle. This was reasonable, because Schlatter's initial experience with the Tübingen students was not positive. However, by that time, Schlatter had established himself as a productive scholar and a popular professor in the southern-German university. Schlatter refused the opportunity to become a candidate for the position. Kähler never expressed bitterness that Schlatter had refused the offer, but he wanted to be certain that a like-minded theologian would carry on the position he originally received from his own mentor, Friedrich August Tholuck.[101]

The anti-credal movement within German theology profoundly affected both Schlatter and Kähler. On June 3, 1892, the government of the Kingdom of Württemberg relieved the minister, Christoph Schrempf, of his position because of his unwillingness to use the Apostles' Creed in the baptismal ceremonies. This questioning of the long-standing traditions of the church set off a series of protests and counterprotests that eventually drew Kähler and Schlatter into the fray. Kähler addressed the Schrempf situation as a matter of grave significance in his manifest "Unser Streit um die Bibel" (Our Struggle for the Bible). The same action led to the open support of Schrempf by Adolf Harnack in 1892 in Martin Rade's liberal journal, *Die christliche Welt* (The Christian World). As a result of Harnack's infamous attack against the

99. Neuer, *Schlatter: Ein Leben*, 335; Martin Kähler, *Das Kreuz*, in Beiträge zur Förderung christlicher Theologie, ed. A. Schlatter und W. Lütgert, vol. 15, no. 1 (Gütersloh: Evangelischer Verlag "Der Rufer," 1911).

100. Briefe vonKähler an Schlatter, D 40, #426, letters dated September 9, 1904, December 24, 1910; Adolf Schlatter Archive, Briefe an Martin Kähler, D 40 #426; Neuer, *Schlatter: Ein Leben*, 434–36.

101. Briefe von Kähler an Schlatter, D 40 #426, letter dated March 1, 1910.

Apostles' Creed, conservative churchgoers petitioned the kaiser to open a new theological chair in Berlin for a conservative theologian. The kaiser agreed to their demands and called Schlatter to fill the chair in 1893.[102]

Schlatter used Martin Kähler's writings extensively in his own thought. He was familiar with Kähler's works and quoted Kähler's *Der Wissenschaft der christliche Lehre von dem evangelischem Grundartikel aus* (The Study of Christian Teaching from the foundational Protestant doctrines), *Die sogenannte historische Jesus und der geschichtliche, Biblische Christus*, (So-Called Historical Jesus and the Historic, Biblical Christ) *Zur Lehre von der Versöhnung*, (On the Teaching of Reconciliation) and *Wiedergeboren durch die Auferstehung Jesu Christi* (Born Again through the Resurrection of Jesus Christ) in his *Christliche Dogma* (Christian Dogma).

SCHLATTER AND BLUMHARDT

Schlatter noted himself that his lack of a relationship with Christoph Blumhardt was unusual for somebody in his position. Although Blumhardt's Bad Boll was only a short trip from Schlatter's Tübingen, the professor never met the famous preacher. Schlatter did have a deep friendship with both the younger and elder Friedrich von Bodelschwingh, who ran a retreat center similar to Bad Boll. Both Bodelschwingh's Bethel and Blumhardt's Bad Boll served as centers for spiritual reflection and counseling; however, Bodelschwingh's and Blumhardt's personal relationship was sometimes contentious.

Schlatter may have been tempted to travel to Bad Boll early in his tenure at Bern, especially since both Blumhardts were well known in Switzerland. However, the Bern faculty's intense distrust of Schlatter's interaction with Pietism made him wary of creating any connection to the renowned spiritual healer. Thomas Nippold, Schlatter's dissertation adviser at Bern, submitted a newspaper editorial contesting the way in which the Bern Pietists influenced the hiring of Schlatter. In Nippold's condemnation of the Pietists, he cited their usual belief in demons and spiritists (*Hexenglauben*). The elder Blumhardt's own claim to have played a role in the healing of the demoniac Gottliebin Dittus in 1842 led Schlatter to steer clear of the Blumhardts' spa in Bad Boll. Later Schlatter received another critique of the Blumhardts that may have ultimately kept Schlatter from ever initiating the relationship. While still in Swiss ministry, Schlatter formed a deep friendship with the free-church pastor Edmund Fröhlich, who acted as a spiritual mentor for the young Schlatter,

---

102. Neuer, *Schlatter: Ein Leben*, 292; Martin Kähler, *Aufsätze zur Bibelfrage*, ed. Ernst Kähler (Munich: Kaiser Verlag, 1967), 21–22.

who found no such relationship within the fellowship of the Swiss state church. Fröhlich needled the Blumhardts' theology, noting that the elder Blumhardt preached for a new outpouring of the Holy Spirit. Fröhlich's response to this theological statement was cutting. He replied that the problem with modern Christianity was not that Christians did not have an adequate amount of the Holy Spirit, but rather that they had an overabundance of it. Fröhlich noted that modern Christians still received the Holy Spirit, but they no longer felt obligated to obey it.

Indeed, what separated Schlatter from Blumhardt most likely involved differences in pneumatology, or at least misunderstandings of each other's doctrine of the Holy Spirit. Schlatter's sister Dora asked him for advice during a bout with sickness in 1887. She asked him whether she should go to the Swiss healer Otto Stockmayer or to Christoph Blumhardt. Schlatter replied to Dora through his mother that if she chose to go somewhere, she ought to head to Bad Boll, since he thought little of Stockmayer. However, his greatest reservation about both healers was his strongly held belief that God listens to the prayers of all the faithful, not just to the famous healers. Blumhardt himself would take up this call around the same time as Schlatter's advice to his sister, as he moved himself and the rest of Bad Boll away from their emphasis on spiritual healing.[103]

Schlatter's relationship with Blumhardt and Kähler testifies that they were well acquainted with each other's work but suggests that they were not intimately attached. This makes their parallel thought and careers all the more astounding. It suggests a much broader, common sentiment among believing church figures that spanned all of German-speaking Europe. Perhaps most remarkable is Schlatter's welcome into the broader academic environment following his publication of *Glaube*. He did not need to seek relationships with the conservative leaders of the church; they found him. And this was following publication of Schlatter's most ambiguously conservative theological work (Harnack was an admirer of the work, as were Cremer and Kähler). Elements of Schlatter's relationship with Blumhardt remain more troubling. Schlatter's distance from Blumhardt certainly showed scholars' wariness to be associated with controversial politics or expressions of faith. Nevertheless, Schlatter's relationships with Stoecker and Bodelschwingh show that he was not against cultivating relationships with well-known preachers. Blumhardt's comparative isolation from the university faculties is unfortunate. Admittedly, at the end of his life, he did cultivate relationships with the rising Swiss

103. Neuer, *Schlatter: Ein Leben*, 208–209. Neuer refers to Schlatter alluding to the elder Blumhardt. This must be a mistake of either Neuer or of Schlatter, since in 1887, the elder Blumhardt had been dead for seven years; Schlatter, *Rückblick*, 84–85.

theologians, but he never was close to any of the truly prominent nineteenth-century theologians. We have little indication what sort of interaction he could have had with them.

THE MODERATE REACTIONARY: SCHLATTER IN THE CLASSROOM

Like many accomplished scholars, Schlatter received only mixed marks for his classroom performance. He set high expectations for his students and for himself. He taught in an unorthodox manner that led many students from the far corners of the empire to pursue a chance study under him, and led others to reject him as a teacher. These latter students only took his courses reluctantly when they were required by the university. Nowhere was this more pronounced than at his arrival at Tübingen. The University of Tübingen was no longer the flagship university for academic theology in Germany; that title had passed to Berlin. But it possessed a storied history of theologians and theological students. Tübingen had provided some of the greatest minds in both the believing and critical traditions of theological scholarship. Two of the leading lights of Pietism, Johann Albrecht Bengel (1687–1752) and Friedrich Christoph Oetinger (1702–1782), were associated with Tübingen. Bengel taught there, and Pastor Oetinger studied theology there. Following them and their tradition were Johann Tobias Beck and Adolf Schlatter, who were the principal figures at the theology school during their day. On the critical side, Tübingen was the location of writing for David Friedrich Strauss's monumental *Das Leben Jesu* (The Life of Jesus), and his teacher Ferdinand Christian Baur provided the first critical system of church history, which sent shock waves through all fields of academia. Finally, in the generation between Beck and Schlatter, the theology department was led by Carl Heinrich von Weizsäcker (1822–1899), a church historian and successor to Baur's Tübingen School.

As the most prolific scholar at Tübingen during his time, Schlatter lived up to his predecessors, critical and liberal alike. Therefore, his reputation was enormous, but that may have been too much for some students. Bruno Meyer, a student from Germany's northernmost province, Schleswig-Holstein, spent a semester at Tübingen for the purpose of studying under the famed New Testament scholar. He later recalled, "Unlike most of the other Tübingen theology students, I did not find what I had hoped from Professor von Schlatter. Above all his wholly unsystematic thinking bothered me greatly." In response to this, the unnamed Kiel professor who read his curriculum vitae penciled in next to the comment, "Quite true."[104]

Schlatter's took his teaching philosophy from his philosophy professor at Basel, Karl Steffensen. Steffensen refused to provide clear answers for his students. Instead, he opted for a Socratic method of teaching that required students to find their own answers. Schlatter tried to adopt this approach for biblical studies. He saw his responsibility as professor to teach his students how to read the Bible. He hoped they each individually had the wisdom to choose the right interpretation of it. Here his method greatly differed from the historically based curriculum developed during the Weiszäcker chancellery of the department. During the period directly preceding Schlatter, professors trained the students principally in historical interpretations of the New Testament, using carefully detailed lectures. His approach also differed from Martin Kähler's detailed lectures. As a result of this decision to leave the conclusions open for his students, Schlatter's lectures (like his published works) were less vehemently polemical than those of his Halle colleague. This also resulted in his own students' varied viewpoints, which covered the spectrum from the very conservative Wilhelm Lütgert to the more critically open Paul Althaus.[105]

Despite his attempt to teach the methods of biblical interpretation neutrally, Schlatter was aware of a significant cultural battle being fought in university theology departments. This was his motivation for his scathing attack on Paul Jäger's attempt to create an atheistic theology. The purpose of theological education would necessarily continue to be the teaching and education of future leaders of the church. Theology was a professional degree. He would not allow it to be reduced to an abstract theoretical study. He believed that the theological truths it professed had practical and long-standing ramifications for the way students would carry on the ministry after they left their education. The fact that some theologians including Jäger proposed "atheistic" theology made Schlatter sympathetic to the growing number of church members who began to reject university training altogether (as Schlatter nearly did in his own life). So while Schlatter believed his first responsibility was to teach the manner in which students could learn to read the Bible for themselves, he eschewed a value-neutral classroom and still professed his views to his students. He offered them his own best judgments. He showed them how they were the product of the critical apparatus he taught them and believed they needed to best understand the Scriptures. However, he did this in a way that students were not required to parrot back his opinions.[106]

104. Nordelbische State Church Archive, Kiel, Bruno Meyer, Bestand 42.07 #262.

105. Schlatter, *Rückblick*, 209–210.

106. Schlatter, "Atheistic Method," 213, 225.

While at Tübingen, Schlatter taught the two-semester New Testament Seminar to nearly every theology student at the university. He used his other rotating seminars to address some of the issues he found most pressing in theological debates. These courses addressed the critical views of Jesus and of the Scriptures. His extant lectures on the life of Jesus, the veracity of the Gospel of John, and the character of the early church testified to his desire to expose his students to the most contentious doctrines of the church. They also portray a professor who was unafraid to challenge the received norms of modern critical theology. His teaching was not nearly as polemical as Kähler's was at Halle, but it still carried the mark of a believing theologian who thought highly of defending his perspectives for the next generation of church leaders for Baden-Württemberg.[107]

Schlatter's semester course on the life of Jesus offered fewer succulent moments than one would expect from reading a believing scholar of the early twentieth century. He never surprised with the gossipy conjectures of the extreme critical wing, but he seldom provided a self-righteous tongue-lashing to those who did. His course was much like his entire teaching career. In university after university, Schlatter was brought in because of office politics. He was continually called on to be the conservative savior in an increasingly secular, cynical, and unbelieving environment. As soon as he arrived at each of his schools (the already-conservative Greifswald being the exception), camps had already formed to either welcome him as their savior or shun him as an interloper. Yet at each university, Schlatter spent significant efforts fighting against these preconceived notions, winning over some of his critics but also losing a significant portion of his supporters. He struggled to create a quiet compromise. He wanted to be a believing scholar, and he desired the same for his students. He envisioned himself and his students as people who took their biblical studies seriously with the highest level of respect and effort and who applied and made use of the newest means of study available.[108]

Despite Schlatter's insistence on the importance of a solid training for pastors in the theology department, he respected his defined responsibilities and made no effort to teach his students homiletics. He left that responsibility to the Tübingen professor Friedrich Traub (1860–1939). Instead, he taught his courses in the confidence that good ethical preaching comes from right

107. State Church Archive, Stuttgart, Adolf Schlatter Archive, Vorlesung zur Leben Jesu, D 40 #1987; State Church Archive, Stuttgart, Adolf Schlatter Archive, Rede über Johannesevangelium, D 40 #193/9; State Church Archive, Stuttgart, Adolf Schlatter Archive, "Die älteste Christenheit und die Bibel," D 40 #193.

108. State Church Archive, Stuttgart, Adolf Schlatter Archive, Vorlesung zur Leben Jesu, D 40 #1987.

doctrinal understanding. In so doing, however, Schlatter may have missed out on truly influencing the Christianity of common Germans, who would never read theological treatises. The uniformity of German sermons showed that students continued to model their sermons on their professors' didactic systems long after they left the university and that reaching people in the idiom of the modern era was low on the list of priorities in most homiletics classrooms.

Conclusion: The Ivory Tower and the Practical System of Adolf Schlatter

Schlatter was particularly suited to create a modern believing theology. He lived his life on the front lines of the controversy between critics and conservatives. He was a major figure in defining the points of the controversy about the nature of the Scriptures as the word of God. He understood that the weakness in post-Enlightenment theology's critical research came in the question of authority. How could the church continue to guide and lead society in a modern era that no longer trusted the foundation of the sacred history?

Schlatter's position as a professor of theology lent him considerable prestige in late-Wilhelmine Germany. It was a Germany that possessed a hierarchy, whose highest ranks were filled with the professorship in a sort of meritocracy following the descent of the aristocracy following Germany's unification.[109] So he was in a considerable position of prestige, considering that he was widely recognized as a foremost spokesman for the Protestant church, still the largest popular institution in Germany. Furthermore, his Swiss Reformed background gave him an outsider's opportunity where he could sidestep the long-standing church rivalries within the empire. Believing theology was ripe for a system of theology that looked forward to a reinvigorated faith as it entered the twentieth century.

109. Fritz K. Ringer, *The Decline of the German Mandarins: The German Academic Community, 1890–1933* (Hanover, NH: University Press of New England, 1990), 3, 5–8.

5

Views from the Kingdom of God
The Life and Preaching of Christoph Blumhardt

The miracles of Jesus are also a sign for the future. . . . From my youth on, I lived amongst signs and wonders. The life of my blessed father was evidence for me and awakened the thought: Our savior is coming! Jesus is near. Jesus is victor over all the evil that comes on Earth. Today we are standing again amongst the signs of the victory of Christ. Even with all the evil things that are taking place in the nations. The peoples lie, as on their deathbeds, and many small nations lament because they suffer so much from the violence of war.

Even the dead must experience Christ's victory. . . . For this reason the time must come, when Jesus makes himself known amongst the dead and will show his greatest wonders. The word of Jesus Christ will even be brought to the graves. Both the dead and the living will rejoice. They will not concern themselves with questions of who died and who lived. No, they will all rejoice that Christ lives. They will rejoice that the hour comes into which the voice of the Son of God calls and great signs will transpire calling to those who are already dead. So the miracles of Jesus guide us on

> *our way in the sufferings of life and in the*
> *sufferings of death. Again and again they*
> *tell us: be comforted!*
>
> —CHRISTOPH BLUMHARDT, SERMON
> DELIVERED OCTOBER 24, 1915[1]

In 1899, at a meeting of workers in the industrial town of Göppingen in Württemberg, Pastor Christoph Blumhardt openly expressed his support of the workers' social democratic ideals and demands. As he was a well-known local religious figure, Blumhardt's attestation was a sensation. The Social Democrats realized the potential of tapping Blumhardt's renown and persuaded him to run for the Württemberg legislature. The German Protestant state church was incensed and rescinded his title as minister. Blumhardt won the election and from 1900 to 1906 sat as a delegate for the Social Democrats in Stuttgart. He claimed that, as a man waiting for the kingdom of God, he had no other choice available than to join the aggressively secular German Social Democratic Party (SPD).

During his lifetime, Blumhardt was a well-known pastor and spiritual healer in his local Württemberg and his beloved Switzerland. However, Blumhardt never published his sermons or wrote any books during his lifetime. He was also not in enduring correspondence with any of the other figures in this study. In that sense, he might not be considered a contributor to modern believing theology. However, he was a unique example of the use and ramifications of a thoroughly modern believing worldview. Blumhardt showed one extreme in the spectrum of possibility for conservative Christian thinkers at the turn of the twentieth century. For Blumhardt, the Bible's veracity was unquestionable. Its content was ontologically certain. He situated himself in a theological world where the invisible realities of God were more present and certain than the tangible realities of his empirical surroundings. His theology also suggested this in that his main points of faith revolved around the unseen power of God that shapes all history. As a whole, Blumhardt's theology of biblical interpretation conversed more with the pietistic thinkers of the eighteenth century than with critical questions of contemporary scholars, both positive and liberal. However, his ethical actions were a product possible only

---

1. CHRISTOPH BLUMHARDT, *ANSPRACHEN, PREDIGTEN, REDEN, BRIEFE, 1865–1917: NEUE TEXTE AUS DEM NACHLASS*, ED. JOHANNES HARDER, VOL. 3, *GELIEBTE WELT, 1907–1917* (NEUKIRCHEN-VLUYN: NEUKIRCHENER VERLAG DES ERZIEHUNGSVEREINS, 1978), 188–89.

in the modern environment of Germany following the Second Industrial Revolution.

Blumhardt was able to combine his eighteenth-century pneumatology with his twentieth-century practice through his self-acknowledged role as a prophet for the modern world. He never meant he was a prophet in the sense that he knew the future. He was a prophet because he received a special message from God and a new interpretation of the Scriptures for his own time. He modeled himself on the Old Testament prophets, who saw their ministry as a call to the people to return to God and to pursue God's will. This manifested itself in his proclamation of the imminent arrival of the kingdom of God. Unlike the Pietistic fathers in whose theological footsteps he trod, Blumhardt the modern prophet saw that the ethical outcome of the belief in the unseen was to act in the everyday empirical world. Only in that way could the invisible realities of God become visible, and only in that way could Christians begin to usher in his promised kingdom.

Growing Up in the Kingdom of God: A Sketch of Christoph Blumhardt's Life

Christoph Friedrich Blumhardt was born in Möttlingen in the duchy of Baden on June 1, 1842. His father, the Reverend Johann Christoph Blumhardt, was in the midst of the most exciting and tumultuous portion of his own ministry. Beginning in 1842, the elder Blumhardt began the spiritual care of Gottliebin Dittus, who had suffered under demonic possession for two years.[2] Although Blumhardt originally tried to assist in finding some medical cure, it soon became apparent that the sickness was spiritual in nature. For nearly two years, the elder Blumhardt visited Dittus and fought with the spirits who lived within her. Finally, at Christmas 1843, with her words, "Jesus is Victor, Jesus is Victor," the long spiritual battle was closed, and Dittus was released from her ailments.[3]

---

2. Dittus's demonic possession manifested itself in times of unconsciousness, night unrest resulting in banging sounds loud enough to bother the neighbors, and the feeling that her body was being forcibly moved and contorted. Johann Christoph Blumhardt, *Blumhardts Kampf: Die Krankheits- und Heilungsgeschichte der G. Dittus in Möttlingen*, 5th ed. (Stuttgart-Waiblingen: Verlag der Plakatmission, n.d), 16–17. Some writers have attempted to explain Dittus's ailment in terms of psychological disorder. However, since this spiritual conflict was the cornerstone of both Blumhardts' ministries, the empirical exercise only belittles their lives' work. Furthermore, psychological explanations of historical characters and ailments are suspicious at best. I have chosen to continue to refer to her condition as a demonic possession, since no other indisputable or more helpful alternative can be proposed.

3. Ibid., 24–25, 77, 80.

Dittus's sufferings and the manifestations of her possession became a well-known spectacle in the town. After her healing, a revival took place in Möttlingen. Not only the townsfolk, but people from surrounding areas and even from other countries came to the small village church to confess their sins and to ask for forgiveness. Many also came asking for prayer and spiritual care for their own sicknesses and spiritual troubles. To observers and to Johann Christoph Blumhardt himself, it appeared as though the healing was just the first miracle of a new apostolic period. The elder Blumhardt began to pray for a new outpouring of the Holy Spirit and committed himself to the spiritual care of whomever came asking for help.[4]

Christoph Blumhardt was born into this environment of spiritual awakening and his father's own awakening to the powers and presence of the Holy Spirit. In this sense, he differed from many of the other influential Christians of his day. The elder Blumhardt even attended the University of Tübingen at the same time as D. F. Strauss, but the trajectories of their careers could not differ more. Johann Christoph Blumhardt would never ask the same sorts of critical questions about the Scriptures that his contemporaries did.

Over the next decade, Johann Christoph Blumhardt felt growing pressure to leave Möttlingen. The parsonage no longer had the capacity necessary for the volume of guests and appellants. Furthermore, the town church grew unsettled at the change required for Blumhardt's continued work. In 1852, with the help of large gifts from Alsatian industrialists and Stuttgart merchants, Johann Christoph Blumhardt bought the spa and resort at Bad Boll near Göppingen, southeast of Stuttgart. The new surroundings spared the elder Blumhardt the typical responsibilities of a village pastor and gave him a new environment in which to continue the ministry that began in Möttlingen.[5]

Little has been written about Christoph Blumhardt's early experience at Bad Boll, and Blumhardt himself only referred to it sparingly. Bad Boll was presumably an opportune place for him to grow. His own memories later in life were that he was a rambunctious child with little to indicate he would later follow in his father's footsteps. However, no evidence remains that he was in any way a prodigal or rebellious son. By the time he began his studies, he was willing to follow the admonition of his father to study theology, despite his own lack of interest in the subject.[6]

4. Friedrich Zündel, *Johann Christoph Blumhardt: Ein Lebensbild*, 8th ed. (Giessen: Brunnen-Verlag, 1921), 149, 151–52.

5. Albrecht Esche, "Reich Gottes in Bad Boll: Vorwärts mit Blumhardt—mehr als ein Spaziergang," in *Warten und Pressieren: 150 Jahre Blumhardt in Bad Boll*, ed. Albrecht Esche (Bad Boll: Evangelische Akademie Bad Boll, 2002), 17, 20.

He began his first vicariate in 1866, the year of the Austro-Prussian War. Although he indicated his desire to join the war effort, he was allowed to advance to his vicariate without military service. His experiences as a vicar were discouraging for the young student. He found that, by comparison, he could not match his father in preaching. At the time, Blumhardt wrote of his father in reverential terms, heaping praise on his father's skill as a pastor and preacher. Furthermore, the ministers with whom he worked limited his service as a pastoral counselor, the role in which he felt the most comfortable. He later recalled that he undertook his study to be a minister only because of his father's encouragement.

The university years were not stimulating, and his vicariate was stifling. His only spiritual mentor was his father, who continually wrote him advice and admonitions from Bad Boll. In 1869, during the Franco-Prussian War, Blumhardt finished his first vicariate but opted not to take the state exam to receive full ordination and instead opted to return to Bad Boll to assist his father in the administration of the spa.[7]

In 1870, Blumhardt married Emilie Bräuninger. Together they had seven daughters and four sons in Bad Boll. For the most part, their marriage seems to have been a happy one with a deep sense of cooperation. At one point, Blumhardt even contradicted the writings of the apostle Paul to compliment his wife. In 1 Corinthians, Paul described marriage as a distraction in ministry, and while Paul admitted that marriage was necessary for some people, it was not advantageous. Blumhardt roundly criticized Paul's writings and suggested that he was more productive in his ministry working and cooperating with his wife than he could have been if he had remained alone. However, during the last few years of Blumhardt's life, the two lived separately, with Emilie traveling around the world, visiting their expatriated children. After he gave up his full-time duties in 1906, Blumhardt moved out of Bad Boll to the nearby village of Jebenhausen and lived there with his spiritual partner, Sister Anna Gräfin von Sprewitz. There is no reason to believe that this later relationship was anything but platonic, but the relationship certainly suggests an unusual degree of intimacy with Blumhardt's wife away.[8]

Shortly before his death in 1880, Johann Christoph Blumhardt called in his sons, Theophil and Christoph. He laid his hands on them and said, alluding to his struggle over Gottliebin Dittus, "I bless you for victory."[9] After the

6. Blumhardt, *Ansprachen*, vol. 1, *Von der Kirche zum Reich Gottes: 1865–1889*, 40.

7. Eugen Jäckh, *Blumhardt Vater und Sohn: Und ihre Botschaft* 2nd ed. (Berlin: Furche-Verlag, 1925), 93; Blumhardt, *Ansprachen*, 1:28–29; Esche, "Reich Gottes," 26.

8. Blumhardt, *Ansprachen*, vol. 2, *Seid Auferstandene, 1890–1906*, 57; Esche, "Reich Gottes," 26, 28.

death of Johann Christoph Blumhardt in 1880, Christoph took over his father's responsibilities as the head of the resort. Where the younger Blumhardt had been uncertain and troubled about his call to the pastorate during his studies, he quickly found his feet and his voice as head of Bad Boll. Within a short time, he was able to develop a reputation as a formidable speaker and healer in his own right.[10] Bad Boll never suffered a significant drop in guests during the transition. In the first decade after his father's death, his ministry echoed that of his predecessor. It was centered on the same message of the kingdom of God and the outpouring of the Holy Spirit that the elder Blumhardt had developed during the revival at Möttlingen. Characteristically, during this period, his sermons also often appealed to his father's ideas to lend his own message legitimacy.

By the last decade of the nineteenth century, Blumhardt's focus began to shift outward. In 1889, he took a trip to Italy for health reasons. The trip acted as a catalyst for change in his life and preaching. The perspective from Catholic Italy gave him new insights on Protestant culture in his homeland. After his return, his ministry and his sermons focused more on the prophets of the Old Testament, and his own preaching notably adopted their style. Blumhardt began to use his position at Bad Boll to critique the idleness of German Christians.

In 1894, he abandoned his pastoral privileges and ceased giving Communion, administering marriages, and wearing the traditional church robes. At that time, he told the guests at Bad Boll that the church duties would be handled by his brother, Theophil, minister in the Boll parish church. His justification for this was that he was to take commands from God alone, and not from the state church. He hoped that by leaving the responsibilities of the pastorate, he would find more time to actively pursue the kingdom of God. He never meant his decision to be seen as a separation from the state church. He thought of it merely as a chance to free himself from the time-consuming responsibilities that came with his position. He thought that by removing himself from the liturgical rites, he would be a good servant of the German state church. By leaving, he would prevent people from using his critiques to create new Protestant sects.[11]

9. Blumhardt, *Ansprachen*, 1:37.

10. Interestingly, while firsthand accounts of Bad Boll suggest Theophil's continuing importance to the family ministry, his work was never preserved and published in the same way as that of Johann Christoph and Christoph.

11. Blumhardt, *Ansprachen*, 1:193; 2:35–36; Esche, "Reich Gottes," 27.

Blumhardt's decision to enter politics in 1899 separated him from his church and from what his father would have wished. He understood that his father could never join the Social Democratic Party. Johann Christoph Blumhardt's ministry had concerned itself with the unseen spiritual sufferings around him. For this reason, the elder Blumhardt's ministry at Bad Boll had focused on prayer, separation from the world, and building up inner piety. Christoph Blumhardt later recalled that his father reacted joyously when a strong Christian died, because then the believer could intercede with God face-to-face on behalf of the spiritually suffering on earth.

Blumhardt concluded that his father's decisions and motivations were the right ones for the time. However, he asserted that the times had changed, and new pressures and sufferings of humanity were visible and present. As a result, the younger Blumhardt changed his own path and the path of Bad Boll into a center of political activism. His entry into politics also necessitated his separation from the state church. In the fall of 1899, the Württembergischen Konsistorialrat (Consistory Leadership of Württemberg), the overseers of the regional state church, rescinded Blumhardt's ordination. He never contested the decision, since he already had voluntarily abandoned his pastoral ministry in 1894. He was never reinstated into a pastoral office.[12]

Blumhardt's theological core remained the same during this transition, but the sermons of this time showed a great faith in politics to resolve many of the spiritual injustices of the world. The move was the logical outcome of his decade-long critique of the church. Throughout his six-year political career, however, other socialists questioned Blumhardt's adherence to the party line. He never received a reprimand from the party, but the accusations may have discouraged his political career. His choice not to pursue an additional term in the parliament came as quickly as his choice to run in the first place.[13]

For the rest of his life, Blumhardt never abandoned his association with the SPD, but the political message of his sermons decreased significantly in the last decade of his life. These years possessed his richest theological thought. He was able to recollect a long ministry and put it into better perspective. His sermons and devotions displayed a milder, more contemplative spirit. Blumhardt's thought late in life returned him full circle to his early years and to the thought of his father. He no longer possessed the optimism that modern political action would solve spiritual troubles. Instead, he held out hope for a sudden and dramatic act of God that would transform history and the world. In his last decade, he returned to the more passive faith of a traditional pietistic hope in

12. Blumhardt, *Ansprachen*, 2:202, 229, 234, 256–57.
13. Ibid., 2:219, 314–15, 332.

God, but he coupled this with the wisdom achieved from years of activism. He returned to his father's simple call of "waiting and rushing (*warten und pressieren*)" for the dramatic arrival of the kingdom of God.[14]

In 1906, after leaving politics, Blumhardt traveled to Palestine and the Middle East. After his trip, he developed a severe case of malaria. He recovered but continued to have health woes for the rest of his life. At this time, he moved his residence away from Bad Boll to a villa in nearby Jebenhausen. He continued to come to Bad Boll with regularity to give devotions and sermons to the guests and staff. He appointed Eugen Jäckh to be his successor in the everyday administration of Bad Boll. Jäckh's succession also marked the transition of Bad Boll's leadership out of the hands of the Blumhardt family (although some of Blumhardt's daughters stayed on long afterward in various administrative duties). Finally, he sold Bad Boll to a foundation made up of some of his friends. In 1917, after facing three years of the First World War, Blumhardt had a debilitating stroke that completely ended his public ministry. He died two years later on August 2, 1919, having lived just long enough to see his SPD win the first national democratic election of a republican Germany. He was buried near his father in Bad Boll. Jäckh oversaw the funeral and on Blumhardt's wishes merely read Psalm 43 instead of offering a eulogy. Blumhardt's funeral was attended by several members of the SPD but by no official representatives of the state church.[15]

Biblical Realism and Natural Supernaturalism: Christoph Blumhardt's Hermeneutic

At first glance, Christoph Blumhardt's hermeneutics seemed to be worlds separated from the perspective of his fellow theological conservatives, Adolf Stoecker, Martin Kähler, and Adolf Schlatter. Blumhardt questioned the teachings of the Epistle to the Hebrews on its doctrine of the Holy Spirit. He outright challenged the apostle Paul's doctrine of marriage and even Paul's Christology. At times, his separation of a God of wrath from a God of love sounded more like Adolf Harnack's return to Marcionism than Schlatter or Kähler's careful biblical exegesis. Blumhardt's sermons were free from any conscious hermeneutical principles and often ranged far from the contextual

---

14. Johann Christoph Blumhardt's call to "waiting and rushing" was intentionally contradictory as it referred to a sense of eschatological patience for God's action while responding to the immanence of the Holy Spirit's presence. Christoph Blumhardt's use of the term as a move past his political activism and a return to an inward piety fits well with his ideological return to his father's eschatological worldview.

15. Esche, "Reich Gottes," 28.

meaning of the Scriptures. On closer inspection, however, Blumhardt's understanding of the Scriptures picked up where Schlatter and Kähler left off. Blumhardt may have questioned individual passages, but he never challenged the fundamental foundation of the Scriptures for all Christian belief.[16]

Blumhardt scholars termed his hermeneutical principle "biblical realism." What they meant was that he began with the elemental belief that the Bible is real. For him, the Bible was not something to be critically questioned, it merely was as it existed. He approached the Bible the way a cartographer approaches a familiar continent. Cartographers do not question the origin of the coastlines or the mountains; rather, their job is to describe them to assist travelers in finding their way. Likewise, Blumhardt saw his own role with the Bible as similar to that of a cartographer, describing the terrain of Christianity to his listeners.

Although he never indicated any familiarity with the writings of modern conservative theologians, the conservative academic community laid the intellectual foundation for his hermeneutic. Those academics showed (or attempted to show) that the Scriptures were trustworthy for living a life pleasing to God and authoritative for the Christian walk. Blumhardt never assumed that he also needed to defend the value of the Bible to his listeners. Instead, he spent his life explaining how it could be lived out.

For this reason, Blumhardt would never fit in a theological faculty. He never asked the questions that theologians of the time posed. Academic theology in the late nineteenth century sought to explain scriptural belief in terms of Enlightenment thinking. Blumhardt's theology, however, was flip-flopped. He had no problem believing in miracles; he saw them every day all around him. For Blumhardt, it was nature and the empirical world that needed explanation in terms of the Bible.

In his reading, the world portrayed in the texts of the Bible was more real than the world portrayed by the empirical senses and the modern sciences. He wrote that he could not "read the stories of the Old Testament without getting a terrible case of home-sickness, it is the same with the New Testament. Everything in the Bible, including the Epistles of Paul, contains the message: 'There is one above who does everything, nothing comes to pass without him.' Everything in the Bible speaks of the acts of God."[17] He believed he saw his

16. Blumhardt, *Ansprachen*, 2:57, 195, 225, 314; 3:15–16, 67; Christoph Blumhardt, *Eine Auswahl aus seinen Predigten, Andachten und Schriften*, Ed. R. Lejeune, vol. 3, *Ihr Menschen seid Gottes!* (Zürich: Rotapfel-Verlag, 1928), 50; Christoph Blumhardt, *Gottes Reich Kommt!: Predigten und Andachten aus den Jahren 1907 bis 1917*, ed, R. Lejeune, vol. 4, *Eine Auswahl aus seinen Predigten, andachten und Schriften* (Zürich: Rotapfel Verlag, 1932), 195.

17. Blumhardt, *Ansprachen*, 1:81.

world from the viewpoint of God's revelation. Even in his deepest interaction with socialists, he possessed the stubborn conviction that his party comrades were on the verge of seeing everything as he did. He waited for them to realize their tremendous opportunity to play a role in ushering in the kingdom of God.[18]

Blumhardt lived in the perfect environment for such a worldview. Bad Boll was separate from the rapidly secularizing Germany. He lived in an environment where everyone who surrounded him believed that all health, money, and relationships were directly delivered from God. For this group and for Blumhardt himself, the Bible was the source of answers to the confusion of the world, even in times of great stress or war. He was not unfamiliar with atheistic explanations of the world's phenomena, but in his environment and his circle of influence from childhood on, the Enlightenment interpretations were inferior to the belief that God dictates the fate of everything.[19]

In Blumhardt's thought, the reality and presence of miracles went hand in hand with the unquestionable reality of the Bible. The miracles of the Bible showed the power and character of God, and miracles in the modern world were proof that God was still at work. Like the reality of the word of God, the miracle accounts of the Bible were without question true. A God who could create the world could also intervene in history. Blumhardt's use of miracles as evidence for the Bible's veracity was a subtle but important difference from the approach of believing scholars of his era. Whereas Kähler and Schlatter accepted miracles because of the authority of the Bible, Blumhardt believed in the Bible because it gives testimony to the supernatural qualities that God necessarily possesses. The result of this difference was that Blumhardt never shied away from alluding to miracle. He never felt obligated to explain or defend the miraculous to religious skeptics.[20]

For Blumhardt, the reality of miracle was the supreme test of faith for modern Christians. Christianity would not and could not exist without a clear and literal incarnation of God into man in Jesus Christ and without Jesus' death and resurrection. This separated him from his liberal colleagues in the pastorate who believed that Jesus's teachings had ethical power wholly unrelated to the story of his resurrection. Blumhardt asserted that Jesus' death and resurrection were the essence of Christianity and the start of personal transformation.

Blumhardt's certainty about the Bible's supernatural message came due to his own personal experience with miracles. His firsthand encounter with

---

18. Ibid.

19. Ibid., 1:125; 2:37; Blumhardt, *Christoph Blumhardt*, 4:388.

20. Blumhardt, *Ansprachen*, 1:99; 2:95.

miracles came as a youth in the midst of the revival in Möttlingen. Blumhardt saw logic in the miracles of the Bible. The miracles testified to him about a God who acted in history to bring his salvation to the world, most notably in Jesus Christ. It made perfect sense, then, when the Bible taught that the establishment of the kingdom of God and the miraculous resurrection of the dead at the end of the world were the ultimate destination for God's beloved people. These were not points of esoteric dogma; this was the obvious conclusion to God's long history of activity. These beliefs in God's dramatic action in the world provided the cornerstone for his theology on the kingdom of God.[21]

After his father died, Blumhardt ascended into the role of spiritual healer at Bad Boll. Then he saw the active hand of God in the healings that took place under his care. Furthermore, he believed that this activity should be present in the lives of every Christian. Even late in his career in 1908, Blumhardt reiterated:

> I have this constant distress when people come to me asking, "pray for me!" Oh, how often I have groaned; am I the only one through whom God can work?—This is how I see it: people very much want to see an act of God. . . . It was the same with our Savior; the people came to him in their troubles. And great signs and miracles took place! If we are supposed to be children [of God], as Jesus was a child of God, then we can also see miracles transpire. I will go so far as to say; the present time needs an extraordinary intervention from God . . . . Today with so much evil fighting against the good, I believe that—when it is necessary for God's work and as it advances the salvation of humanity—indeed *something extraordinary will come to pass*.[22]

While Bad Boll's emphasis on spiritual healing decreased as he moved more actively into solving social ills, he never abandoned his foundational beliefs that came with his firsthand experience of God's active role in the present world.[23]

In Blumhardt's interpretation of the Bible, its miracles gave the Christian Scriptures authority and power for his present day, but they still needed to be interpreted to a world suffering from sin. When it came to hermeneutics, he was anything but systematic. Because his God was a dynamic God whose hand was active in history, his interpretation of the Bible was similarly dynamic.

21. Ibid., 1:64, 110, 153–54.
22. Ibid., 3:21. Emphasis in original.
23. Blumhardt, *Christoph Blumhardt*, 4:23–24.

Because times changed, God's interaction with the world changed.[24] Therefore, Blumhardt's interpretation of the Bible was not literal, in the sense used by a defender of verbal inspiration.

BLUMHARDT'S SUBJECTIVITY IN HERMENEUTICS

Blumhardt's disagreements with the Scriptures were wholly different from anything else seen in his day in Germany. When scholars of the late-nineteenth and early-twentieth centuries questioned the truth of the Bible, they contested its supernatural accounts. For Blumhardt, in contrast, those were the narratives beyond question. When he questioned the Bible, he questioned its ethical and religious principles.[25] The Bible, as the medium through which the word of God comes to believers, is useful and timeless, but its meaning varies from epoch to epoch and even day to day and needs to be continually reinterpreted by new prophets and apostles as God deems it necessary. This new revelation trumped and changed the old. He admonished his congregation, "One will find nothing dumber than tradition. My father was a great personality, greater than most people who knew him even realized. But if I were simply to follow the tradition of my father, I would be pushed to the side. . . . The things that my father knew, are not enough for us today. . . . We need to be people who continually struggle forward and expect a new revelation. . . . For our present time we need a new revelation to know God's command for today."[26]

24. God's changing interaction with the world bears remarkable similarity to dispensationalist theology, which was gaining followers in English-speaking Christianity at the time. Indeed, a comparison of Blumhardt to Darby and Schofield would provide an interesting and valuable comparative history. The main points of commonality between the two would be, first, a belief in God's changing interaction with humanity in different epochs. Second, both Blumhardt (especially late in his life) and dispensationalism possessed an eschatological outlook that expected God's imminent breakthrough into world history to establish the eternal kingdom of God (dispensationalism's premillennialist doctrine). The two theologies differ dramatically, though, in their understanding of the charismatic gifts such as prophecy. Dispensationalists defended the character of the Scriptures by arguing that the direct communication of God to the church through prophecy ended with the closing of the canon, Blumhardt, in contrast, anxiously expected God's active communication. In any case, it is certainly a surprise that much of Blumhardt's theology shared more with English-American radically conservative theology than with the debates of his own countrymen and women.

25. Interestingly, Blumhardt's major challenge to the Bible's teachings was the characteristic of God as a God of judgment. Blumhardt's doctrine of salvation was never clearly stated but had strong elements of universalism. After the turn of the century, he even divided the two, the God of Judgment (*Zorngott*) from the comforting God (*Trostgott*). As he did this, he stumbled into an unusual commonality with Adolf Harnack's neo-Marcionist theology. However, their arrival at this common place came from wholly different paths; see Blumhardt, *Christoph Blumhardt*, 3:50.

26. Blumhardt, *Ansprachen*, 2:50–51.

Therefore, Blumhardt told his listeners, when the will of God was hidden or unknown, the only recourse for Christians was to wait for God to reveal God's present will through those to whom God chose to disclose it. Even if it took years, God was trustworthy to make God's will known to those who sought it.[27]

For this reason, Blumhardt considered the Bible the mere starting point of Christian revelation. His biblical realism also changed the meaning of the "word of God." The result of any act of God was a "word of God." Certainly, Blumhardt affirmed that the Bible fell into this category as the written account of any number of acts of God. However, he also believed that just as God's revelation of God's self did not stop at the Bible, neither did the "word of God" stop at the Scriptures. Instead, he often used "word of God" to describe the intricate character of nature that also indicates the hand of God and reveals God's character to the world. In Röntgen's discovery of the X-ray, Blumhardt saw a "word of God." The X-ray was a part of the creation God had made. Likewise, any flower, any star in the heavens—all of these were "God's words" that the sensitive spiritual observer could make sense of to better understand God and to better comprehend his or her own responsibility in the world.[28]

BLUMHARDT AGAINST OBJECTIVE HERMENEUTICS

Blumhardt believed that academic theology's narrow realm of biblical interpretation stifled true spiritual Christian belief and practice. As a holder of conservative theological viewpoints, Blumhardt made some of his attacks against the growing liberalism and the modern Protestant's attachment to the university professor. In a characteristically blunt sentence, Blumhardt condemned learned Christianity as "an evil thing."[29] In his mind, university theology departments replaced a holy Christianity with a list of creeds and bits of information. In the process, Blumhardt accused Christians of losing their principal call; they were to be different from the world. He reminded his listeners that God was open to hearing everybody's prayers and requests. The simple function of conversation between the believer and God needed no intercession from professors or pastors.[30]

At its worst, according to Blumhardt, academic theology destroyed faith in God's ability to work in the world. In this, he attacked believing and critical scholars alike. The believing theologians, especially the biblicists among them, had reduced God's revelation to the written word. The Bible was sacred and

27. Ibid., 3:37, Blumhardt, *Christoph Blumhardt*, 3:156–57; 4:34–35, 266–67.

28. Blumhardt, *Ansprachen*, 3:171–72.

29. Ibid., 1:110.

30. Ibid., 1:98, 110, 182.

had its origin from God, but Blumhardt insisted that anybody who read the Bible would know that God's ability to reveal himself was not limited to the Holy Writ. Moses and Abraham were true to God before any Scriptures were written, and God had no difficulty showing himself to them. Blumhardt preached that even if all the Bibles of the world were gone, God would still be able to reveal himself to the church. True Christianity was a process of moving beyond university theology. True faith did not stop at the mere inspection of the Scriptures, but it began with accepting them as truth and living them out in day-to-day practice.[31]

Blumhardt's critique of liberal theologians was similar. He questioned their Enlightenment view of the miraculous. They were so convinced of the superiority of reason that they forgot the most elemental truth of theology: they were dealing with God. If God is the same God who could create something out of nothing, then it is not difficult for God to act miraculously today. Blumhardt said, "I am often laughed at because I still pray and believe that God still performs miracles. Some talk about miracles, but people do not even know what miracles are. It is the most natural of the natural that we humans can live in the power of God and not merely in nature."[32] If God is the creator of everything, then it is wholly natural when God behaves in ways incomprehensible to humans.[33]

Blumhardt believed that the Bible was a true and accurate account of God's actions in history because it was consistent with the way he experienced God's continued work with people in the present. In a way, the Bible filled in the blanks of God's purpose in the world. So while the Bible was not fundamentally essential for faith, it was the clearest explanation of God's will and God's work in the world. Blumhardt saw God acting miraculously in Bad Boll and even in the SPD, but the Bible supplied the answers and interpretations for God's purposes in those actions.

Exactly this understanding of the Bible and of the continuing revelation of God's word through history made the Bible the beginning and foundation of all theology. Conservative scholars such as Kähler and Schlatter spent their careers addressing the all-encompassing belief in the Bible. For them, the Bible contained all fundamental truths about God for Christian believers. For Blumhardt, the Bible was no less true, but it could not encompass all that God was and all that God wanted to tell God's children. This did not mean that Blumhardt considered God's revelation incomplete. He saw room for God to

31. Ibid., 1:165, 166, 182; 2:19, 68; 3:97–98.
32. Ibid., 2:95.
33. Ibid., 3:171.

act and to bring the culmination of history to pass. Blumhardt spoke about the importance of Christians being open for God's revelation: "In every Christian congregation, where people come together to hear the Word of God, even when the reading and discussion of the Biblical passage is simple, in every one of these churches is a point, a seed, and there assembles the church of Jesus Christ."[34] But the church of Christ did not remain at this point; it moved on, and the seed grew into a mature plant and bore fruit in the form of a force to change the world.[35]

AWAKENING THE SLEEPING GIANT: CHRISTOPH BLUMHARDT'S ART OF PREACHING

Blumhardt left behind only his sermons and a handful of letters as an estate for later historians to gain an understanding of his theological beliefs and developments. As a rule, Blumhardt played down his most notable claims to fame. When he was still active in a healing ministry, he never made public any of the miraculous healings, not even as illustrations for his sermons. Generally speaking, he frowned on the open publication of his sermons. This did not arise out of his modesty, but rather as a defense of Bad Boll and its place in German Christianity. Throughout his and his father's career, various people, usually other Protestant church leaders, attacked both Blumhardts' theology. These affronts often came in public and embarrassing ways. In the introduction to a short book that introduced Bad Boll and the elder Blumhardt's ministry to the public, Christoph Blumhardt asked that any theological disputes be handled privately, rather than in the newspapers.[36]

Blumhardt had reason to be concerned. His sermons were not the carefully measured homilies encouraged in most of Germany at the time. He was a firebrand. Like most German sermons of the late nineteenth century, his sermons were devotional rather than exegetical explanations of the biblical passage's meaning. He took liberties with the Scriptures and extrapolated their teachings in questionable ways to be of use for the important issues of his day. What is more, he was aware that he was going beyond the accepted frame of interpretation. He felt free to level his critiques on those whom he thought deserving, and he had no problem making his listeners feel uncomfortable.

---

34. Blumhardt, *Christoph Blumhardt*, 4:329.

35. Ibid., 4:35; Blumhardt, *Ansprachen*, 3:45–46.

36. Christoph Blumhardt, *Gedanken aus dem Reiche Gottes, im Anschluß an die Geschichte von Möttlingen und Bad Boll, und unsere heutige Stellung: Ein vertrauliches Wort an Freunde* (Bad Boll: Bad Boll, 1895), 4.

Blumhardt wished that his sermons would motivate Christians to get ready to change the world. Often, in doing this, he would make claims of questionable orthodoxy. At times, he went so far as to state that the Bible should not be available to anyone who wished to read it, that individual passages of the Bible were greatly mistaken, that he was receiving special messages from God, or that the entire institutional church had abandoned its responsibilities. However, in the context of all his sermons, every unorthodox, shocking statement was outnumbered by others that fit within the traditional beliefs of Protestantism.[37]

For his opponents, Blumhardt was easy to condemn. He realized, however, that for his listeners to truly understand him, they needed to be committed to spending long periods of time with him to hear his various views before they made any rash condemnation. For this reason alone, he played down the publication of his sermons. The first characteristic to recognize in Blumhardt's sermons was that, instead of following the systems of sermon making he had learned in his studies, he modeled his own sermons and his career on the prophets of the Old Testament.

Calling Germany to Repentance: Prophecy in the Ministry of Christoph Blumhardt

Blumhardt's conviction that God was still giving the world new revelation awakened in him the expectation that the Holy Spirit would unveil to him new meanings in the Bible's ancient texts.[38] He differed from the mainstream Protestantism of his day in his love for Old Testament prophecy. German sermons of the period were drawn almost exclusively from the New Testament with the occasional Psalm as a text. When academics did look at the prophets, it was to look at their textual content, not to use them for advice in spiritual living. Blumhardt, in contrast, used them with great frequency and gusto. "I cannot help myself," he said, "as rocky as the Israelite history was, I enjoy it more than the history of Christianity. In Israel every now and then there came

---

37. Blumhardt, *Christoph Blumhardt*, 3:50; Blumhardt, *Ansprachen*, 1:105, 107; 2:56, 57.

38. A note on the footnotes concerning Blumhardt's theological beliefs: As mentioned earlier in this chapter, Blumhardt's sermons are unsuitable or at least difficult for prooftexting. Unfortunately, some such evidence is needed for a fair treatment of his theological views. For the most part, I have attempted to focus on major themes he repeated in his sermons and to give an accurate, if unsystematic, portrait of his theology. The following footnotes are to portions of Blumhardt's sermons that are demonstrative of the theology being described, but they are by no means exhaustive. Likewise, some passages in his sermons contradict others; in those cases, I have tried to find Blumhardt's general meaning within the larger body of his work and to hold those as Blumhardt's opinions.

somebody with an incredible message, and spoke—not only spoke, but showed it in himself—'The Lord is my strength.'"[39]

Blumhardt often repeated his hope that new prophets would arise to call modern Christians back to true worship of God. Since God had called prophets to present his message in the Old Testament, Blumhardt remained convinced that God would continue this work in the era of the New Covenant. This was the reason why he felt no shame in changing his father's call. He thought that to merely honor his father and continue his ministry would be the greatest failure possible at Bad Boll. Instead, he sought something prophetic. He understood that such a prophetic ministry would alienate modern culture. Prophetic ministry and the prophetic books of the Bible were the words of God that could be heard on earth. These messages were seldom easy but always true. So Blumhardt proclaimed that even though modern-day prophets could expect persecution and rejection, they would be comforted with the wonderful knowledge that they had the privilege of carrying the true message of God.[40]

Blumhardt soon gave indications that he was receiving such a prophetic call from God. His certainty in the special prophetic ministry of Bad Boll came from its origins. In the movement of revival and return to God, Bad Boll showed itself to have special supernatural resources. Three biblical proofs showed that Bad Boll's ministry was from God. First, the ministry of both Blumhardts in Bad Boll led to the honest confession of sins. Second, the confession was followed by a move away from heathenism and superstition. The final manifestation of their prophetic call was that it showed itself in the power to heal and to cast out demons.[41]

Since Blumhardt's ministry continued to call for a return to a theocentric life more than forty years after his father's struggle with the demons of Gottliebin Dittus, he could state that he built on the original foundation laid in Möttlingen by his father. Blumhardt never wanted to be a prophet of the future, but one of the present; that is, he desired to be one who proclaimed God's truth to the modern world.

As with the prophets of the Bible, his prophetic teaching brought misunderstanding and differences with the institutional religion. To some degree, Blumhardt understood the origin of these attacks. Bad Boll's tripartite mission as a retreat center for Christians, a center of prophetic speech, and a place of spiritual healing was difficult to place in the highly structured state-

---

39. Blumhardt, *Ansprachen*, 3:88–89.

40. Ibid., 1:125; 2:50–51.

41. Blumhardt, *Gedanken*, 2–3; Blumhardt, *Ansprachen*, 2:55; 3:29–30.

church institutions. As understandable as these attacks might have been, they shook his faith in the church structures of his homeland.[42]

Like the prophets of the Old Testament, Blumhardt found that the hardest attacks to handle were the ones that came from others who shared the same religious core beliefs. Bad Boll was attacked during the elder Blumhardt's leadership and again when the son assumed responsibility. In 1894, Friedrich von Bodelschwingh, pastor and leader of a similar Christian spa in Bethel near Bielefeld, openly challenged Blumhardt's ministry and his orthodoxy in a letter. Bodelschwingh wrote, "If Miss Kraft relayed your perspective to me properly, then we have the responsibility and the right to object to your teaching which has no foundation in the Word of God. Because in this case you did not work from the Word of God but rather from personal revelation, we must act against you and your false teachings. . . . I will not conceal that I do not consider you merely mistaken, but rather sick."[43] Instead of being a close ally, Bodelschwingh attacked Blumhardt's prophetic ministry. Blumhardt refused to answer Bodelschwingh's letter but allowed his brother to do so. Theophil Blumhardt alluded to the apostle Paul in his response, writing, "Believe me when I say that my brother is physically and spiritually wholly healthy: but to the honor of his Lord and master, he will happily be seen a fool by the pious and impious of the world alike."[44] The attacks from Christians wore on Blumhardt over his career and played a significant role in his abandonment of the pastoral responsibilities in 1894 and his movement into the anti-state-church SPD in 1899.

Blumhardt never allowed the critiques to stop his own preaching. He turned the skepticism of his fellow Christians into both motivation for his own ministry and ammunition in his censure of the church's social impotence. Indeed, his main prophetic message was aimed against the church and its social inactivity. As Klaus-Jürgen Meier showed, Blumhardt never left the realm of Württemberg pietism. His critiques came from one who loved the church and loved the religiosity of his region. However, this piety had turned stagnant.

Perhaps because of their fundamental differences on the nature and reality of the Bible, Blumhardt and the liberals were too far apart to have any fruitful interaction. Blumhardt reserved his harshest prophetic critiques of modern Christianity for his fellow pietists and theological conservatives. He accused these pastors and laity of committing the cardinal sin of Protestantism: they had replaced God's grace with human rules. The modern pietist pastors dwelled

---

42. Blumhardt, *Ansprachen*, 1:44.

43. Ibid., 2:44.

44. Ibid., 2:45.

only on the punishments of God instead of on God's forgiveness of sins and God's unending love. Blumhardt disagreed with this take on Christianity. He argued instead that God is "enormously liberal."[45]

For Blumhardt, going to church was not about reaching salvation, but about going above and beyond. The rules and laws of the Bible were there for the Holy Spirit's role of perfecting the individual believer. They played no role in salvation. He confronted pietism with his prophetic calling that Christianity had become weak because Christians failed to love as Jesus loved. Modern Christianity and modern pietism took a religion of grace and mercy and turned it into a religion of damnation and condemnation. The lack of love from the pulpit led to the lack of results in bringing the new generation to Christ.[46]

As Blumhardt's prophetic ministry matured, he narrowed his critique of the church's general lack of love to its specific lack of compassion in social problems. In his experience with pietists, he found a deep-seated compassion, but he also discovered that they expressed it only with other pietists. These Christians brought their confessional arguments into their humanity and refused to help those who suffered but thought differently. Blumhardt pointed out that Jesus was known as a friend of tax collectors and sinners, as one whose love reached all, even those who rejected him. His call to his co-confessionalists was to act like Jesus, to go into the world living the gospel. God did not send Jesus for Christians to sit on their hands. Christians were called into the world.[47]

Once Blumhardt came into contact with the socialist movement, his call to arms became even more specific. Christians were to motivate themselves to help the poor and downtrodden as an exercise to usher in the kingdom of God. He continued to motivate his fellow believers to action, using the socialists to shame the Christians. Even though the socialists did not have the example of Jesus to follow and the strength of Jesus to accomplish their task, they were still out in the world, working to improve it. While the socialists were bettering the world, Blumhardt jested, the Christians stayed home and prayed their pious prayers. Blumhardt asserted, "The Kaiser is nothing compared to Rothschild! In Mammonism everything is coming to its climax. Mammonism is the anti-God that can only be defeated by God. Marx was a prophet! What he said fifty years ago has been fulfilled today."[48] The Christians abandoned their moral responsibility and replaced it with the views of the outside, worldly culture.

45. Ibid., 1:105.

46. Ibid., 1:91–92, 105–106, 154; Blumhardt, *Christoph Blumhardt*, 4:53.

47. Blumhardt, *Ansprachen*, 1:181; 2:73–74, 94.

48. Ibid., 2:264.

Once Blumhardt joined the socialist party, his blending of his Christianity, his prophetic call, and his actions was complete.[49]

Perhaps surprisingly, considering the political overtures of Blumhardt's message, Blumhardt's prophetic ministry never dealt on the same level of blessings and curses that Stoecker famously developed in the wake of the Franco-Prussian War in 1870. Blumhardt never tied God's kingdom to a particular moment or show of piety. The key to his separation from Stoecker's message is that he had little use for a particular national orientation in his politics or preaching. The kingdom of God would not be an extension of Germany, as it was for Stoecker, and therefore it could not be initiated by a particular war. Likewise, it would be inevitable and larger than human actions, rather than the summation of them. Here Blumhardt removed the charge of sectarian power that Stoecker had. The kingdom would be a universal blessing, not because it would ensure conversion, but because God is good.

The Real and Future World: Blumhardt and the Kingdom of God

The best way to study Blumhardt's theology is to focus on his preaching concerning the kingdom of God. The idea of the kingdom characterized and shaped his entire ministry from beginning to end. His prophetic style of preaching never aimed to portray a well-rounded, thorough dogma, but it did return time after time to build up a portrayal of the kingdom of God. Through his career, he preached with remarkable stamina a few themes that lay close to his heart and ignored many others. Therefore, this chapter may leave many important theological questions unanswered, but it will remain truer to Blumhardt's own intents than much of the historiography that tries to pin down Blumhardt's central theological beliefs.

Blumhardt's Kingdom of God Placed in Nineteenth-Century Theology

The proclamation of the kingdom of God was Blumhardt's central theme throughout his preaching career. Theologically speaking, Blumhardt could not have hit on a timelier message. The questions concerning Jesus's preaching of the kingdom of God and the character of the kingdom were popular theological topics for the majority of German Christian thought of the era. During Blumhardt's lifetime, the liberal theologian Albrecht Ritschl portrayed Jesus' kingdom of God as the moral/ethical community that collects itself around the

49. Ibid., 2:168–69, 216.

teachings of Jesus Christ. Some two and a half decades later, Johannes Weiss questioned Ritschl's portrayal, writing that Jesus Christ's own proclamation of the kingdom was future-looking and had little to do with present ethical standards.

Conservative dogmatists kept the two extreme views of the kingdom of God in a continuing tension. They wrote that some elements of the kingdom of God were already present, and some were yet to come with the return of Jesus Christ. On the whole, however, the conservative theologians chose to remain silent on the kingdom's exact character. Blumhardt's depiction of the kingdom paralleled this conservative view, but he brought into the preaching and thinking about the kingdom of God a passion that was unique.

The character of Blumhardt's preaching of the kingdom of God was thoroughly romantic. It fit in well with the Biedermeier sentiment of the second half of the nineteenth century. In his spa, separate from the world, he could create a perfectly peaceful environment. This was a portion of the kingdom of God before the consummation of the world. His mind turned on the expectation of an imminent, dramatic renewal of the world. His expectation was not merely optimism that progress was being made. He was certain that God's triumph was imminent.

Eventually, as he found his calling in the SPD, his romanticism bloomed to encompass the whole modern world. The kingdom of God was being born from the sufferings of the industrialized workers. However, when his political dreams failed to come to fruition, he retreated once again, like the romantics before him, into his private sphere that he could control. The spa at Bad Boll again became a haven of Christ's kingdom in a heathen world.

Blumhardt's theology of the kingdom of God began with the Bible's portrayal of the corruption of the world. Blumhardt had little room in his pastoral care for self-pity. Humanity got what it deserved. Sin was the human rebellion against the goodness of God, and since everyone was sinful, no one should be surprised when God removed the divine blessing. Concerning prayer, Blumhardt exhorted:

> Prayer is not some kind of coercive power over God that we can force him to serve us . . . . A much better prayer is to realize why we have these troubles in the first place. *We* are the guilty party, not God. And our problem is not that we are not praying properly, but that we are not in a right relationship with him. We act as though everything is perfectly fine when we pray. But God is not going to do anything when we have no desire to change. Whoever seeks the

Kingdom of God will find God's help, but if we are outside of the Kingdom, then we can expect nothing.[50]

Blumhardt described prayer as a microcosm of true Christianity. Prayer, as well as the Christian life, was a three-step process. First, the supplicant acknowledges his or her own culpability in personal suffering. Then the believer asks God to assist and remove the person's troubles, despite his or her sin. Finally, the Christian acts according to the will of God in response to the answered prayer.[51]

However, despite unanswered prayers, Blumhardt was confident in his faith that God desired to help. God was active in the world and wished to send out the blessings of the Spirit to modern Christians, even as God had sent the Spirit to the early church.[52] The work of the Holy Spirit was a principal focus of the early part of Blumhardt's ministry. He described the Spirit's role as twofold. First, the Spirit was active in Christians through prayer to bestow God's gifts and healing to the world. This description of the Holy Spirit's work built on the healing ministry of his father. The second (and more important in his own career) of Blumhardt's descriptions of the Holy Spirit's work in the world was that the Spirit is responsible for shaping history in order to prepare the way for the arrival of the perfect kingdom of God.[53]

The centrality of the Holy Spirit in Blumhardt's theology of the kingdom of God contrasted sharply with the predominant theology of the day. In his thinking, the Spirit played a more prominent everyday role than even Jesus Christ. Other streams of Protestant thought of the era treated the Holy Spirit's role as difficult to define and hazy at best. To make a generalization, conservative theologians acknowledged the triune God and the presence of the Holy Spirit in the Godhead. However, they found little practical application for the Holy Spirit and focused much more on the atoning work of Jesus Christ.

Critics, in contrast, wholly abandoned the theology of the Holy Spirit as a product of the early church's mythological zeitgeist. For them, when the term *Spirit of God* was used, it meant God's mind-set and will such that the spirit of a man or woman may be lined up and brought into unity with the Spirit of God. This was more a description of an ethical quality than a supernatural one. For

50. Ibid., 2:3.

51. Ibid., 2:2–3.

52. In this sentiment, Christoph Blumhardt and his father anticipated the Pentecostal revival that would begin on Asuza Street in 1907 and soon spread to the entire world. Some Pentecostal writers go so far as to say that the Blumhardts were a sort of founders of the movement. This claim may not be wholly unfounded; however, there is no mention of glossolalia (speaking in tongues), the key characteristic of the Pentecostal revival, in Bad Boll.

53. Blumhardt, *Ansprachen*, 1:49, 68, 89, 159–60.

Enlightenment theologians and their successors, there was no Holy Spirit in the Godhead with a function or existence separate from God, the Father.

THE CHARACTER OF THE KINGDOM OF GOD

Certainly to his listeners, Blumhardt's theology of the Spirit's role in the kingdom of God was novel and surprising. Yet it was not in any way at odds with his scriptural understanding. Reading the Bible with its accounts of the supernatural work of God and the Spirit in the world, he saw a particular plan and logic in history. He saw God's sweeping plan for God's people from their origin in sin up to the restoration of their holiness in the last days. History was the progress toward sinlessness. This movement was set into motion first through the atonement of Christ, then through the transformation of the world through the Holy Spirit; it finally culminated in the coming of the kingdom of God.[54]

Blumhardt's kingdom of God was the coming of God's righteousness to earth. This righteousness would come with the return of Jesus Christ from heaven. Blumhardt's depiction of the kingdom, being both political and physical, differed greatly from the abstract morality and spirituality that was the common view among most liberal and many conservative theologians of his era. Blumhardt described the kingdom of God as the completion of the work Jesus began. In preparation for Jesus' return, this work was continued by Jesus' church through the power of the Holy Spirit.

Blumhardt often compared the coming kingdom with the kingdoms of this world. He saw in the wake of the 1848 movements an era of growing nationalism that was characterized by war and bloodshed. The coming kingdom would be completely different. The kingdom of God was a kingdom of peace. Blumhardt motivated his listeners to strive for the kingdom with this cry: "We protest against everything that ever happened in history up to this point in the name of our Christ, in the name of the unnumbered masses, and for God who sent Christ so that all may receive their proper due."[55] Whereas the society Blumhardt knew was one led by the powerful and the rich, the coming kingdom would be ushered in by a groundswell of the common people, who would realize the value they had for God.[56]

As Blumhardt moved toward the socialists, his call for the advancement of an earthly kingdom of God became clearer. His portrait of the kingdom bore

54. Ibid., 2:292; Blumhardt, *Christoph Blumhardt*, 4:143, 153–54, 245–46, 321.

55. Blumhardt, *Ansprachen*, 2:214.

56. Ibid., 1:190; 2:213–14, 231; Blumhardt, *Christoph Blumhardt*, 4:9–10.

remarkable similarity to the workers' utopia of Karl Marx and August Bebel. In one speech shortly after his entry as a candidate for the SPD, Blumhardt drove the point home:

> The Kingdom of God is a new society that requires a new way of life. . . . We must strip off any honor, any fame, and take these things far from our heart and proceed all the way down [to the masses], completely free from everything. Why did Jesus go the bottom? Because the roots were there. Greed, covetousness, selfishness is the sin of the world. It is the root of all tyranny, all cruelty and all murder. That's why Jesus went to the bottom. Today Christians are just as greedy as any Jews; they sell everything just to make money.[57]

Blumhardt believed that the Christians forgot their humble origins and swapped them for the grand pursuits of the world. He accused them of forgetting that Jesus came to the people, not just to the Calvins and Luthers of the world. When Blumhardt was in the SPD, he was convinced that Jesus' first act when he returned to earth would be to remove all the lords and authorities from their positions of power. He described the kingdom of God as a groundswell movement that would begin from God and move through the people to create a new and just society.[58]

For Blumhardt (and here he separated himself from the predominant conservative theological thought of his time), the kingdom of God was a universal good. Blumhardt's kingdom of God was so big and so total that its blessing spread to believers and skeptics alike. God's final entry into the world would be so magnificent and awesome that everybody would acknowledge God's goodness and blessings. Eternal happiness and the provision of God were not limited merely to those few who willingly accepted it. Blumhardt's God was too big to think that an arbitrary mediator such as the human will could have sway over the hand of God.[59]

Blumhardt's universalism in his kingdom of God portrayal turned him into the guardian of God's blessings and salvation for the non-Christian and even outright opponents of Christianity. They, too, would be recipients of God's generosity. Blumhardt often preached this or similar sentiments: "I still want to have something to do with Mohammedans and Buddhists because I want to bring them into heaven. Obviously God must do it, but I am praying for it, and

57. Blumhardt, *Ansprachen*, 2:154–55.
58. Ibid., 2:156–57, 213; Blumhardt, *Christoph Blumhardt*, 4:10.
59. Blumhardt, *Ansprachen*, 3:69.

I tell him daily: Dear God, I want to be last! I do not want to ascend into heaven when there are others who have to descend into hell."[60]

Blumhardt defended open lines of communication between the Christian communities and the outside world. When believers ignored those who thought differently, they risked missing God's messages to them. Just as Blumhardt thought God's revelation was not merely restricted to the Bible, he also believed that Jesus was not limited to showing himself only through Christians. God often expressed God's will to the world more clearly through liberal theologians, through Karl Marx, and through Leo Tolstoy than through the pious preachers who did nothing to relieve the pain of this world from their listeners.[61]

Certainly Blumhardt believed that the kingdom of God was not limited to any nationality. He eyed borders and nationalism skeptically. He was critical of tying Christianity too much to Germanness. He described the God who only loved Germans: "God is a World-God, a God of the entire creation. What the Germans, the English, and so forth have made into their God, those are national gods, they are idols. And they gain strength proportionately to the level of nationalist enthusiasm in the land. . . . What is war? It is nothing other than the outcome when the true God is hindered from being seen."[62] War was the embarrassing outcome of Europe's lukewarm Christianity. If citizens of all nations could worship God equally, then war and animosity between these groups was unjustifiable. In his opinion, the beginning of the kingdom of God would mark the end of worldly nations.[63]

In these points, Blumhardt approached the extreme Calvinist view of God's omnipotence. However, he differed from the Reformer because he chose to hope for universal salvation. After all, he asked, what was the harm of people who were incapable of belief? Without God first making God's self known to the individual, all humans were incapable of knowing or believing in God. Those people should not be judged simply because they had not received the gift to feel and see God. Blumhardt contended that those who attempted to restrict God's grace were more harmful to the kingdom than the unbelievers were. In this sense, Blumhardt exercised remarkable tolerance. It was better to believe than not to, and he hoped to bring those who did not believe into belief. However, he refused to take it on himself to judge and condemn others. Blumhardt passed on to his listeners some advice he had received from his

60. Blumhardt, *Ansprachen*, 1:151.

61. Blumhardt, *Ansprachen*, 1:150–51; Blumhardt, *Ansprachen*, 2:226.

62. Blumhardt, *Ansprachen*, 2:25.

63. Blumhardt, *Ansprachen*, 2:25–26; Blumhardt, *Christoph Blumhardt*, 4:13–14.

father. They should assume everybody they met was a believer and a just person. With this perspective in life, they would be more able to see clearly the work of God in everyone they contacted.[64]

Despite his universalism, Blumhardt still made an important distinction between believers and unbelievers. The difference was the presence of God in their activity. Everyone was made in the image of God, and for this reason, people were able to have sympathy and to help others in time of need. However, only a select number of people had God's Spirit acting in them. They were privileged because God had chosen them. He compared these believers to a ray of light in a shadow; they made the contrast between earthly evil and heavenly good apparent in all things. They acted as the catalysts to give the impulse and the drive for all humans to act in their godly image rather than in their sinful nature. So while Blumhardt made no distinction of reward for believers and unbelievers, there was a clear distinction of place and responsibility in the world. The responsibility Blumhardt gave to believers was not difficult. Serving God and being able to accomplish God's work because of the Holy Spirit was a privileged position.[65]

In the end, Blumhardt warned his listeners that no matter what they were called or what dogma they held, God was looking first and foremost for those who were willing to do the work for God's kingdom. At no point could a Christian rest on his or her laurels, confident of God's good grace. Christians must remain vigilant to seek and practice God's will. No matter what religious title one might have had, God would judge human violence and power (*Gewalt*) severely. At the same time, God was willing and able to move in and through whomever God desired. Everyone was capable of being a worker for God's kingdom. For Blumhardt, a well-lived life weighed much more in eternal significance than a proper dogmatic stance. The time of the kingdom of God was nearing. Christian evangelism no longer bore the responsibility to find and destroy enemies of the faith. The time had come to prepare the world for the kingdom of God.[66]

Blumhardt's portrayal of the future kingdom of God was coupled with a firm optimism about the direction of humanity. He saw the history of Christianity and modernization as a progression toward God's kingdom. In this social optimism, Blumhardt fell comfortably into the normative historical outlook of nineteenth-century theology. He also paralleled the social outlook of

64. Blumhardt, *Christoph Blumhardt*, 4:14; Blumhardt, *Ansprachen*, 2:21; Blumhardt, *Ansprachen*, 3:1, 14–15.

65. Blumhardt, *Ansprachen*, 3:47; Blumhardt, *Christoph Blumhardt*, 4:29.

66. Blumhardt, *Ansprachen*, 2:226, 292; 3:69.

Stoecker's 1870 vision and the social outlook of Kähler and Schlatter. Blumhardt believed there was little that Christians could not achieve if they held their focus on the coming kingdom of God. He saw evidence of the coming kingdom everywhere he looked. He pointed to the growth of Christianity in European empires and the cessation of persecution against it as evidence for the advancement of the world. Joining these with the advancement of evangelization of areas that were formerly hostile to the gospel, he saw God's hand in the ability of the West to civilize and moralize the non-Western world.

Before the First World War, Blumhardt also proudly proclaimed the coming end of war as evidence for the advancement of society. During his first forays into socialism, he went so far as to say that it was God's intention that industry would mechanize, and in turn, the separation of workers from the means of production gave workers a voice and class consciousness. These were indisputable proofs of God's preparation for God's kingdom. Building on Jesus' call for workers to reap the spiritual fields of the masses white with harvest, Blumhardt preached:

> In earlier centuries people had to fight without real hope for the simplest good thing. They died for every little step forward for God's work. They suffered every punishment through persecution, imprisonment and torture just because they wished to make the smallest movement forward towards the Kingdom of God . . . . Whenever we see the monstrous power of men's accusation and the satanic charges by which all humans were judged, and we compare them to our own present day, we come to the conclusion; we are no longer in the time of immature wheat, we are already in the era where the fields are becoming ready to harvest.[67]

God was actively at work molding the world for God's kingdom. As Blumhardt put it, not even the "idiocy" (*Dummheiten*) of humanity—that is, their wars—could slow God's hand.[68]

No matter how far the world had come toward achieving the kingdom of God, much still needed to come to pass before Christ returned. Blumhardt motivated his listeners with the thought that the church was responsible for finishing the advancement of society and ushering in the kingdom of God. Even as outward war was decreasing, inner war continued to rage. The souls of men and women everywhere continued to fight the battles of sin and

67. Ibid., 3:154.
68. Blumhardt, *Christoph Blumhardt*, 4:151, 153, 302; Blumhardt, *Ansprachen*, 1:117–18; 2:106, 213.

righteousness. In this struggle, Christian faithful were privileged to be able to fight alongside God. In Blumhardt's picture of Christian living, every simple act was the act of a worker for the kingdom of God. Nearing the end of his life, he preached:

> We are now workers for the coming of the Kingdom of God; our savior is the work, and we are the workers. . . . Now let it out! Say, "Kingdom of God!" Say, "Kingdom of God!" when you learn something. Say, "Kingdom of God!" when you read a book and want to teach. Say, "Kingdom of God!" when you are searching for your place in the world. Say, "Kingdom of God!" when you are rich. Say, "Kingdom of God!" when you are poor. Say, "Kingdom of God!" when you are healthy and strong. Say, "Kingdom of God!" when you are sick. Say, "Kingdom of God!" in the storm. Say, "Kingdom of God!" in the darkness. Say, "Kingdom of God!" in the deep; say, "Kingdom of God!" in the heights. Then you, too, are a worker. And the work needs workers.[69]

Every Christian had his or her role within the kingdom of God, and every role was essential for success.[70]

Living the Kingdom of God on Earth: Blumhardt's Ethics

Christoph Blumhardt's unusual response to his Christian belief, especially his participation in socialist politics, has made him fascinating to historians and historical theologians over the past eighty years. Blumhardt lived his Christianity with a fervency seldom seen in Christian leaders.

Ethics as a Response to Christ

In his consistency of belief and action, Blumhardt paralleled the liberal scholar Albert Schweitzer. Both Blumhardt and Schweitzer felt called by Jesus to respond radically to the evils of the present world. They both moved in directions frowned upon by their own respective theological schools of thought. Blumhardt left the comforts of his pietistic surroundings, his pastorate, and his retreat center to join the adamantly secular socialists. Schweitzer left the nurturing centers of liberalism—his university seat and his urban pastorate—to join the theologically conservative Paris Mission in Lambarene, Gabon. Both

---

69. Blumhardt, *Christoph Blumhardt*, 4:279.

70. Ibid.; Blumhardt, *Ansprachen*, 2:106.

attempted to follow the example of Christ as they saw it and separated themselves from the religious status quo. Both saw themselves struggling for the eschatological kingdom of God. Yet, however similar their actions appeared on the surface, the roots of their ethics were worlds apart. While Schweitzer attempted to live the ethical purity of Jesus and to mirror his love of neighbor, Blumhardt was using every avenue possible to warn people to prepare their hearts and their lives for the coming of God's supernatural kingdom.

Like Kähler and Schlatter, Blumhardt believed that ethics was the best response to the relationship and salvation offered by God. His strong theocentric theology suggested that a relationship between God and an individual was possible only when God initiated it. God was responsible not only for beginning the relationship, but also for providing the strength and motivation for a changed, ethical life. The glorious thought that God wanted a relationship with creation in the first place—and this in spite of the individual's sinful rebellion—gave the recipient his or her first impulse to live an ethical life.

Blumhardt pointed out to his congregation that God was the creator of their whole beings; God gave them the proper musculature to laugh and gave them legs to jump or even to dance. God wanted to take men and women as they were. If not, God would have created people differently. Ethical living for Blumhardt was a response to this relationship. He did not believe that ethics was a series of restrictive rules. God never wanted the creation to lose the joy and happiness that came from the little activities in life. On the contrary, God wanted to be alongside God's children in everything they already enjoyed doing.

This was no trying task. Blumhardt described the intimate tie between his relationship with God and personal ethics as a symbiotic relationship. God called people to be in the most intimate, wonderful relationship. God called people to be God's children, and for Blumhardt, the Christian response was proper obedience to God's call and God's work in the person's life. Once again, Blumhardt put a different spin on obedience. He preached that every action of humanity could be done with two motivations. One was to act out one's own selfish desires, for one's own gain. The other possibility was that, under the influence of God and in relationship with God, men and women could act in order to praise and thank God. Ethics and obedience did not entail changing the act, but rather changing the motivation behind every work.

The tension between these two motivations of actions was intense. Without the Holy Spirit's complete transformation of the soul, individual Christians were incapable of changing their mind-set. It was out of the constant tension of the Christian to destroy his or her own selfish desires and to embrace a relationship with God that Blumhardt coined one of the principal phrases of his career: "Die, so that you may live!" Death was the Christian's only experience comparable to the extreme conversion from living for oneself to living for God.[71]

Therefore, Blumhardt held that the worldly pursuit of pleasures was not the only faulty response to God's relationship. He was just as frustrated by and critical of Christians who set up extreme rules of piety that limited the freedom of relating to God. When Christians made rules about proper godly activities, or when they demanded a certain liturgy, then they actively limited other people's opportunities to rejoice at God's creation. Instead, Blumhardt suggested that every Christian ought to be overjoyed at the intimacy they had with the creator God, whether they were attending a moving church service or observing the smallest beetle.[72]

Since God desired that joy be found in every aspect of creation, ethics was a form of worshipping God. Blumhardt portrayed true worship as that which grew out of the enjoyment of God, God's creation, and God's relationship with his people. The practical outcome of such worship entailed emulating God's primary actions and goals with humanity. It began with forgiveness of one another and moved on to aiding others who were experiencing times of trouble. Finally, the worshipper humbled himself or herself to realize that the capability to worship arose from the forgiveness that he or she received from God. The true worshipper of God had no rights to anything but joy and thankfulness for salvation.[73]

A Christian's ethical life separated him or her from the sinfulness of the world and testified to God's power to change lives. Blumhardt compared sin to a covering of clouds in the night sky. Sin was not the total corruption of humanity. It was merely that which separated people from knowing their true essence that they had received when they were created in God's image. Sin kept the world from seeing the beauty of God's power and love. Christians' greatest response to God's powerful, saving love was to testify of this love to

---

71. Blumhardt, *Ansprachen*, 1:157, 163; 2:8–9.

72. Ibid., 2:164–65. This thought of Blumhardt's also lends a fruitful comparison to Albert Schweitzer's ethical philosophy that he termed "reverence for life." As also mentioned earlier in the chapter, Blumhardt termed every act of God and every facet of creation a "word of God." Logically following the divine origins of all creation, Blumhardt concluded that all creation should be treated with the respect due to its divine creator. Schweitzer's philosophy paralleled Blumhardt's almost to a tee. Schweitzer also wrote that since all life originated from God, all ethics is entailed in the reverence for life. Albert Schweitzer, *Civilization and Ethics*, 3rd ed., trans. C. T. Campion and L. M. Russell (London: Adam & Charles Black, 1946), 17.

73. Blumhardt, *Ansprachen*, 3:121, 171–72; Blumhardt, *Christoph Blumhardt*, 4:78.

other people who had not yet discovered it. When they did this, they removed the covering of sin and showed others the great universe of God's compassion. Ethics was not a matter of persuasion (and certainly not of coercion); it was the free response to God's wonderful relationship.[74]

If God's relationship was the motivation for ethics in Blumhardt's theology, saving the world was its goal. To show God's true love, believers needed to be separated from the sins of the world. Yet Blumhardt did not desire his listeners to gravitate toward the traditional ascetic separation of Christians from the world. The separation from the world should be shown in their radically different pursuits. The followers of Christ were to have no interest in the typical worldly goals of society—wealth, fame, and power. Their goal ought to be to win the world for God. He advised his listeners to win the world by fighting injustice. When changed people did God's will, they were a light to the world and saved others from the internal death of sin. This saving mission was the principal goal of ethics.[75]

Blumhardt argued that true ethics required more than the mere belief in Jesus. Belief and discipleship were two radically different ideas. The difference between the two was found in their results. Anybody could believe in Jesus, but that did not require people to change their behavior. There were people who believed in God yet continued to start wars and cause bloodshed. Blumhardt berated such people because they were more concerned with their own honor than the honor of God.

SOCIALIST ETHICS

Blumhardt was unparalleled at putting his abstract beliefs in godly ethics into practical application. In a sense, his ethics, more consistently than in the case of most Christians, could not be understood out of the context of his actions in the world. However, unlike the abstract motivation for his ethics that remained consistent through his career, his practical ethics changed dramatically over the various phases of his ministry. Blumhardt's ministry following his father at Bad Boll during the 1880s and 1890s saw the development of his biblical realism. In his sermons and his actions of the time, he called for a spiritual ministry against the forces of the devil and of sin in the world. Especially during the first decade of his ministry, he fought this spiritual warfare in the same manner as his father had—through prayer for the sick and distressed visitors of Bad Boll. Writing to a pastor in 1882, two years after succeeding his father, he described his ministry at

74. Blumhardt, *Christoph Blumhardt*, 4:102.

75. Blumhardt, *Ansprachen*, 2:106, 165–66; Blumhardt, *Christoph Blumhardt*, 4:37.

Bad Boll this way: "We have never before had so much interest in our ministry as we do today. Many are coming just to ask to be blessed so that they may convert. They are coming even when they do not have physical problems. I can perceive a great work of salvation in the invisible world . . . . More and more the history of the world is being freed from its Satanic influences so that God can lead his creation to its goal. For this reason the syncretism between God and the World must come to an end."[76]

Following this, his ethical exhortations of the time were largely spiritual. He called his listeners to spiritual freedom and told them they could be free from illnesses, possessions, and even the overly restrictive rules of the church through offering their lives to the leadership of God. This sacrifice of one's life to God was not a passive act. The believer needed to go and grasp God's good plan and good wishes. Blumhardt used his father as an example. His father had known that God wanted to heal Gottliebin Dittus from her demons. God only needed a faithful servant to intervene and stop the evils of the world. Quoting the prophet Isaiah during the early Bad Boll years, Blumhardt challenged his listeners to say to God, "Here I am, send me!"[77]

Over the next twenty years, especially through the finding of his prophetic call, the focus of his ministry changed radically, even when the expectation remained that his congregation would offer itself wholly to God's will. Initially, Blumhardt was skeptical of all party politics. In 1884, shortly after Adolf Stoecker's founding of the Christian Social Workers' Party, Blumhardt wrote a letter to a friend in which he said Stoecker's activism appeared contrary to David's lack of politicking during Absalom's rebellion and to Jesus' acceptance of his responsibility to die on the cross. Both of these biblical heroes allowed God to give them their glory; they did not question God when God seemed to be taking away their power. Blumhardt concluded his letter by writing, "The Savior must have lied if party politics is the path to victory."[78]

Blumhardt's entry into politics surprised many of his contemporaries. His preaching up to that point had been largely apolitical, and his critiques were leveled against the church, not the state. However, he was never wholly separated from at least a passing political interest. Blumhardt had a good relationship with Stoecker, who acted as host for Blumhardt when Kaiser Friedrich III invited the Bad Boll healer to come as the emperor lay dying. The relationship with Stoecker allowed Blumhardt to gain admittance to observe the kaiser's closed funeral ceremonies. Like Blumhardt, Stoecker was interested in

76. Blumhardt, *Ansprachen*, 1:59.
77. Ibid., 1:143; 2:43, 44.
78. Ibid., 1:74.

helping the downtrodden workers. Both of these famous preachers also became actively involved in working-class-oriented politics later in their careers. However, here the similarities end.

As court preacher, Stoecker was intimate with the royal family and their politics throughout his whole career. He also had enormous respect for Chancellor Otto von Bismarck. He worked in urban Berlin and experienced more of the suffering of workers firsthand. Finally, when he began the Christian Social Party, Stoecker desired to create an explicitly Christian and state-church alternative to the secular Marxists. In contrast, neither Blumhardt nor his father showed much interest in politics before his entry into the SPD. He had been suspicious of Bismarck and of other leaders with great power (excepting the pious kaiser). His experiences were shaped by his rural surroundings, and his circle of influence was mostly middle and upper class. Finally, when he joined the socialists, he saw that move as the ultimate critique against the church. His participation in mass politics put into practice his prophetic arguments that secular and unchurched socialists like August Bebel were doing more for the kingdom of God than his fellow pastors were.[79]

Seventeen years after his initial meeting with Stoecker, as Blumhardt entered the Social Democratic Party, he was aware of the monumental change in his own thinking. He repented of his earlier beliefs and acknowledged that God's call to him was significantly different from the one his father had received. Blumhardt's work of the time differed from that of his father because he felt called into the physical world, not just the spiritual one. He looked at the pietism of his youth and was shocked that while the Christians around him were outwardly so holy, they never took the time or effort to change the world. Such religion was useless, remonstrated Blumhardt. At his second political speech in Göppingen, he said to his socialist listeners, "I am hoping for a wholly new society. From early in my life, I found that religion has no value for me if it does not change society and does not bring the greatest fortune to Earth. That is how I have understood my Bible and my Christ. For this reason, I feel related to the people who are fighting for a Utopia."[80] He used Jesus to explain his motivation for this change. Jesus, too, left the spiritual realm in order to come help people in their everyday cares. Since Jesus was God's active ministry to the world, then God must desire that Blumhardt's ministry be a similar one.[81]

79. Esche, "Reich Gottes," 27–28; Blumhardt, *Ansprachen*, 1:46, 107, 136.

80. It is important to note in these early political speeches that, for a candidate for the party, Blumhardt showed a remarkable misunderstanding of socialism. He still saw the Social Democratic Party as a utopian party working for a millennial future, when most Marxists (including Marx himself) had earlier abandoned this vision for scientific materialism. Blumhardt, *Ansprachen*, 2:180.

After preaching with little success that the church should reform itself to actively resolve society's ills, Blumhardt found that his message was similar to the socialist critique of modern politics. Both socialists and he called for immediate action to help the poor, both critiqued the status quo, and most importantly, socialism had a legacy of a millennialist hope for the future. Blumhardt's understanding of a socialist utopia blended well enough with his own vision of the kingdom of God that he had little trouble ignoring the aspects of their beliefs that clashed. Blumhardt's unique position as a clergy member in the SPD faction made him a celebrity for the party. SPD head August Bebel even visited him at Bad Boll and is reported to have said, "When I am with Reverend Blumhardt in Bad Boll, then it is easy for me to believe in God."[82]

Through the 1880s and 1890s, Blumhardt became convinced that God was moving through political change. He preached with regularity that Jesus never wanted to found a religion with its rites and rules. Rather, Jesus came to change the world and fix its social problems. He contended that Jesus concerned himself with the social and physical illnesses of those around him. In the modern era, these questions had moved from spiritual care into the political realm. Therefore, to accomplish the Christianity of Jesus, Blumhardt needed to be involved in the political institutions and to make sure they were properly administrated. To justify his leap into politics, Blumhardt argued that ethics was a situational phenomenon. He said people behaved according to where they were in life. For this reason, he suggested that Christianity could not produce one single, general ethic for everyone, non-Christian and Christian alike. In the depths of poverty, people were not capable of hearing or obeying God's will properly. So during this time, he saw his role change to one of helping people ascend into a position in life where they could begin to be responsive to God's voice. Blumhardt summed up the goal of Christianity as the elevation of the whole of humanity. Here he came into line with the socialists and argued that the future paradise on earth could come only when all human needs were met. Only when this was accomplished, he believed, would all people finally be in a place where they could be receptive to God's will.[83]

Blumhardt's experience in Bebel's SPD was the pinnacle of his practical ethical mission. During these seven years, Blumhardt most explicitly attempted to model his ministry after that of Jesus Christ. He found a striking number of similarities between his own expectation for the kingdom of God and Bebel's and Marx's ideology. Of this similarity, he said at a socialist meeting in

81. Ibid., 2:161–62, 169, 257; Blumhardt, *Christoph Blumhardt*, 3:302.

82. Esche, "Reich Gottes," 33.

83. Ibid., 289–90; Blumhardt, *Ansprachen*, 2:288.

Göppingen, "No one should wonder when a man who belongs to Jesus stands by the working class today. Christ belonged to the poor. He was crucified because he was a socialist. He made twelve proletarians into Apostles. The people who say that I am abandoning God when I want to be a proletariat are only fooling themselves."[84] He saw in Jesus a fellow fighter against the spirit of capitalism. He testified to Jesus' radical socialism because Jesus revealed himself to everybody equally, and everybody had an equal share of his salvation. Here, Blumhardt's anti-hierarchical Christianity, which he had possessed from the earliest days in his ministry, found its ideology. Jesus the Proletarian Messiah did not need pastors or professors to regulate the people any more than Marx or Bebel did.[85]

During his political career, Blumhardt also believed he had a responsibility to negotiate between Christians and socialists. Following the lines of the socialist, he told his Christian listeners that the socialists were against neither belief nor religious conviction. They were merely against the institutional attachment to the state and against the destructive social relationship when the state and the church were combined. To the socialists, Blumhardt proclaimed that communism could only be built on a foundation laid by Jesus. Socialism had a footing and a potential only in the lands of Christendom; Asia and other countries of the world were neither ready for nor capable of a socialist revolution. The unique quality that made the West ripe for a socialist revolution was its foundation on the Christian belief that all humans were equally loved by God and given an equal amount of grace in salvation. For these reasons, Blumhardt concluded that Christianity and socialism were fully compatible beliefs.[86]

However, this marriage of Christian belief and socialist dogma was a hard sell. From early on in his political career, questions about his beliefs came not only from the state church that had defrocked him, but also from his political comrades. Some socialists questioned Blumhardt's combination of religion and Marxism. In an article concerning one of his campaign speeches, one socialist wrote, "At the end, Blumhardt gave a picture to the comrades, of what a true socialist should be. That Blumhardt's portrayal indicated that the socialists were still far away from their goals will not please every Social Democrat listener. Is Blumhardt the one who can bring the Party to these goals? On his earnest and selfless conviction there can be no doubt, but there certainly are questions about his eventual success. He seems to take people too much as they *ought to be*,

---

84. Blumhardt, *Ansprachen*, 2:184.

85. Ibid., 2:194; Blumhardt, *Christoph Blumhardt*, 3:302.

86. Ibid., 3:445–46; Blumhardt, *Ansprachen*, 2:166, 186, 189, 272, 279.

rather than how they *really are*."[87] Blumhardt's views on his party showed that he also felt this division between the socialists' practicality and his own idealism. In dinner discussions at Bad Boll, he commented about his political colleagues:

> The German Social Democracy does not offer us any particularly pleasing option. They lack the love of their enemies. They are practical enough; their problems lay more in the theoretical. One should always think and speak like the Party. It is a lot like the church. As it is now, I do not expect anything from them. The movement to love one's neighbors must come from the people. They will decide that it must never come to violence. Every now and then you can box the ears of a friend, but never an enemy! One must say truth to an enemy with love! Then be silent! Never fight with violence![88]

The original questioning of Blumhardt's perspective by some socialist party members erupted into a full-blown skepticism of his religious socialism during his tenure in the provincial legislature. By late 1904, he was obligated to stand at a meeting of the Social Democratic Party and defend his party loyalty and his adherence to the party platform. The socialists accepted his explanation of his political viewpoints, but from his sermons, it became clear that he was beginning to separate his political and religious expectations for the kingdom of God.[89]

In September 1906, Blumhardt announced that he would not seek a second term. Letters he wrote in the following years indicate that although he no longer coupled religion and politics, he also was not embittered by the socialists. He continued to see them as the best possible political option, and he remembered his time in the Württemberg Parliament positively. But his preaching concerning the social ills of his time changed radically after his departure from the legislature. After he left politics, his sermons began to emphasize humanity's helplessness in trying to resolve the world's social problems. How different it sounded from his socialist years when he said, "No one can change the human society one iota, unless the light of the Kingdom of God is already shining in. In today's emotional times, everybody has become very tired of searching for new life in the social questions, even working on the foundation of Christendom, they believe that nothing can be done . . . frankly it

---

87. Blumhardt, *Ansprachen*, 2:219. Emphasis in original.
88. Ibid., 2:314–15.
89. Ibid., 2:317–19, 332.

cannot be done by us, but only through the light of God."[90] After Blumhardt's departure from the SPD, his focus shifted away from the belief that the kingdom of God could be grounded in human activism.[91]

With the exception of his criticism of the war, his prophetic career critiquing Christianity and society as a whole was also largely laid to rest. However, like the last twenty-six chapters of Isaiah, where Isaiah's prophecy of Israel's impending destruction became a prophecy of Israel's salvation, Blumhardt's message changed to one of hope for the future and for God's salvation of humanity. Although Blumhardt never lamented his participation in politics, he came to the point where he acknowledged that the effort did not accomplish what he originally had hoped. As a devoted prophet who discovered his prophecies unfulfilled, Blumhardt reappraised his message and found a new wonder for God's grand plan for the world.

POST-POLITICS ETHICS

The final decade of Blumhardt's ministry was a return to his ethical roots. His call to action grew more passive. Instead of holding followers of Christ responsible for enacting God's plan for the world, he adopted a reformed vision of God. He portrayed God as the principal actor in history. Christians were fortunate merely to be used by God for the divine plan. God was beholden to bring out the goodness of humans that was in them because they were created in God's image. At this point in his life, he challenged his listeners to wait for God to show them their own godliness as well as that of their neighbors. He thought it impossible without this enlightenment to follow Christ and to worship him truly. Once a person's godliness was clear, then it was easy to love him or her. With the right perspective, Blumhardt encouraged his listeners, love of neighbor became a simple commandment.[92]

During these years, Blumhardt preached that the principal role of the disciple of Christ was to wait in preparation for the call of God and to wait for God's kingdom. Whereas earlier in his ministry, he called for immediate action, first from the church and then from political institutions, his later preaching called for the church to wait for God to initiate the actions that would save the world. Waiting for God became his principal ethical encouragement. He preached, "Waiting is a significant act. To wait, in every darkness, in the cruelest death, where the most painful and forlorn cries arise: that is where the

---

90. Blumhardt, *Christoph Blumhardt*, 4:174–75.

91. Ibid.; Blumhardt, *Ansprachen*, 3:1–2, 7–8.

92. Blumhardt, *Christoph Blumhardt*, 4:15–16.

Son of Man will come! . . . But we must be waiting: we must have the strength to wait; to wait in hope and to struggle with the world."[93] In this final phase of his ministry, Blumhardt bestowed upon God the duty to initiate the coming of God's kingdom, and his ethics paralleled this new passivity.[94]

While he saw waiting as dependent upon God's action, it was not an inactive state where the Christian no longer had responsibilities in the world. In Blumhardt's preaching, waiting was still coupled with acting and responding. The difference, though, in this later separation was that the result of discipleship was less clear than it had been earlier in his ministry. Discipleship meant trusting to God's leadership even when God's goals were not clear. It seems at this point Blumhardt was satisfied with his past actions. It had been right for him to advance into politics, despite the result that God did not reward him with the kingdom coming through his political pursuits, as he had expected at the time. The earlier agitator of discontent for the world spoke of the quality of a disciple's contentment at Bad Boll in 1908, saying, "So many believers complain today, the present unresolved world does not please them anymore. But, I have never heard a true disciple ever complain."[95]

Late in his career, he continued to preach that God expected his disciples to follow Christ's example of loving their enemies, forgiving others of their transgressions, and helping others in their distress. He also began to reassert the importance of evangelism, mission work, and communicating the gospel to the lost. He still held to the universalism and predestination that had marked his time in the SPD, but he began to state more clearly than before that it was better when people knew that the work they were doing was for God. Living out these simple mottoes was what he saw as the mark of true discipleship in his last decade.[96]

Blumhardt in his final years even tempered his critique of the church. He noted that the church still possessed a role in the proclamation of the gospel to the whole world. The church had a unique duty and a unique place that were never eclipsed by political parties such as the SPD. He encouraged his nephew to join the pastorate and wrote to him that the church was still the bearer of God's will. He asked his nephew, Who else takes on the responsibility for the proclamation of the gospel to the lost in the world? His view of the church in these years had softened dramatically since the zenith of his criticism of the church late in the nineteenth century. He was again proclaiming the unending

93. Ibid., 4:14.
94. Ibid., 4:15–16.
95. Blumhardt, *Ansprachen*, 3:25.
96. Ibid., 3:24–25, 121; Blumhardt, *Christoph Blumhardt*, 4:47.

victory of the church. He was heard saying once again that Jesus Christ would prevail through the triumph of the church.[97]

It was not merely coincidence that led Blumhardt to use a catchphrase of his father, "waiting and rushing" (*Warten und Pressieren*), during his postpolitical career. Indeed, his final phase of preaching was colored by a return to his father's emphases and style of ministry. This phenomenon was all the more remarkable due to the decisive and intentional break he had made from his father during his stint with the SPD. By the end of his life, the younger Blumhardt returned to a diffident respect for his father. His sermons returned to a focus on Bad Boll as a retreat from the world, a pocket of holiness separated from the outside sinfulness. He once again began to rouse up the expectation for personal miracles in the life of his congregation. These miracles were the fuel for the belief that God is capable of all things.

Even in his very last sermons, Blumhardt held fast to the expectation of the imminent arrival of the kingdom of God. Even though the type of preaching and ethical motivation had changed over the years, the goal of God's kingdom remained permanently in the forefront of Blumhardt's teaching. To the end, he continued using his father's other main aphorism, "Jesus is victor," and this victory would culminate in Jesus' transformation of the world.[98]

CONCLUSION: BLUMHARDT AS AN EXAMPLE OF THE POSSIBILITIES OF BELIEF IN LATE-NINETEENTH- AND EARLY-TWENTIETH-CENTURY THEOLOGY

Typically, historians of Blumhardt have focused on his active years in the SPD to gain a picture of his theology, ethics, and portrayal of the kingdom of God. For many reasons, this was often the best method available. Historians covered the development of his social activism because Blumhardt's politics so effectively inspired others to seek a similar active role as Christians pursuing social justice. Many of these same scholars downplayed the details of his theological development, because theologically speaking, Blumhardt never started a school of thought or had well-known disciples. After all, Blumhardt was far too unsystematic to have people follow his theology, but he was charismatic enough to have people follow his actions.

However, this research perspective turned Blumhardt's last decade of ministry into a mere epilogue in most histories and overlooked Blumhardt's theological advances over his last years. At the end of his life, he was a more

---

97. Blumhardt, *Ansprachen*, 3:132: Blumhardt, *Christoph Blumhardt*, 4:329, 332–33.

98. Blumhardt, *Christoph Blumhardt*, 4:23–24; Blumhardt, *Ansprachen*, 3:93, 201.

mature leader, more understanding of human weakness and more capable of comforting those who were suffering. These qualities came out most remarkably in his handling of the First World War, which will be discussed in depth in chapter 7. Blumhardt's optimistic view of history and his expectation of the kingdom of God helped him console his listeners at Bad Boll as they struggled with immense suffering and loss of life.

Blumhardt's biblical realism built a hodgepodge theology from the most diverse elements in German religious belief that more than made up for his lack of systematic thought. He began with a sensual, experiential understanding of God the Father and the Holy Spirit. His personal experiences authenticated the veracity of the Scriptures for him and justified their continued importance in the modern world. He bypassed the foundation of biblical hermeneutics being debated by the day's brightest conservative scholars. Instead of merely building a defense of the Bible's historical authenticity, he went so far as to argue that God was still dynamically revealing God's self to modern-day apostles and prophets. He was so confident in his method of biblical interpretation that he felt neither the need to defend it nor the desire to ground it in any explicit philosophy. He turned his archconservative interpretation of the Bible to the quintessentially liberal principle of the ethical, universal kingdom of God. This unusual combination led him even to break with both theological traditions to find a home in the Marxist SPD. He found the true pursuers of this ethical millennium in the Social Democratic Party.

Only when even the most zealous communists were shown incapable of living up to or establishing the kingdom of God did his theological framework shake. Instead of losing all faith in humanity and in his entire system, he began with renewed vigor to find God's message to God's people in the new century. He ended with his most profound (and paradoxically for Blumhardt) most passive discovery. He could remain fully confident in God's direction and plan for God's creation and kingdom even in the midst of the full destruction of the previous century's progress by a few months of war and in the midst of his own uncertainty about God's specific actions.

Even though Blumhardt had little noticeable effect on the widely held theological beliefs of his day, he showed the breadth of possibility and the diversity of opinion within the believing Protestant community. He showed that conservative Protestants of his day were not merely fighting to keep ground against the advancement of theological and political liberalism. They, too, possessed an aggressive agenda of social action. He demonstrated that pietists and conservatives of the period were capable of a self-critical appraisal of the church and of their cherished dogmas. He testified to the possibility of Protestants forming a loyal opposition to the administration of the state. Blumhardt's loyal opposition manifested itself both in his advancement in the ranks of the opposition Social Democratic Party and in the admission of Germany's responsibility and guilt for the First World War. As the war ended and the exodus of the masses out of the church increased, those leaving could have pointed to Blumhardt's tradition to testify that the church need not have been the unquestioning supporter of the state in imperial Germany.

6

The Friends of Job
German Sermons, 1888–1914

By the beginning of the First World War, the believing theologians developed an effective community and apparatus for political influence through the work of Adolf Stoecker and the other court preachers. Through Kähler, Schlatter, and their ally Hermann Cremer, the believing theologians had a plastic, able theology that responded creatively and powerfully to the threats of modernity. In Stoecker and Blumhardt, they had a class of celebrity preachers who were able to give examples of creative preaching utilizing this subjective, devout belief in a world of skepticism and challenges from socialists, liberals, scientists, academics, and print media.

The politically active wing of this movement made a calculated risk to invest these resources in making certain that the clergy remained orthodox. They had lost the ability to dictate the orthodoxy of the theological faculty. Initially, challenges to orthodoxy were banned from theological faculties. Popular outrage and activism by clergy forced leading biblical scholars such as D. F. Strauss and Julius Wellhausen out of theology faculties and into philosophy or philology departments. As the century wore on, however, the liberal school of Albrecht Ritschl and Adolf von Harnack so dominated the field that theological liberals could no longer be excluded from all theology departments. Conservative faculties sequestered themselves at Erlangen and Greifswald, while theological liberalism reigned supreme at most other universities. To protect the upcoming clergy, the leadership of the state church used its influence to spread the believing faculty to the broadest number of universities. Instead of creating a separate, fundamentalist culture in a few faculties, they chose to require representation of believing faculty. The logic presumed that if conservative theologians were at each institution, then the largely conservative theology students would be reaffirmed in their traditional faith. Furthermore, the influence of the conservative church hierarchy would exercise its authority over candidate pastors to keep heterodoxy out of the parish church. The church leaders therefore gambled that believing theology would thrive and be victorious within the state church over the opposing critical theology in university faculties, rather than through a decisive fundamentalist break, as happened in America.

If this plan were successful, it should follow then that the sermons of the pastors coming out of the universities would bear markers of the conflict between believing and critical theology that the competing faculty members played out before their eyes. This chapter puts this logic to the test by inspecting and analyzing the theology and biblical interpretation of sermon makers during the reign of Wilhelm II. The results of the church leaders' gambit had, at best, mixed results, and then only at the end of the era. Generally, the influence of either critical or believing theology was lost behind traditional Lutheran platitudes and nationalist enthusiasm.

This and the next chapters look at the relative failure of believing theology to incorporate itself into the culture of churches in Germany. While the attempt on the part of church hierarchy to limit the influence of theological liberalism seems to have succeeded at keeping critical scholarship out of churches, the church culture failed to adopt the positive changes that the theology of Schlatter, Kähler, and Blumhardt offered to adapt to modernity.

In 1890, Pastor Paul Langbein of Würtingen published a collection of historical sermons. Langbein meant this anthology for popular devotional reading at home. He believed that the sermons were as true for his readers as they were to their listeners on the day they were preached. Included in the collection was a sermon by the late general superintendent of Celle, Dr. Max Frommel, who had delivered it following the successful victory over the French at Sedan in 1870. It read nearly identically to the sermons being preached by Adolf Stoecker elsewhere in the empire. The sermon summed up the religious fervor following that battle. For Frommel, the Franco-Prussian War was principally spiritual. God had determined its results even before the fighting took place. Frommel told his listeners that the French could blame their ignominious defeat on the judgment of God. Frommel and many other German pastors who followed him believed that Germany's future success would be proportional to its citizenry's faithfulness to God. If the people remained true to God, Germany would continue to advance and succeed in the world. France's defeat was to serve as an example to Germany. If Germans abandoned their calling as a Christian people, they could expect a defeat at least as horrible as that which France had received.

Frommel proclaimed that war originating from human greed and pride was sinful. France's aggression against Germany was one clear example. In France's case, God's judgment was shown when God turned their warmongering sin against them. Speaking of the war, Frommel said, "Let us not believe that God gave us the victory because we are in some way more God's people than the French due to our piety and morality. . . . Everyone with eyes can see Germany's own idolatry of the self. . . . However, we may say, and we desire to say: God built one more dam against the flood of the Revolution to protect his holy [political and social] order. For this, every Christian in every nation ought to thank him."[1] France's defeat was both a blessing for God's people and a warning to those who had abandoned God.[2]

The desire of revolutionaries to overturn the God-given social and political order mystified Frommel. The long-standing social order flowed naturally from God's love. Order and peace were characteristics of God.

Frommel praised God for victory over France, noting that God's message of judgment on the evil of human pride was clear. God's role in upholding German order was indubitable to him and countless other devout believers. He warned his listeners to be vigilant in their continuing support of God's order and God's gospel to assure Germany's continued blessing. He admonished Protestants to block Germany's growing religious apathy. He concluded with these words: "Therefore, O Germany, you beloved land, you nation of our fathers great and mighty. You were once known as the land of the faithful, the army of the Gospel, from which the faith's flames spread through the world. From the farthest north to the distant west, you were nurtured from God's miraculous hand. O nation, nation, hear the Word of the Lord: Blessed is the land, whose God is the Lord!"[3] Frommel was confident that when Germans recognized God's blessings of 1871, they would turn in prayer and love to their God and creator.[4]

Frommel poetically put into words the driving theological message of pastors in late-nineteenth-century sermons. These pastors proclaimed that individual Germans and indeed the whole German state stood at a crossroads.

---

1. Max Frommel, "Am Vaterländischen Gedenktag," in *Evangelisches Haus-Predigtbuch: Eine Sammlung auserlesener Evangelien-Predigten aus alter und neuer Zeit auf alle Sonn-, Fest- und Feiertage des Kirchenjahrs*, ed. Paul Langbein (Reutlingen: Enßlin und Laiblin, n.d.), 1095.

2. Ibid., 1094–95.

3. Ibid., 1100.

4. Ibid., 1099–1100.

One path continued the growing trend away from the Christian faith of their forebears, but it led to an impending doom. The other road was for Germans to repent from sin and return to God's lordship over their state and their personal lives. The clergy promised that the right decision would bring blessings unheard of in the modern world. Their theology of blessings and curses dominated the church's ethical teaching for the whole generation preceding the First World War.

German Sermons at the Beginning of the Effectiveness of Kähler, Schlatter, and Blumhardt, 1888–1895

Hierarchical structures and an archaic rhetorical style had calcified German sermon making in the late nineteenth century. These stylistic relics of a bygone era proved impervious to the efforts of Schlatter, Kähler, and Blumhardt to modernize the sermons of believing pastors and motivate German Protestants to lives reflecting their gratitude to God. In the end, the prejudice of class privilege and the weight of the Reformation tradition gave the pastoral institution too much inertia to be flexible in the face of a rapidly changing society in late-nineteenth- and early-twentieth-century Germany. Although Kähler and Schlatter attempted to provide their students with alternative models that were more useful for contemporary theology, their direct influence can be seen in only a minute portion of the students who studied under them. Despite Blumhardt's celebrity, his example found few followers. As a result, German Protestantism relied on ministers whose sermons implied a stratified society, an authoritarian church, and a God whose generosity was tied directly to the nation's obedience. As Germany democratized and left the institutional church, the pastors' social conservatism proved unable to stem the tide. On the eve of World War I, Germany's believing ministers offered ineffectual sermons with few answers for modern problems. This set up a catastrophic finale as World War I offered a bloodbath that nobody expected and a defeat that no theologian could explain.

Sermon Sources and Methodology

Extant unpublished sermon sources are rare. This is unfortunate, since handwritten sermons are the best examples of typical sermons of the period coming from pastors of relatively little prominence or historical note. Pastors often wrote in shorthand, and few families preserved their collections, especially as the handwriting systems were reformed at the beginning of the twentieth century. This makes it nearly impossible to trace the thought of parish pastors over a long time. Nevertheless, one source provides a broad sampling of sermons. Some of the state church archives collected examination sermons from each of their clergy members.

To be ordained in the German state church, pastoral candidates were required to pass two examinations. The first came upon completion of university training, when the university faculty administered the test. Following the successful completion of the first theological examination, the students would enter a three- to four-year vicariate. During this training time, they received practical training on the art of pastoral care and practice in giving sermons. The second examination tested the candidate's preparedness for entering full-time, independent service to the church, sponsored by the state. The examinations tested theoretical knowledge with sections in theology, ethics, and Old and New Testaments, and they measured practical ability, based on a sermon, a catechism course, and an essay on practical theology. These examinations provide a glimpse of the period's art of sermon making as performed by those who were not among the church elite. Despite the limited number of surviving materials, they most likely give a more representative picture of German sermons from the era than published collections do. These sermons were by pastors who were writing their sermons week in and week out, applying the talents they trained during their four to five years of university education. Sampling sermons from the period has proven to be disappointing, although instructive. The majority of these theological candidates showed only a clumsy and faulty understanding of the modern ideas they had encountered while undertaking their university education.

The confusing cacophony of voices at the universities complicated this situation. Most schools had faculties with varying views. Some professors would be strict adherents to the newest critical ideas, others sought to find a mediating position, and still others defended the traditional doctrines of the faith. This combination of widely varying positions was enough to confuse the most able students. Furthermore, a lack of clear guidelines from the church hierarchy and widely varying doctrinal positions from one province to another removed all but the last vestiges of theological guidance and accountability for new pastoral candidates. Each province had an overseeing committee, which was responsible for determining when certain pastors were theologically unfit to shepherd a church. This defrocking occurred very rarely for matters of theological opinion (Blumhardt was thus disciplined for his membership in the Social Democratic Party). This atomized the provinces into a patchwork of autonomous parishes, some adhering only to the loosest definitions of Christian faith and others condemning such pastors. Generally speaking, liberal clergy pastored larger city parishes, and traditionalist clergy were prominently represented in small rural churches, but exceptions in both cases were common.

THE ART OF SERMON MAKING

The principal reason that churches did not become the battleground for theological opinion was the clergy. For the lion's share of clergy, the theological divides were less important than their social standing. The state-church pastors were figures of prominence in their respective communities, although they were often poorly paid. Since theological study was open to students from a broad background and considerable funds were available for college scholarships, the church was a common profession for those with social aspirations who might not have any particular devotion to the religious aspects of the church. These pastors would not have as great an interest in the ideas of modernity (or of the faith of the fathers) as they had in retaining the prestige and power of the church in the state.

For reasons such as these, pastors put as much emphasis thwarting threats to the social order as they did threats to right doctrine. The sermons and ethical writings of the time attacked revolution and the threat of Marxism. They praised the state and monarch and elevated the German sense of order and discipline. More than anything else, however, the sermons railed against the growing secularism in Germany that damaged the continuing authority of the church. Germany was a Christian nation, they said, and without the continued guidance of the church, moral anarchy loomed on the horizon.

German sermon oratory at the end of the nineteenth century was a finely honed and carefully taught skill. With the exception of length, sermons varied little regionally or through the years. University education for theology students included extensive training in pastoral rhetoric. In their education, the pastors were taught to outline the biblical text on which their sermons were to be taken. (Most pastors followed the state church's assigned passages for each Sunday.) The university faculty taught their students to first use the outline to determine the sermon text's message and its authorial intent. The sermons were not exegetical text studies, however; instead, the pastor was encouraged to find one single thought, a morsel from his study of the text, from which he could deliver a sermon. What resulted were sermons that combined theologizing and moral teaching. They often strayed far from the meaning of the text without really introducing the congregations to the meaning or problems of the text.

Certain characteristics were common among pastors of all stripes. For example, all sermons bore the same fundamental structure. They were based on an abstract religious principle (often starting from the essential Reformation doctrines instead of the sermon text) and developed into moral injunctions. However, even these conclusions usually remained abstract. They seldom identified or discussed particular sins, deferring instead to the individual consciences of their congregations. With the exception of a general condemnation of modern secularism, moral guidance was not associated with modern issues or problems. The abstraction of ideas and the lack of specificity in moral teaching made the sermons timeless. With little exaggeration, the spiritual teaching in sermons given in 1900 would have been welcome and understood by churchgoers in 1750. Such sermons were unable to aid parishioners in developing a theological understanding of their modern world.

Sermons commonly carried nationalist sentiment or indicated the pastors' growing sense of fear that religion was subsiding from German public life. They had, in other words, little direct interaction with the themes and problems of the principal university theological debates of the time, such as the character of Jesus' preaching of the kingdom of God, the critical appraisal of the Scriptures, or the modern interpretation of the life of Jesus.

THEOLOGICAL DEBATE IN GERMAN SERMONS

The debates over the place and interpretation of the Scriptures that was embroiling the universities certainly manifested itself in the pulpits. However, it was never as explicit as it was at the universities. The personal beliefs of the pastors, whether traditionalist or critical, did show themselves in certain aspects. Liberal pastors, for example, either separated themselves from the miraculous accounts of the Bible or removed those stories from the physical world of causation. As an example, some critical pastors recognized Jesus' resurrection from the dead as wholly spiritual. In their view, the eyewitness sightings of Jesus were simply visions that had no tie to physical reality. Others attributed the miracles of the early church to outpourings of enthusiasm that had psychological explanations.[5]

While critical sermons of this period rarely explicitly challenged the traditional doctrines of the church, the critical pastors did attempt to justify their own beliefs in light of church history. Liberal theological candidate Albert Dierolf built his sermon from the Reformation doctrine of justification by faith alone. However, he separated himself from the Reformation creeds. Belief, he wrote, appealing to the liberal sentiment of the day, was the knowledge that

5. Hermann Strasosky, *Wahl-Predigt über Apg. 8, 14-24: Gehalten am 9. Sonntage nach Trinitatis 26. Juli 1891, in der St. Pauli Kirche* (Hamburg: Rüter, 1891), found at Nordelbische State Church Archive, Kiel (NSCA), Bestand 94, lfd. Nr. 486, 4.

the individual's life lay in the hands of a loving God. Belief that saved was the certainty that God would not hold sins against the individual. "This trust [in God's forgiveness]," said Dierolf, "is the belief that the Apostle meant when he said, 'now, we are righteous through faith.' In this faith we have peace with God. This faith is not adherence to a collection of truths that we need to have to become children of God but to have peace in our hearts." For Dierolf, the liberals, with their abandonment of condemnation and doctrinal absolutism, were the true successors of the spirit of Martin Luther.[6]

Traditionalist pastors tended to be more outgoing in their convictions. They expressed their distrust of rationalism's influence on modern theology. Instead of defending their beliefs against the attacks of modernity, however, these pastors turned their scorn on critical scholars and pastors. They showed a distrust of academic thinkers and lumped liberal Christians in with the threat of secularism. Some went so far as to blame secularism on the rise of rationalist Christianity at the end of the eighteenth century.

In 1889, pastoral candidate Gottlob Berner saw the Christian message being eaten away from within. He opined, "Many of the so-called Christians are actually anti-Christian, or else unquestioningly on the track of the ideas and authorities of the time. The so-called Christians suffered from the question Pontius Pilate asked, 'What is truth?'" Obviously, for Berner, Christian truths could not be synthesized with the iconoclastic philosophies of the day. Five years later, Berner wrote his second examination. He once again used his sermon to question the philosophical outlook of his liberal colleagues. He railed against the simplicity and selectiveness of the critical Christian message. He began by quoting Jesus,

> 'I am come.' Notice this small word, 'I.' Jesus from Nazareth is the one who said it; he said 'I am the light of the world.' The light of the world is not the humanity or the love of neighbor, or any other idea that Jesus taught this dying world. The light of the world was the living Jesus. Jesus did not mean just a part of his person, but the whole person when he said, 'I am come to be a light to the world.' Not his teaching alone or his acts of love alone are the light to the world. It is the whole Jesus with his teaching with his acts of love with the history of his life, suffering, resurrection and salvation.[7]

6. State Church Archives, Stuttgart (SCAS), personalakte, A27 #503: Albert Dierolf.
7. SCAS, personalakte, A27 #197: Gottlob Berner.

For Berner, the only Jesus acceptable was the Jesus as literally interpreted from the word of God; to question this was to become one of the "so-called Christians."[8]

While issues surrounding Jesus and the miraculous caught the focus of the pastors, the character and origin of the word of God played only a minor role in the sermons of the period, considering the importance of this topic in the theological debates. The pastors referred to the Bible as the word of God to underscore the authority of their statements. In their sermons, however, they did not define those aspects of the Scriptures that made it the word of God, nor did they aid their listeners in scriptural interpretation. Surprisingly, of the selected sermons of the period, exhortations that the listeners ought to read and interpret the Bible for themselves were extremely rare.[9]

The sermons' lack of appeal to the Scriptures or to their authority stands out because of the importance of debates about Scriptural authorship and hermeneutics in the pastoral training of the time. Leading scholars on both sides encouraged their students to share these debates with their congregations. Questions about the nature of the Scriptures and inspiration appeared in some form on most theological exams. In answering the questions, students showed an aptitude to understand the historical Christian approaches to the Scriptures. Only a few showed significant ability to defend the Scriptures as the unquestionable word of God or to attack the theological foundations of the doctrine of inspiration. Students of both camps who defended their particular belief received better marks on the exams than those who simply recounted the historical manifestations of doctrines of the Scriptures.[10]

The foundation of ethical behavior was another point of conflict between critical and traditionalist clergy. Liberal clergy redefined the understanding of the Holy Spirit so that it was no longer considered an independent person of the Holy Trinity. Instead, the Holy Spirit was the spirit of God that was found in every person. It was the spirit of goodness and self-sacrifice for the good of

8. Ibid.; NSCA, personalakte, Bestand 25.01, lfd. Nr. 144: Friedrich Heinrich Gustav Paul Clemen.

9. SCAS, A27 #197: Gottlob Berner; Pastor Niese in Flensburg u. Consistorialrath Ahlfeld in Hannover, "Zwei Predigten beim Jahresfest des schleswig-holsteinischen Hauptvereins der Gustav-Adolf-Stiftung am 9. Und 10. August 1892 in Meldorf", (Kiel: Schmidt & Klaunig, 1892), found at NSCA, Bestand 94, lfd. Nr. 396,3; SCAS, personalakte, A27 #645: Nathanael Elsäßer; SCAS, personalakte, A27 #647: Theodor Elsäßer.

10. Johannes Weiß, *Die Nachfolge Christi und die Predigt der Gegenwart* (Göttingen: Vandehoeck & Ruprecht, 1895), 105; Niedersachsische Staats- und Universität Bibliothek, Göttingen, Cod. MS. Martin Kähler, Box 12: "Ansätze und Entwürfe," 16d, "Theologie," March 13, 1900, 1–3. For two excellent examples of exam answers, conservative and liberal, of the time, cf. SCAS, personalakte, A27 #197: Gottlob Berner; SCAS, personalakte, A27 #581: Wilhelm Eberwein.

others that rooted out the opposing spirit of selfishness. Liberals saw in Jesus the highest manifestation of the Holy Spirit. More than anyone before or since, Jesus understood that individual lives lay in God's protection and care. Jesus also taught humanity that God would lead the surrendered soul well because every person was a child of God.

Because Jesus had this unequaled connection with the Spirit of God, he was endowed with particular wisdom, and his example would continue to guide Christians. Liberals taught that as individual Christians imitated Jesus's spiritual lifestyle, they would develop a love for God. According to these pastors, the purpose of ethics was to create a place of stillness in the heart in a world of pressure and difficulty. With this, they placed a greater emphasis on the motivation of the heart to be godly and devalued the correct knowledge of doctrine or Scripture. The result of the ethical life for critical pastors was truly liberal. They hoped to be liberated from the desire to sin. The love of God offered hope and power to overcome all evil motives in their lives.[11]

The conservative motive for ethics centered on the love of Christ. This love was born out of gratitude to Christ for the atoning sacrifice on the cross. Jesus was more than an example of how to love God; his sacrificial atonement was the direct act of a loving God. True freedom from sin for conservative pastor Adolf Kuhlgatz could come only from a direct action of God—and the sacrifice of God's divine and sinless son. He contended that a belief in God that truly accepted forgiveness for sins necessarily accepted the highest view of Christ possible—namely, that he was fully divine as well as fully human.[12]

ETHICAL TEACHING AND NATIONALISM

While the ethical motivations differed between traditionalist and critical pastors, the ethical mandates they offered their congregations were similar. The majority of ethical teaching in the sermons remained abstract, presumably so it could be applicable to all members of the congregations. Pastors praised the return and repentance of prodigal sons to loving fathers. They lauded families of peaceful and nurturing homes. To individuals, they encouraged the prevention of sin and the defeat of temptation. The virtue of repentance was likewise universally admonished. The idea of a life changed for the better held universal appeal. Certain specific actions were clearly understood as amoral by all clergy: thievery, lying, waste, and hedonism.[13]

11. Strasosky, *Wahl-Predigt*, 3, 9; SCAS, personalakte, A27 #503: Albert Dierolf; SCAS, personalakte, A27 #41: Paul Heinrich Andler; SCAS, personalakte, A27 #27: Gotthilf Nathanael Adolf Ammon; SCAS, personalakte, A27 #1260: Hermann Viktor; SCAS, personalakte, A27 #581: Wilhelm Eberwein.

12. SCAS, personalakte, A27 #100: Johannes Bauder; SCAS, personalkte, A27 #698: Adolf Kuhlgatz.

Like Frommel and Stoecker before them, German pastors at the beginning of Wilhelm II's reign warned that God's blessing would remain only as long as Germany was careful to protect its religious heritage. Universally, the pastors looked with suspicion at their contemporary religious culture. The German clergy had a strange ambivalence about the moral character of their people. On the one hand, they were the spiritual heirs of Luther and Gustavus Adolphus. This showed itself in God's blessings seen in Germany's victorious political rise to preeminence on the continent, the piety of its monarchs, and the success of its industry. On the other hand, the growing moral decay shown in the decadence of the rich, the intellectuals' mockery of all things religious, and the general apathy toward Christianity found in the population as a whole flummoxed the German pastors. All in all, they saw such irreligion as a remarkable lack of gratitude to the God who had brought them such wealth and political success.[14]

The pastors warned against the culture's growing apathy toward discerning between religions. They were appalled to see some voices in the culture arguing that all Christian confessions and, indeed, all religions were equally valid. They implored their hearers to reject such religious indifference. Religion, they argued, required the whole determination and participation of every person. Its differences were matters of eternal life or death and could not be shrugged off in the pursuit of wealth and power. These pastors reminded their listeners that the church and state were a unity in Protestant Germany. The unity of Germany demanded the unity of confession within its borders. Peace and prosperity depended on the success of Protestantism.[15]

Protestant conservatives emphasized their confessional heritage with respect to Catholicism. Fresh on the heels of Bismarck's unsuccessful *Kulturkampf*, the Protestant clergy continued to question German Catholic patriotism and Catholics' intentions toward Germany's Protestant majority. The Protestant mission organization Gustav-Adolf-Stiftung (Gustavus Adolphus Foundation), founded in the mid-nineteenth century, trained and financially supported Protestant clergy to move into Catholic countries, specifically the Austrian Empire. Although the foundation was intended principally to support Protestants already in these areas, the member pastors warned that their Catholic counterparts had devious intentions. They reminded

---

13. SCAS, personalakte, A27 #126: Karl Heinrich Paul Baumgärtner; SCAS, personalakte, A27 #100: Johannes Bauder; Strasosky, *Wahl-Predigt*, 5–6.

14. SCAS, personalakte, A27 #1553: Gustav Katz; SCAS, personalakte, A27 #1075: Eugen Häußler.

15. Paul von Zimmermann, *Zwei Predigten bei der 44. Hauptversammlung des Evangelischen Vereins der Gustav-Adolf-Stiftung* (Leipzig: Centralvorstandes des Evangelischen Vereins der Gustav-Adolf-Stiftung, 1890), 22; K. W. Doll, "Predigt," in *Gustav-Adolf-Stiftung*, 11.

listeners of the destruction Catholics had brought to Protestant territories during the War of Palatine Succession, as well as the destruction brought to Germany by Catholic armies in the Thirty Years' War. They recounted multiple tales of modern persecution of Protestants, as well as the papal acceptance of them. They were certain that "the world power in Priests' habits waited for an easy victory" over the northern Protestant states.[16]

Liberal pastors were every bit as suspicious of cultural trends as the traditionalist clergy. They lamented that the church, previously esteemed, was no longer looked to on questions of social importance. The critical pastors believed that Christians were unfairly judged as being closed to new ideas. They argued that the ethical ideals they found in Jesus' teachings not only paired well with any supportable truth, but also advanced the proper application of those truths. Hermann Strasosky, a liberal pastor in Hamburg, encouraged his listeners to boldly confront any person who claimed that Jesus' teachings were no longer applicable to modern knowledge. He claimed that when Christians boldly proclaimed their ethical beliefs, every open-minded person would acknowledge Christianity's superiority to any other moral teachings.[17]

Despite suspicion of religious apathy in Germany, sermons at the beginning of Wilhelm II's reign universally lauded the German nation, as Frommel and Stoecker had done more than fifteen years earlier. The German unification in the 1870s was unequivocally accepted as part of God's greater plan. Liberal pastor Hermann Strasosky used Germany as proof of God's goodness in history. Strasosky proposed that Germans might not have understood God's good plan when they suffered under the domination of Napoleon I and his nephew, but it was at exactly these moments that the German nation was born. He told them that under Napoleon I, the germ of a unified German mentality formed, and Napoleon III's pomposity sparked the successful war that forged the nations together into an empire.

Paul Clemen, a missionary in training and an ideological antipode to Strasosky's critical theology, also blended his national sentiment with his theological understanding of history. He argued that Napoleon's occupation of Germany was God's punishment for the German rational Christianity of Lessing and Reimarus. God brought the armies of France through Germany because German Christians rejected the Bible as God's word and refused to acknowledge Jesus' divinity. Both camps, despite their opposing prognosis of the events of history, believed that God had a specific plan for Germany directly related to the spiritual health of its Protestant Christians.[18]

16. Doll, "Predigt," 1; von Zimmermann, "Predigt," 25; Niese, *Zwei Predigten*, 2, 8.
17. Strasosky, *Wahl-Predigt*, 2.

The general praise for German military success spilled over into spiritual metaphors in the sermons. Several pastors compared faithful Christianity to military service. The Christian, like the good soldier, needed to be disciplined and ready for sacrifice. Good preparation and diligence in training promised a successful Christian campaign against their bitter enemy, sin. This spiritual soldiering also required accepting one's spiritual, social, and political superiors, with the ultimate submission being to God.[19]

These pastors carried over their theology of blessings and curses into the personal realm as well. They claimed that personal piety and faithfulness to God directly influenced success in life, business, and happiness. Lack of faithfulness led in turn to failure. Many pastors suggested to their congregations that if they were suffering or unhappy, they ought to reappraise their lives. They asked them to inspect their souls to see if they were living their lives fully for God. Though they would never suggest that it was universally true, they taught that God's punishment for sin would often manifest itself in personal suffering.[20]

In the sermons' critiques of culture, the pastors made a clear distinction between their church, or at least their congregations, and the sins of other Germans. They perceived a wall of righteousness and moral superiority for themselves over the rest of the population. German culture, especially in its evils, did not include like-minded Christians. Moral injunctions were aimed at congregations, but only at a personal level. Calls for repentance were made for the nation without directly connecting these calls to the sins of the parishioners. This trend continued up to the war; moral guidance for clergy in the late nineteenth and early twentieth centuries was not self-critical. Here Christoph Blumhardt showed his maverick nature. His sermons were readily open to self-criticism and questioning the motives of his congregation, although he likewise seldom confessed his personal failings.[21]

THE SERMONS DURING THE ASCENDENCY OF KÄHLER, SCHLATTER, AND BLUMHARDT, 1895–1904

While Schlatter, Kähler, and Blumhardt were becoming the leading figures of the believing community and gaining their greatest notoriety, they were still only making the smallest dent in the sermon-making culture of Germany.

18. Ibid., 8–9.

19. SCAS, personalakte, A27 #1553: Gustav Adolf Kaz; SCAS, personalakte, A27 #1075: Eugen Häußler; SCAS, personalakte, A27 #1645: Theodor Klaiber.

20. NSCA, personalakte, Bestand 25.01, lfd. Nr. 144: Paul Clemen.

21. Cf. SCAS, personalakte, A27 #1311: Richard Hildenbrand; SCAS, personalakte, A27 #197: Gottlob Berner.

The changes in sermon culture in the following decade were minor. The most important themes from the beginning of the reign of Wilhelm II continued unabated. The rhetoric of the sermons relied heavily on sentimentality and, at times, awkward turns of phrase in an attempt to find a Wilhelmine religiosity in the Christian message.

CONSPICUOUS ABSENCE OF THEOLOGICAL CONFLICT

The sermons of this era still were mired in a conspicuously middle-class language that praised German culture. In appealing to the kingdom of God, poet and pastor Otto Gittinger mused, "What is the Kingdom of God? Answer: it is the community of God come to us, a piece of heaven in this poor world. If you seek it you will find it. Come to Jesus. He is the Kingdom of God, he is the righteousness." He then continued, after contrasting the riches of God to the poverty of this world, "Does that not call and move your heart? Can you remain cold and unfeeling without desire? Does not your heart burn when you see him from a desire to be like him? Would you not give all your money and all your possessions to live like he did, if you could die once as he did?"[22]

Such sentimentality of religious devotion could even go so far as to hypothesize wholly indefensible biblical interpretations. Pastoral candidate Friedrich Kübler ruminated on Psalm 19 to open his examination sermon: "The old Psalmist sat in a small chamber. He had locked the door tight behind him. His sins weighed heavily on him so that he could not find peace. He sat long in inner struggle until finally comforted he could cry out victoriously, 'The Lord will save me from all my sins!'"[23] Sermons delivered in Wilhelmine Protestant churches showed considerably more effort on the part of the pastors for verbal effect than careful study or clarity of message.[24]

Roughly one-third of the sermons were full of such obfuscation that the theological viewpoints of the pastors were indecipherable. With such theological disputes that raged between theological conservatives and critical thinkers, this was admittedly quite an accomplishment, since their viewpoints varied markedly on fundamental Christian themes like the resurrection, atonement, the value of the Scriptures, the foundation for the Christian life, and the very historicity of their faith. There could be several explanations for this theological uncertainty. One is that, since many of the extant sermons were

22. SCAS, handschriften, HS 22: Otto Gittinger, "Predigten 1899/1900," sermon given December 3, 1899.

23. SCAS, personalakte, A27 #1840: Friedrich Kübler.

24. SCAS, handschriften, HS 22: Otto Gittinger, sermon given December 3, 1899, 4; SCAS, A27 #1840: Friedrich Kübler.

connected to theological examinations necessary for receiving placement in the state church, the pastors might have felt encouraged to be vague in order to keep from offending any of their listeners, liberal or conservative. However, the examination sermons that were the clearest in their defense of their respective beliefs received consistently higher marks from the graders.

A second possibility is that the pastors understood the higher theological issues to be beyond the understanding of their congregations, whose members seldom had higher education. If this were the case, they would hide their sophisticated, complex understandings of theology and God from their simple congregations. This would explain why sermons were devotional instead of exegetical. This idea naturally suggests a plausible class-based suspicion that would have been likely in the nineteenth century. Germany's universities were in their heyday. Degree holders of all levels received unprecedented prestige in political and social realms. The pastors of rural parishes would have likely been the only person in the community with a higher education. They expected respect from their neighbors and enjoyed portraying themselves as esoteric and learned. Since the critical ideas of theological education were difficult subjects at the university level, they must have seemed far too complex for their rudimentarily educated parishioners.

Problems still exist, even with this explanation. With Harnack's *What Is Christianity?* selling unprecedented numbers of copies, a basic form of critical ideas must have filtered down even to the simplest Germans. A far more potent likelihood for the intentional avoidance of the schemes is not the inability of the people to understand the concepts, but the perceived inability. The class-based biases were notable even in those who did not share the practice of avoiding difficult subjects. Schlatter consistently referred to his parishioners in Kesswil-Uttwil as "his farmers," who had a simpler understanding of the world around them.

A final possibility was that the pastors did not fully understand the ramifications of the differing theological viewpoints. Indeed, some of the students, who generally learned the various viewpoints through rote memorization of historical theology, combined the varying viewpoints in an awkward mixture and were unable to present clear defenses of any one particular stance. They were unclear of how their university education fit into the proper pastoral care of their flock. And they were uncertain about how to incorporate it into the traditional liturgy and sermon format that had characterized German Protestantism for generations. Some combination of these last two possibilities must have played a role in every community where the critical questions of the Bible's character as the word of God were not discussed. For the health of the Protestant church, the deeper modern ideas were too central to the faith and too often the subject of their university education for pastors to simply ignore these debates in their professional careers. Nevertheless, this seems to be exactly the case.[25]

POLEMICAL SERMONS OF THE GEMEINSCHAFTSBEWEGUNG

However, stoking the coals of the critical-traditionalist debates were the seminaries of the burgeoning *Gemeinschaftsbewegung* (Community Church Movement). *Gemeinschaften* (literally, communities) were congregations formed within the auspices of the state church but in opposition to the growing liberalism of the universities and the urban clergy. The *Gemeinschaften* formed in close interrelation with the church in the more pietistic south, offering extra activities and mission opportunities for devout Christians. In the north, the *Gemeinschaften* grew as a denomination within the state church. They met weekly on Sunday afternoons to offer a conservative glance at the weekly text. The idea was that members would continue to attend the state-church services but would get their teaching from the *Gemeinschaften* preacher. The sermons coming out of the *Gemeinschaften* seminaries bore a polemical tone that paralleled the same phenomenon in the early years of the American fundamentalist-modernist debates. For these sermon makers and for the teachers at their schools, the defeat of dangerous theological issues received a much more consistent and one-sided treatment. Correspondingly, their students showed a clear, if predictable, understanding of the debates and incorporated them into their sermons.[26]

Some of the sermons delivered by *Gemeinschaften* seminary candidates and by guests at the schools revealed the disgust that these theologically conservative circles felt for modern biblical scholarship. In an Easter exam sermon in the seminary at Kropp in northern Germany, Carl Masius combined many of the

---

25. Cf. Weiß, *Die Nachfolge Christi*, 105–106. One excellent example of the simplification of sermons for the lesser educated came from Albert Schweitzer. Following the First World War, Schweitzer wrote a series of sermons in which he outlined the themes that would form the foundation for his philosophical work, *Civilization and Ethics*. Schweitzer simplified his concepts to an almost comical degree. These sermons are included in an English translation in Albert Schweitzer, *Reverence for Life*, trans. Reginald H. Fuller (New York: Harper & Row, 1969); cf. Albert Schweitzer, *Civilization and Ethics*, 3rd ed., trans. C. T. Campion & L. M. Russell (London: Adam & Charles Black, 1946).

26. Nic. Jessen-Thiessen, "Zur Geschichte der Gemeinschaften in Schleswig-Holstein," in *Lesebuch: Erlesenes aus der Geschichte der Gemeinschaften in Schleswig-Holstein*, ed. Manfred Tugemann and Hans Repphun (Bünsdorf: Verband der Gemeinschaften in der Landeskirche in Schleswig-Holstein, 2001), 12–13.

distinctive characteristics of sermons at the time and mixed with it a burning desire to purify Germany's theology. He argued that Germany had fallen back into the heathenism of its Gothic forefathers. Yet this heathenism was different: "This new heathendom is much wilder, more mean-spirited, more violent, rawer, and more impudent than the old one ever was. This one is worse because it had the truth and has fallen from it. This culture had the truth of the Word of God, but they walked away from it and fell back into the old lies, and they serve him who is the father of all lies."[27] Three students at the seminary in Kropp, Jurgis Purvins, Paul Clemen, and Richard Beuhsel, echoed Masius's warnings in their examinations about Germany's apostasy in the name of culture, honor, and science. They promised God's punishment if the country did not return to its earlier faith. Like Masius, these three identified the greatest threat to the tradition of faith in their country as the appearance of rationalistic Christianity that removed the supernatural elements from their faith.[28]

TRADITIONALISM AND NATIONALISM IN SERMONS

Sermon candidate Herman Breitweg's examination sermon in 1902 shed light on a characteristic of some conservative pastors in the state church at the end of the nineteenth century. His sermon was an example of an immaculately formulated service that eschewed modern religious idioms. His logic and theology were lifted straight from the Reformation and would have been at home in the sixteenth century. He elevated the word of God alongside Communion as God's sacramental means of creating community straight out of the theology of Luther and Melanchthon. The sermon was void of any mention of the particular issues of modern theology or the influences of the theological debates of the preceding century. Even as Martin Kähler's early work continued to build a systematic theology from the central tenets of the Reformation, some conservative pastors bound themselves to the defensible theology of the Reformation to avoid the weighty conflicts of the present.[29]

Nationalist sentiment continued to build during this period as well. Two examples were particularly poignant in the growing belief of German ascendancy and the close interaction of church, state, and the beneficent will

27. Carl Masius, *Wandelt wie die Kinder des Lichts! Predigt zum Examen Ostern 1900 im Predigerseminar zu Kropp* (Schwerin i.M.: Sandmeyersche Hofbuchdruckerei, 1900), found in NSCA, Bestand 25.01 lfd. Nr. 69, 4.

28. NSCA, Bestand 25.01 lfd. Nr. 69: Masius, *Kinder des Lichts!* 4–5; NSCA, Bestand 25.01 lfd. Nr. 391: Jurgis Purvins; NSCA, Bestand 25.01 lfd. Nr. 144: Paul Clemen; NSCA, personalakte, Bestand 25.01 lfd. Nr. 121: Richard Beuhsel.

29. SCAS, personalakte, A27 #327: Hermann Breitweg.

of God. Flensburg pastor F. Andersen gave his views of God's role in German history at a service dedicating a memorial church on the grounds of the First War of Schleswig's Battle of Idstedt that took place in 1850. In the sermon, he remembered the bitter loss by the German nationalist revolutionaries and the swift retribution from the Danish government, which he compared to the Babylonian captivity of the Jews. While he remembered the struggles of ethnic Germans following the war, he marveled at how God had thwarted the Schleswig Germans only to allow them a greater victory in 1864. He reminded his listeners (more than fifty years after the battle) to forgive their Danish neighbors and to avoid any desire for revenge. The new church built on the site of the bloody battle was to be a church of peace. Most importantly, Andersen hoped his congregation would take the lesson of Idstedt to remain true to their faith in difficult times. He told them, "This church should remind you. The purpose of life is not to be successful but to fulfill our obligations. Above all we are to retain our faith in God, even when thoughts of God seem only to be thoughts of suffering."[30] Idstedt reminded them of this because of their own history which he recounted:

> And then it came, the glorious end! The bells tolled the death of Friedrich VII, and it sounded like Easter bells. Wake up, get up! . . . Those who once abandoned you are now coming to free you. Then came the great moments of history one after the other. The day from Oeversee, from Düppel—where from the pain from Idstedt was quenched—: from Königgrätz—, there is Austria (once again God's judgment in history!) forced into a corner; the day of Sedan, and of Versailles—, until finally the German emperor's crown is awarded. And in all of this Schleswig-Holstein helped as a strong link in the chain. . . . Now it was there, the glorious end—God's thoughts were not those of suffering, but thoughts of peace."[31]

For Andersen, Germany's history was the triumphant story of God's enduring blessings.[32]

Otto Gittinger also memorialized the beginnings of the empire as a testimony to true faith. Gittinger used the final days of Kaiser Wilhelm I to

30. F. Andersen, *Gottes Gedanken in unsrer Geschichte verkörpert in der Kirche bei Idstedt: Predigt bei der Einweihungsfeier am 24. Juli 1903 gehalten von F. Andersen Hauptpastor an St. Johanis in Flensburg* (Schleswig: Julius Bergas, 1903), found in NSCA, Bestand 98.019 lfd. Nr. 1, 10.

31. NSCA, Bestand 98.019 lfd. Nr. 1: Andersen, *Gottes Gedanken*, 11–12.

32. Ibid., 6–12.

illustrate Christ's faithfulness unto his death in the Good Friday sermon of 1900. Gittinger encouraged his listeners' untiring faithfulness to their calling by reminding them of the kaiser's words, "I have no time to be tired" as he "shakily wrote his name with his last ounce of strength"[33] on a piece of legislation. The nationalism of the pastors elevated the kaiser who had accomplished the final unification of the German Empire to a status reserved for the saints of the faith.[34]

The Sermons of Kähler and Schlatter

Kähler and Schlatter, as university professors, had the possibility of the greatest impact on the art of sermon-making during their career. They not only instructing their students on the proper methodology for Biblical study in preparations for their Sunday services; they also prepared sermons on a regular basis to be given in the churches of the Halle, Greifswald, Berlin, and Tübingen. These sermons provided models for their young protégés.

KÄHLER

Kähler's art as a preacher differed greatly from his style as a teacher. Surprisingly, even as Kähler filled his teaching with sharply phrased opinions and marked convictions, his sermons were noncombative. They included none of the harsh tirades against the Catholics, atheists, and liberal Protestants that colored his lectures. Apparently, he did not wish to involve his lay listeners in the fine details of the day's theological disputes. Kähler certainly had marked skill as a poetic orator. His sermons possess an unmistakable rhetorical beauty. However, in his sermons, he avoided the controversial subjects he loved to debate in his lectures. In the pulpit, he stuck to the traditional themes of Christianity and saved his marked opinions about theological orthodoxy for the teacher's lectern.[35]

Certainly, his sermons were not devoid of theological partisanship. Although he did not actively expand on the current theological disputes in his sermons, his starting point for his sermons came from the perspectives he derived from his theological work. As in his theology, Kähler remained true to the traditional claims of Christianity and the miraculous accounts of Jesus Christ. He preached about Jesus' resurrection, miraculous works, ascension, and eventual return.

---

33. SCAS, handschriften HS 22: Otto Gittinger, "Predigt on Karfreitag."

34. Ibid.

35. SCAS, handschriften HS 22: Otto Gittinger, "Predigt am Osterfest"; SCAS, personalakte, A27 #269: Wilhelm Bochterle; SCAS, personalakte, A27 #382: Hugo Bunz.

In one of his sermons that was later published in the newsletter *Monatsblatt für die Diaspora in Oberschwaben* (Newsletter for the Diaspora in Upper-Swabia), Kähler explicitly worked to move the focus of his listeners away from the scientific viewpoints common in university theological departments. In this sermon, covering a text in which Jesus' disciples asked their teacher whether a man born blind was in that state because of his sins or the sins of his parents, Kähler said the disciples were asking a modern question, the academic scientific question of causality, namely, *why* did this happen?

Kähler observed that Jesus never answered the why question; instead, Jesus explained that the man's blindness would serve a purpose. He used this text to show that Jesus turned the scientific question of causality into a metaphysical statement: the man was born blind to show the glory of God. Instead of responding by answering the modern question of his disciples and ignoring the suffering of the blind man, Jesus helped the blind man and miraculously returned his sight. The historical questions of causality were important, but the questions of faith took precedence in Christianity. The overtones of the sermons were similar to the topics covered in his most famous work, *The So-Called Historical Jesus*. Jesus the teacher was superseded by Jesus the supernatural, superhistorical savior. Likewise, the conclusions Kähler drew from the text appealed to the subjectivism he so diligently worked out in his argumentation in *Unser Streit um die Bibel* (Our Struggle for the Bible). Yet it missed that work's clearly delineated justification for his subjectivism. The sermon lacked the broad picture of modern thought, both ultracritical and archconservative, given in his theological works and in his lectures. In lieu of this, Kähler's sermons provided a simple interpretation wherein he merely pointed to the dogmatic impact of Jesus' example without any explanation for his certainty about its continuing validity.[36]

Kähler's assessment of the modern world was largely missing within his sermons. He spoke of spirituality and the Christian life in abstract biblical terms that were not given in concrete modern forms. He freely spoke of sin and temptation within the world, but he avoided its specific evils. Although he freely gave his advice and direction to his students in all subjects, Kähler in his sermons concerned himself primarily with his parishioners' spiritual well-being, rather than their political or theological purity.[37]

36. Lower Saxony State and University Library, Göttingen, Cod. MS. M. Kähler, Box 11, #18.
37. Ibid., Boxes 11 and 15.

SCHLATTER

Sermon making remained particularly important throughout Adolf Schlatter's professional life. He continued to preach regularly, even after his appointment as professor. In fact, Schlatter recalled in his memoirs that he would never have agreed to leave the pastorate if Samuel Oettli had not presented him with the prospect of continuing to preach after he became involved at the University of Bern. It is little wonder that he loved it, since he was a gifted orator. His sermons show that he illuminated difficult concepts eloquently and simply. During his final tenure at Tübingen, Schlatter rotated every fourth Sunday with other preachers at the university's theological chapel. His Sundays proved particularly popular with the chapel's attendees, student and nonstudent alike. He continued to preach there well after he ceased teaching at the university. Preaching the word of God from the church chancel was a lifelong passion for Schlatter.

Schlatter brought all of his themes and ideas from his major systematic works consistently into his sermons. In this, he differed from Kähler and the overwhelming majority of German Protestant clergy during his lifetime. He believed that even though he could not adequately address the debates in all their complexity, his congregation was capable of following and learning from Christian thought at the highest level. In this respect, Schlatter was a unique leader of the Protestant church in the early twentieth century. He felt free to address the ethical dilemmas that many in his congregations were facing. He used his sermons to question the comfortable lives of the modern materialist culture. He also boldly took on the false worship of some Christians. With all the trappings of spirituality, he believed that some Christians turned the focus of worship services on themselves—in effect, worshipping themselves instead of God. It is not clear whether Schlatter meant to point his rebuke toward liberal churches that no longer recognized the omnipotent and just God in their doctrine. He could have been speaking to a congregation that worshipped its own piety instead of worshipping God through sacrifice and acts of mercy; he attacked both practices in numerous sermons.

Schlatter used his sermons to question the modern faith in nature. It seemed to him that modern Germans continually demanded signs and wonders from God. When they saw these events, however, Schlatter noted that they bent over backward to find a natural explanation. He called such naturalism faithlessness and egotism. It arose out of the desire for humans to control their own destiny. According to the naturalist's logic, if the miraculous in the world could be explained naturally, then it could be controlled and manipulated. For this reason, Schlatter called for a new, modern reformation of the German spirit that would bring it back to the certainty of the word of God. Schlatter warned that nature is a cruel master. When the miraculous was removed from a person's will, and then, when nature failed to be manipulated, then all faith in something good in nature melted away. All possibility of seeing the benevolent hand of God was destroyed. Nature might indicate God, but it could never lead a person to God. For this reason, the modern human still stood in need of the revelation of God through his son, Jesus Christ. Schlatter made the contrast for his listeners: Jesus Christ offered hope in all trials and offered community in all human loneliness.[38]

Schlatter's sermons also addressed the liberal theology of some German Christians. He warned his listeners that religion without a divine and powerful Christ was empty and worthless:

> One cannot say it enough in our time: please do not find out what will happen when we separate humanity from Christ. We have tried it enough to find out what the result is. The answer is apparent. People become confused when they try to understand the glory of nature without the Lord.... What will religion become without Christ? Dreams and phrases. What will happen to our sociability without him? It will turn into a pursuit for trinkets that tickle one's fancy. What will become of our money and property? A worthless household full of stuff that helps with nothing, but can often destroy everything. What will become of our love? Egotism, even if it is perfumed egotism.[39]

Although Schlatter found himself in awe of the progress of modern society, he knew it could all evaporate into mist once the West stopped continually purifying and renewing its faith.

He particularly defended the bodily resurrection of Jesus. The critical theologians of the *Religionsgeschichte* (History of Religions) school were willing to admit that Jesus was resurrected from the dead. However, they argued (against the tradition of the church) that the resurrection was a spiritual resurrection and the resurrection sightings were visions. Johannes Weiss went so far as to claim that the New Testament narratives understood them as such. Schlatter could not accept this viewpoint and openly challenged it in

---

38. Adolf Schlatter, *Der Ruf Jesu: Predigten von D.A. Schlatter* (Stuttgart: Verlag der Vereinsbuchhandlung, 1913), 180–85; Adolf Schlatter, *Predigten in der Stiftskirche zu Tübingen* (Tübingen: Schnürlen, 1902), sermon 4, "Landesbußtag" (March 1, 1903), 5–6.

39. Schlatter, *Ruf Jesu*, 35–36.

his sermons. He compared the ecstatic vision experience of Isaiah's calling in Isaiah 6 with the Gospel of Mark's narrative of the resurrection. Isaiah's image was larger than life and clearly unnatural, but Mark described the day and the surroundings in plain language. Schlatter integrated basic biblical criticism into his sermons to argue that Mark, at least, understood the resurrection sightings of Jesus to be natural in the most basic way. The resurrection of Jesus, according to Schlatter's sermon, was a natural phenomenon that took place in the physical world.[40]

One sermon, entitled "Wesen des Christentums" (The Essence of Christianity), deserves a closer appraisal. Certainly, Schlatter knew that his sermon bore the same title as two works that sent shockwaves through German Protestantism, both at the academic level and among a general readership. The first *Wesen des Christentums* (*Essence of Christianity*) was published by Ludwig Feuerbach in 1841. In this work, Feuerbach took on the whole tradition of Christianity. He claimed that Christianity (and religion as a whole) was created by the transference of human characteristics onto a "God" myth. Feuerbach stated that Christians were not worshipping God in their church services; they were worshipping themselves or at least a perfected version of themselves. The second *Wesen des Christentums* (*What is Christianity?*) was printed in 1900 by Adolf von Harnack. Although Harnack believed in the presence of an outside God and had a high esteem of Jesus Christ, his version of traditional Christianity was no less cutting. He defined Christianity as a religion with a pure ethical core that had added layer after layer of counterproductive tradition in the same way that pipes add layer after layer of residue until they can no longer function as they were intended.

Schlatter brought his own addition to *Wesen des Christentums*. He never named the works of these two previous writers in the sermon text, but their influence was certainly present both in his mind and the in the minds of his listeners. His text was John 10:22-30, in which Jesus' listeners confront Jesus, demanding him to state explicitly whether he is the Messiah. Schlatter looked at the text and stated that, by asking Jesus in the way that they did, Jesus' listeners made themselves judges over Jesus' claims as the Christ. They inverted the natural hierarchy and put themselves into God's authority. They demanded that Jesus make his plans clear so they could opt to choose him or reject him.

At that moment when Jesus's sinful listeners made the most outrageous claims, Schlatter said, Jesus acted decisively and magnanimously. He gave them the response he needed to give without bending to their expectations of him.

40. Ibid., 35–36, 306.

Then he stepped away from that crowd. Schlatter commented that Jesus did not need the crowd to validate his authority. He received his station directly from God. In this short dialogue, Schlatter argued that Jesus gave the true essence of Christianity (*Wesen des Christentums*). The essence was not where the people sought it (and certainly was not a creation of the human fantasy, as Feuerbach would have it). Jesus' incarnation as the Christ challenged their expectations and undermined their deepest-held convictions. Schlatter stated (in direct opposition to Harnack's pronouncements) that Jesus' purpose in his earthly, human ministry was to build a spiritual community that would last for eternity. Schlatter believed that Jesus clearly stated that Christianity was more than Harnack's moral code. It relied on the calling and the instigation of God. In response to Jesus' saying, "My sheep hear my voice," Schlatter told his listeners, "We do not build up our own certainty. We do not elect our own belief. We do not create our own Christ. We do not produce our own piety and religion through our own excellence. Everything begins with God. When he does not start everything, there is no progress and no completion."[41]

Christianity and the Christian faith, Schlatter told his congregation, were not the product of human effort or study, but the product of God's self-revelation. Schlatter proclaimed that Christianity was a religion of hope because it was a religion of revelation. He preached that Jesus came to reveal God to God's creation. Christianity was not the blind quest of humans to find God but the revelation of God through Jesus Christ as he is portrayed in the Bible.[42]

This sermon, like many others of Schlatter's, was not filled with specific practical examples of ethics and right behavior, but was a continual reappraisal of a theocentric religion focused on God's instigation and sustenance. This was Schlatter's popular answer to the anthropocentric definitions of Christianity from Feuerbach and Harnack. He returned to the reformed doctrines of Protestantism to state that Christianity was not measured by the acts of humanity, but by the grace of God. He knew that his answer would be unsatisfactory to both Feuerbachian and Harnackian apologists, but he perceived no need to address them explicitly in his sermons. He only responded to the need to rephrase and reappraise the traditional doctrines of Christianity for his listeners in confidence that they already had the relationship with God that would make his words ring true. In so doing, Schlatter attempted to redefine the *Wesen des Christentums* for the orthodox.

---

41. Ibid., 21.
42. Ibid., 20–21; Schlatter, *Predigten*, sermon 4, pp. 5–6.

Schlatter also used his sermons to address the specific subjects that interested and troubled his listeners. He took on the cultural impatience of modern Germany. He told his listeners that the modern world was fascinated and enthralled with death. A modern person pursued the heart's fancies and lusts of the flesh because the person could see only the imminence of his or her own death. Christianity offered a different picture. It promised a world where life is eternal and value is seen in the long, slow growth of the spirit toward godliness.

In similar terms, he took on the avaricious pursuit of wealth. As lives' focus turned to monetary wealth, Schlatter told his listeners, everyone's spirit yearned only for the workaday world. All the while, they missed the true treasures of life. These treasures were found in the eternal word of God. Schlatter promised his congregation that when they wrestled with and encountered the Bible, they would learn the true value of perfect forgiveness and love above the pursuits of worldly wealth.

Schlatter also encouraged more participation in the life of the church. Church offerings were more than monetary, he said. A member of the church ought to give money freely, but also ought to sacrifice time and effort to advance the saving work of the church. He questioned the growing pragmatic view of religion in the Germany of his day. Religion was seen as the ordering mechanism on which the social structure of Germany was constructed and because of which the power of German industry excelled. Yet, Schlatter warned his listeners, that faith was an end in itself, and it ought not be understood as the means to a better economy. Industriousness was advantageous, but he saw it as something to put into service for the church.

Schlatter used his sermons to make political points as well. During an election campaign, Schlatter used Jesus' teachings to contrast political pursuits. Jesus told his followers that whoever wanted to be greatest in the kingdom of God ought to be the servant of all others. Schlatter reminded his listeners that the politics of the kingdom of God were greatly different from the politics of the German Empire. This was a freeing truth he announced. The members of the kingdom of God had eternal security and no longer needed to worry about the status of their lives. They no longer needed to worry about governments that could take their lives. In all situations, economic, political, and ecclesiastical, Schlatter called his congregation to a steady, continual purification of their faith and called them to repentance in those moments where they failed God.[43]

In these practical applications, Schlatter painted the life of the true believer. A faithful Christian in his view was industrious and faithful in work and

43. Schlatter, *Ruf Jesu*, 45, 85–86, 155, 163, 220, 225–26; Schlatter, *Predigten*, sermon 4, pp. 2–3.

allegiance to church, state, and society. Yet he or she yearned for an eternal gratification of the desires of the spirit. A true Christian, in Schlatter's sermons, did not seek the wealth of the world but remained an active and helpful participant in it. As a guide, Schlatter offered the basic tenets of the Protestant faith: repentance of sins, interaction with the Scriptures, and prayer. He encouraged his listeners by reminding them that the first followers of Christ had to follow their lord individually. These early Christians faced the ridicule of the social and religious leaders around them. If the early disciples could show such fortitude, then modern believers could also hold to their Christian convictions. Schlatter acknowledged that Germany had also progressed to the point where Christianity was no longer the guiding principle of the nation. He encouraged his listeners that Christ still called brave individuals to follow him when they knew in their consciences that he was their salvation and hope.[44]

Schlatter did not break fresh ground with his sermons. They followed the same themes and ideas that were already present in his theology. As was seen in his teaching to his students, he believed that right doctrine led to right Christian belief and practice. His sermons show that he believed that his congregation also needed to have the highest level of preparation necessary to live the Christian life. His preaching testified that Schlatter saw no qualitative difference between the Christian who read and understood his esoteric work, the student in his classroom, or the layperson in his congregation. Schlatter believed that Christians of all levels were capable of understanding the word of God as the complete revelation of God.

SERMONS AT KÄHLER AND SCHLATTER'S HEIGHT OF INFLUENCE, 1907–1914

In the years leading up to the First World War, German sermon making experienced a renaissance. New influences from both the conservative and critical schools of thought inspired some pastors to change the face of sermon making. Critical pastors especially grew in their confidence to create explicitly modern sermons. They answered the sharp rebuke given them by Schlatter and others who claimed that, despite the power of academic theological liberalism, such theology was impossible to transfer into the pulpits.

SENTIMENTALISM

Some of the notable weaknesses of the earlier period lingered, however. A large number of sermons remained mired in sentimentalism. This tendency

---

44. Schlatter, *Predigten*, sermon 9, "8. Sonntag nach Trinitatis" (August 2, 1903), 3–4.

affected pastors on both sides of the theological divide. While some pastors followed Schlatter's and Kähler's modern defense of traditional doctrines and rallied around their interpretation of the Scriptures, those who continued in the pattern of sermon making from the late nineteenth century seemed to move even further into a shallow play of rhetoric. The certainty that one would expect in a church divided by fierce theological battles was replaced with a confusing ambivalence, and the pastors' ignorance of the issues was covered with sentimental recreations of biblical accounts and flights of fancy.

Some of the sentimentalism in the sermons of the period was used to emphasize the stark spiritual contrasts in modern theology. One such example came from liberal theologian Theodor Bungenberg. Although his sermons were fine examples of critical exposition, he used sentimentalism to shock his congregation into action. He wrote, "Even the warm, loyal heart of our savior, full of friendly, generous love showed in these words a painful, bitter anger—and **we** think we are supposed to use Jesus as an excuse for our ambivalence?"[45]

Liberals were not the only pastors to fall into sentimentalism. Conservative pastor Theodor Knolle of Wittenberg used sentimental illustrations to set the mood for his sermon on Easter 1913. He described the idyllic spring day with "golden glimmer that shined over the morning mist in the city of Jerusalem." To this he contrasted the dark feelings of the women heading to anoint their dead teacher. The preachers used sentimentalism as a rhetorical tool to initiate emotional attachment to their sermons. The practice was common, and extrabiblical flourishes to sermon texts were commonly used to aid a particular interpretation, conservative or liberal.[46]

NEW INFLUENCES: INNOVATION IN GERMAN SERMON MAKING

Critical and believing pastors alike continued to define the church as separate and at times as opposed to the larger and increasingly secular culture. They recognized that modern society gave Germans an increasing number of alternatives to the Christianity of their past. Pastors looked askance at the surrounding masses who rejected the proscribed Christian life. They also noted that many Germans who claimed to be Christians did little to show the influence of Christ in their lives. Modern science and philosophy created a new vocabulary for many to express their doubt. The city's cultural amusements competed with the church for the hearts of the populace. The pastors showed

45. Theodor Bungenberg, *Gleichnisse Jesu*, ed. E. Rolffs, Moderne Predigt-Bibliothek, vol. 9, no. 4 (Göttingen, Vandenhoeck & Ruprecht, 1912), 3. Emphasis in original.

46. NSCA, Bestand 98.011 lfd. Nr. 53: Theodor Knolle.

no patience with the objections they heard. They claimed that the doubt of modern Germans was insatiable. While Germans claimed they would believe if they saw a miracle, the pastors echoed Schlatter and retorted that the doubters would find a rational explanation for even the most exceptional miracles.

In all the modern demands for proof, pastoral candidate Felix Paulsen rebuked the skeptics for missing the miraculous all about them. He stated that everything that could be understood and explained by human reason was always marred by sin and sickness. The greatest miracles and mysteries of the universe were too great for reason to grasp. They were indisputable proof of the existence of an immanent God. Paulsen added that the greatest of these miracles, the resurrection of Jesus, showed a God who acted powerfully without flaw.[47]

These pastors noted wryly that many secular Germans were proud of their independence from the church. Clergy lamented that the modern rebellion against authority was built on a faulty understanding of freedom and independence. The modern man or woman claimed to be free from submitting to the authority of state, military, marriage, church, religion, morality, and education. Somehow they believed that this independence showed a greatness of character. The pastors warned that such hubris promised a world of chaos and self-destruction. True freedom, wrote Swiss pastor Robert Aeschbacher (whose confirmation courses inspired Karl Barth to study theology), was freedom from one's base desires. It was shown in self-control and sacrifice. If Germans gave up this freedom in favor of their own evil, warned Aeschbacher and others, then there would be social atrophy.[48]

Regardless of society's claims to superiority over Christian superstitions, the pastors posited that the give-and-take of philosophical claims made modern society nervous and unstable. Critical and conservative German pastors agreed that by abandoning the true God of Christianity, Germany opened itself to new gods and new ideologies that blew it this way and that. The German people lost their anchor and opened themselves to multiple evils and a new heathenism. Devotion to Jesus had protected society from its base desires, greed, and hedonism. The culture's rejection of Jesus in the face of scientific and philosophical objections let society devolve into materialism. Pastor Thomas

47. Ottmar Schönhuth, *Die Wunder Jesu*, ed. E. Rolffs, Moderne Predigt-Bibliothek, vol. 9, no. 3 (Göttingen: Vandenhoeck & Ruprecht, 1911), 16–17; Theodor Kaftan, *Von der Kirche: Predigt gehalten zur Eröffnung der Außerordentlichen Gesamtsynode der evangelisch-lutherischen Kirche Schleswig-Holsteins am 5. Dezember, 1907* (Schleswig: Julius Bergas, 1908), found in NSCA, Bestand 94 lfd. Nr. 80, 8; NSCA, personalakte, Bestand 12.03 lfd. Nr. 902: Felix Jacob Paulesen.

48. Robert Aeschbacher, *Ich lebe, und ihr sollt auch leben* (Basel: Friedrich Reinhardt, 1911), 399–400; Zentralarchiv der evangelischen Kirche der Pfalz, personalakte, Abt. III, Akt. 160: Emil Lind.

Breit (who would later gain fame as a coauthor with Karl Barth of the anti-Nazi Barmen Declaration) wrote in 1912 that as Jesus became less important, "things" became more central to modern people. Germans were abandoning the core characteristics of an enduring society—morality, piety, and humility—at an alarming rate. There was enough reserve left for this generation, but he feared for the following one. Friedrich Daur saw a particularly malevolent form of this materialism in Communist agitation. Communism fed on the dissatisfaction that grew from people's material inequality. He proposed the alternative of Christian faith. Christian contentment and trust in God for one's material needs were fundamentally opposed to the Communist goals and claims.[49]

Despite the continued motifs of the pastors against German materialism and amorality, their teachings bore a marked change from the earlier sermons. The newer sermons were moving away from the theology of blessings and curses that had so defined the first generations of post-unification German Protestantism. In these new sermons, God established moral order because it brought its own rewards. Amorality promised future catastrophe for its own evils, not because God would bring down curses on the people. In this new thinking, ethical proscriptions were gifts from God. God gave these rules because God knew that they would bring blessings to people. Thus, the blessings that came from ethics were independent of God's direct reward. God was still integral in this picture of ethics because God gave the believer and the society the power to do good.

For conservatives, this was a direct empowerment of God through the Holy Spirit. Liberal thinkers and those of the history of religions school saw this power coming from the example of Jesus and the spirit of sonship. The phenomenon that arose on both conservative and critical sides came from a changing emphasis on ethics at the university level. Schlatter's *Ethik*, published in 1914 but taught as a course for several years preceding its publication, certainly had low opinion of a theological outlook that saw the outpouring of God's grace and love in proportion to human obedience. This shift in sermon making was to be short-lived, however. The return of war brought with it the return of blessings-and-curses theology.[50]

49. Bungenberg, *Gleichnisse Jesu*, 5; Schönhuth, *Wunder Jesu*, 7; Wilhelm Lueken, *Die zehn Gebote*, ed. E. Rollfs, Moderne Predigt-Bibliothek, vol 9, no. 2 (Göttingen: Vandenhoeck & Ruprecht, 1911), 7–8; SCAS, personalakte, A27 #704: Heinrich Eytel; Thomas Breit, *Lieben, Leiden, Leben* (Augsburg: Schlosser, 1912), 22; SCAS, personalakte, A27 #460: Friedrich Daur.

50. Aeschbacher, *Ich lebe*, 401; Bungenburg, *Gleichnisse Jesu*, 12–13, 16; Schönhuth, *Wunder Jesu*, 6–7, 9; Lueken, *Die zehn Gebote*, 9; SCAS, personalakte, A27 #376: Adolf Bürk.

CLASH OF CULTURES

Specific admonitions for ethics followed familiar tropes in the years preceding the war. Sermons attacked the universally recognized failings of hypocrisy, disorder and rebellion, hedonism, hatred, and lies. The sin of greed was central to the sermons of the period. The pastors encouraged their congregations to display true generosity and sacrifice. They taught that generosity was not the same as a vow of poverty. Good Protestants ought to seek to provide for themselves and their families, but they also ought to aim to provide for the broader circles of their community. Some went so far as to call money the new idol of Germany. They claimed that Germans who praised themselves for abandoning superstition and freeing themselves from religious spiritual crutches had, in fact, only bound themselves to a new spirituality of avarice. True Christianity, they argued, was shown in a generosity of spirit and selflessness with possessions.[51]

Not all observations from the pulpit of the surrounding culture were negative. Certain aspects garnered the highest praise; for example, the royal family continued to be lauded for their Christian service. Württemberg pastoral candidate Karl Berckhemer used Wilhelm I as an example of godly leadership. He pointed to Wilhelm's humility and resourcefulness in granting Bismarck and Moltke authority over those elements of government at which they excelled. He continued heaping his praise on the former chancellor, stating that no Christian ideal could be said better than Bismarck's campaign slogan, "I offer myself to serve." Berckhemer tied these high leaders to his listeners, stating, "In exactly the same way the factory worker can be a ruler just like the king so long as they fulfill their calling faithfully." It must be noted that Wilhelm II never gained such praise from the pastors during his reign, but considering the overwhelming support of the imperial system, this was probably because he could not be canonized while he was still alive.[52]

Unlike his fellow members of the clergy, Berckhemer seemed little concerned that so many people were leaving the church. He argued that Christianity did not need to be observed in the church for it to be true religion. He stated that the greatest Christian truths had been absorbed into the German character and the German family. Those who rang the death tolls of Christianity forgot to notice the Christian character of Germans—their loyalty

---

51. Lueken, *Die zehn Gebote*, 8; Schönhuth, *Wunder Jesu*, 19; SCAS, personalakte, A27 #880: Adolf Gehring; NSCA, Bestand 12.03 lfd. Nr. 902: Paulsen; NSCA, personalakte, Bestand 42.07, lfd. Nr. 104: Martin Fischer.

52. SCAS, personalakte, A27 #192: Karl Berckhemer.

and good moral standards. So long as Germany remained strong, Christianity would live in the hearts of Germans.[53]

INNOVATION IN CRITICAL SERMON MAKING

Theological confrontation advanced to a new level in the pastorate in the decade preceding the First World War. Particularly noteworthy were the changes in critical theology. The development of the history of religions (*Religionsgeschichte*) school of thought in universities gave new inspiration to critical sermon writing. The writings of a young generation of theologians created new means of discussing religious experience without referring to the traditional interpretations of Christianity. The few years preceding the war saw a significant increase in liberal sermon publications, including the Göttingen-based *Moderne Predigt-Bibliothek* (Modern Sermon Library), and *Die Festpredigt des Freien Christentums* (Celebration Sermons of Free Christians), published in Berlin. The latter collection justified its publication as proof that modern theology could produce sermons of the highest level.

The history of religions school breathed new life into the ideas of Jesus' Messiah-consciousness and the development of his God-consciousness. In the last decades of the nineteenth century, Ritschlian liberals had demoted these ideas, originally developed by Friedrich Schleiermacher and D. F. Strauss, to levels of secondary importance theologically. The new methods of the history of religions school, coupled with the new ideas of psychology, brought these ideas once again to the forefront and gave pastors new tools to explain religion as a phenomenon of genius and spiritual consciousness.

The long-standing difficulty with these ideas was that they required a more subtle interpretation of the biblical passages, especially when members of the congregation knew the Bible as it was interpreted traditionally. The history of religions school's ideas of development in Jesus' thought and teaching came as much from the gaps in the story as from the texts themselves. At a theological level, the critical tools used to develop these ideas were sophisticated and persuasive; however, translating the ideas of Messiah-consciousness and God-consciousness to the lay level were difficult tasks for a pastor working with parishioners who were not familiar with textual criticism and did not spend their days analyzing the Bible.

An elemental change at the end of the nineteenth century and the beginning of the following century enabled liberal theologians to draft more effective sermons. Through these decades, the move away from close biblical

53. Ibid.

exegesis and the limited expectation that lay Christians would individually read the Bible paved the way for liberal efforts. The critical pastors felt free in their sermons of the immediate prewar years to change and reword biblical passages. As the scriptural texts from which the sermons were based became less central in the pastors' teaching, the onus of explaining why modern theology broke from the more easily understood literal interpretation of the Bible disappeared. The modernist pastors replaced the close study of the text in their sermons with sweeping systems of history that encompassed all religious experience. German Protestants were finally open to adopting new ideas into their traditional faith and their immutable liturgy.

Ottmar Schönhuth, deacon of Langenburg in Württemberg, used this technique to his advantage in his series of sermons on the miracles of Jesus. Most critical scholars were unwilling to attribute to Jesus supernatural control over the natural and physical cosmos, but that did not preclude them from acknowledging Jesus' special kinship with God and his control over spiritual matters. One of the first miracles recorded in the Gospel of Mark, the oldest gospel account, was the cleansing of a demon-possessed man in Capernaum. Schönhuth gave the passage his own interpretation in his sermon, filling in the gaps where the Bible claimed a miracle. The picture he gave was of an enraged man whose outpouring of wrath on Jesus led others to believe he was possessed by demons. This interpretation changed the whole meaning of Jesus' act.

For Schönhuth, Jesus showed his religious genius by remaining calm and collected through the event. His choice words cooled the situation. Schönhuth admitted that while there was no exorcism performed, Jesus' actions still showed an extraordinary leader and example for all Christians who followed. Schönhuth and other like-minded pastors emphasized that the miracles of the Bible were not evidence of Jesus's divinity, but were teaching tools, ways to clarify the message of his teaching. This sort of extrabiblical logic and reinterpretation of the miraculous in the Bible—which critical scholars had used since the earliest biblical criticism—finally matured in sermons during the last years preceding the First World War.[54]

STATE-CHURCH REACTION TO CRITICAL THEOLOGY

Even as the critical pastorate was coming into its own, the churches in Germany forced them to walk a finer line on issues of the Scriptures and doctrine. In 1892, the church in Württemberg excommunicated Christoph Schrempf for refusing to state the Apostles' Creed at a baptism. Shortly thereafter, Adolf

---

54. Schönhuth, *Wunder Jesu*, 2, 4.

Harnack wrote a treatise supporting Schrempf's theological statements. It was noteworthy that Harnack never condemned the church for defining itself theologically. (This controversy sparked Kähler's tract *Unser Streit um die Bibel* (*Our Struggle for the Bible*), and Harnack's response brought Schlatter to Berlin.)

Similar events continued to take place through the Wilhelmine era. In 1911, two cases developed around Carl Jatho and Heinrich Heydorn, who were defrocked from their respective provincial churches for heretical teaching. Heydorn grew particularly attached to Adolf Harnack through his university studies in Berlin and certainly was aware of the elder theologian's opinions on the matter that had led him to side with Schrempf in attacking the Apostles' Creed almost two decades earlier.

In 1910, Heydorn accepted a pastorate in Hamburg and began publishing a paper for like-minded Christians. In the style of Martin Luther, Heydorn penned one hundred theses for the reform of the modern church. These theses were listed in terms of "right" and "wrong" doctrines. Heydorn used them to argue, among other things, that the Bible was solely the result of human actions and not the revelation of God. He stated that God is not personal and that Jesus was not divine. The moderate churchman Theodor Kaftan, general superintendent of the state church in Schleswig, played a major role in excommunicating Heydorn in 1911. He defended his grounds in a short pamphlet written in the same year. Kaftan's brother, Julius, had taught Heydorn during his studies in Berlin, so Kaftan was familiar with Heydorn's situation personally beyond the ecclesiastical trial. Kaftan argued vehemently that Heydorn's antibiblical theses broke first with the spirit of the fundamental Lutheran doctrine that the church is to be a church of word and sacrament. Kaftan's second, and more damning, critique was that Heydorn's beliefs about Jesus broke with the central claim of historical Christianity that Jesus was the son of God.[55]

Once Kaftan completed his justification for his actions against Heydorn, however, he needed to define how most liberal pastors could remain within the church he oversaw. Kaftan disputed the claim of some archconservative thinkers that liberalism as a philosophy was fundamentally antichurch. These conservative thinkers claimed that liberalism's individuality was impossible to reconcile with an institutional church that demanded unity of belief and doctrine. Kaftan responded that liberalism, especially in its theological form, retained its affinity and ties to the centrality of Jesus Christ. Its adherents might

55. Theodor Kaftan, *Wo stehen Wir? Eine kirchliche Zeitbetrachtung verfaßt in Veranlassung des Falles Heydorn bzw. des Falles Jatho* (Schleswig: Julius Bergas, 1911), found in NSCA, Bestand 94 lfd. Nr. 80., 4–6, 11.

not wholly agree with the Gospels, but they remained faithful to the elemental beliefs of the church—the centrality of the Scriptures and the supremacy of Jesus. Heydorn and Jatho, in contrast, negated these central elements and therefore defined themselves against the church.[56]

Kaftan held to his decision even under significant pressure from the liberal theologians and pastors throughout Germany who came to Heydorn's defense. They argued that Christian clergy must have the liberal freedom to follow their consciences. Against this, Kaftan appealed to an unlikely ally, Harnack, who supported the church's right to defend itself from heresy. Although Heydorn was eventually able to be reinstated in another church province and found many like-minded thinkers throughout Germany, the actions against him and Jatho (and Schrempf before them) kept freethinking theology on a short leash.[57]

During these years, conservative leaders continued to warn their congregations about the mistakes of critical theology. Robert Aeschbacher told his listeners that a movement was afoot that tried to separate Jesus' teaching of "love your neighbor as yourself" from the rest of Christian doctrine. These liberal scholars claimed that traditional Christianity restricted Christians from noticing their neighbors' needs because they were too concerned with pleasing God. Aeschbacher remarked that such thinking was unjustified, since love of God meant submitting oneself to God, which included caring for others in need. Sermon candidate Gerhard Herrmann compared modern critical study of the Bible to polishing a precious stone. In the attempts to create something more beautiful than the raw stone, these critics cut and polished until they found that they were left with nothing.[58]

While the effects of Schlatter and Kähler and the other believing university professors changed the shape of some conservative pastors, it is crucial to restate that the largest percentage of young pastors continued to show little inclination toward one side or another. They left their university studies unaware of the significant chasm in worldviews and interpretations of Christianity that divided the theological camps. Largely, these pastors were conservative by inclination but critical in their training. The results were confusing and superficial amalgamations of varying ideas and philosophies.

---

56. Ibid., 26–27.
57. Ibid., 28.
58. Aeschbacher, *Ich lebe*, 20; SCAS, personalakte, A27 #1267: Gerhard Herrmann.

THE TRACES OF KÄHLER AND SCHLATTER IN THEIR STUDENTS

A small number of Kähler's and Schlatter's students indicated the effects of their teaching. Theodor Daur, a student from Korntal, Württemberg, studied under Schlatter and Cremer in Greifswald in 1891 and 1892. While his motivation for traveling from southern Germany to its northern coast has been lost, his conservative answers to the largely liberal examining faculty of Tübingen suggest that he was drawn by the conservative nature of the Greifswald faculty. While there, he took four courses from the young Schlatter. The sermon given for completion of his second theological exam indicated that some of Schlatter's most distinctive ethical teachings were already developed early in his career during his Greifswald tenure. In describing God's unconditional love, Daur incorporated Schlatter's historical understanding of revelation. He explained to the congregation that God specifically revealed himself in history (the account of which was in the Bible) in order for the picture to be clearest originally to his people Israel, then additionally to the church through Jesus Christ. No theological viewpoint was so uniquely Schlatter's as his explanation of the necessity of God's historical revelation. It was his distinctive teaching through his career.[59]

Daur also showed elements of Schlatter's ethical teaching several years before the publication of Der christliche Ethik. He told his listeners, as Schlatter wrote later, that God's grace through revelation culminated in the calling (Berufung) of the individual to be a child of God. This calling, for both Schlatter and his student Daur, gave the Christian power to live the ethical, good life, in confidence of God's enduring love and salvation through the atoning sacrifice of Jesus Christ. Daur concluded with words that could have come straight from Schlatter's writings: "So it is with us when we experience the love of God. It *humbles* us but at the same time elevates us so that we must confess: What am I, that you, God, accept me and call me? . . . In this way the individual person will become ever lesser and God ever greater. Amen."[60] Daur also followed Schlatter's lead in the specifics of his ethics, writing in his exam that a Christian state was possible only when the majority of citizens faithfully sought a Christian politics in cooperation. Only as Christianity pervaded the state's life was a Christian state possible.[61]

The thought of Schlatter and Kähler pervaded Herman Böhner's 1907 exam sermon for entry into the pastorate in the Bavarian Palatinate. During

---

59. SCAS, personalakte, A27 #462: Theodor Daur.

60. Ibid. Emphasis in original.

61. Ibid.

his academic study, Böhner spent a year at Tübingen with Schlatter and the following year at Halle with Kähler. Böhner's sermon used the text Acts 5:34–42, which records the words of the Pharisaic rabbi Gamaliel when he recommended that the Sanhedrin not kill the apostles Peter and John for their claims that Jesus was the Christ. Böhner used Gamaliel's discourse to discuss the Protestant's political role. In the text, Gamaliel chose not to use violence to counter the spiritual claims of Jesus' disciples. Böhner saw this as an eternal truth: spiritual wars were to be fought with spiritual weapons, and physical wars with physical weapons. The church and the state existed in different realms and possessed their different tools for different purposes.

Böhner, like Daur, anticipated Schlatter's discouse in *Ethik* on church and state relations. He told his congregation that Christians were to respect their political superiors. They had the example of Jesus Christ, who submitted to his own wrongful death rather than rebel against the Roman Empire. He admonished Christians to resist the many voices in his contemporary culture that encouraged populations to rise up against their superiors. Böhner pointed to the same evidence as Gamaliel in the passage in Acts. Many Jews tried to rise up against the Romans, but their movements were forgotten. Jesus accepted the imperial authority, and his movement swept the world. Christians had certain obligations to their authority, but using Schlatter's logic, Böhner insisted that they were hierarchical. A believer's first responsibility was to God, then to the state, and then to all other authorities. If these three came into conflict, as in the case that the state would not allow worship of God, then the believer must accept the state's authority to execute judgment against them when they fulfilled their first responsibility to God.

Böhner reminded his congregants to thank God that they did not face such choices in modern Germany but encouraged them that if they should experience this type of conflict, they would receive supernatural strength from the Holy Spirit. (Apparently, Böhner did not believe that the previous generation's *Kulturkampf* was out of the spirit of the state's religious tolerance.) Since Germany had a God-fearing, Christian government, he told his listeners, they were in an ideal situation. For them, serving their government was serving God. Böhner's and Daur's sermons showed a small but dedicated group of believing theologians who were willing to reassess their role as pastors in the light of Kähler's and Schlatter's reappraisal of traditional Christian doctrines.[62]

---

62. Zentralarchiv der evangelischen Kirche der Pfalz, personalakte, Abt. III Akt. #895: Herman Böhner.

CONCLUSIONS

On the whole, German sermons changed relatively little over the nearly three decades preceding the First World War. The rhetoric and ethical exhortation of the majority of sermons through this period were superficial and abstract. Even the modern, progressive-leaning pastors proved conservative in their craft. As a collection, the sermons portrayed a church uneasy about its position in the modern world and reluctant to question the foundation and benevolence of the power hierarchy of Germany.

The sermon also exposed a hierarchical pecking order between the university structure, the institutional church, and its congregation. With the exception of the extreme adherents of both sides, the clergy seemed unwilling and unable to express the deep fissures and the changing Christian self-identity that took place when the foundational principles of the faith were questioned by so many inside and outside the church. While university theologians wrote volumes of polemical literature defending their respective viewpoints as essential for the continued survival of the Christian faith in Europe, the pastors either misconstrued the ideas, avoided the issues by remaining mired in the ideas of Reformation Germany, or adopted a position but delivered it fully realized, as though the debate did not exist. The huge questions of spiritual authority and the interpretation of the Bible in the modern world were issues for educated, sophisticated thinkers, not for the casual church member, who would not have the resources to process these radical changes safely.[63]

There were points of change and adaptation even within the conservative church community, however. By the last decade before the war, a break from the antiquated debates of the Reformation and the overly simplistic theology of blessings and curses seemed to signal a new era of believing Christianity for a new generation. With opportunities for a high-quality conservative education in Greifswald, Halle, and Tübingen at the turn of the century, pastors had the opportunity to learn new methods that borrowed the techniques of modern knowledge and combined them with the cherished beliefs of the ancient church. University professors Schlatter and Kähler, alongside Herrmann

---

63. Apparently, the institutional church also recognized the care of its pastors over the interests of the congregations. Adolf Kuhlgatz, a conservative pastor in Lägerdorf in Schleswig-Holstein, was asked to leave by his congregation in the industrial town. He often closed the church because of low attendance, and visiting state-church observers from the church consistory frequently recommended that he was ill suited for such a congregation and ought to be moved to a rural seat. Instead of moving him to a position where he would no longer be expected to pastor a congregation, the church consistory recommended foisting him on a smaller congregation that would not be a great loss if his services were poorly attended. NSCA, personalakte, Bestand 12.03 lfd. Nr. 698: Adolf Kuhlgatz.

Cremer, Wilhelm Lütgert, and others, coupled with renowned preachers Christoph Blumhardt and Friedrich von Bodelschwingh, were gaining in renown even while a new generation of liberal scholars was (in their opinion) growing in infamy. As the First World War came, however, these minor changes were lost, and the theologians who inspired them were forgotten in the tumult of the war and the radical changes to society and religion that followed.

7

Confident in Jesus' Victory

Germany's Protestant Clergy's Spiritual Guidance during the First World War

But since Christianity is now proved impossible as an ethic, or rather, since the ways of European man are now proved impossible in relation to the ethic of Christianity, we are faced with a need and placed before questions which make us think that the difficult asseverations of the Christian dogma of the old style correspond far more closely to the actual situation than does our predecessors' confident assertion that "following Jesus" is a simple task.

–Karl Barth, "The Problem of Ethics Today"[1]

The Changing Clerical Stance during World War I

Beginning in 1730, the Herrnhuter Brüdergemeinde (better known to English speakers as the Moravians) published a yearly devotional with short excerpts from the Bible for every day of the year. They produced the book so that their members throughout the world could daily read and contemplate the same Bible passages. The regular reading of this little book became a staple of German piety even outside of the small Moravian church, and some began

---

1. Karl Barth, "The Problem of Ethics Today," found in Karl Barth, *The Word of God and the Word of Man*, trans. Douglas Horton (New York: Harper & Row, 1957), 147–48.

to read the texts as a sort of Christian horoscope that guided them through their day. Naturally, the importance of this text grew on the national day of repentance on August 9, 1914, the first major Protestant religious holiday after the beginning of the First World War. So when the Moravians' New Testament text for that day, chosen months earlier, was Rom. 8:31 ("If God is for us, who can be against us?"), many clergy understood it as a clear message for the Christians of Germany that God supported their side in the war.[2]

Other than a few notable exceptions, Germany's Protestant theologians and its clergy uniformly supported and advocated the government's participation in and justification for World War I. In lending their support for the war, the clergy instilled spiritual interpretation, justification, certainty, and purpose into the war effort. Their spiritual pursuits paralleled the imperial government's temporal goals exactly. As the war moved into a battle of attrition, however, the clergy had few resources available to comfort their churches after their promises of a quick and glorious victory proved false. The sermons at the end of the war bear a markedly different quality from those at the beginning in their understanding of the great suffering involved in such a wearying war. Nevertheless, none of them dared face the possibility of German defeat.[3]

2. Cf. O. Gruhl, "Gott für uns," delivered in August 1914, *Ein Feste Burg*, vol.1, *Das Wort Gottes im Kriege: Predigten und geistliche Reden aus der Kriegszeit* (Berlin: Schmidt & Co., n.d.), 39; A. Herwig, "Erste Kriegsbetstunde," delivered on August 9, 1914, *Drei Preigten, gehalten bei Ausbruch des Krieges 1914* (Asperg: Karl Wolf, 1915), 17.

3. Karl Hammer's *Deutsche Kriegstheologie*, Arlie Hoover's *God, Germany, and Britain in the Great War*, and Nicholas Hope's article "Prussian Protestantism" addressed German war jingoism. The first two works drew from published sermons and theological writings from Germany at war. They addressed the convergence of religious fervor with nationalism in the First World War. For Hammer this grew out of the theological teaching and experience of the Franco-Prussian War, when an initial hand-wringing and call for repentance turned into a jubilant feeling of providential blessing. Hoover found that the First World War took on the character of a holy war, which he believed to be an unacceptable perversion of faith. The religious leaders combined their parishioners' base hatred with holy fervor to drive the nationalistic fighting in the war. These two works added to the general historiography of the era by showing the close relationship between the church and the nationalistic fervor growing in Germany after its unification. The church leaders in general were unable to separate their responsibilities and loyalties to their beliefs from their loyalties to their state. Hammer and Hoover were two rare examples of historians whose work used sermons to shed light on religious moral leadership. Hope's article drew more on the long-standing traditions of German clergy that made them play such an influential and self-destructive role in the First World War. The German Protestants not only supported the war, but they became the most important mouthpiece of the Supreme Army Command. This came at the same time as the war was stripping the churches of their treasures, their bells, organ pipes, and other ornamentation. After the fall of the government in 1918, Hope found it unsurprising that many in the church yearned for the Spirit of 1914, when the church was full and playing an important role in the direction of the state. Hope's contribution helps explain why the churches acted so vehemently during the war and why they refused

MOBILIZED CLERGY

As the First World War broke out in August 1914, the church mobilized along with the rest of the population. The clergy got caught up in the same excitement that electrified Germans everywhere. Young pastors raced to join the military for both active and chaplaincy duties. The theological departments in universities held emergency exams for students who desired to complete their studies early so they could join the fighting. Many of the greatest voices in academic theology—Adolf Harnack, Adolf Schlatter, Wilhelm Hermann, Reinhold Seeberg, Josef Mausbach, and Sebastian Merkle—joined with eighty-seven other leading academics to sign the war manifest "An die Kulturwelt" (To the Civilized World) on October 4, 1914.[4] These theologians and countless lesser-known pastors throughout Germany also lent their support to the German war effort in the best way they knew how. They delivered sermons to their congregations to steel them for the sacrifices that needed to be made for a German victory. As the most influential ethical voice in Germany at the time, the Protestant Church's unanimous support of the government's call to arms gave the imperial leadership a powerful ally in the mobilization of Germany's resources to go to war.

Certainly the alliance between state and church proved a boon to both sides. All of the difficulties that had plagued the church for decades seemed to vanish in an instant. The mobilized population turned to the church to ascertain God's will for the nation in war. Churches were filled again, and a common support of the military effort united both critical and believing church leaders. The war seemed to be a direct blessing from God to both reinvigorate the church in the land of Luther and to form Germany into a stronger, unified nation with a stronger, unified faith. This optimism that the war was a blessing to the nation was affirmed in the war sermons.

In the first two years of fighting, Protestant ministers used their sermons to give the war a spiritual significance beyond the earthly pursuits of the warring governments. The vast majority of the period's sermons shared a common

to give up hope for victory even as the war dragged on. Their very survival and integrity depended on German victory. Karl Hammer, *Deutsche Kriegstheologie, 1870–1918* (Munich: Deutsche Taschenbuch Verlag, 1974), 14–18; A. J. Hoover, *God, Germany, and Britain in the Great War: A Study in Clerical Nationalism* (New York: Praeger, 1989); 129–31, Nicholas Hope, "Prussian Protestantism," in *Modern Prussian History, 1830–1947,* ed. Philip G. Dwyer (New York: Longman, 2001), 199–200.

4. "An die Kulturwelt" was a letter from the German intellectuals to the intelligentsia of the rest of the world, and it aimed to be an explanation and justification of the German war as it claimed, "against the lies and slanders" of their national enemies. Werner Neuer, *Adolf Schlatter: Ein Leben für Theologie und Kirche* (Stuttgart: Calwer Verlag, 1996), 563.

thread. The preachers told their congregations that the war was part of God's plan for the earth and for the German nation. The earthly war had cosmic, eternal importance; it was a war fought as much with weapons of faith and prayer as with machine guns and biplanes. The sermons' redefinition of the First World War lent it a theological interpretation that filled in the gaps where the temporal justification for the war fell flat.

NATIONALISTIC SERMONS OF BLESSINGS AND CURSES, 1914–1915

The Protestant sermons delivered in the opening phases of the war were uniform in message and focus. Therefore, it is possible to inspect these sermons as a single body of literature with a unified message to the German nation as it prepared for and marched into war. In their rhetoric of God's divine role in the war, the justice of the German war effort, and the sacrifice necessary from the German people, the sermons paralleled each other significantly, with only minor differences in points of emphases.

The foundation for this unified picture of the war in the sermons of 1914 and 1915 was the common Protestant understanding of God. For German pastors of the early twentieth century, critical and believing alike, God was the omnipotent ruler of the earth. God orchestrated the political world events as part of a larger spiritual plan of world evangelism and transformation into the coming kingdom of God. This led the theologians to believe that the pain and sufferings of political turmoil were mere birthing pains for a perfect and painless future world. This viewpoint blended political and spiritual. Christians therefore could actively participate in both kinds of activities as an act of worship and full devotion to their God. Even a mundane political war such as the First World War (mundane in that it lacked the great ideological tensions of the other wars of the twentieth century or the religiously motivated wars of previous centuries) became a "holy war" in the pulpit rhetoric. God was using God's servants in the political and military arenas to accomplish the divine earthly plan.[5]

According to the war sermons, God used the war to send a message to creation about humanity's sin. The pastors reflected that the years of peace had led to complacency and contentment, which in turn led people to trust their own capabilities and strength. As people were no longer dependent upon

---

5. Otto Zurhellen, "Mobilmachung," given August 2, 1914, in *Kriegspredigten* (Tübingen, Mohr, 1915), 5; Pastor Karstens, "Predigt für den aus Anlaß des Heldentodes der ersten 7 Gefallenen der hemmingstedter Kirchengemeinde angesetzten Gedächtnisgottesdienst am 22. nach Trinitatis, den 8. November 1914," found at Nordelbische State Church Archives, Kiel (NSCA), Bestand 94 lfd. Nr. 182, 4–5.

God for their physical well-being, they left the church, and their faith faltered. However, as the war came, God spoke to people through their distress. The war reminded them of their own weaknesses. As the events of the war swallowed up the comforts of prewar life, people were being reminded of the right place of God in their lives. The war was a taste of God's judgment of a people who had forgotten God in their everyday life. As Pastor Herwig of Asperg, Württemberg, colorfully described,

> In this way as life got better for our people, the more enjoyable the things of this world became, the more they believed that they did not need to fear God or to take his command. And once they were set loose they could not get enough of their heapings of sin and guilt. . . . The [German] people were poisoned with novels, vulgar shows and plays, and cinemas and theaters of a doubtful character in their attempts to satisfy their ravenous hunger [for sin]. . . . The war came as a warning to our German people to repent from their false ways.[6]

This condemnation of sin should not be viewed in a negative light. The war was an incredible opportunity. It was a second chance for those who had forgotten God to find God again. The pastors proclaimed that the First World War was a blessing, an act of God to return God to the rightful place as the central love of everyone's life. The war gained a spiritual importance beyond any political success each time a soldier on the front cried out to God in the heat of battle and as each parent prayed for a son's safety on the battlefield.[7]

Since the war was an act of divine revelation, the pastors and theologians of Germany openly acknowledged that God played an active role in the orchestration of the war. Pastors either ascribed to God full responsibility for the war or said God permitted the war to take place in the divine wisdom and plan for the world. God's role in the origin of the war provoked various responses from German preachers as they sought to interpret the great events around them.

6. A. Herwig, untitled sermon delivered August 9, 1914, in Herwig, *Drei Predigten*, 12–13.

7. Friedrich Rittelmeyer, "Krieg!" delivered on August 7, 1914, in *Christ und Krieg: Predigten aus der Kriegszeit* (Munich: Kaiser, n.d.), 6; Reetz, "Bußtag nach Kriegsausbruch," delivered in August 1914, in *An meine Soldaten: Ansprachen und Predigten während der ersten Kriegsjahres* (Leipzig: Im Xenien-Verlag, 1916), 32–33; Gittinger, "Rede beim Feldgottesdienst," delivered on August 5, 1914, in *Kriegspredigten aus dem großen Krieg: 1914 und 1915 von verschiedenen Verfassern*, ed. Paul Wurster, (Stuttgart: Evang. Gesellschaft, 1915), 87; Reetz, "Vom Vergehen der Völker," undated sermon, in Reetz, *An meine Soldaten*, 111.

A war with spiritual origins needed spiritual action. The war was described as a burden to be dutifully carried by the Germans; it was a test of their loyalty and service to God. In response to their faithful obedience, the clergy promised, God would use the war to heal the German nation from its sin. They hoped the war would remind Germany of the meaning of true peace and righteousness. Most of all, they expected the war to inspire a fervency to follow God's will in a people who had been wooed by the long peace and prosperity into thinking only of their material gain and their satisfied stomachs. For the pastors at the beginning of the great year, the war was not a product of human will, but God's calling of God's people to steadfast loyalty and service.[8]

The preachers gave their call for repentance with a promise of forgiveness. The war had shaken them, but God was giving them another chance. If the people turned toward God, God would faithfully guide them through the war and protect them from the evil that surrounded them. They would become God's people if they turned from their sins. And God would reward and protect them in the entirety of their lives—in their jobs, in relationships, and in family life, even beyond the success God promised in war.[9]

Certainly, the central focus of the war sermons was not gloom and destruction. Ultimately, God's role in the war provoked hope among the Protestant clergy. If God was responsible for the war, God was also in control of its outcome. The whole purpose of war, for the faithful Christian, was to inspire trust that God would bring a satisfactory and successful victory to God's people. The German pastors rallied their listeners. Once they were chastened and returned to true devotion, then God would show true divine power and bring the war to a successful end.[10]

The sermons of the period were fiercely nationalistic. God was using the war to speak to Germany alone. The other nations were peripheral, used

8. Zurhellen, "Mobilmachung," 3, 5; Gittinger, "Rede beim Feldgottesdienst," 88; Herwig, untitled sermon delivered August 9, 1914, 13–14; Wilhelm Hadorn, "Weh der Lüge," in *Er ist unser Friede* (Neukirchen: Buchhandlung des Erziehungsvereins, 1915), 406; Johannes Hauri, "Der Segen des Krieges," in *Nicht Frieden, sondern das Schwert: Acht Kriegs-Predigten* (Basel: Friedrich Reinhardt, 1914), 46–47; Zurhellen, "Landesbettag," delivered on August 5, 1914, in Zurhellen, *Kriegspredigten*, 15; Lülmann, "Deutsches Volk Gottes Volk," delivered on November 18, 1914, in *Ein Feste Burg*, 60; Landeskirchliches Archiv Stuttgart (LAS), personalakte A27 #1480: Edward Julius Richard von Jan; Gustav Benz, "Am vorabend des Krieges," delivered on August 2, 1914, in *Dennoch bei Gott: Predigten aus den Kriegsjahren 1914–1916*, 2nd ed. (Basel: Friedrich Reinhardt, 1916), 20.

9. Paul Wurster, "Opfer!" delivered on September 13, 1914, in Wurster, *Kriegspredigten*, 205; Herwig, untitled sermon delivered on August 9, 1914, 13–14; A. Herwig, sermon delivered on August 2, 1914, in Herwig, *Predigten*, 5; Lülmann, "Deutsches Volk," 64.

10. Karstens, "Heldentodes," in NSCA, Bestand 94 lfd. Nr. 182.

as God's tools to bring about the divine will in the German people. God may have been condemning the sins of Germany, yet Germany's religious leaders imagined little possibility that God intended their country's defeat. The cleansing of the German people's sins required sending their troops into danger and sacrificing some of their sons in battle. But God's punishment would be only of short duration.

Even the fighting could be done out of spiritual devotion. The pastors told their congregations that the march to the front was an act of faith that showed the Germans' trust in God and their hope for a victorious resolution. After all, the pastors had already established that God's will and justice would ultimately determine the outcome of the war. Therefore, the war would not be decided by the race to encirclement, but by the race to find and satisfy God's holy will. A glorious victory would pay dividends beyond the sacrifices of war. As garrison chaplain Otto Gittinger informed his troops, "This is God's will for us now, that our men-in-arms be a pious, brave, modest, human, and brotherly people. When this desire of God is satisfied, then even if the whole world stand against us, we will remain secure in the belief: 'If God is for us, who can stand against us!'"[11] God's control over the victory was certain, even over seemingly insurmountable opposition. Germany's role was simply to enter the war and fight for God's will, secure in the certainty of God's (pro-German) sovereignty and justice. Put simply, these preachers promised their congregations that God would not let a Christian Germany fall.[12]

JUST WAR: GERMAN INNOCENCE AND CITIZEN PARTICIPATION

The Protestant clergy were so confident in God's support because of their certainty in the justice of the German war effort. Even though the clergy were united in acknowledging that Germany struggled with sins of unbelief and cultural fragmentation, all clergy were likewise uniformly agreed that the Germans were not responsible for the war. Their nation entered the war with a clean conscience before God. The Germans neither wanted war nor provoked it. They also agreed that of all the nations involved at the war's beginning, Germany had done the most to prevent it. Since they believed that the war proceeded despite the best efforts of German diplomacy, the sermons determined, the German claims in the war must be fully just. Germany's

---

11. Gittinger, "Rede beim Feldgottesdienst," 92.

12. Zurhellen, "Mobilmachung," 6–7; Benz, "Am vorabend," 17; Lülmann, "Deutsches Volk," 58; Rittelmeyer, "Krieg!" 8; Herwig, sermon delivered on August 2, 1914, 7–8; Herwig, "Erste Kriegsbetstunde," 17; Gruhl, "Gott für uns," 44.

Christians now had the obligation to fight the just war to defend the honor and freedom of Christian Germany from their surrounding enemies.[13]

The clergy also encouraged their congregations to fight heartily because it would show their thankfulness to God for the blessings they received in Germany. One pastor asked his parishioners what gratitude they would show God if they simply allowed the French and the Russians to overtake their land. For these clergy, true love of God was indistinguishable from the true love of their fatherland, which was a gift from God.[14]

The German clergy also justified individual Christians' full participation in the war. Eduard Beitter from Weldenstein near Crailsheim in Württemberg took his second clerical exam in 1914, shortly after the outbreak of war. His ethics essay question asked about Christian participation in war. His response was a typical one. He acknowledged that the question posed difficulties, since one of Christianity's central ethical tenets is that Christians ought to love their enemy, whereas war's purpose is "the merciless destruction of the other."[15] Even so, Beitter wrote that a Christian could fight with a clear conscience on three points. First, Jesus told his listeners to "give to Caesar what is Caesar's." Therefore, the worldly governments had the right to exact military service from their subjects. Beyond this, Christians could freely volunteer for such service while still being faithful to God because the German culture was the keeper of many Christian treasures. If Germany were to be destroyed, these treasures would be lost. When Germany was victorious, these Christian characteristics would be spread to the world. Beitter's final point grew out of the mystical connection he saw between individuals and the state. Since the body is God's temple (1 Cor. 6:19), and since the German people were one united body, then Christians concerned about the inner health of the nation would never allow the destruction of the German body, the German temple of God, from outside forces. The defense of the body by Christians would prove beneficial

13. Rittelmeyer, "Krieg!" 3; Herwig, sermon delivered on August 2, 1914, 5; Gittinger, "Rede beim Feldgottesdienst," 88–89; Gruhl, "Gott für uns," 40–41. The early sermons of the war stated that Germany was brought into the war through the treachery of its opponents. The Germans' only guilt in the origin of the war was their efficiency and industriousness. The pastors asserted that their success made their opponents envious, which brought open aggression. The clergy damned Germany's enemies for misusing Germany's love of peace, which these foes hoped to exploit for their own gain. None of the Germans' sins were directly responsible for the origin of the war. That responsibility lay solely with their enemies. Zurhellen, "Landesbettag," 15–16; Gittinger, "Rede beim Feldgottesdienst," 89; Wurster, "Opfer!" 205; Reetz, "Vom Vergehen der Völker," 106; Herwig, sermon delievered on August 2, 1914, 3–4; Gruhl, "Gott für uns," 40–41.

14. Rittelmeyer, "Krieg!" 3.

15. LAS, personalakte, A27 #172: Eduard Beitter.

for the whole of Germany, because the war would bring other individuals out of their moral stupor and reinvigorate the people as a whole. The individual participation in war by devout Christians would begin a chain reaction that would end with a strengthened, pious, and powerful Germany. Victory, Beitter promised, would allow Germany to establish an enduring peace and a powerful, godly people.[16]

Some of the pastors brought their worst condemnation to bear against the enemies of their state. The sermons accused France of pettiness, arguing that the French were merely acting out of revenge for their defeat in the Franco-Prussian war of 1870–1871. The description of the Russians by some sermons was even more extreme. Russia was called a half-barbarous nation led by a "godless, amoral, conscience-less, scavenging aristocracy who want to turn our blooming, orderly people and land into wasteland."[17] Both nations were simply warmongers who knew no higher law of morality and whose cultures were vastly inferior to the superior German Christian civilization. Interestingly, the German pastors seemed unconcerned about the moral or Christian characteristics of their Austrian and Ottoman allies.[18]

For the pastors, France and Russia were cruel, stunted cultures, which made their aggression explainable, but Britain's opposition to Germany was the most odious example of treachery. Germany's intellectual leaders had long praised and admired England as the co-bearer of the best of European culture and civilization. Like Germans, the British were moral and religious, industrious and fair. Since the German clergy registered no serious flaw in breaking the neutrality of a Belgian government that already had clearly sided with the French at the outbreak of war, the British justification for themselves that they joined the war to defend Belgian neutrality sounded hollow and worthless.

The pastors saw only one possible explanation for Britain's hostility: simply put, England cared little for sharing prestige and honor with Germany. The British were obviously envious of Germany's growing military, economic, and cultural power, and sought to defeat the Germans by siding with less-than-reputable allies. The religious character of the British had clearly been greatly overestimated. The clergy now claimed that the British faith was merely ceremonial decoration and that the core of the British people's lives remained untouched by Christianity. The German pastors and theologians were quick

---

16. Ibid.

17. Gittinger, "Rede beim Feldgottesdienst," 87.

18. Rittelmeyer, "Krieg!" 8–9; Adolf Harnack, "Address by His Excellency, Professor von Harnack," *German-American Meeting of Sympathy in the Berlin City Hall, August 11, 1914* (Berlin: Liebheit & Thiesen, 1914), found in Staatsbibliothek zu Berlin, Adolf Harnack Nachlass, Kasten 11, #1187, 18–19.

to condemn what they considered Britain's haughty confidence that it could destroy Germany.[19]

WAR AND A GERMAN AWAKENING

The opening months of the war gave German pastors grounds for confidence beyond the first victories in Belgium. Germany appeared on the verge of a spiritual reawakening and seemed ready to repent and turn from its sin. The first such sign was that the whole nation was moving as one single body, one entity free from the social fissures that had increasingly brought interclass, interparty, and intrareligious strife. The ministers praised the selflessness of citizens who, at the beginning of the war, shared their resources and sacrificed individual comforts, describing these acts as a great sign of Germany's penitence and spiritual preparedness for the war. Many pastors especially lauded the working-class abandonment of the international alliances that had formed around socialist idealism. Such signs were a clear result of God's mighty work in the German people.[20]

The second cause for the clergy's optimism in the war was the perceived pious beliefs and religious leadership of the kaiser. Great spiritual strength was essential for the success of the German armies, and the kaiser had the ultimate responsibility in calling his nation to war. When, therefore, Wilhelm II called out the German armies and defended the clear conscience of the German government and leadership, the Christian leadership was elated that he was concerned for the empire's spiritual well-being. The Protestant clergy also gladly accepted the task the kaiser had set out for them, to turn their congregations to prayer and repentance. The pastors knew that this spiritual leadership from the top would influence the whole country to seek God's will in the time of battle. The ministers gushed about the kaiser, who lent his spiritual leadership and led by example. They spoke with awe that he sent his son to the front, where the prince was wounded. The clergy were confident that such leadership would find favor in God's eyes.[21]

19. Theodor Kaftan, *Die gegenwärtige Kriegslage und wir Christen* (Ratzeburg, Schleswig-Holstein: Christenvereins, 1916), found in NSCA, Bestand 94 lfd. Nr. 80, 16; Lülmann, "Deutsches Volk," 63; Reetz, "Vom Vergehen der Völker," 105–106; Harnack, "Address by His Excellency," 19–20, 23; Adolf Harnack, "Antwort auf das Schreiben von 11 Großbritannischen Theologen," in Staatsbibliothek zu Berlin, Adolf Harnack Nachlaß, Kasten 11, #1189, 1.

20. Zurhellen, "Mobilmachung," 10; Gittinger, "Rede beim Feldgottesdienst," 88, 91; Gruhl, "Gott für uns," 42–43; Lülmann, "Deutsches Volk," 58–59; LAS, A27 #1480: von Jan; Hauri, "Der Segen des Krieges," 49–50; Johannes Hauri, "Die Vaterlandsliebe des Christen," in Hauri, *Nicht Frieden*, 55, 58–59.

21. Wurster, "Opfer!" 205–206; Rittelmeyer, "Krieg!" 3; Herwig, sermon delivered on August 2, 1914, 4; Gruhl, "Gott für uns," 39.

Seeing Germany as blameless in the outbreak of war and as ready to seek God and repent of its societal flaws gave the Protestant ministers confidence in a quick and decisive German victory. Otto Zurhellen summed up this sentiment, preaching, "So let us go armed with the serious but joyful spirit [of the cross on Golgatha] into the difficult battle and only worry about this one thing: that we are good, with pure hearts and full of the Holy Spirit in the heat of battle and in the work of loving aid, then we will be victorious, then we must be victorious!"[22] Zurhellen followed his own advice and joined the military. He was killed a few months after the war began, but his wife carried on his work, publishing his war sermons in 1915.

Just Warriors and Brave Citizens: War Ethics

The German clergy's confidence in God's aid to the Germans determined their ethical mandates. In their view, God was in control of the beginning and the end of the war, and the Germans' war piety and clear conscience gave them reason to believe in a decisive victory for their armies. Therefore, the pastors called the German army to protect Germany's reputation and to endure the war in Christian morality. They charged their congregations with bravery, self-sacrifice, and moral behavior.

First of all, they spoke to the soldier, for whom bravery and self-sacrifice were highly esteemed and promoted ideals. The preachers praised soldiers for their willing advancement to the front to protect their homeland from their cruel enemies. These soldiers stood as examples for the German Christians because of their willingness to lay their life on the line for their parents, wives, and children, for their houses and land, and to protect their throne and their altar. This sacrifice followed the example of Christ their Lord. Pastor Gittinger determined bravery to be part of God's will; he told his soldiers, "God commands that we fight bravely . . . . No cowards may hide in our lines, ... 'Win! Win or die!' . . . God wants brave German men who will shock the enemies with their attacks."[23]

The soldiers were reminded as they headed out to war that they were the bearers of German culture and morality. Jesus' commandment to love one's enemy was not eclipsed by the war. Therefore, the pastors counseled soldiers to behave appropriately and Christianly in foreign fields of battle. They were to be ambassadors of the best of German qualities and to spread these good characteristics in the lands they would conquer. They had the responsibility

22. Zurhellen, "Landesbettag," 20.

23. Gittinger, "Rede beim Feldgottesdienst," 90; Karstens, "Heldentodes," 3–4.

for modesty and morality. It was appropriate to fight in righteous anger at the unrighteous aggression of their enemies, but they must not act in hatred or malice. Despite the crimes and aggression shown against Germany, the pastors warned the troops in their midst not to turn their dutiful opposition into hatred. They were not to blame the poor common foot soldier in the opposing trenches for bringing the blight of war against them. German soldiers needed to maintain justice and love, even in the midst of conflict. If they could do this, the pastors told the troops, they would keep the dirt of cruelty against the defenseless from besmirching the proud banner of the German Empire.[24]

The Protestant clergy also admonished self-sacrifice and industriousness on the home front. They told their congregations to make every possible sacrifice to aid the German war effort, which would keep their nation whole and their people strong and healthy. They encouraged their parishioners to sacrifice their luxuries as an act of worship and piety. This willingness to offer the small comforts of life meant as much for the general success in war as the soldier's willingness to offer his life. The obligation of the German people was to refrain from selfish pursuits and from questioning their own suffering and difficulties for the duration of the war. Sacrifice would be repaid, and work offered would accomplish feats that the worker never dreamed possible. The preachers were united in their expectation that the willingness to sacrifice would be Germany's greatest strength and the greatest assurance of a quick victory over the nation's enemies.[25]

More than the justice of the war or the bravery and idealism of the war excitement, the hope of a greater and better Germany inspired the clergy to full support of the German war effort. In the opening year of the war, the Protestant clergy of Germany promised their listeners that as a result of their bravery, sacrifice, and morality, the German victory would bring undreamed-of glories and spiritual riches. The German victory promised to protect and advance the Protestant Christian belief that found its center in Germany. This meant more than simply the rites and practices of German Lutheranism. The religion they cherished was spiritually superior to all others. It alone brought true morality and a free, real faith. In the clergy's thinking, it was the religion that brought about the penitence that cleansed Germany after the war began. This religion

24. Rittelmeyer, "Krieg!" 2; Herwig, sermon delivered on August 2, 1914, 6–7; Zurhellen, "Mobilmachung," 2, 9; Wurster, "Opfer!" 206; Gittinger, "Feldgottesdienst," 91; Hauri, "Vaterlandsliebe", 55-56, 61.

25. Zurhellen, "Mobilmachung", 8; Gittinger, "Rede beim Feldgottesdienst," 88; Wurster, "Opfer!" 203, 205; Gruhl, "Gott für uns," 40, 45; Reetz, "Vom Vergehen der Völker," 108; Rittelmeyer, "Krieg!" 5, 8–9, 11; Herwig, "Erste Kriegsbetstunde," 17.

invoked temperance in the pursuits of pleasure. And the faith sparked a closer dependence on and interaction with God.

THE HOPE IN THE VICTORIOUS WORLD TO COME

The wartime sermons expressed a conviction that this religion would grow even stronger after the German victory. It would be cleansed by the war from its sinful impurities and would be more genuine than ever before. Pastor Rittelmeyer quoted a soldier in a sermon. The soldier wrote, "I have wanted to live with the purpose that the spirit of Christ would rule in the world. Now I head out into the battlefield for my fatherland, so that we can accomplish what I have wanted for so long! Yes, when the war is over we want to be able to give our fatherland the greatest thing it can be given, the spirit of Jesus Christ."[26] The protection of this religion was the greatest promise the clergy invoked to inspire courage for a quick victory.[27]

At the same time as it protected German religion, victory would also accomplish what was, in many pastors' minds, exactly identical: it would protect the superior German culture from being overrun by Germany's inferior neighbors. These two powerful assets of German life, its culture and its religion, would then expand from the German heartland into the neighboring states. This would advance the moral character of the other countries, and it would establish an enduring peace both internally and internationally.

Indeed, a return to an enduring peace was a common theme running through most of the sermons. Specific political goals were seldom mentioned in the sermons as pursuits of the military venture. However, on occasion, some pastors could not resist imagining the future world after German victory. Tübingen professor of theology Paul Wurster encouraged a hope in a unified German state that would encompass both Germany and Austria. This state would preserve German culture and religion for generations to come in true godly peace. Later in the war, Theodor Kaftan, bishop of Schleswig-Holstein, echoed Wurster's earlier claim that the Germans would restore their place as the preserver and originator of culture in the Polish and Baltic lands. Therefore, Kaftan argued, the German Empire had the right to put these peoples under its dominion in order to protect those lands (as well as the German center) from the brutality and amorality of the Asiatic Russians. Sermon candidate

---

26. Rittelmeyer, "Krieg!" 14.

27. Zentralarchiv der Evangelischen Kirche der Pfalz, Abt. 150.20: Johann Jacob Griess; LAS, A27 #1480: von Jan, 8–9; Rittelmeyer, "Krieg!" 5; Wilhelm Hadorn, "Pons non ruit," undated sermon, in Hadorn, *Er ist unser Friede*, 420; Lülmann, "Deutsches Volk," 61; Benz, "Am vorabend," 20; Hauri, "Der Segen des Krieges," 48, 53–54; NSCA, Bestand 42.07 #262: Bruno Meyer; Zurhellen, "Landesbettag," 14.

Bruno Meyer from Scheswig-Holstein summed up the political goals of the early war in his student exam in the spring of 1916: "Shouldn't we always sing with thankful excitement and accord out of the depths of our hearts the words of the song: 'Germany, Germany, over everything, over everything in the world'? Yes, friends, Germany over everything, but just over everything **in the world!** There is nothing more beautiful or glorious in the world, nothing more valuable or priceless as our German fatherland with all of its goods and truths and beauties that it possesses, all of its ideal goods: German science, German art and German culture!"[28] Insofar as the clergy could determine political goals during the war, these goals were closely tied to the benevolent German religious destiny to spread Christian morality and religion to the ends of the earth.[29]

THE ENDURING FAITHFUL: SERMONS OF 1916–1918

As the expectation for the war transitioned from a quick, bloody, but decisive maneuver into a war of endurance and attrition, the emphases of the German-speaking clergy changed along with it. The publication of war sermons in Germany dropped as the war became more difficult and the losses more overwhelming. This was likely due to a number of factors, including censorship and the limited resources allocated for publication. However, published and unpublished sermons indicate psychological factors as well. The general outline of the first sermons remained, but underscoring them was a newfound weariness and disappointment as the optimistic prognostications of the initial years failed to be fulfilled.

The most noticeable characteristic of the sermons from the latter half of the war was their war weariness. The long, unceasing fighting and the lengthening tallies of the dead from each community weighed heavily on the pastors' messages. The daily needs of their congregations as they faced the naval blockade from Great Britain also began to appear in sermons. The pastors sympathized with their parishioners who faced overinflated prices on food due to war profiteering. All the hopes they had borne at the beginning of the war seemed to melt away into an unending suffering and powerlessness. The German pastors were anxious to stem the tide of doubt and anger with God that grew out of the crushing hardships. They reminded their congregations that God was still present, still loving, and still sovereign over everything. Whereas

28. NSCA, Bestand 42.07 #262: Meyer. Emphasis in original.

29. Zurhellen, "Mobilmachung," 5, 9; Gennrich, "Reformation," published in *Ein Feste Burg*, Vol. 1, *Das Wort Gottes im Kriege: Predigten und geistliche Reden aus der Kriegszeit* (Berlin: Schmidt & Co.,n.d.) 166; Rittelmeyer, "Krieg!" 4; Hauri, "Der Segen des Krieges," 49–51; Wurster, "Opfer!" 208.

early in the war, the pastors had proclaimed God's will with confidence to their congregations, as the war went on, they simply expressed hope that one day God would make God's actions clear to everyone who suffered. They still encouraged patience and endurance, but gone were the echoes of the success of the Franco-Prussian War that had so colored the earlier sermons.[30]

The sermons of the latter half of the war still expressed a belief that the war was the critique of God on a sinful and apostate nation. However, the new sermons looked increasingly skeptically at the German claim that Germany possessed an elevated culture. The new sermons denounced any culture that had no recourse to prevent such a war.[31]

Reports of faith from the front had a powerful effect on the clergy as the war ground on. The accounts of soldiers' piety amazed the preachers, who had difficulty fathoming the horrors of the front, and the pastors showed sympathy for those whose faith weakened. In these illustrations of stories from the front, they found the greatest encouragement for continued faith in victory amidst the war suffering. They praised the soldiers for their selfless sacrifice of their lives as they died, confident in knowing that the earth was not their eternal home. Reports of their somber celebrations of religious holidays, Christmas and the Day of Repentance (*Bußtag*), in the trenches inspired the clergy in their faithfulness to God.[32]

Many of the pastors in the latter half of the war still promised a glorious victory for the German people, but the message was thick with allusions to hard testing and purification through fire. These pastors described the war as a testing ground for God to determine the dedication and endurance of the

30. LAS, personalakte, A27 #897: Erich Gerbeth; Paul Kalweit, "Aus der Tiefe," undated sermon, in Otto Dibelius, *Er ist bei uns wohl auf dem Plan: Festtagspredigten*, 3. Heft, [vol. 3?] *Bußtag und Totenfest* (Berlin-Lichterfelde: Edwin Runge, 1917), 6; Gerhard Heinzelmann, "Wert des Lebens," sermon delivered August 4, 1918, in *Vom Bürgertum im Himmel: Fünfzehn Predigten aus den Jahren 1917 und 1918* (Basel: Verlag von Kober C.F.Spittlers Nachfolger, 1918), 201–202; Gerhard Heinzelmann, "Kriegslehre," sermon delivered on March 11, 1917, in Heinzelmann, *Bürgertum*, 5; Max Braun, "Der Sieg über den Tod," sermon delivered in 1917, in Dibelius, *Er ist bei uns wohl auf dem Plan*, 22; LAS, personalakte, A27 #1407: Theodor Holzapfel; Dibelius, "Warum wollt ihr sterben?," in Dibelius, *Er ist bei uns wohl auf dem Plan*, 14; LAS, personalakte, A27 #3147: Karl Spengler; Kaftan, *Die gegenwärtige Kriegslehre*, 6.

31. Friedrich Rittelmeyer, "Vom Gotterleben im Krieg," sermon delivered on February 6, 1916, in Rittelmeyer, *Christ und Krieg*, 240; Dibelius, "Warum sterben?," 13–14; Heinzelmann, "Kriegslehre", 2; Heinzelmann, "Wert des Lebens," 209; Kaftan, *Die gegenwärtige Kriegslehre*, 39–40.

32. Dibelius, "Warum sterben?," 16; Rittelmeyer, "Vom Gotterleben im Krieg," 236–37; NSCA, Bestand 42.07 lfd. Nr. 262: Meyer; Braun, "Der Sieg über den Tod," 24–25; Kalweit, "Aus der Tiefe," 6–8.

German people, to see whether they had the stomach for the hardship of the world, and to find whether they loved God enough to remain faithful through years of hardship.[33]

Even more present than victory in the later sermons was simply the yearning for peace. Here Jesus and the love of God replaced the allusions to the Old Testament that had marked the sermons preached earlier in the war. The sermons from the end of the war no longer mocked the pseudo-peace of prewar Germany. Rather, they longed for the end to the sufferings and death that the war brought daily. In these sermons, the prayers to the God who was sovereign over the war still hoped for victory, but they petitioned for an honorable peace.[34]

The deep yearning for peace gave new impetus for the verbal attacks against Germany's enemies in the latter years of the war. The pastors seemed shocked and upset that the Allied enemies of Germany rejected the kaiser's overtures of peace. To the clergy at the end of war, that response spoke of those nations' arrogance and abject hatred. Despite the yearning for peace, their opponents' recklessness eliminated surrender as an option, lest the unjust aggressors claim the victory. The clergy spoke out against the clear resolution of their enemies to obliterate any semblance of Germany, and they prayed that God would wreak judgment on their enemy's conceit.[35]

The clergy's spiritual goals at the end of the war were muted and individual. Peace and trust in God became the central themes of an expected internal growth after the war. They often alluded to the peace and trust Christ had as he sacrificed himself on the cross; it was a peace born of suffering. Their description of the character of the kingdom of God changed. In the opening phase of the war, they had described the kingdom of God as a political institution that would bring peace to the world through benevolent but coercive force. By the end of the war, they referred to it as an internal kingdom and an internal peace in the hearts of those who trusted in God.[36]

One who had a deeper, firsthand understanding of the need for peace was the pastoral candidate Daniel Buck. Buck, the son of a miller and farmer, was born August 6, 1892, in Blaubeuren in Württemberg. He studied theology

---

33. Dibelius, "Warum Sterben?," 13, 19; LAS, A27 #3147: Spengler; LAS, A27 #1407: Holzapfel; Kaftan, *Die gegenwärtige Kriegslehre*, 9–10.

34. LAS, A27 #3147: Spengler.

35. Ibid.; LAS, A27 #897: Gerbeth; Kaftan, *Die gegenwärtige Kriegslehre*, 7–8.

36. It is important to note that both of these interpretations had important precedent in both the critical and believing traditions of biblical hermeneutics before the advent of the war. LAS, A27 #1407: Holzapfel; LAS, A27 #3147: Spengler.

at Tübingen and Marburg but broke off his studies in 1914 to volunteer for military service. He fought as an infantry lieutenant in twelve battles in France including the Sommaisne, the Somme and Verdun, and in the process he earned the Iron Cross, first and second class, as well as the Württemberg Golden Medal for Military Service. He reapplied for his pastoral examinations in 1918, writing that he had been at times the impromptu chaplain for the burials of his comrades in arms.[37]

His examination sermon was an exemplary text of war sermons at the end of the war. He delivered his thoughts to other troops and took up their hope for peace. Much, he said, became a riddle in the war. Life had been brought into question. Comrades he had seen only moments before died in a flash. The war made the people around him so much more serious. They yearned for peace, not merely two weeks of home leave, but true and enduring rest.

But a Christian, Buck said, could not merely hope for peace; he needed to fulfill his obligations first. As a medal winner, Buck continued his sermon by saying there was a time when every young man wanted to go and do something extraordinary, and young men embraced the chance for heroics in war. They wanted to be recognized for their bravery, intelligence, and courage. After enduring the war, they were more mature, more modest. They realized that the great accomplishments of war could be done only when all the little necessary tasks were completed. Yet everybody's experience in the war included a long litany of personal failures and lapses of courage. He knew that many in his congregation, as he had, realized their need for God only as they first encountered the thunderous sound and shock of the battlefield.

Nevertheless, Buck encouraged the troops to fight on. The faithful life was not made up only of times of enjoyment and comfortable peace. The Christian faith was a struggle and a fight that achieved peace only through vigilance and hard work. His listeners faced a greater enemy than those in the other trenches; the greatest enemy of peace was the personal sin of each member. However, Jesus Christ offered power and strength for all the struggles and battles of life, temporal and spiritual. For Buck, this strength was the origin of joy and peace in his heart on the battlefield. The young pastoral candidate who had entered the war with visions of greatness and heroics was by the end of the war preaching a staid faith in a personal salvation. This faith, he promised, would bring Germans to a positive conclusion of the long war. After his successful completion of the examination, Buck returned to the front. On March 27, 1918, he was killed instantly by a bullet to his head.[38]

37. LAS, personalakte, A27 #353: Daniel Buck.
38. Ibid.

In November 1918, the capitulation of German forces to their Allied enemies meant that the unthinkable took place in Germany. The powerful German army was humbled after four years of fighting, and the government collapsed in revolution. The church's sufferings began shortly thereafter. The exodus from the church that had been underway before the war's beginning in 1914 began again with renewed vigor. Over the next few decades, the majority of the great churches of Germany would become mere skeletons of their former selves. The voices of the clergy for ethical and moral guidance became weak, drowned out in the increasingly secular Germany.

LOSS OF THE WAR AND THE CLERGY'S LOSS OF INFLUENCE

In the Weimar period and the Nationalist Socialist Germany to come, political parties and secular ideologies determined the moral direction of the German people. Not only was the clergy's promise of a German victory unfulfilled, but their prophecies of a new pious, penitent Germany also failed to come to fruition in the wake of the devastating treaty negotiated at Versailles. Clearly the German clergy's inability to provide a spiritual understanding of defeat in the First World War crippled their continuing influence in Germany.

The question remains whether any single action or any different message could have preserved the prestige of the Protestant Church in Germany. But some conclusions can be drawn from the sermons of the First World War. The first fatal flaw was the failure to recognize a real possibility of loss in the war. As Christians, the pastors had to maintain their belief in the sovereignty of God, but their narrow nationalistic conception of God could not be the only interpretation possible. As it was, the church possessed no valid theology wherein Germany could lose without it being the result of hidden sin or without it besmirching the justice of God.

The failures of their theology were the result of the second major flaw in the German Protestants' ethical leadership in the First World War, namely, the total acceptance of the government's propaganda and justification for the war. The church proved incapable of questioning the government's actions. No voices were raised concerning the vague purpose of the war in the first place. Furthermore, the Christian leadership accepted fully the German government's explanation for invading Belgium (due to its clear sympathies with France) and even the sinking of the ocean-liner *Lusitania* that was the main motivation for the American entry into the war (America was sending arms to Great Britain).[39] They blindly accepted the claims of foreign armies' brutalities while shrugging

---

39. Kaftan, *Die gegenwärtige Kriegslehre*, 16, 19.

off reports of the same from those marching under the German flag. The church's support for and theological buttressing of the German war information system gave the government an air of infallibility that was overturned only when the government collapsed. By that point, the church was already in too deep; the uncritical support of the government could not be explained away, and for the many families in Germany who had suffered losses, there was no comfort from a sense of achieving any lasting purpose of the war. The theologians who grew up around the war, such as Karl Barth, chose to reject the whole of nineteenth-century theology solely because of its incredible impotence to question the government's values and justification for the war. Facing the same impotence, the German people simply rejected the church.

ADOLF SCHLATTER AND THE FIRST WORLD WAR

Adolf Schlatter's experience of World War I paralleled that of the rest of the German clergy of the period. He began as an ardent supporter of the war, but in the years that followed, he repented and declared that the war was a folly. His war experience was one of personal anguish and theological wrestling. The war was a significant turning point in Schlatter's life, his works, and his ethics. Schlatter's new sense of calling and responsibility in the wake of the war was apparent from his writings during and after the conflagration. Following the outbreak of war and the death of his son a few months later, the sixty-two-year-old Schlatter never regained the prolific academic writing output he had produced before the war. Most of his work from that point on—and he continued to write several volumes right up until his death—focused on teaching basic biblical understanding to individual (non-expert) believers and on revising his earlier masterworks.

PERSPECTIVES AT THE WAR'S START

In the opening months of the war in 1914, Schlatter clearly showed his support for the German government. He signed the war manifesto "An die Kulturwelt," which was printed in the newspaper *Frankfurter Zeitung* on October 4, 1914. Although there is some doubt whether he knew the exact content of the fiercely nationalistic memorandum, there can be no question that he agreed with its general intentions, even if he might have balked at some of the wording.[40]

However, Schlatter's clearest defenses of the German government came through two public presentations. The first was on August 9, 1914, when Schlatter as a preacher in the Tübingen *Stiftskirche* (University Church)

---

40. Neuer, *Adolf Schlatter*, 563–64.

delivered a sermon on the national day of prayer and repentance. This sermon, along with a paper he presented on the kaiser's birthday in 1915, outlined his ideological support for the German war effort. Schlatter's pro-German thought in these two works echoed that of the vast majority of Germany's theological leadership. However, his ethical justification for the war differed in that it expressed an understanding of the Allies' reasons for war and empathy for the states that chose armed neutrality over participation in the war.

From the pulpit of the *Stiftskirche* in Tübingen, Schlatter brought his politics into his sermon delivered two days after the outbreak of the war. He joined with the congregation in the general excitement and expectation that great things would come from the war. They would be able to see the German nation grow, unified and powerful. However, no amount of hope for good things could on its own bring victory. Schlatter's message was that human efforts were powerless against the will of God. God made the ultimate decisions that would determine the war's outcome. Furthermore, God's decisions would be the best for the whole world. Schlatter noted the importance of this quality from God:

> It is apparent from the history of our neighboring countries, who started and created the schisms, . . . that one race (*Geschlecht*) prepares the path of another and that all influence each other in community. That is why it is so crucial that one [God] is ruling, whose government has no borders, and whose eye is not focused solely on one region of the world, but sees everything. It is of the utmost importance that one will rules and that does not change with the years or vacillate with each generation, but remains to the perfection of all things in eternal justice and eternal grace.[41]

For Schlatter, God's absolute control over the destiny of the world was a matter of comfort and confidence for the outcome of the world.[42]

Schlatter preached that Germany was fighting two wars. One was the earthly war against France and Russia. However, this earthly war was simply a manifestation of a larger cosmic, spiritual war between good and evil, which was fought in every individual's life. Because he believed that God was sovereign over all earthly developments, he maintained that Germans could approach God for help in fighting both wars. Due to the large importance

---

41. Adolf Schlatter, "Am Bettag beim Beginn des Kriegs," sermon delivered August 9, 1914, in Paul Wurster, *Kriegspredigten*, 3.

42. Ibid., 1, 3.

of the worldly happenings, the war needed to be fought both physically and spiritually. He encouraged his parishioners to approach God humbly in the opening days of the war precisely because they were strong and because they expected military victory. Their confidence in their military strength was no reason to go into war. Rather, they should build up their spiritual fortitude. Germany would advance on the Western Front only when its people addressed the underlying spiritual issues. Spiritual strength grew as people turned to God; that was the key to bringing Germany victory in its temporal war.[43]

Since the communal prayers to God would constitute the spiritual aspect of warfare, Schlatter did not tell his listeners that God would exclude them from physical obligations and sacrifice in the war. Prayers lifted to God requesting removal of all pain in the war were cowardly and inappropriate. Since he saw the war as part of God's plan, Schlatter steeled his congregation to accept suffering in war without doubting God's continued grace. True faith would see them through pain and sacrifice, and God would constantly renew their faith in supernatural joy. He told his listeners, "We submit our entire existence to the will of our God, saying, use us as you will, we are ready!"[44] The war would be a blessing to the German people because it would be an opportunity for every German in his or her setting to wholly devote himself or herself to the sovereignty of God.[45]

Schlatter warned that the spiritual campaign of good against evil was just as pressing as the ongoing physical war. It, too, was a life-or-death struggle. Even as the nation mobilized to march to the front, he exhorted his listeners to prepare themselves for war against their inner enemies. Individuals' internal sin would keep them from being able to approach God with petitions for military success. He beseeched members of his congregation to repent of their vengeful, bloodthirsty hatred of their opponents, because God would not answer prayer inspired by repugnant malice. Once the people purified themselves of their sins, they could have confidence in God's quick resolution of the war and correspondingly of the pain it brought.[46]

Schlatter painted a picture of the world after the war. He gave his listeners hope for victory on both the spiritual and political fronts, confident that God would give them victory over their egotism and their false confidence in the strength of this world. While the best attempts of politicians could not prevent war, God had the power to restore and strengthen the community of nations

43. Ibid., 2, 4–5.
44. Ibid., 5.
45. Ibid.
46. Ibid., 5–6.

(*Völker*). God's centrality in the new peace would allow God to give the world true community and justice.[47]

Schlatter had great hope that God would use the war to accomplish mighty works in the German people. They already saw a dramatic increase in productivity from the work of their hands in the early days of the war. He maintained that they could continue to count on such blessings. Schlatter asserted that Germany fought this war for exactly this hope of a greater, better world. He preached this in the full confidence that the sovereign God, whose power and justice would determine the outcome of the war, would bless Germany's good cause.[48]

Schlatter concluded his sermon with a thought that he would later voice at his son's funeral service: "None of us live for ourselves."[49] This German war was a war entered into reluctantly by a powerful, godly nation, which fought for neither individual goals nor individual successes, but rather struggled on in the hope for successes that would aid the whole German nation and that would bring blessings to the whole world.[50]

THE DEVELOPMENT OF SCHLATTER'S WAR INTERPRETATION, 1915

In 1915, after Schlatter had already experienced his greatest personal losses in the war, he took up his pen to defend the German war goals in a paper entitled "Recht und Schuld in der Geschichte" (Rights and Guilt in History). He presented the work to the University of Tübingen faculty on the kaiser's birthday.

Schlatter opened with recognition of the right of states to enter into war. Schlatter historicized political morality. He upheld that moral laws guided nations and determined the justice of war. These laws were the result of the whole scope of a nation's past rather than a natural, eternal law. A nation's moral standards were the collective will of the citizenry formed by the nation's unique history and the people's foundational principles. Despite the extreme nature of Germany's present situation, war could only shift the direction of a nation's moral compass. It could not create morality anew. Therefore, this war was not the result of one nation's single act of evil, but the product of nations' vastly different histories and values.[51]

For Schlatter, the two complementary forces of personal decision and the national will determined how righteously or unjustly a country acted in war.

47. Ibid., 6–8.
48. Ibid.
49. Ibid., 9.
50. Ibid.

Every modern person participated in both of these decisive wills. The national will was the collective choices of the nation's citizenry. He added justice to his definition of the war by explaining that the second moral will that every citizen participated in and that delimited the merits of the First World War was the individual will. Certainly the national will and the national context influenced the individual's decision making, but the individual remained on the whole independent of national sentiment. The state and the citizens lived in a symbiotic relationship, each one for the other, so the state had the responsibility to call its citizens to its defense when threatened. Correspondingly, the citizens had the right and obligation to fight on the nation's behalf. Justice in war came from the proper balance and foundation of these two forces. For Schlatter, any nation deficient in the upright moral character of these two forces was incapable of fighting a just war. Nations that were disunited were incapable of succeeding in the great feats of history. Likewise, nations that robbed their citizens of their individual wills were incapable of acting justly or with moral conviction.[52]

Schlatter also noted that a war like the First World War expanded the definition of guilt. It began because of the common volition of the whole people in each of the Western nations. The war was not simply the desire of a few leaders, but rather the common will of every participant nation. Therefore, when he ascribed guilt and innocence, he conceived of it in the broadest possible categories. Judgments of justice and guilt in this war would be carried by every member of every nation touched by the war. Therefore, Schlatter argued, whole nations needed to be commended or condemned for their acts.[53]

---

51. Adolf Schlatter, *Recht und Schuld in der Geschichte: Rede vor der Universität Tübingen am 27. Jan. 1915, am Geburtstage des Kaisers*, ed. A. Schlatter and W. Lütgert, *Beiträge zur Förderung christlicher Theologie*, vol. 19, no. 1 (Gütersloh: Evangelischer Verlag "Der Rufer," 1915), 5–6, 25.

52. Ibid., 15–16, 23.

53. Ibid., 12. Schlatter understood the challenge of discussing ethics while a war of unparalleled technology raged around them. Mechanically and materially, the war took on a life of its own. It pitted two opposing technological economies working with all their might against each other. Seeing the war simply as a race to technical supremacy, the war could be reduced to some formulaic logical outcome based on technical merit. Schlatter summed up the materialist explanation for the war that he heard around him. If one country knew itself to be technologically hemmed in, it would declare war simply for economic and technical mastery. However, such a view of the war was irresponsible because it ignored the importance of the will in war. The materialist reduction removed the human power to create, or avoid such wars. War was still produced by an act of thinking and willing before the mechanical elements ever engaged. For Schlatter, the human will was the foundation point for all epic moments of history, and therefore that war could not be defined in simple terms of stimulus and response. He demanded the recognition that the human will could implement such terrible destruction. At the same time, he also defended the fundamental belief that human decision could create and defend cherished

Schlatter asserted that the judgment of war guilt was based on the war's ability to create or destroy community. A war was just if it created and built up the community. (Schlatter would have understood the Franco-Prussian War's creation of the German Empire as just such a constructive result.) Contrarily, a nation's wars were unjust when the war destroyed the community that led it. (The Napoleonic Wars proved an example of wars that destroyed more than they created.) However, community was not only found within national boundaries. He suggested that there were important international, universal obligations that further complicated judgment. As a member of the clergy, he could not be exclusively German, because the Christian church was a universal, open community. Likewise, the universal ideals of knowledge and the university did not preclude pro-German sentiment but did make provincialism unethical. War was capable of hindering these communities, as it could destroy national bonds. Any war that preserved the community of the state while destroying the universal communities of faith and learning was just as guilty in Schlatter's definition as one that broke down the cultural and social fabric of a sovereign nation.[54]

Having established the continuing importance of ethical judgment and the corporate responsibility for the war, Schlatter set out to establish the partial justice of the German war effort. Whenever one nation threatened any other nation's essential principles, then Schlatter supported the nation's right to defend those principles by any means necessary. These foundational principles were the glue that knit the whole national fabric together. If they were undermined, then the nation would dissolve into millions of disenfranchised individuals. Schlatter understood Germany's participation in World War I as this sort of act. As a war to defend the essential ideological and spiritual foundation of the German Empire, the First World War was wholly justifiable. He praised the moment of German decision, declaring, "The hours, in which the 'thou shalts' call to the nations and they answer, 'I will do' make the epochs of history."[55] For Schlatter, the German nation internalized the moral standards of historical justice and guilt, so that in a time of crisis such as the First World War, it responded powerfully and righteously.[56]

Although Schlatter determined Germany's cause in the war to be just, he acknowledged that Germany's opponents could make the same claim. Because

---

values. Despite the mechanized character of war in the twentieth century, the ethical appraisal of war remained essential in the modern world. Ibid., 7, 14.

54. Ibid., 19–20.

55. Ibid., 14.

56. Ibid., 14–16.

the ethics of war were determined by each country's national characteristics, Germany's enemies' motivation for war was likewise just. Unlike most other theologians in Germany, he did not cast blame on other nations; rather, he described the war as the inevitable product of colliding ideologies and state fundamentals. The war, though it was the outcome of the righteous national will, was an unavoidable conflict of many justifiable nations whose national interests collided into each other and whose citizens were unwilling to bend to the other country's morality and will.[57]

This historical understanding of ethics separated him significantly from the majority of thinkers in Germany of the period. He allowed that the ethical practice of war and politics was historical and variable from community to community. He explicitly rejected an absolute moral guideline for such significant events other than to say that every community, every nation has the right to defend its core values. Christianity, then, had little direct influence in the engagement and continuation of war, but it guided the interaction between the warring parties.[58]

Schlatter made it clear to his listeners that the ethical mandates of war were as much individual as corporate. A nation made up of people who possessed clear consciences would only enter a just and constructive war. Even against the greatest movements of national wills, an individual never lost his or her individual will. Even though the national will could drown out individuals' voices, the same individuals never forfeited their responsibility for their own actions. Schlatter brought in theological justification for his political statements only at the point of individual responsibility. His interpretation of the religion of Jesus gave relatively few guidelines for the direction of nation-states. However, it did provide clear direction for individual believers as they brought their will in line with God's perfect will.

For Schlatter, the just state and the just individual were inseparable. He used the symbiotic nature of the relationship between the individual and the state to defend his naturalized homeland's honor from the slanderous attacks of Germany's enemies. The full-hearted, industrious support of the war proved that the German people were anything but the militarized automatons of the ruling class that their opponents portrayed. Any state that coercively bent the will of its citizenry would not long remain the friend of its subjects. The state would become the people's enemies and would be ineffective in war. For Schlatter, the effectiveness of Germany's armies proved the moral fortitude and unanimity of the German populace.[59]

57. Ibid., 16–17.
58. Ibid.

Schlatter praised the kaiser for his leadership in the war, suggesting that the kaiser was the personification of the national will. Although Schlatter attributed military willingness to the collective will of the masses, he knew they needed a focal point to coordinate their efforts. As a mob, the masses could not determine the direction and goals of the military. The kaiser was the conduit who took the formless collection of individual wills and formed it into a fervent, unbreakable national will. In a war of the magnitude of the First World War, the utmost hierarchy was necessary, and the position of kaiser was crucial to manage the energies of the nation's people, who so unanimously joined in the war.[60]

In the end, Schlatter concluded that Germany could stand proud: a unified nation of citizens confident in their good consciences as individuals and in their support of the national will. The German nation's action and devotion to its foundational principle convinced Schlatter that the war was just and justifiable. In support of this, Schlatter took up the defense of his king against the verbal attacks of the nation's enemies. He stated, "Now since our history has its ethical foundations and effects, our relationship to the kaiser is a personal connection made complete through that wholesome love that leads to our loyalty. Were this connection incomplete, then our history would be ridden with guilt, but in that we have that completion, we know the justice we receive from our history."[61] Confident in the German hierarchy and the core of German history from which it evolved, Schlatter concluded with the brash statement, "Even when the other nations may compare our kaiser to a Caesar Augustus or a Napoleon, we can answer: we do not have such a Kaiser here, but you cannot take the German Kaiser from us. We call today with unbroken courage and devout loyalty: long live the German Kaiser!"[62]

ADOLF AND PAUL SCHLATTER

The early months of the war gave Schlatter a terrible blow. His son Paul, a doctoral student who was writing his dissertation on Napoleon, was called to service immediately after the war commenced. He joined the western front within two weeks. The elder Schlatter took up a correspondence with his son at the front. His letters combined the news from the front as he received it, optimism for his son's success, and encouragement of his son's faith in the midst of the brutal fighting. At the end of September, Paul was wounded by shrapnel

---

59. Ibid., 22–23.
60. Ibid., 12–13.
61. Ibid., 24.
62. Ibid., 24.

in the shoulder. He was transferred to a military hospital away from the front lines.

Initially, Schlatter was encouraged that his son would recover and could shortly return home. His letters dated from the first days after the news encouraged Paul because he would have time to rest and recover away from the fighting. The elder Schlatter was aware that his son might lose an arm, but he seemed unaware of the wound's location near Paul's chest. He also wrote Paul of his thankfulness that all his children would soon be united in Tübingen, since his daughter Ruth, who had been in England as the war broke out, was home after being part of a civilian exchange with Britain. Paul lingered for a few weeks, but his father's hopes for his recovery proved false.

Schlatter borrowed a car to retrieve his son. Unfortunately, Paul died before he could be picked up. Schlatter drove the coffin home and gave the funeral sermon himself. The loss of his son among the incredible losses of German life at the opening of the war sent Schlatter into a depression, but his support of the war never wavered, as his 1915 discourse on the justice of the German war testifies.[63]

The brief correspondence with his son Paul on the front shows Schlatter's lively interest in the war proceedings and displays his implicit acceptance of the German information authority. He regularly filled much of his letters with the current news from the front. In his first significant letter to Paul, he proclaimed the victorious advancement of the German troops and their allies in France, Serbia, and Austria, and the repulsion of the Russian army in Prussia. He wrote to his son, "The government offered peace to the Belgians that would respect their sovereignty. They offered that when the war allowed it, the Belgian borders would be recognized again. The Belgians rejected the offer. They seem to continue to hope for a French victory in Brussels."[64] Even after his son was wounded, Schlatter sent him information that the German line was holding against the British and French combined forces. He had little hope that Russia could change for the better, but he believed that a German victory would establish a brotherly community among the civilized powers of Europe.[65]

Schlatter's letters to his son also indicate a complete awareness of the serious nature of the war. He delivered no naive odes to heroism but chose to share with his son news of friends and former students who were killed in the war. At no time was this as clear as after he heard of his son's misfortune. He begged his

63. State Church Archive, Stuttgart, Adolf Schlatter Archive, D 40 #458: Briefe aus der Tübingen Zeit an den Sohn Paul, 1905–1914, letters dated August 7, August 17, and September 30, 1914.

64. Ibid., letter dated August 19, 1914.

65. Ibid.

son to inform him of everything important, even if the news were painful and difficult.[66]

In the funeral oration for his son, Schlatter offered a wholly different perspective on the purpose of the war. He portrayed the war as a chance for youth to find God and to rely on God for their comfort and peace in a time of loss and death. A war that led young people to God would prove to be a valuable war. However, not only the youth on the battlefield needed to rely on God in such trying times. The war was quite as much an opportunity for those who remained at home to learn to rely on God. He encouraged his listeners to find God because their war was more than simply a fight against Russians, French, and British. They were involved in a larger, cosmic war against the sinful world and against the destructive elements of nature and history. In this mystical war against the dark and evil cosmic forces, they needed supernatural armor to trust in God's holy plan for the universe.[67]

For Schlatter, military service for a Christian was not merely an option, but even a Christian calling. Since the believer accepted God's blessings from the state, then the Christian citizen was responsible for the state's defense. The Protestant participation in the military was doubly important for Schlatter because a believing presence would also police the state from turning to evil intentions. A Protestant military in a Protestant state would resist the sinful tendencies of some toward power hunger, pride, and war mongering.[68]

SCHLATTER'S REFLECTION AFTER NATIONAL DEFEAT

Schlatter's opinion of the war eventually changed. He stuck doggedly to his defense of German righteousness despite the death of his son and the enormous loss of life. Yet when the German army returned defeated and the peace of Versailles brought about no justice or goodness, Schlatter's opinion of the whole war changed dramatically. He admitted that he had misjudged the war's merits at its beginning, and he regretted the entire conflict.

After the war, his recollections of the hard times from 1914 to 1918 expressed a markedly different impression from those of his orations during the fighting. His memoirs painted a different picture of the German Empire than was found in his fiercely nationalistic speech "Recht und Schuld." In one such anecdote, Schlatter recalled his experience in imperial Germany. As chair of

66. Ibid., letters dated September 30 and October 10, 1914.

67. Adolf Schlatter, quoted in Udo Smidt, ed., *Regem Habemus: Bilder und Zeugnisse au seiner deutschen christlichen Studentenbewegung* (Berlin: Im Furche-Verlag, 1925), 146–48.

68. Adolf Schlatter, *Die christliche Ethik*, 3rd ed. (Stuttgart: Calwer Vereinsbuchhandlung, 1929), 138–39.

the theological department in Berlin, he had been expected to participate in a parade for the dedication of a memorial to Wilhelm I. The ceremony included many leaders of the regime, but the military presence dwarfed all the others. In 1924, he recalled that the parade had acted as a testimony to the military might of the German Empire. His own participation in such a spectacle certainly had made him nothing more than a decoration piece that symbolized the Christian trappings of a militarist state.[69]

After the peace treaty was signed, when his memories of the war turned bitter, Schlatter thought of the war with pain. In his memoirs, Schlatter wrote of having had a growing awareness of aggression between the European states before the actual outbreak of war in 1914. Yet he also recognized his own naïveté because he had allowed his daughter to attend missionary preparation courses in Edinburgh for the summer. In 1914, he had not believed it possible that England would enter the war as an enemy. Even as the Schlatters understood that war was approaching, they had little idea that they were preparing for a "world war." However, the end of the war surprised him even more than the beginning. He recalled that when war broke out, he had expected the eventual return of peace, but at the time, he could conceive of only two possibilities: either a peace earned by a German victory or a peace resolved upon by the complete exhaustion of the fighting nations. During the war, he had never considered the possibility of a German defeat.[70]

In retrospect, Schlatter expressed a deep anger at the British strategy in the war. He had held Britain in high esteem because of its advancements in technology, natural science, and politics and even for its forms of Christian piety. However, his respect for England was shaken by its embargo. Schlatter never understood how a war between standing armies could demand the destruction and elimination of the civilian population. The hardships from the embargo continued to haunt Schlatter long after the war had concluded. He recalled without regret that he had taken up the prayer of many in Germany at the time: "God punish England." Although Germany was not the tool that God used to punish the British embargo, Schlatter remained confident in God's justice and the eventual fulfillment of their petition.[71]

Schlatter also deeply regretted that Germany's downfall was all in the pursuit of Austria's honor. Even before the war, Schlatter had been rebuked by Württemberg's royal house for criticizing its open diplomacy with Austria.

69. Adolf Schlatter, *Erlebtes*, 4th ed. (Berlin: Im Furche-Verlag, 1926?), 14–15.

70. Ibid., 18–19; From Adolf Schlatter, *Rückblick auf meine Lebensarbeit*, 2nd ed. (Stuttgart: Calwer Verlag, 1977), 243, 245.

71. Schlatter, *Erlebtes*, 20–21; Schlatter, *Rückblick*, 243–44.

Schlatter had referred to the Austrian court as a dark sphere where the royal family ruled with little concern for their citizenry. Schlatter felt distressed, even after the war, that Germany had tied its fate so tightly to the Austrian questions of succession. In the end, he regretted the loss of so many German youth, including his own son, for the pursuit of Habsburg justice.[72]

Despite his anger about the war, Schlatter continued to defend the German people's response in the war. He praised their resolution to win the war. He honored their sacrifice of food and luxuries, and he expressed thankfulness that they undertook the long war without bitterness and hatred toward their enemies. Even after the war, Schlatter wrote that the Germans lived by Jesus' rule of loving one's neighbor. Even when the rest of the world tried to starve them and killed their youths, the Germans lived in love for their erstwhile enemies. He also lauded the German youths' willingness to return to their work when the war was decided. He was grateful to see the students return to his classroom with excitement and vigor to complete their studies.[73]

Only after the war was already decided did Schlatter recognize Germany's sins and faults in the First World War. He saw the returning troops marching through the streets with decorated weapons as though their return was one of honor. The return of troops, rejoicing at the cessation of the war they had lost, made the guilt of the nation clear to him. Furthermore, he recognized his own culpability in the guilt because of his support for the war. Of his own impressions of 1918, he wrote, "I say with deep regret, that I too needed the difficult experiences from 1914–1918 to understand my own participation with the state and the pressing necessity of repentance."[74] He hoped that this communal recognition of sin would reunite Germany, fragmented by war, because recognized sin would lead to a communal repentance.[75]

Although Schlatter found peace with the resolution to the war, he never felt comfortable with the outcome of the Versailles Treaty. He saw the treaty as the product of French revenge for that nation's humiliation in 1871. He wrote in retrospect, "Our entry into the war was a morally justifiable act and did not restrict our connection with God but strengthened it. The peace of Versailles, on the other hand, was a crime that had a poisonous result that touched me as well. During the war I never came to hatred, nor was I tempted to murder, but after the peace I fought to protect my soul from the destructive thoughts and dark emotions."[76]

---

72. Schlatter, *Erlebtes*, 17–18; Schlatter, *Rückblick*, 242.

73. Schlatter, *Erlebtes*, 20, 22–23.

74. Ibid., 22.

75. Ibid., 22.

He was also uncertain about the political manifestations of the Weimar Republic. He regretted the loss of conservative morality. He lamented the poverty of the schools and the separation of the church from the schools. He grieved for the rising use of alcohol and the open eroticism in the young republic. He also mourned the growing power of banks to make some wealthy while impoverishing others. However, he also refused to romanticize Germany's aristocratic past. He openly disagreed with a decision by the Tübingen faculty to award the former King of Württemberg an honorific doctorate and title as the "supreme bishop" of the Protestant Church. Schlatter hoped believers would make the best of the situation. He called for a greater presence of the church in political culture to establish a true morality for a new epoch in Germany's political culture.[77]

In his memoirs, he looked back on the sadness of the war in the empty classrooms and on the days he accompanied his son to his train and brought his dead son back to Tübingen. Despite the loss of his son, Schlatter expressed no regret that his son had died for his naturalized country. Even after Germany's defeat, Schlatter continued to affirm the state's right to demand that its citizens fight in its defense.[78]

SCHLATTER'S POSTWAR REVISION OF ETHICS

After the war, Schlatter took up his pen to revise his work *Die christliche Ethik* (Christian Ethics), adding his new revelations from the war about the believer in the modern state and in war. His warning to Christians to refrain from encouraging war remained the same as they were before the First World War. However, he changed his argument when it came to participating in war itself. The very nature of war had changed in 1914. Up to that point, he had felt justified in echoing other theologians who recognized war as a political solution when all other attempts failed to retain peace. Before the First World War, he had believed that war was a means to procure the long-term peaceful coexistence of nations. Since this end was supposed to be the hope of both nations going to war, earlier wars kept the fighting between the armies and away from the civilian populations. This earlier form of war making also ceased its brutality when an individual soldier or the whole army surrendered. In such wars, Schlatter agreed, military service and war were wholly permissible for Christians.[79]

---

76. Schlatter, *Rückblick*, 252.

77. Ibid., 250, 252; Schlatter, *Erlebtes*, 23.

78. Schlatter, *Erlebtes*, 19; Schlatter, *Rückblick*, 246.

79. Schlatter, *Die christliche Ethik*, 165–67.

The First World War made such logic insupportable. For Schlatter, the First World War was a return to pagan warfare that took up the aim to completely destroy opposing peoples through starvation and wanton killing. The First World War was fought without an aim at peace. The war was undertaken solely with the aim of crushing the opposing nation into submission and imposing an unequal armistice.

In the wake of the First World War, war was no longer a means to diplomatic ends. Its barbarity made it impossible to support ethically. Schlatter despaired of such a war. The only hope at its onset would be to pray that God supernaturally "dam the flood of evil that would destroy the nations."[80]

The results of the war also forced Schlatter to reconsider his theological description of the state. In his revisions, Schlatter recognized that the state, like its individuals, was organic and plastic. The state changed its shape and its manifestation to match the qualities and characteristics of the individual. As in his initial edition of *Ethik*, he said the state and the individual lived in a symbiotic relationship. The state's forms could be built anew as the nation's constituency transformed and renewed. Using this logic, Schlatter recognized the rights of a monarchical German Empire to transition into a republic. He was theologically able to recognize the newly formed Weimar Republic, even though he continued to assert that it was unethical for believers to be involved in revolutions and civil wars. The role of Protestants in the state changed relatively little when their government was a republic. Believers were still called to follow the state obediently. His belief that the state still retained its authority over its individual citizens remained unchanged after enduring the war and revolution.[81]

Schlatter encouraged the church to work against the influence of the large cities after the First World War. He had long been suspicious of cities for their impersonal, unfriendly atmosphere and their anonymity. His own experience in Berlin had been confusing and unsettling. After the war, he saw the major urban centers as both the seat of power for the major states and as the nest for revolutionary discontent. Because he saw urban centers as containing the paradoxical keys to unity and disunity, he called the church to minimize cities' destructive tendencies while advancing its unifying forces. The teachings of the church and the community of the Holy Spirit could contain and control the divisive power of urban centers better than any coercive police force. After the war, with the rise of urban culture and urban mass politics, Schlatter called for the church to renew and strengthen its moral voice in the increasingly chaotic

80. Ibid., 167.
81. Ibid., 136–37.

cities. He saw the ideal Germany arising from a just republic with a Christian character.[82]

After the loss of the war, Schlatter struggled to come to grips with its ramifications. However, he eventually came to terms with the peace of 1918. He wrote about the war's outcome in retrospect, saying, "The outcome showed us that we fooled ourselves about the state of our people's inner poverty. We believed only in the courageous bearing of our nation at the outbreak of fighting and we ignored the sensual lust that our people carried and the shackles of their egotistical thoughts that only concerned itself with their own happiness. The outcome of the war destroyed our illusions and thus became a blessing, because the destruction of our illusions is a work of God's grace."[83] In the end, Schlatter welcomed the outcome of the war because it testified to the fragility of human ethics and goodness in a sinful world.[84]

BLUMHARDT AND THE WAR

If Blumhardt's participation in the Social Democratic Party was the climax of his practical ethics, then his experience during the First World War was the culmination of his theological thought. Granted, his theology no longer possessed the unchecked optimism that had fueled his prophetic ministry and his political career from 1890 to 1906, but his thought during the first three years of the war was complex, subtle, and still hopeful. It was full of the wisdom gained from a long life spent shepherding believers, but also colored by disappointments as he watched the Germany he knew and loved collapse in the war.

He understood the various motivations for the war. For some, war inspired the dream of creating a new class of heroes like those that arose out of Bismarck's wars in the 1860s. For the masses, this was the only way for them to have any real involvement in political power and the shape of the world. However, for Blumhardt, war was fundamentally unjust. He condemned the great European powers who thought to use their militaries to try to destroy one another. He recognized this years before Schlatter echoed his statements. He rebuked the states for going against the rule and law of love of enemy that they received from Jesus and from their Christian heritage.

Blumhardt's professional life was bookended by war. He never fought in any of the wars, but his brother Theophil was an officer during the Franco-

82. Ibid., 137–38.

83. Schlatter, *Erlebtes*, 22.

84. Schlatter, *Erlebtes*, 21–22.

Prussian War of 1870–1871. Already at this point in his life, Blumhardt showed himself to be suspicious of the merits of war. He was appalled by the German press's demonization of the French people. In correspondence with his brother, he indicated that he was happy that Theophil had met courteous and honorable French officers. Despite questioning the war, Blumhardt joined in the general exaltation of the unification of the German Empire that ensued from the united German victory over the French. Indeed, throughout Blumhardt's political and theological career, he would hold the same sentiment: a strong support of German patriotism coupled with a distrust of Germany's wars and nationalism.[85]

When Germany and its allies took to the battlefield during the world war, Blumhardt saw the same errors taking place once again. From the start, he perceived the war as the bankruptcy of politics and power. His own political activity, which he had hoped would usher in the kingdom of God a decade earlier, instead ushered in the golden moment for Satan to exert his influence once again. As the battle lines formed, the German press attacked the opponents' character and culture again. Blumhardt exhorted his listeners to be different and to withhold judgment. In a 1915 statement radically different from the vast majority of German sermons at the time, he told his listeners, "Who started the war? Who is responsible? We always want to put the guilt on others. But we want to be people of the Kingdom of Heaven, and as such, even when we read the newspapers, we should not judge others."[86] The war showed how important it remained for Christians to stay separate from the world. Despite all appearances of progress, the events of 1914 showed the world's incapability to stop the outpouring of evil and the coming of war.

THE KINGDOM OF GOD VERSUS THE KINGDOMS OF THIS WORLD

Instead of reacting with bitterness, Blumhardt responded with hope and with his belief in the power of the kingdom of God. The followers of Christ were capable of living life differently within the sinful world. Christians were indeed involved in a war, but the war of the followers of Christ had nothing to do with the physical weapons and bloodshed. In Blumhardt's sermons of the First World War, he referred to the Christian war as internal struggle against the darkness of death and hell. Alluding to the apostle Paul's spiritual armor, Blumhardt called his listeners in this modern era to gird themselves with the shield of faith, the helmet of salvation, and the sword of God's word. Blumhardt declared that "the

---

85. Christoph Blumhardt, *Ansprachen, Predigten, Reden, Briefe, 1865–1917: Neue Texte aus dem Nachlaß.* Herausgegeben von Johannes Harder. vol. I, "Von der Kirche zum Reich Gottes: 1865–1889" (Neukirchen-Vluyn: Neukirchener Verlag des Erziehungsvereins GmbH, 1978), 1:31–32.

86. Blumhardt, *Ansprachen*, 1:187.

Word of God is a sword; with it we can defend ourselves and keep ourselves free from all earthly things. We can live in God's Spirit and approach the Kingdom of God in Jesus Christ, our lord, where we will be free from all restrictions of time and place and from the world's struggles and its suffering."[87] Unlike the German military on the field, Blumhardt was certain of the victory of his side in the spiritual war, so long as they fought alongside Jesus Christ.[88]

Indeed, Blumhardt's most idiosyncratic interpretation during the war was not that he recognized the war's shortcomings and its evil; rather, it was his twist on understanding the world war as part of God's cosmic plan. Where others perceived God's plan manifesting itself in the positive outcome of the war, Blumhardt saw the war as the encroachment of Satan on the world. Blumhardt's spiritual interpretation meant that God's kingdom would not achieve victory when Germany claimed victory. The kingdom of God was being prepared by the war as each believer grew in his or her ability to trust in God's strength regardless of the war's outcome.

Blumhardt's interpretation of the spirituality of the war differed from the common view of Germany as the upholder of all good Christian character. No matter the suffering his listeners were enduring, their troubles were only short-lived. To comprehend the mindlessness of war, Blumhardt held to his biblical expectation of the imminent coming of the kingdom of God. In so doing, he saw in the darkest hours of war a reason to rejoice and to celebrate God's plan for history.

His initial optimism was both for the coming kingdom of God and for a victory for the German Empire. Blumhardt's warning not to judge the enemy did not make him any less a patriot for the German people. In August 1914, Blumhardt had somber words for his Bad Boll guests. War was an evil, and

---

87. Christoph Blumhardt, *Gottes Reich Kommt!: Predigten und Andachten aus den Jahren 1907 bis 1917*, ed, R. Lejeune, vol. 4, *Eine Auswahl aus seinen Predigten, andachten und Schriften* (Zürich: Rotapfel Verlag, 1932), 4:406.

88. Blumhardt, *Christoph Blumhardt*, 4:405–406; Blumhardt, *Ansprachen*, 3:187. Blumhardt's condemnation of the war from its origins was remarkable considering the nearly unanimous support for the war by the German Protestant clergy. Outside of Schweitzer (and excepting the already-deceased Kähler), all of the other prominent theologians of this study openly supported Germany's entry into war. But Blumhardt's condemnation of the war has been used in nearly hagiographic terms. One writer even claims that Blumahrdt prophesied the coming of war. Albrecht Esche, ed., *Warten und Pressieren: 150 Jahre Blumhardt in Bad Boll* (Bad Boll: Evangelische Akademie Bad Boll, 2002) 35. But if mystical foresight is implied, one must note that in the decades around the turn of the century, Blumhardt also made various statements about war coming to an end. It is clear, however, that Blumhardt was against war and militarism and certainly modern propaganda during his entire career, beginning at the time of the Franco-Prussian War.

many would die. However, he held out hope that, like the Franco-Prussian War, this war could still be a boon for the empire. He used Christ's words and described the war as a cross for soldiers to bear, both for their present fatherland, the German Empire, and for their future home, the kingdom of God. If these soldiers were aware of God's role in the war, Blumhardt believed, then they could be comforted that it would all turn out for the best.[89]

Directly from the start of the war, however, Blumhardt preached that the war's goals were not defined by kaisers and kings, but by the God of the universe. God was in control of nations' fates. Even if the war looked bleak, he was confident that God was using it for divine purposes. As the war turned into a standstill, Blumhardt continued his hope that the war would bring with it great spiritual results. As the soldiers saw the severity and cruelty of war on the battlefields, they would also see the hand of God. In their times of distress and suffering, they would turn to God, and God would comfort them. The war was the coming of spiritual renewal of Germany, beginning with the soldiers comforted in their distress. When they saw an outpouring of the spirit of war, God would respond with an outpouring of the Holy Spirit. Blumhardt prepared those around them with the news: the kingdom of God was coming to replace the woes of this world. His stubborn optimism for the acts of God through the follies of humanity continued even in his bleakest hours. He wrote his brother, Theophil, in 1916 that he could no longer see the will of God in the war. However, he still hoped for good to come from the war, even if it was not in the way that many had expected.[90]

THE WORLD WAR AS BACKDROP TO BLUMHARDT'S THEOLOGY

The war provided Blumhardt with the contrast necessary to begin his most complete portrait of the coming kingdom of God. Blumhardt considered the present world with its moral bankruptcy to be a world of bloodshed and pointless conflict. In contrast, the kingdom of God was a kingdom of peace in which the world was ordered properly under God's will. The discontent with this world that Blumhardt had tried to instigate during his time in the SPD never rang as true as it did during the war, long after he had left politics and abandoned the hope that it could change the world for the better. Deep into the war, Blumhardt simply said, "God's will is peace on earth."[91] He told his listeners that this was always God's will, and God always worked for this peace.

89. Blumhardt, *Christoph Blumhardt*, 4:361, 363.
90. Ibid., 4:364, 372, 390; Blumhardt, *Ansprachen*, 3:170, 193.
91. Blumhardt, *Christoph Blumhardt*, 4:413.

Therefore, Blumhardt could say that the war was not caused by God but would be used by God to bring true, real peace. In this last sentiment, Blumhardt echoed Schlatter's interpretation of just war.

Blumhardt continued to contrast this world with God's kingdom. During the war, he asserted that when Germans claimed they wanted peace, they really meant they hoped for a return to their own comfort from earlier times. God's peace was much different, much deeper. God's peace was the complete removal of suffering and conflict. In October 1915, Blumhardt preached to his listeners, "There is so much more that we do not yet understand. Perhaps for this reason our dear Lord allows such a war to come . . . that we may be reminded to think about the peace that he wants to give. This is the peace that is greater than our understanding and all of our culture. For we have seen that even in the most advanced culture conflict still arises so easily between people and everything remains so wicked."[92] In the kingdom of God, there would be only one law: the law of loving one another with God's love. This law, this love, he said, provided true satisfaction for the human soul, and this love knew no national boundaries.[93]

The contrast Blumhardt drew between his present world and the future kingdom of God led him to call for nationwide repentance. Everybody involved in the war, from state rulers to lowly workers, possessed guilt for the coming of war, if for no other reason than that all were so quiet when it came. He caricatured the prewar culture as sitting in its parlor room and lamenting that nothing new ever came to pass. This apathy toward peace constituted guilt as much as the greatest aggression. If people were to respond to the war with repentance, then something great, something from God, would take place. Blumhardt proclaimed that the war was a message from God to their conscience. They were to turn to God and to trust in God. In response, Blumhardt added, God would give them a pure conscience, a new faith, a new certainty, and a new hope.[94]

Blumhardt's family was touched by the catastrophe of the war only after its armistice. Blumhardt's son Georg survived the actual conflict of the war but became sick on the return trip and died shortly thereafter in Stuttgart. Blumhardt, who was already approaching death himself, took the death of his son and the defeat of his nation with a stillness and certainty that in it lay the perfect will of God.[95]

92. Ibid., 4:414–15.

93. Ibid., 4:413–16; Blumhardt, *Ansprachen*, 3:183–84.

94. Blumhardt, *Ansprachen*, 3:176.

Believing Theologians and the First World War

The interpretation of the First World War offered by Blumhardt and Schlatter differed vastly from that of the majority of German clergy. Of course, Blumhardt and Schlatter differed from each other as well. Blumhardt was years ahead of Schlatter in comprehending the futility of the war for the advance of the church. Blumhardt also offered a considerable critique of German society and its government during wartime, something Schlatter failed to do.

Nevertheless, the writings of Schlatter and Blumhardt bore some important similarities. Both believed, alongside the rest of the church, that God had great cosmic plans for the war. However, both also divorced God's plans from an interpretation stating that any good that came out of the war would mean the expansion of the German state and its culture. God was free to work as God willed. Both affirmed that believers could be confident in God's good guidance of the church. Furthermore, both contested the belief that Germany's opponents were driven by evil intentions. Both acknowledged equal guilt, or equal justice, in their interpretation of war guilt. Finally, both acknowledged that the role of the believer's responsibility to the state did not change with the character of the state. Blumhardt's stroke kept him from stating his response to the revolution, but his political thought and his theology lead one to expect that it would not have differed greatly from Schlatter's. Believers needed to submit to the state as the arbiter of justice in the new republic as they had needed to submit to the former empire. Neither theologian would have had space for the archconservative sentiment of the 1920s that the republican government had been illegitimate from its inception. If more Protestants had acted on the thought of Blumhardt and Schlatter, then perhaps a greater challenge to Nazi ascendancy would have risen along with Hitler.[96]

The Rejection of His Elders: The War's Impact on Karl Barth

Karl Barth epitomized both the rejection of the earlier century's theology and the desire to salvage ties to the Protestant Christian faith, but in a greatly changed form. Historical theologians have thoroughly recounted Barth's biography and theology, and an in-depth recitation here is unnecessary. Yet he made brief encounters with the themes of this study. They illuminate

95. Eugen Jäckh, *Blumhardt Vater und Sohn und ihre Botschaft*, 2nd ed. (Berlin: Furche-Verlag, 1925), 174–75.

96. Despite this optimistic interpretation, it ought to be mentioned that Schlatter, who lived until 1938, never joined the Confessing Church protest movement against the Third Reich. It is also impossible to know how Blumhardt might have reacted to Hitler's regime.

Protestantism before the war and the attempt of the band of believing Christian leaders to recast traditional doctrines in light of the best and most productive methods of theological inquiry.

Barth was born in 1868 in Switzerland but went to receive his higher education in Germany. Even though he was a student of Schlatter's at Tübingen for a short time, his formative theology came from the liberal theological tradition. He studied in the finest liberal Christian tradition under Wilhelm Herrmann at Marburg and Adolf Harnack in Berlin. At this time, he worked as an assistant editor on the preeminent liberal theological journal *Christliche Welt* (*Christian World*). When he concluded his university education, shortly before the First World War, he went to join the pastorate in Switzerland. Barth's experience of the First World War came in Safenwil, Switzerland, in the canton of Aargau. From his position in the safety of Switzerland, he saw the war show itself to be barbaric and everything that modern European culture had claimed was impossible.

The brutality and uncivilized carriage of modern Europeans during the war presented Barth with a crisis. If Europe was Christian, its subjects should behave in a manner befitting their faith. If they behaved in a way pleasing to God, then God would not rain destruction on them. God was not a deity who took pleasure in Europe's destruction. Barth stood at a crossroads as he decided how he was supposed to preach the morality and liberality of the Christian faith to his parishioners at a time when Europe, the seat of Christianity, showed itself to be acting against the character of its Christian heritage. Indeed, it was not the internal theological issues that gave him pause, but the practical application of sermon making. The practice of preaching that seemed most resistant to change elsewhere in Germany during the war proved to be Barth's sticking point.[97]

Barth noted the separation between how Christians ought to behave according to the liberal Protestant moral code and how they truly behaved in war and peace. This, in turn, led him to contemplate the difference between God and humanity. The difference was unfathomable. Barth decided that his new preaching would have to focus on the incomprehensible holiness of God. In his mind, this meant a return to an older understanding of the Bible as the word of God. God spoke to men and women through the Bible. As Christians encountered the Scriptures, God transformed them. The responsibility of the pastor in the writing of sermons consisted of bringing the listener to the Scriptures and enabling him or her to encounter the holy God.[98]

---

97. Barth, *Word of God*, 22, 99–100.
98. Ibid., 99–100.

As he faced his weekly duties to prepare sermons, Barth hammered out the outlines to a new understanding of traditional doctrines, and he attempted to return to the theology of the seventeenth century with new perspectives. He called his new theology dialectical or crisis theology. The crisis of humanity, shown so catastrophically in the war, was its sinfulness and separation from God. In the face of an omnipotent and holy God, human efforts were intrinsically flawed and miserable. True Christianity was the recognition of this fact and the submission to God's mercy and grace through Jesus Christ.[99]

The war convinced Barth that the principal pursuits of nineteenth-century Protestant theology were misguided. Dialectical theology was defined as much by its attempt to negate the theology of the nineteenth century as by its new reappraisal of older perspectives of God's holiness and human depravity. He asserted that the Bible could not be intended for the pursuits that nineteenth-century theologians ascribed to it. Most critical theologians from Ritschl to Troeltsch argued that the Bible laid the groundwork for the highest human morality.

Barth commented that this view was flawed. The people in the Bible were sometimes good, but with the exception of Jesus, they were never ideal examples. All of the great leaders and prophets of the Old Testament, from Abraham through David, and those of the New Testament, notably Peter, were flawed and sinful, even self-destructive. The Bible stories could not compare to local legends and heroes who represented national ideals more comprehensively. What the Bible revealed was God's act to restore and strengthen these people despite their shortcomings.[100]

Barth found many sympathetic listeners to his theology during the first years following the war. Emil Brunner, Eduard Thurneyson, Dietrich Bonhoeffer, Rudolf Bultmann, and Paul Tillich all accepted Barth's fundamental critique of the nineteenth century and used it for their own purposes, even when they did not correspond with Barth's new theological creation. However, it is important to note that Barth's critique was leveled against critical Christianity. His sweeping rejection did not include the sort of Christianity encouraged by Schlatter and Kähler. He was certainly familiar with them. His rejection of Schlatter's teaching of ethics proved that he would never accept prewar believing theology absolutely. Yet his break was complete enough that he believed he could not simply pick and choose the elements of nineteenth-century theology that suited him or agreed with him. Even the believing

99. Karl Barth, *The Epistle to the Romans*, trans. Edwyn C. Hoskyns, 6th ed. (London: Humphrey Milford, 1933), 1–2.

100. Barth, *Word of God*, 37–39.

Christianity of the nineteenth century still grounded its efforts on modern critical interpretations of the Bible and so on an incorrect understanding of God's infinitude.

Barth had to break from everything in the nineteenth century because the First World War was such an all-encompassing catastrophe. He turned the attention of his bile to theological liberalism, since that was the story of his own biography. However, Barth's true break was from the meaningless sermons and practical Christianity that sprang from conservative and liberal clergy alike. German Protestantism as a whole had grown too comfortable with its religion and its God. Had the German pastors who were already of a conservative conviction adopted Kähler's, Schlatter's, and Blumhardt's modern piety, then this break might have proven unnecessary. Despite Schlatter's support for the war, the faith of Kähler, Schlatter, and Blumhardt was not tied to the national character of Germany. It adapted a self-critical outlook that sought to be separate from the world.

Barth's influence on twentieth-century German Protestant theology cannot be overstated. For good or ill, his early work defined the shape of theology for the following century, as Strauss's had for the previous century. The result was that the picture of nineteenth-century theology was defined as the movement from which he broke. Subsequent thinkers continued to relegate Stoecker, Kähler, Schlatter, and Blumhardt to the periphery of thought and ignored their influence and their representation of nineteenth-century believing theology except insofar as it influenced the generation of the crisis theologians.

Ironically, it was probably Stoecker (whose theology and nationalist impressions would have been the most disagreeable to Barth) who provided the most important influence on Barth. When Barth was confronted with a distressing political situation in the Third Reich, he built a coalition of like-minded theologians to take on church political and later secular political issues. In so doing, he followed the path of the believing Positive Union movement of the nineteenth century and provided in it one of the most remarkably successful protest movements against Hitler's influence on the church.

8

Conclusion
The Relics of the First Modern Believing Theology

The effects of the First World War on theological currents were immense. Some intellectual historians like to find proto-twentieth-century thought before the war to diminish the thesis that the war changed Europe's character of thought. Undoubtedly, such early precursors of the new century's leading ideas were to be found in the nineteenth century, but these were certainly not widely held. For the popular Protestant conscience, the war was a watershed event. After congregations had listened for four years to preachers insisting on God's particular plan for German victory, a credibility gap arose that was simply insurmountable. German Protestant clergy's continued insistence on God's favor during the war undermined the church's moral authority as a result of their inability to cope with the destruction and sorrow of the First World War. As the biblical friends of Job proved unable to comfort their friend in suffering, the clergy of Germany were unable to devise a proper response to their own nation's plagues. After the war, Protestantism needed to radically reform itself or be abandoned.

For this reason, the development and evolution of theological ideas that had been progressing in the decades before the war were abandoned. From the university theologians to the lay parishioners, Protestants disregarded the alternative viewpoints that might have grown to prominence, had the war never taken place. The prewar generation, even in a theological field littered with innovative giants from both the critical and believing camps, was remembered principally for being non-epochal. The postwar generations reduced even Adolf Harnack, Ernst Troeltsch, and Albert Schweitzer (or at least his theology) to minor players in the modern era. These brightest names of the generation only continued to be studied within the specific fields of historical theology. It is therefore not surprising that Stoecker, Kähler, Schlatter, and Blumhardt have been likewise ignored by all but the narrowest histories.

In one example, the most notable characteristic of Karl Barth's *Protestant Theology in the Nineteenth Century* is that fully half of the book is an extended introduction covering the theology of the eighteenth century. When Barth finally arrives at the nineteenth century, he includes some orthodox theologians from the middle of the century: August Tholuck, Johann Tobias Beck, and Johann Christoph Blumhardt. However, he spends the most ink outlining the developments of critical and liberal theology. Most subsequent historians of the era have done likewise. Their story of the nineteenth century is one of new developments in liberalism and the slow demise of traditional piety. This story possesses many merits. The new university model epitomized by Berlin in the nineteenth century advanced innovation over orthodoxy. Particularly by the 1870s, the most prominent university theologians no longer affirmed many of the important historical doctrines of the church. However, this is a one-sided look at the church. From the perspective of the pastorate, this theological challenge to orthodoxy was a fringe movement. The pastorate remained strongly devoted to a traditional interpretation of the Scriptures even as the clergy's prominence within society was diminishing.

A reappraisal of this nineteenth-century theology from the perspective of the pastorate finds that the story of the conservative response to the critical challenge needs its own analysis. Here the believing theologians arrived not as a rearguard action against the inevitability of the liberal movement, but rather as individual thinkers in their own right whose audience and message were shaped by the practical needs of the majority of the pastorate. Their theology likewise was not defensive (even if some of their political actions were).

Whether Stoecker, Kähler, Schlatter, and Blumhardt have any insight to bring to modern theology is beyond the scope of this book. They were men of their age who developed their picture of God from the general ideas of their nineteenth-century environments. Their theology certainly appears anachronistic in many of its most important ethical and national assertions. Nevertheless, this cannot overshadow their considerable creativity and breadth of influence as believing Protestants sought to define themselves within and against modernity.

Albeit inelegantly and only in political terms, Adolf Stoecker realized the precarious situation of Protestant belief as it entered an unprecedented era of skepticism. The threat from intellectual skepticism, working-class antagonism, and industrialization were threatening to overthrow the long-held responsibility of the Protestant state church to offer Germany moral direction and social stability. In response, Stoecker rallied the remaining resources of the church in an attempt to build up levees against the rising water of modern secularism. In total, Stoecker's work was truly productive. He raised the visibility of the church hierarchy in government through church politics and the creation of the Christian Social Party. He advocated and achieved the placement of sympathetic professors in the leading universities of the empire. Finally, he gave voice and structure to an informal organization (which took the name of the allied church political group, Positive Union) that could formulate a successful response to the culture threatening its existence. However, even as he succeeded at creating all of these, he also sowed the seeds of the same movement's destruction. He brought into church leadership and politics a populist bigotry that undermined the gravitas called for by the ethical questions that inevitably formed in the forging of a new state. Likewise, he perfected a simplistic moral preaching style that proved the template for pastors who preferred retreating into obscurantist nationalism over responding to the real intellectual challenges of their congregations.

Despite the weaknesses of the system, Martin Kähler, Adolf Schlatter, and their university allies adopted Stoecker's vision of a robust, self-confident state church for their own. They utilized the platform of a contested nature of the Scriptures to sweep aside traditional doctrines of verbal inerrancy and unquestioned devotion to Lutheran scholasticism in favor of a subjective hermeneutic. Their system allowed the modern skeptic to challenge traditional biblical interpretations, to question the Bible's origins, and to embrace the newest historical research while at the same time maintaining the Protestant centrality of Scriptures to faith. Their example of top-level research and collegiality allowed a peaceful coexistence between themselves and critical theologians in university faculties. Most importantly, as Blumhardt, Schlatter, and Kähler showed, this theology enabled interesting, refreshing sermons that addressed contemporary cultural issues in a modern idiom.

They acted on the hope that they could reach enough students with their ideas and beliefs to reshape the contours of the German pastorate. Indeed, on the eve of the First World War, it looked as though they might have been successful. New vitality and energy were evident in German sermon making. Students of Kähler, Schlatter, and their allies were able to develop theological teaching that moved beyond a simple theology of blessings for good national behavior and curses for sinful behavior. Their sermons were nuanced, humble, and innovative. Yet the remains of this theology are difficult to uncover today.[1]

---

1. Ironically, the clearest line of influence of these theologians lay in the neoliberal schools of Paul Tillich and Rudolf Bultmann. These theologians appropriated ideas from Martin Kähler's *The So-Called*

The intellectual environment of post-Enlightenment Germany created monstrous challenges for Christians of all stripes. Reason was valued above revelation, and empirical objectivity became the standard for all fields of knowledge. This intellectual milieu shaped and defined Stoecker, Kähler, Schlatter, Blumhardt, and their colleagues. But they never wavered in their belief that the best advancements of their modern age could be reconciled with their admiration of the prominent traditional doctrines of the church. They forged a new piety that unabashedly accepted the ideal of modern empiricism that scientific inquiry could broaden Protestants' understanding of their faith. They did not shy away from the close inspection of the biblical texts' origins and the biblical authors' intent and identity. They accepted these methods so long as the scholar accepted the possibility of God's active participation in the Bible's formation. Modernity's reason could not be allowed to hinder God's revelation. So long as modernity accepted the Bible as the word of God, they perceived no inherent contradictions between scholarship, hermeneutics, and faith.

This understanding of God's authority and the limits of human reason offered a moral direction wherein good action consisted of the finite creature's pursuit of the infinite creator's will. The perfect will of God could be grasped as God was allowed to transform the individual believer. Morality, too, was placed on the same level as the knowledge of God. It was malleable to the situation and event, and it was based upon the believer's connection to God. As Blumhardt suggested, this might even mean questioning the divine authority of the kaiser and supporting radically democratic socialists.

The failure of this modern, believing theology was its limited effect on the students and pastors of Germany. Schlatter and Kähler certainly received much support and garnered respect from much of German-speaking Protestantism. One must remember, after all, that the majority of German Protestants of the time looked askance at the radically critical views issuing from the universities. But questions still arise how Kähler and Schlatter, who dedicated themselves to crafting the art of teaching pastors, could have had so little real influence on the

---

Historical Jesus and the Historic, Biblical Christ in the formation of their central ideas of the separation of *Historie* and *Geschichte* in the life of Jesus. (Both words mean *history* in German, but *Historie* was used by Bultmann and Tillich to suggest an objective, factual history as understood in post-enlightenment categories. *Geschichte*, which is both *history* and *story* in German, was used to connote stories or myths of a higher truth. They borrowed this dichotomy from Kähler's *So-Called Historical Jesus and the Historic, Biblical Christ*; the German title uses the terms: *Der sogenannte historische Jesus und der geschichtliche, biblische Christus*.) They also adopted Kähler's description of the central responsibility of the preaching (*kerygma*) of the gospel.

faith of their age. The damning cause of their limited influence came from their separation of theology from faith. Their theology was modern, but their faith was pietistic. They never demanded their students accept their new theology; they simply offered it. For this reason, their students could reject the theology while still expressing considerable sympathy for them as spiritual mentors.

Despite the common viewpoints and doctrine, the German clergy of the early twentieth century proved incapable of reforming liturgical preaching and expression of the faith. Individual pastors and parishioners might have agreed wholly with Schlatter and Kähler, but they were unable to find creative ways to incorporate their modern ideas into their highly formalized sermons. Christoph Blumhardt found a way to change the nature of worship, but only in his personal sphere. His adherence to the Social Democratic Party showed a willingness to question the Christian claims of his society and his government, but it alienated him from other clergy, who were unable to see past their deep suspicion of Marxist atheism. The logic of these three examples of believing Christian leadership was consistent, but it required a reformation of the mind. It required a thoroughly modern understanding of Christian doctrine. It could not coincide with sermons built wholly from Reformation-era themes, because the Reformers never questioned the authority and foundation of the Scriptures. Only a modern Christian could have a supple enough faith to respond to the moral challenges of the twentieth century.

Bibliography

Unpublished Sources

State Church Archive Speyer (Landeskirchliches Archiv Speyer)

Handwritten Documents

Abt. 150.20: Johann Jakob Griess.

Personal Files

Abt. III Akt #160: Emil Lund.
Abt. III Akt #895: Hermann Böhner.

State Church Archive, Stuttgart (Landeskirchliches Archiv Stuttgart)

Adolf Schlatter Archive

D 40 #193: Die älteste Christenheit und die Bibel.
D 40 #193/9: Rede über Johannesevangelium.
D 40 #193/10: Die biblisch-theologische Darstellung der Lehre Jesu.
D 40 #420: Briefe an Martin Kähler.
D 40 #426: Briefe von Kähler an Schlatter, Briefe von Harnack an Schlatter.
D 40 #427: Briefe von Weiss an Schlatter.
D 40 #458: Briefe aus der Tübingen Zeit an den Sohn Paul, 1905–1914.
D 40 #1233: Briefe an Martin Kähler.
D 40 #1237: Briefe an Adolf Harnack.
D 40 #1987: Vorlesung zur Leben Jesu.

Handwritten Documents

HS 22: Otto Gittinger.

PERSONAL FILES

A27 #27: Gotthilf Ammon.

A27 #41: Paul Heinrich Andler.

A27 #100: Johannes Bauder.

A27 #172: Eduard Beittler.

A27 #192: Karl Berckhemer.

A27 #197: Gottlob Berner.

A27 #269: Wilhelm Bochterle.

A27 #327: Hermann Breitweg.

A27 #353: Daniel Buck.

A27 #376: Adolf Bürk.

A27 #382: Hugo Bunz.

A27 #462: Theodor Daur.

A27 #503: Albert Dierolf.

A27 #507: Ernst Dieterich.

A27 #581: Wilhelm Eberwein.

A27 #645: Nathanael Elsäßer.

A27 #704: Heinrich Eytel.

A27 #880: Adolf Gehring.

A27 #897: Georg Erich Gerbeth.

A27 #1267: Gerhard Herrmann.

A27 #1407: Theodor Holzapfel.

A27 #1480: Edward Julius Richard von Jan.

A27 #3147: Spengler, Karl Wilhelm.

LOWER SAXONY STATE AND UNIVERSITY LIBRARY, GÖTTINGEN (NIEDERSÄCHSISCHE STAATS- UND UNIVERSITÄTSBIBLIOTHEK, GÖTTINGEN)

MARTIN KÄHLER PAPERS

Cod. Ms. M. Kähler, Box 11, Späne von der theologischen Hobelbank, Predigten.

Cod. Ms. M. Kähler, Box 12, Ansätze und Entwürfe.

Cod. Ms. M. Kähler, Box 15, Predigten.

NORDELBISCHE STATE CHURCH ARCHIVE, KIEL (NORDELBISCHE LANDESKIRCHLICHES ARCHIV)

Bestand 42.07 #262: Bruno Meyer.

Bestand 94 lfd. Nr. 80: Kaftan, Theodor, *Die gegenwärtige Kriegslage und wir Christen*. Ratzeburg, Schlew.-Holst. Christenvereins, 1916.

Bestand 94 lfd. Nr. 182: Karstens.

National Library, Berlin (Staatsbibliothek zu Berlin)

Adolf Harnack Papers

Kasten 11, #1187, Harnack, Adolf. "Address by His Excellency, Professor von Harnack." *German-American Meeting of Sympathy in the Berlin City Hall, August 11, 1914.* Berlin: Liebheit & Thiesen, 1914.
Kasten 11, #1189, Harnack, Adolf. Antwort auf das Schreiben von 11 Großbritannischen Theologen.

PUBLISHED SOURCES

Aeschbacher, Robert. *Ich lebe, und ihr sollt auch leben.* Basel: Friedrich Reinhardt, 1911.
Andersen, F. *Gottes Gedanken in unsrer Geschichte verkörpert in der Kirche bei Idstedt: Predigt bei der Einweihungsfeier am 24. Juli 1903 gehalten von F. Andersen Hauptpastor an St. Johanis in Flensburg.* Schleswig: Julius Bergas, 1903. Found in Nordelbische Landeskirchliches Archiv, Bestand 98.019 lfd. Nr. 1.
Althaus, Paul. *Adolf Schlatter: Gedächtnisheft der deutschen Theologie.* Stuttgart: W. Kohlhammer, n.d.
Althaus, Paul, Gerhard Kittel, and Hermann Strathmann. *Adolf Schlatter und Wilhelm Lütgert zum Gedächtnis.* Beiträge zur Förderung christlicher Theologie 40, 1, edited by Paul Althaus. Gütersloh: C. Bertelsmann, 1938.
Barth, Karl. *The Epistle to the Romans.* Translated by Edwyn C. Hoskyns. 6th ed. London: Humphrey Milford, 1933.
———. *Ethics.* Edited by Dietrich Braun. Translated by Geoffrey W. Bromiley. New York: Seabury, 1981.
———. *Protestant Theology in the Nineteenth Century: Its Background and History.* Translated by Brian Cozens. London: SCM, 1972.
———. *The Word of God and the Word of Man.* Translated by Douglas Horton. New York: Harper & Row, 1957.
Beintker, Horst. *Die Christenheit und das Recht bei Adolf Schlatter: Unter besonderer Berücksichtigung des Kirchenrechts.* Edited by Hans Urner. Theologische Arbeiten 4. [East] Berlin: Evangelische Verlagsantalt, 1957.
Benz, Gustav. *Dennoch bei Gott: Predigten aus den Kriegsjahren 1914–1916.* 2nd ed. Basel: Friedrich Reinhardt, 1916.

Bergmann, Peter. *Nietzsche, "the Last Antipolitical German."* Bloomington: Indiana University Press, 1987.

Blumhardt, Christoph. *Ansprachen, Predigten, Reden, Briefe, 1865–1917: Neue Texte aus dem Nachlaß.* Edited by von Johanes Harder. 3 vols. Neukirchen-Vluyn: Neukirchener Verlag des Erziehungsvereins, 1978.

———. *Eine Auswahl aus seinen Predigten, Andachten und Schriften.* Edited by R. Lejeune. 4 vols. Zurich: Rotapfel Verlag, 1924–32.

———. *Gedanken aus dem Reiche Gottes, im Anschluß an die Geschichte von Möttlingen und Bad Boll, und unsere heutige Stellung: Ein vertrauliches Wort an Freunde.* Bad Boll: Bad Boll, 1895.

Blumhardt, Johann Christoph. *Blumhardts Kampf: Die Krankheits- und Heilungsgeschichte der G. Dittus in Möttlingen.* 5th ed. Stuttgart-Waiblingen: Verlag der Plakatmission, n.d.

Bockmühl, Klaus, Herausgeber. *Die Aktualität der Theologie Adolf Schlatters.* Giessen: Brunnen-Verlag, 1988.

Brazill, William J. *The Young Hegelians.* New Haven, CT: Yale University Press, 1970.

Breit, Thomas. *Lieben, Leiden, Leben.* Augsburg: Schlosser, 1912.

Brezger, Rudolf. *Gelebte Theologie: Adolf Schlatter 1852–1938.* Stuttgart: Quell Verlag, 1983.

Bungenberg, Theodor. *Gleichnisse Jesu.* Edited by E. Rolffs. Moderne Predigt-Bibliothek Volume 9, no. 4. Göttingen: Vandenhoeck & Ruprecht, 1912.

Class, Helmut. "Blumhardt Vater und Sohn—Anruf und Anstoß heute." In *Leben in Gang halten: Pietismus und Kirche in Württemberg*, edited by Theo Sorg. Metzingen: Ernst Franz Verlag, 1980.

Collins Winn, Christian T., *Jesus Is Victor! The Significance of the Blumhardts for the Theology of Karl Barth.* Eugene, OR: Pickwick, 2009.

Conser, Walter H. Jr. *Church and Confession: Conservative Theologians in Germany, England, and America, 1815–1866.* Macon: Mercer University Press, 1984.

Cremer, Ernst. *Hermann Cremer: Ein Lebens- und Charakterbild.* Gütersloh: Bertelsmann, 1912.

Davis, Natalie Zemon. *Society and Culture in Early Modern France: Eight Essays.* Stanford, CA: Stanford University Press, 1975.

Dibelius, Otto, ed. *Er ist bei uns wohl auf dem Plan: Festtagspredigten.* Volume 3. *Bußtag und Totenfest.* Berlin-Lichterfelde: Edwin Runge, 1917.

Diephouse, David J. *Pastors and Pluralism in Württemberg, 1918–1933.* Princeton, NJ: Princeton University Press, 1987.

Doll, K.W., and Paul von Zimmermann, *Zwei Predigten bei der 44. Hauptversammlung des Evangelischen Vereins der Gustav-Adolf-Stiftung.* Leipzig: Centralvorstandes des Evangelischen Vereins der Gustav-Adolf-Stiftung, 1890.

Dwyer, Philip G. ed. *Modern Prussian History, 1830–1947.* New York: Longman, 2001.

Eley, Geoff, ed. *Society, Culture, and the State in Germany, 1870–1930.* Ann Arbor: University of Michigan Press, 1996.

Engelmann, Hans. *Kirche am Abgrund: Adolf Stoecker und seine antijüdische Bewegung.* Band 5. *Studien zu jüdischem Volk und christlicher Gemeinde.* Berlin: Selbstverlag Institut Kirche und Judentum, 1984.

Esche, Albrecht, ed. *Warten und Pressieren: 150 Jahre Blumhardt in Bad Boll.* Bad Boll: Evangelische Akademie Bad Boll, 2002.

Evangelisches Gesangbuch: Ausgabe für die Evangelische Kirche in Hessen und Nassau. 2nd ed. Frankfurt/Main: Spener Verlagsbuchhandlung, 1998.

Ein Feste Burg. Volume 1. *Das Wort Gottes im Kriege: Predigten und geistliche Reden aus der Kriegszeit.* Berlin: Schmidt & Co., n.d.

Fritzsche, Michael. "Gottes Mann in der SPD: Christoph Blumhardt (1842–1919)." In *Verletzlichkeit und Vertrauen: Erhard John zum Dank*, edited by Harald Nehb. Ulm: Pfarrerschaft und Mitarbeitern im Kirchenbezirk Ulm, 1985.

Gregory, Frederick. *Nature Lost? Natural Science and the German Theological Traditions of the Nineteenth Century.* Cambridge, MA: Harvard University Press, 1992.

Hadorn, Wilhelm. *Er ist unser Friede.* Neukirchen: Buchhandlung des Erziehungsvereins, 1915.

Hammer, Karl. *Deutsche Kriegstheologie, 1870–1918.* Munich: Deutsche Taschenbuch Verlag, 1974.

Hampe, Johann Christoph. "Kritiker der Kirche: Christoph Blumhardt." In *Kritik an der Kirche*, edited by Hans Jürgen Schultz. Stuttgart: Kreuz-Verlag, 1958.

Harnack, Adolf. *German-American Meeting of Sympathy in the Berlin City Hall, August 11, 1914.* Berlin: Liebheit & Thiesen, 1914. Found in Staatsbibliothek zu Berlin, Adolf Harnack Nachlass, Kasten 11, #1187.

———. *What Is Christianity?* Translated by Thomas Bailey Saunders. Philadelphia: Fortress Press, 1957.

Hauri, Johannes. *Nicht Frieden, sondern das Schwert: Acht Kriegs-Predigten.* Basel: Friedrich Reinhardt, 1914.

Heinzelmann, Gerhard. *Vom Bürgertum im Himmel: Fünfzehn Predigten aus den Jahren 1917 und 1918.* Basel: Verlag von Kober C. F. Spittlers Nachfolger, 1918.

Hengel, Martin, and Ulrich Heckel, eds. *Paulus und das antike Judentum: Tübingen-Durham-Symposium im Gedenken an den 50. Todestag Adolf Schlatters.* Wissenschaftliche Untersuchungen zum Neuen Testament 58. Tübingen: Mohr, 1991.

Heron, Alasdair. *A Century of Protestant Theology.* Philadelphia: Westminster, 1980.

Herwig, A. *Drei Predigten, gehalten bei Ausbruch des Krieges 1914.* Asperg: Karl Wolf, 1915.

Heschel, Susannah. *Abraham Geiger and the Jewish Jesus.* Chicago: University of Chicago Press, 1998.

Hoover, A. J. *God, Germany, and Britain in the Great War: A Study in Clerical Nationalism.* New York: Praeger, 1989.

Hunt, Lynn. *Politics, Culture, and Class in the French Revolution.* Berkeley: University of California Press, 2004.

Jäckh, Eugen. *Blumhardt Vater und Sohn und ihre Botschaft.* 2nd ed. Berlin: Furche-Verlag, 1925.

———. *Christoph Blumhardt: Ein Zeuge des Reiches Gottes.* Stuttgart: Evang. Missionsverlag, 1950.

Jäger, Hans Ulrich. *Politik aus der Stille: Ernesto Cardenal, Dom Helder Camara, Martin Luther King, Christoph Blumhardt, Niklaus von Flüe.* Zurich: Theologischer Verlag, 1980.

Jonas, Raymond. *France and the Sacred Heart: An Epic Tale for Modern Times.* Berkeley: University of California Press, 2000.

Kaftan, Theodor. *Die gegenwärtige Kriegslage und wir Christen.* Ratzeburg, Schleswig-Holstein: Christenvereins, 1916. Found in Nordelbische Landeskirchliches Archiv, Bestand 94 lfd. Nr. 80.

———. *Von der Kirche: Predigt gehalten zur Eröffnung der Außerordentlichen Gesamtsynode der evangelisch-lutherischen Kirche Schleswig-Holsteins am 5. Dezember, 1907.* Schleswig: Julius Bergas, 1908. Found in Nordelbische Landeskirchliches Archiv, Bestand 94 lfd. Nr. 80.

———. *Wo stehen Wir? Eine kirchliche Zeitbretrachtung verfaßt in Veranlassung des Falles heydorn bsw. des Falles Jatho.* Schleswig: Julias Bergas, 1911. Found in Nordelbische Landeskirchliches Archiv, Bestand 94 lfd. Nr. 80.

Kähler, Martin. *Aufsätze zur Bibelfrage.* Edited by Ernst Kähler. Munich: Kaiser Verlag, 1967.

——. *Dogmatische Zeitfragen: Alte und neue Ausführungen zur Wissenschaft der christlichen Lehre*. 3 vols. 2nd ed. Leipzig: Deichert (Georg Böhme), 1907–13.

——. *Geschichte der protestantischen Dogmatik im 19. Jahrhundert*. Edited by Ernst Kähler. Munich: Kaiser, 1962.

——. *Das Gewissen: Ethische Untersuchung; Die Entwicklung seiner Namen und seines Begriffes*. Darmstadt: Wissenschaftliche Buchgesellschaft, 1967.

——. *Jesus und das Alte Testament*. Neukirchen–Fluyn: Neukirchener Verlag des Erziehungsverein, 1965.

——. *Das Kreuz*. Edited by A. Schlatter and W. Lütgert. Beiträge zur Förderung christlicher Theologie 15. Jahrgang. Gütersloh: Evangelischer Verlag "Der Rufer," 1911.

——. *Der Lebendige Gott: Fragen und Antworten von Herz zu Herz*. Leipzig: Deichert (Böhme), 1894.

——. *Neutestamentliche Schriften in genauer Wiedergabe ihres Gedankenganges dargestellt und durch sie selbst ausgelegt*. Darmstadt: Wissenschaftliche Buchgesellschaft, 1968.

——. *Schriften zu Christologie und Mission: Gesamtausgaben der Schriften zur Mission mit einer Bibliographie*. Edited by Heinzgünter Frohnes. Theologische Bücherei: Neudrucke und Berichte aus dem 20. Jahrhundert 42. Munich: Kaiser Verlag, 1971.

——. *The So-Called Historical Jesus and the Historic, Biblical Christ*. Translated and edited by Carl E. Braaten. Philadelphia: Fortress Press, 1964.

——. *Der Sogenannte historische Jesus und der geschichtliche, biblische Christus*. Edited by E. Wolf, Theologische Bücherei: Neudrucke und Berichte aus dem 20. Jahrhundert 2. Munich: Kaiser Verlag, 1953.

——. *Theologe und Christ: Erinnerungen und Bekenntnisse von Martin Kähler*. Edited by Anna Kähler. Berlin: Im Furche-Verlag, 1926.

——. *Wie Studiert man Theologie im ersten Semester? Briefe an einen Anfänger*. 2nd ed. Leipzig: Deichert, 1892.

——. *Die Wissenschaft der christlichen Lehre: Von dem evangelischen Grundartikel aus*. Neukirchen–Fluyn: Neukirchener Verlag des Erziehungsverein, 1966.

Karstens, *Predigt für den aus Anlaß des Heldentodes der ersten 7 Gefallenen der hemmingstedter Kirchengemeinde angesetzten Gedächtnisgottesdienst am 22. Nach Trinitatis, den 8. November 1914*. Found at Nordelbische Landeskirchliches Archiv, Bestand 94 lfd. Nr. 182.

Koch, Grit. *Adolf Stoecker, 1835–1909: Ein Leben zwischen Politik und Kirche*. Erlangen: Palm & Enke, 1993.

Kühl-Freudenstein, Olaf, Peter Noss, and Claus P. Wagener, eds. *Kirchenkampf in Berlin 1932–1942: 42 Stadtgeschichten*. Berlin: Institut Kirche und Judentum, 1999.

Kühne, Johannes, ed. *Ein Vater in Christo: Erinnerungen an Adolf Schlatter*. Berlin: Im Furche-Verlag, 1939.

Kümmel, Georg. *The New Testament: The History of the Investigation of Its Problems*. Translated by S. McLean Gilmour and Howard C. Kee. Nashville: Abingdon, 1970.

Langbein, Paul, ed. *Evangelisches Haus-Predigtbuch: Eine Sammlung auserlesener Evangelien-Predigten aus alter und neuer Zeit auf alle Sonn-, Fest- und Feiertage des Kirchenjahrs*. Reutlingen: Enßlin und Laiblin, n.d..

Lim, Hee-Kuk. *"Jesus ist Sieger!" bei Christoph Friedrich Blumhardt: Keim einer kosmischen Christologie*. Basler und Berner Studien zur historischen und systematischen Theologie 67. Frankfurt am Main: Peter Lang, 1996.

Lueken, Wilhelm. *Die zehn Gebote*. Edited by E. Rolffs. Moderne Predigt-Bibliothek. Volume 9, no. 2. Göttingen: Vandenhoeck & Ruprecht, 1911.

Lütgert, Wilhelm. *Adolf Schlatter als Theologe innerhalb des geistigen Lebens seiner Zeit*, Volume 37, no. 1. Beiträge zur Förderung christlicher Theologie, edited by A. Schlatter and W. Lütgert. Gütersloh: Bertelsmann, 1932.

Macquarrie, John. *Twentieth-Century Religious Thought*. Philadelphia: Trinity Press International, 1989.

Masius, Carl. *Wandelt wie die Kinder des Lichts! Predigt zum Examen Ostern 1900 im Predigerseminar zu Kropp*. Schwerin in Mecklenburg: Sandmeyersche Hofbuchdruckerei, 1900. Found in Nordelbische Landeskirchliches Archiv, Bestand 25.01 lfd. Nr. 69.

McAleer, Kevin. *Dueling: The Cult of Honor in Fin-de-Siècle Germany*. Princeton, NJ: Princeton University Press, 1994.

McGrath, Alister E. *The Making of German Christology: From the Enlightenment to Pannenberg*. New York: Basil Blackwell, 1986.

McLeod, Hugh. *Religion and the People of Western Europe, 1789–1989*. 2nd ed. Oxford: Oxford University Press, 1997.

Meier, Klaus-Jürgen. *Christoph Blumhardt: Christ—Sozialist—Theologe*. Basler und Berner Studien zur historischen und systematischen Theologie 40. Frankfurt am Main: Peter Lang, 1979.

Neill, Stephen, and Tom Wright. *The Interpretation of the New Testament, 1861–1986*. New York: Oxford University Press, 1988.

Neuer, Werner, *Adolf Schlatter: A Biography of Germany's Premier Biblical Theologian*. Translated by Robert W. Yarborough. Grand Rapids: Baker, 1995.

———. *Adolf Schlatter: Ein Leben für Theologie und Kirche*. Stuttgart: Calwer Verlag, 1996.

———. *Der Zusammenhang von Dogmatik und Ethik bei Adolf Schlatter: Eine Untersuchung zur Grundlegung christlicher Ethik*. Giessen: Brunnen-Verlag, 1986.

Niese, —— in Flensburg u. Consistorialrath —— Ahlfeld in Hannover. *Zwei Predigten beim Jahresfest des schleswig-holsteinischen Hauptvereins der Gustav-Adolf-Stiftung am 9. Und 10. August 1892 in Meldorf*. Kiel: Schmidt & Klaunig, 1892. Found at Nordelbische Landeskirchliches Archiv, Bestand 94, lfd. Nr. 396.

Nipperdey, Thomas. *Religion im Umbruch: Deutschland, 1870–1918*. Munich: Beck, 1988.

Reetz. *An meine Soldaten: Ansprachen und Predigten während des ersten Kriegsjahres*. Leipzig: Im Xenien-Verlag, 1916.

Reumann, John. "Introduction." In *The Lord's Supper in Relationship to the Life of Jesus and the History of the Early Church*, edited by Albert Schweitzer. Translated by A. J. Matill Jr. Macon, GA: Mercer Univesity Press, 1982.

Ringer, Fritz K. *The Decline of the German Mandarins: The German Academic Community, 1890–1933*. Hanover, NH: University Press of New England, 1990.

Rittelmeyer, Friedrich. *Christ und Krieg: Predigten aus der Kriegszeit*. Munich: Kaiser, n.d..

Rosenberg, Hans. *Grosse Depression und Bismarckzeit: Wirtschaftsablauf, Gesellschaft und Politik in Mitteleuropa*. Veröffentlichungen der Historischen Komission zu Berlin Beim Friedrich-Meinecke-Institut der Freien Universität Berlin, no. 24. Berlin: Walter de Gruyter, 1967.

Sauter, Gerhard. *Die Theologie des Reiches Gottes beim älteren und jüngeren Blumhardt*. Studien zur Dogmengeschichte und systematischen Theologie 14. Zurich: Zwingli Verlag, 1962.

Schlatter, Adolf. *Die beiden Schwerter, Lukas 22,35-38: Ein Stück aus der besonderen Quelle des Lukas*. Edited by Adolf Schlatter and W. Lütgert. Beiträge zur Förderung christlicher Theologie. Volume. 20. no. 6. Gütersloh: Evangelischer Verlag "Der Rufer," 1916.

———. *Die Bibel Verstehen: Aufsätze zur biblischen Hermeneutik*. Edited by Werner Neuer. Giessen: Brunnen Verlag, 2002.

———. *Das christliche Dogma*. Stuttgart: Calwer Verlag, 1977.

———. *Die christliche Ethik*. Stuttgart: Calwer Vereinsbuchhandlung, 1914.

———. *Die christliche Ethik*. 3rd ed. Stuttgart: Calwer Vereinsbuchhandlung, 1929.

———. *Der Dienst des Christen in der älteren Dogmatik*. Edited by D. A. Schlatter and D. H. Cremer. Beiträge zur Förderung christlicher Theologie, Volume 1, no. 1. Gütersloh: C. Bertelsmann, 1897.

———. *Einleitung in die Bibel*. 5th ed. Stuttgart: Calwer Vereinsbuchhandlung, 1933.

———. *Erlebtes*, 4th ed. Berlin: Im Furche-Verlag, [1926?].

———. *Der Glaube im Neuen Testament*. 3rd edition. Stuttgart: Verlag der Vereinsbuchhandlung, 1905.

———. *Der Glaube im Neuen Testament*. 6th ed. Studienausgabe 1982 text from the 4th edition, 1927. Stuttgart: Calwer Verlag, 1982.

———. "Die mich suchet findet mich." Sermon in *Regem Habemus: Bilder und zeugnisse aus einer deutschen christlichen Studentenbewegung*, edited by Udo Smidt. Berlin: Im Furche-Verlag, 1925.

———. *Predigten in der Stiftskirche zu Tübingen*. Tübingen: Schnürlen, 1902.

———. *Recht und Schuld in der Geschichte: Rede vor der Universität Tübingen am 27. Jan. 1915, am Geburtstage des Kaisers*. Edited by A. Schlatter and W. Lütgert. Beiträge zur Förderung christlicher Theologie. Volume 19, no. 1. Gütersloh: Evangelischer Verlag "Der Rufer," 1915.

———. *Rückblick auf meine Lebensarbeit*. 2nd ed. Stuttgart: Calwer Verlag, 1977.

———. *Der Ruf Jesu: Predigten von D. A. Schlatter*. Stuttgart: Verlag der Vereinsbuchhandlung, 1913.

Schönhuth, Ottmar. *Die Wunder Jesu*. Edited by E. Rolffs. Moderne Predigt-Bibliothek. Volume 9, no. 3. Göttingen: Vandenhoeck & Ruprecht, 1911.

Schumann, Friedrich Karl, and Gerhard Heinzelmann. *Zu Martin Kähler's 100. Geburtstag*. Hallische Universitätsreden 64. Halle (Saale): Max Niemeyer Verlag, 1935.

Schweitzer, Albert. *Civilization and Ethics*. 3rd ed. Translated by C. T. Campion and L. M. Russell. London: Adam & Charles Black, 1946.

———. *The Quest of the Historical Jesus: A Critical Study of Its Progress from Reimarus to Wrede*. New York: Macmillan, 1964.

———. *Reverence for Life*. Translated by Reginald H. Fuller. New York: Harper & Row, 1969.

Smart, Ninian, et al., eds. *Nineteenth Century Religious Thought in the West*. 3 vols. Cambridge: Cambridge University Press, 1985.

Smidt, Udo, ed. *Regem Habemus: Bilder und zeugnisse aus einer deutschen christlichen Studentenbewegung*. Berlin: Im Furche-Verlag, 1925.

Smith, Helmut Walser, ed. *Protestants, Catholics, and Jews in Germany, 1800–1914*. New York: Berg, 2001.

Stadelmann, Helge, ed. *Glaube und Geschichte: Heilsgeschichte als Thema der Theologie*. Giessen: Brunnen und R. Brockhaus, 1986.

Stern, Fritz. *The Politics of Cultural Despair: A Study in the Rise of the Germanic Ideology*. New York: Anchor, 1965.

Strasosky, Hermann. *Wahl-Predigt über Apg. 8,14-24: gehalten am 9. Sonntage nach Trinitatis 26. Juli 1891, in der St. Pauli Kirche*. Hamburg: Rüter, 1891. Found in Nordelbische Landeskirchliches Archiv, Bestand 94, lfd. Nr. 486.

Thurneyson, Eduard. *Christoph Blumhardt*. Stuttgart: Zwingli Verlag, 1962.

Tillich, Paul. *Perspectives on 19th and 20th Century Protestant Theology*. Edited by Carl E. Braaten. New York: Harper & Row, 1967.

Tugemann, Manfred, and Hans Repphun, eds. *Lesebuch: Erlesenes aus der Geschichte der Gemeinschaften in Schleswig-Holstein*. Bünsdorf: Verband der Gemeinschaften in der Landeskirche in Schleswig-Holstein, 2001.

Weiss, Johannes. *Die Nachfolge Christi und die Predigt der Gegenwart*. Göttingen: Vandehoeck & Ruprecht, 1895.

Welch, Claude. *Protestant Thought in the Nineteenth Century*. 2 vols. New Haven: Yale University Press, 1972, 1985.

Wurster, Paul, ed. *Kriegspredigten aus dem großen Krieg: 1914 und 1915 von verschiedenen Verfassern*. Stuttgart: Evang. Gesellschaft, 1915.

Zündel, Friedrich. *Johann Christoph Blumhardt: Ein Lebensbild*. 8th ed. Giessen: Brunnen-Verlag, 1921.

Zurhellen, Otto. *Kriegspredigten*. Tübingen: Mohr, 1915.

Index

Aeschbacher, Robert, 210, 216
Althaus, Paul, 83, 137
Althoff, Friedrich, 99–100
anti-Semitism, 10, 13, 23, 27, 36–38, 39, 41n11, 42, 44
Austria, 25, 26, 50, 51, 193, 200, 229, 233, 247, 249–50

Barth, Karl, 10–12, 13n10, 71, 83, 87, 89, 107n45, 117n62, 130, 131, 210, 211, 221, 239, 258–61, 264
Bauer, Bruno, 64n40, 97
Baur, Ferdinand Christian, 5, 90, 103, 113, 136
Bebel, August, 164, 173, 174–75
Beck, Johann Tobias, 49n9, 50–51, 91–92, 99, 103, 106, 112n55, 136, 264
Beiträge zur Förderung christlicher Theologie, 133
Bengel, Johann, 49n9, 50, 136
Biblicism, 5, 6, 22, 51, 55, 61, 74, 91, 104, 132
Bismarck, Otto von, 12, 25, 27, 28, 30, 31, 33, 34, 51, 52, 101–2, 106n44, 127, 173, 193, 212, 253
Blumhardt, Christoph, 2–4, 6, 8, 10, 15–16, 23, 31, 43, 50, 126n87, 130, 134–36, 141–81, 183–84, 186–87, 195, 220, 253–57, 258, 261, 264–67
Blumhardt, Johann Christoph, 50, 135n103, 143–44, 145–146, 147, 148, 151, 155, 157, 162n52, 171–73, 179, 264
Blumhardt, Theophil, 145, 146, 158, 253–54, 256
Bodelschwingh, Friedrich von, 133, 134, 135, 158, 220

Bonhoeffer, Dietrich, 260
Breit, Thomas, 211
Brunner, Emil, 83, 87, 260
Bultmann, Rudolf, 78n72, 79, 80, 260, 265n1
Burkhardt, Jakob, 90, 92

Caprivi, Leo von, 101
Catholicism, 7, 8, 12, 19, 21, 25–27, 31, 35, 36, 60n34, 61, 75, 76, 85, 106n44, 126, 146, 193, 194, 201
Center Party, 8, 126
Christian Social (Workers) Party, 27, 33–38, 101, 127, 172, 173, 265
christliche Welt, die, 132, 133, 259
Communism, 121, 175, 211
Confessionalism, 5, 22, 29f, 45, 55, 74, 102, 104, 105n42, 106
Cremer, Hermann, 31, 40, 50, 52, 55, 99–100, 102, 106, 131–33, 135, 183, 217, 219–20

Delitzsch, Franz, 50
dispensationalism, 86, 152n24
Dittus, Gottliebin, 134, 143–44, 145, 157, 172

England, 61, 229, 234, 238, 247, 249
Erlangen School, 48, 183
Enlightenment, the, 7, 9, 11n8, 14, 22–23, 54, 55, 56, 57, 60, 61, 75, 104, 106, 107, 112n55, 126, 139, 149, 150, 154, 163, 266
Evangelische Oberkirchenrat, 29, 102

Feuerbach, Ludwig, 97, 109n49, 115, 205–6

First World War, 9–12, 13n10, 15, 16, 26, 29f, 30, 43, 84, 89, 94, 104, 106, 122, 129, 130, 131, 148, 167, 180, 181, 183, 186, 198, 208, 213, 214, 219, 220, 221–61
France, 26, 28, 41, 184–85, 194, 229, 236, 238, 240, 247
Franco-Prussian War, 26, 40, 41, 43, 145, 160, 184, 222n3, 229, 236, 244, 255n88, 256
Friedrich III, 11, 31, 36, 51, 172
Friedrich VII (of Denmark), 200
Friedrich Wilhelm IV, 24, 32
Frommel, Max, 184–85, 193

Gamaliel, 218
Gemeinschaftsbewegung, 14, 198–99
Gustavus Adolphus, 193

Hammerstein, Wilhelm Joachim von, 39
Harnack, Adolf Harnack, 1, 6–7, 30, 83, 100–101, 103, 105n42, 113, 133, 135, 148, 152n25, 183, 197, 205–6, 215–16, 223, 259, 262
Hengstenberg, Ernst, 6, 24, 25, 41n50, 49, 50, 53, 106
Hermann, Wilhelm, 7, 223
Herrnhuter Brüdergemeinde (Moravians), 221
Heydorn, Heinrich, 215–16
History of Religions School, 7, 96, 204, 211, 213
Hitler, Adolf, 27, 258, 261
Holy Spirit, 60, 65–66, 114, 135, 144, 146, 148, 156, 159, 162–63, 166, 169, 180, 191, 192, 211, 218, 231, 252, 256

Inner Mission, the, 23, 25, 26–27, 28, 33, 35, 39
Isaiah, 172, 177, 205

Jäckh, Eugen, 148

Jäger, Paul, 132, 137
Jatho, Carl, 215–16
Jesus, 3, 5, 7, 11n8, 15, 20, 21, 42, 46, 49, 54, 57, 62, 64–70, 78n72, 80–81, 86–87, 89, 92, 96, 109, 111, 112n55, 117–18, 126–28, 138, 141, 143, 150–51, 155, 159, 160–69, 171–75, 179, 189, 190–92, 194, 196, 201–7, 209–11, 213–18, 221, 228, 231, 233, 236, 237, 245, 250, 253, 255, 260

Kaftan, Julius, 215
Kaftan, Theodor, 215–16, 233
Kähler, Martin, 2–10, 15–16, 23–24, 30–31, 39–40, 43, 45–81, 83–84, 87, 91, 94, 100, 102, 104, 106–7, 110–11, 114, 118, 122, 130, 131–34, 135, 137–38, 148–50, 154, 167, 169, 183–84, 186, 195, 199, 201–3, 208–9, 215–19, 255f, 260–61, 264–67
Kant, Immanuel, 47, 68, 89
Kierkegaard, Søren, 111, 116
Kögel, Rudolf, 23, 29n16, 30
Kulturkampf, 12, 27, 31, 106, 193, 218

Lessing, Gotthold Ephraim, 11, 48, 56, 107, 112, 194
Lütgert, Wilhelm, 76, 132–33, 137, 220
Luther, Martin, 22, 31, 34, 38, 40, 43, 53, 68, 70, 106, 164, 190, 193, 199, 215, 223

Marx, Karl, 9, 159, 164, 165, 175
Marxism, 9, 34, 37, 173, 175, 180, 188, 267
Melanchthon, Philipp, 199
Moltke, Helmuth von, 212

Napoleon I, 75, 194, 244, 246
Napoleon III, 194
Nazis, 44, 211, 258
Nietzsche, Friedrich, 9, 10, 60n34, 68, 90, 107n45, 109n49

Nippold, Friedrich, 95–96, 97, 134

Oetinger, Friedrich Christoph, 136
Oettli, Samuel, 95, 98, 203

Paul, (Apostle), 39, 117n62, 128, 145, 148, 149, 158, 254
Positive Union/Positive Theology, 6, 23, 29, 30–33, 39, 40–41, 43, 49, 51, 55, 74, 80, 102–3, 130, 142, 261, 265
Protestant Union (Liberal Party), 29n16, 32

Rade, Martin, 133
Reformation, 5, 9, 23, 29, 32, 36, 53, 61, 66, 70, 74, 81, 83, 92, 103, 106, 107, 115, 186, 188–89, 199, 219, 267
Reimarus, Hermann Samuel, 11n8, 194
Renan, Ernst, 54
Ritschl, Albrecht, 6, 7, 20n2, 54, 84f, 92, 99, 103, 113, 160–61, 183, 213, 260
Röntgen, Wilhelm, 153
Rothe, Richard, 48–50
Russia, 228, 229, 233, 240, 247, 248

Schlatter, Adolf, 2–6, 7n7, 9–10, 15–16, 23, 30–31, 39–40, 43, 55, 58n29, 67–68, 72, 76, 81, 83–139, 148–50, 154, 167, 169, 183–84, 186, 195, 197, 201, 203–8, 209–11, 215–19, 223, 239–53, 257–61, 264–67
Schleiermacher, Friedrich, 11n8, 92, 107, 130, 213
Schniewind, Julius, 76
Schopenhauer, Arthur, 68, 107n45
Schrempf, Christoph, 53, 133, 214–16
Schweitzer, Albert, 57, 78n72, 168–69, 170n72, 198f, 255n88, 263
Social Democratic Party, 7, 8, 11, 34, 37, 38, 126f, 142, 147, 148, 154, 158, 161, 164, 173–81, 256
Steffensen, Karl, 90–92, 137
Stoecker, Adolf, 2–6, 10, 15, 19–44, 45, 52, 55, 72, 80, 101–3, 117, 124, 127,

135, 148, 160, 167, 172–73, 183–84, 193–94, 261, 264–66
Strauss, David Friedrich, 5, 10, 11, 21, 22, 23, 47, 54, 59, 90, 97, 109f, 136, 144, 183, 213, 261

Tholuck, Friedrich August, 49–50, 53, 76, 80, 133, 264
Thurneyson, Eduard, 260
Tillich, Paul, 6f, 78, 79, 260, 265n1
Treaty of Versailles, 11, 238, 248, 250
Treitschke, Heinrich von, 37
Troeltsch, Ernst, 260, 263

University of Basel, 89–90, 93, 137
University of Berlin, 6, 24, 25, 28, 29, 30, 37, 39, 41n50, 43, 91n11, 92, 100–103, 127, 134, 136, 201, 215, 248, 259
University of Bern, 83, 94–99, 101, 102, 131, 134, 203
University of Greifswald, 30, 84n1, 96, 99, 100, 102, 131, 138, 183, 201, 217, 219
University of Halle, 24, 30, 45, 49, 50, 54, 72, 76, 78, 79, 80, 99, 131, 132, 133, 137, 138, 201, 218, 219
University of Tübingen, 50, 52, 53, 55, 91, 92, 101, 103, 104, 133, 134, 136, 138, 144, 201, 203, 217–19, 233, 236, 242, 247, 251, 259

Wagner, Adolf, 37
Weimar Republic, 10, 11, 238, 251, 252
Weiss, Bernhard, 101
Weiss, Johannes, 161, 204
Weizsäcker, Carl Heinrich von, 136
Wellhausen, Julius, 58, 183
Wilhelm I, 8, 11, 24, 36, 37, 51, 200, 212, 248
Wilhelm II, 11, 27n11, 33, 36, 37, 43, 51, 184, 193, 194, 196, 212, 230
Wrede, William, 64n40, 97
World War I. *See* First World War

CPSIA information can be obtained at www.ICGtesting.com
Printed in the USA
BVOW02s1723260114

342762BV00008B/98/P